Cases in International Relations

PORTRAITS OF THE FUTURE

Donald M. Snow
University of Alabama

Longman

New York San Francisco Boston
London Toronto Sydney Tokyo Singapore Madrid
Mexico City Munich Paris Cape Town Hong Kong Montreal

Vice President and Publisher: Priscilla McGeehon
Executive Editor: Eric Stano
Senior Marketing Manager: Megan Galvin-Fak
Media Supplements Editor: Patrick McCarthy
Supplements Editor: Kristi Olsen
Production Manager: Joseph Vella
Project Coordination, Text Design, and Electronic Page Makeup: Electronic Publishing
    Services Inc., N.Y.C.
Cover Manager: Wendy A. Fredericks
Cover Designer: Laura Shaw
Cover Illustration: © Stockbyte/Picture Quest
Manufacturing Buyer: Al Dorsey
Printer and Binder: Maple Vail Book Manufacturing Group
Cover Printer: The Lehigh Press

Library of Congress Cataloging-in-Publication Data

Snow, Donald M., 1943-
    Cases in international relations: portraits of the future / Donald M. Snow. -- 1st ed.
        p. cm.
    Incudes bibliographical references and index.
    ISBN 0-321-08061-0
        1. International relations. I. Brown, Eugene, 1943- II. Title.

JZ1242 .S658 2003
327--dc21

                                                                2002067121

Please visit our website at http://www.ablongman.com

ISBN 0-321-08061-0

  3 4 5 6 7 8 9 10—MA—05 04 03

Contents

Introduction

Portraits of the Future?

As the twenty-first century begins to unfold, it is natural to want to know how it compares to the last century and how it is likely to look. What will be the major changes in how the states of the world deal with one another, and how will things remain the same? What forces are likely to emerge as major agents for change and resistance to change? Where will the world's most serious troubles be? Where will there be sources of hope and positive developments? In which direction does the future lie?

Although we still have trouble articulating the nature and characteristics of the post–Cold War world and its contrast to the days of Cold War, it is reasonably clear that the transition is basically over and that the new trends are discernibly in place. In some cases, the result is remarkable continuity with the past, even if it is sprinkled with change in a different environment. For example, the conflict between Israel and the Palestinians goes back over half a century and continues with little prospect of resolution. The apparent hopelessness of the situation, seen so dramatically on global television over the past few years, shares roots with the Cold War, yet it is different as well. In 2000, the parties came as close as they ever have to peace, only to be rebuffed by the harsh realities of intractable differences. What will the future likely see? We will examine that question in Chapter 6.

We operate in the opacity of the future. Because political science is not a precise science like physics or chemistry, we lack the quality of theory possessed by the hard sciences that might let us predict the future with confidence. Because we lack the lenses to foresee, we can only guess—draw portraits of the present and extrapolate them into a future about which we cannot be sure. It is an imperfect method, but one that can provide insight into our quest.

A word about what this book is and is not is appropriate at this point. As the title suggests, it is a casebook, a presentation of a series of individual cases of problems and trends within the international arena of the early 2000s, chosen because they seem likely to endure for the next several years and to provide at least a partial vision about what the international system will look like. It is not a comprehensive overview of the system or its history, which is the proper province of core textbooks in the field. I have consciously omitted historical cases, for two reasons. First, my concern here is with the future, not the past. Where history informs the present and future (as it inevitably does), I have tried to incorporate the relevant history—for example, the World War II war crimes trials as context for the contemporary emphasis on war crimes. Purely historical (e.g., already resolved) conflicts go beyond my purpose. Second, most of the truly interesting historical cases have already been done and rehashed significantly so that another version would add only marginally to our store of knowledge; we do not need another Cuban missile crisis case study. At the same time, the book is not a systematic exposition of various political science theories explaining international phenomena. While these may be interesting and very valuable, I think they go beyond the concerns and interests of most students in undergraduate college courses, which is where I expect this book mostly to be used.

The book is divided into five parts. In the broadest terms, the parts represent major concerns that one finds in most of the international relations literature and in policy considerations. Some effort was made to align topics with the major means of organization of textbooks in the field, but the diversity of those books made this an imperfect exercise at best. Within each part, I have tried to select individual cases (chapters) that are broadly representative of the issue area and which reflect ongoing problems of importance to students and practitioners in the field. Because there are three cases in each part except Part V (which has four), they cannot possibly provide comprehensive overviews or descriptions without ceasing to be cases. Rather, they seek to look at an aspect of the problem, not its entirety.

A word about pedagogy may help explain this point. Each of the cases begins by identifying a particular problem or dynamic in the international system. The case study on Kashmir, for instance, begins with the observation that there are some international disputes that are so intractable as to be essentially irresolvable. The situation in Kashmir is then examined as an instance of this irreconcilability, by noting and explaining the positions and acceptable outcomes for the various parties, all of which turn out to be mutually exclusive. The case then concludes by looking at the various options available, including maintenance of a status quo that none of the parties finds particularly acceptable but upon which they cannot improve. The cases end with study/discussion questions and references for further reading and research, including a sample of relevant Web sites.

What distinguishes this effort from other supplementary texts—and especially from "readers" composed of selected reprinted journal articles or documents—is that all the essays included are original papers written specifically for this volume. The reason for doing this was to allow more timely coverage of situations that are ongoing than is possible with the lag time involved in publication in journals and the like, and also to allow the cases to be cast within a more standard format than is possible with preexisting materials. In addition, writing original articles meant that it is possible to update and modify materials as events and dynamics change and, hopefully, to facilitate both the freshness and accuracy of the material that appears in these pages. Subsequent editions, should they occur, will hopefully benefit both from the ability to modify the original and to add new materials within the common framework. I hope that doing so will make the materials both more accessible and more germane to the reader.

The rationale for choosing the cases that are included flows from the book's subtitle, "Portraits of the Future." Clearly, it is not possible to present the same breadth of exposure in a casebook as in a core text without either making the casebook encyclopedic and massively long or making the cases so brief as not to be particularly helpful. Rather, a casebook is by its nature a collection of examples presented in sufficient depth to highlight and explain principles, events, and the like in more detail than is possible in a more conventional text.

Why did I choose the cases I did? Clearly, selecting some topics required not choosing others, and I am certain that any reader will find topics that he or she would have preferred in some instances to those I selected and have presented. Such disagreement is inevitable in an area of study as diverse in content as international relations.

Beyond their amenability to case treatment, I used five criteria in choosing the subjects that are included in this volume. The first was that the subject was important and represented an issue or problem that will endure. Cases as diverse as the terrorist attacks of September 11, 2001, the fate of Israel and the Palestinians, the direction of China, and AIDS in Africa meet this criterion. Second, I wanted to look at problems that are fresh, timely, but not covered extensively in other places. The Millennium Summit, which convened for a few days in late summer 2000, made a large number of promises, and then faded from view, fits this criterion; so does the problem of resource scarcity and the future role of nongovernmental organizations in peacekeeping.

Third, I wanted subjects that represent real world problems with which the international system will have to come to grips and about which students need to know in order to be informed citizens. Missile defense as an international problem clearly fits this criterion, as does the problem of state building discussed in the case on Haiti and the one on the future of war crimes. Fourth, I wanted subjects that are future oriented and that will likely endure as problems for a period of time. The precedential value of how the world deals with the African AIDS epidemic meets this criterion, as does the question of how Indonesia deals with globalization and what that means to the future of democratization in the world. Fifth, I wanted subjects that were inherently interesting, so that the reader would approach and consume them with some enthusiasm that, hopefully, will translate into a broader interest in international relations. At a practical level, the intractability of the Kashmir question and how the rules of globalization are enforced fall into this category. At a more abstract level, the question of the future of sovereignty and the future of war meet this criterion.

The modal term in all these criteria is "future." My overriding interest and purpose in this volume is to deal with problems and issues that exist today and will likely continue to be topics of concern in the next five to ten years—or even beyond. If I succeed, it is my hope to give students an enhanced background on real issues, which will allow them to extrapolate some of that knowledge into understanding the dynamics of international relations more broadly.

Individual cases were selected with these criteria in mind. My intention was to select substantive topics that both illustrate important principles operating in the international system and that exemplify important concerns in the contemporary environment. In doing so, I decided that there were visible themes that needed to be included. I selected four general topics—new forces and evolutionary changes in the post–Cold War world, globalization, national and international security, and transnational issues—and then proceeded to try to find cases that would provide illustrations of these dynamics.

It is not, of course, to be expected that the choices I made would be identical to those of any individual instructor. Each of the themes I have chosen is broad in its nature, with an abundance of individual cases that could have been chosen, and some were included and some were not. In picking the cases I did, I tried to invoke the five criteria cited above—importance, freshness and timeliness, real world importance, endurance, and interest.

Each case meets these criteria. For the problem of new forces and change, I chose three cases that are not unique to the post–Cold War period, but have attracted increasing importance since the fall of the Soviet empire. The first three look at forces much more prominent now than during the Cold War. Thus, the case on China reflects both the growing economic and political importance of China and provides some criteria for looking at how China will evolve and participate in the future on issues as diverse as the status of Taiwan and the American plan for a national missile defense (itself a topic of a case that could be used in tandem with "China Rising"). Nongovernmental organizations (NGOs) are not a new phenomenon, as already noted, but they are becoming more prominent and even obtrusive actors in diverse settings, such as peacekeeping. Similarly, the dynamics of democratization began to emerge as an important force in the 1990s, but the experience of how and why democratization occurs represents a long intellectual and practical tradition. The dynamics of change come through strongly in Chapters 4–6. The roots of the problem of war crimes and how to deal with them emerged originally after World War II but have been reenergized by atrocities in diverse parts of the Third World and the Balkans. It is an evolving problem that has yet to be resolved and to which the United States is a major barrier because of its failure to ratify the International Criminal Court statute. The reason for this opposition has to do with the American contention that a war crimes court would potentially infringe upon the sovereign rights of Americans and their government. The assault on national sovereignty is an important theme that will continue to reverberate through the 2000s and beyond. Finally, the issue of the Palestinian-Israeli conflict, which seemed near resolution but which continues to sear the international relations of the Middle East, remains a testimony to the difficulty of resolving extraordinarily difficult situations that may be impossible to settle satisfactorily.

The other concerns are more discrete, although I have attempted to choose my "portraits" from aspects of the subject area that are not typically found in mainstream textual coverage. Thus, Part III deals with aspects of globalization as they affect those to whom globalization is being sold as a major means to improve their conditions. Haiti, for instance, is one of the classic failed states, and creating prosperity in that island country through the extension of globalization is often seen as a way to solve Haiti's problem. The case explores whether this is the answer. The "New Trinity of Globalization" looks at how the "movers and shakers" of globalization operate by examining the dynamics of the triangular relationship between the International Monetary Fund, the United States, and target countries, and what effects this relationship has on countries attempting to enter the global economy. One of the countries that entered that process with absolutely unforeseen and damaging consequences has been Indonesia, and the bruises to the Indonesian system set off by the East Asian crisis of 1997 may be instructive for others. In combination, the three globalization cases raise cautions on the easy assumption that globalization is the direct answer to everyone's problems.

The next concern, captured in Part IV, is with security in the contemporary environment. There is general agreement that the security environment is different and, before September 11, 2001, seemed less threatening than it was during the Cold War. The question is how that environment is indeed transformed. The section begins with an assessment of what future war will look like, drawing from a comparison between projections made during the twentieth century as opposed to those made while facing the future. The extensive investigation of this problem by the Bush administration suggests its enduring importance. The problem of how the proposed actions by one power to increase its security can decrease the security of its neighbors—the classic security dilemma—is investigated through the vehicle of the national missile defense proposal being debated by the United States. To demonstrate the endurance of some problems and their intractability, I have chosen the case of Kashmir, which, along with the Israeli-Palestinian confrontation, has been one of the most difficult to resolve.

My logic in choosing cases for Part V on transnational issues parallels my thinking about the security section. It has become traditional to look at "standard" instances of problems that states cannot individually solve; the environment and human rights come immediately to mind. My intent was to find cases that have not been overdone or which have not been treated particularly as transnational issues, even though thinking of them that way might be helpful. I began with the Millennium Summit held in the summer of 2000, because it brought together a broad range of world leaders who solemnly swore to attack a number of difficult problems without attracting much attention. The case provides a kind of scorecard of their seriousness. Conflicts over scarce resources other than petroleum represent a second global problem that can be viewed as a transnational issue. Similarly, there has been a great deal of attention given to the problem of AIDS in Africa, but not much to how it is a transnational issue and the precedent that will be set for dealing with future similar tragedies. International terrorism is the overriding problem of our day and is one that can only be surmounted by a concerted international effort.

What I have provided is a stack of portraits of the future that I hope the reader will find both broad and enriching. In concluding this introduction, however, I would like to make a comment on the dedication of this book to my longtime friend, the late Eugene R. Brown. Gene and I met in 1989 and shared an office at the United States Army War College for two years before he returned to Lebanon Valley College and I to the University of Alabama. Our initial work together led to a longer-term collaboration that resulted in several book projects brought to fruition. In most cases, Gene was the ideational force who suggested new projects that were then brought to a conclusion by a collaborative effort.

Cases in International Relations is the result of that same pattern of collaboration and was, in some sense, intended to be the culmination of our joint efforts. The idea of an original casebook consisting of original essays was Gene's; unfortunately, he was unable to complete the task we had set out for ourselves, and I had the burden of completing the work after my good friend and colleague left us over the Thanksgiving holiday, 2000. I hope Gene would have been pleased with what turned out to be our final collaboration.

I would also like to than the reviewers who made useful comments on the manuscript. They include Ruth Ediger, Lee University; Larry Elowiz, Georgia College and State University; Linda Petrou, High Point University; Brian Potter, Tulane University; Michael A. Preda, Midwestern State University; Abdoulaye Saine, Miami University of Ohio; and Michael E. Smith, Georgia State University. Finally, I would like to thank Saskia Bunting, my graduate research assistant, for her cheerful and unstinting help in "dotting the i's and crossing the t's (in the words of my editor, Eric Stano).

Donald M. Snow
Tuscaloosa, Alabama

To the memory of
Professor Eugene Brown,
Friend, Colleague, and Collaborator

PART 1

"New" Forces in International Relations

Acommon theme in the post–Cold War international environment is change, both in terms of the extent to which that environment is somehow different than it was before and the implications of those changes for the operation of international relations. The opposing theme is continuity, the extent to which trends and events that may appear unique to the present may represent phenomena from the past, although possibly mutated by differences in the contemporary environment.

The clearest element of change in the contemporary environment is the implosion of the Cold War bipolar confrontation between the coalition of Western countries led by the United States and the coalition of communist states led by the Soviet Union. The Soviet Union no longer exists, and its successor Russia is a pale force by comparison. In this void, the United States has emerged as the sole remaining superpower, or what former Secretary of State Madeleine Albright has called the "indispensable nation" and what others have referred to as the "hyperpower."

A major concern of international relations scholarship has been to try to determine what difference these changed circumstances make. It is the question of continuity versus change and is why the heading of this part puts the term "new" in parentheses. There are, broadly put, three possible answers to the question:

The first possibility is that international politics was fundamentally transformed by the end of the Cold War and that truly new and unique forces have been unleashed by the collapse of the system that would not have been present had the Cold War not ended. This position, of course, is impossible to demonstrate conclusively, because we lack the ability to observe a continued Cold War and compare whether, say, a globalized economy would have occurred if the Cold War had continued. So too might the international terrorism that currently consumes our attention have arisen had the Cold War lingered.

The second possibility is that, aside from the demise of the East-West confrontation, nothing has changed much at all. Since the demise of the communist world (and the end of Marxism as a vital and vibrant ideological alternative to Western-style democracy) is in of itself such a momentous occasion that one can hardly argue that the change is insignificant. At the same time, one can make the argument that the global economy, for instance, would have emerged, possibly pretty much the way it has, regardless of whether the Cold War ended or not.

There is a third possibility between the extremes. That possibility is that there were and are elements of both continuity and change at work in the Cold War and post–Cold War worlds. This position accepts the notion that most, if not all, of the trends present today can be traced back to the earlier period, but that they may have developed differently in the current environment than they would have otherwise. This position would appear to be more moderate and thus appealing and would argue, for instance, that although globalization most likely would have occurred regardless of whether there was a Cold War or not, the nature of globalization is different than it would otherwise have been—e.g., China would probably not been such a prominent member had the Cold War not ended.

Part 1 identifies three substantive areas in which change has appeared to have occurred in the international system. There is nothing systematic or inclusive about the changes included in the three cases. Instead they seek to be illustrative of the ways in which change and continuity are apparent in the system. The three cases look at three aspects in which change is alleged to have occurred: the changing nature of the power of individual states, the emergence of new actors in new roles in the system, and new dynamics in the politics within and between states.

The major burden of each case is whether it represents more continuity or change in the new system, and it is left to the reader to render a judgment in that regard. In Chapter 1, "China Rising," the emergence of the People's Republic as a major player in the system, a so-called rising power, is the subject. Clearly, China was a force in the Cold War period. The question is what kind of force it will be in the changed environment and whether that role is different now than it would have been had the Cold War not ended. Chapter 2, "The Growing Significance of NGOs," looks at the nongovernmental organization (NGO), a form of actor that has become an increasingly prominent part of international interactions since the end of the Cold War. The focus of the case is on how these international organizations make a difference. Chapter 3, "The Democratic Peace," looks at a prominent new emphasis in the post–Cold War international environment: the spread of democratization worldwide.

CHAPTER ONE

China Rising:

A LOOMING THREAT?

PRÉCIS

One of the ways in which the international system appears different than it did before the end of the Cold War is the increasingly prominent role played by the People's Republic of China. Clearly, China was a consequential country during the Cold War, but its significance was overshadowed by its relative position in the communist world. With the demise of the Soviet Union and the adoption of different policies—especially in the economic realm, but increasingly militarily as well—China has become a much more important factor in international politics for the new century.

The question is how China will fit into the international politics of the twenty-first century. With its growing economy and increased military might, will China be a force for stability and peace, or a disruptive force? Will China challenge American world leadership or become a productive part of the globalizing international scene? As issues as diverse as Chinese membership in the World Trade Organization and military confrontation over Taiwan swirl in daily headlines, an assessment of what kind of power China is rising to be is an important concern for the international system.

A rising major power inherently presents challenges to the international system. These ascending states may either deliberately or unintentionally destabilize existing international arrangements, ignite suspicion and fear, and trigger action-and-reaction cycles which can all too readily lead to confrontation or even war, according to a construct known as the "uneven development thesis." As early as the fifth century B.C., the Greek historian, Thucydides, invoked what amounted to the uneven development thesis in his classic book, *The History of the Peloponnesian War*, to explain the origins of the series of wars of 431 B.C. to 404 B.C. in which the Spartans dealt a devastating blow to the once brilliant Athenian city-state. "What made war inevitable," he wrote, "was the growth of Athenian power and the fear which this caused in Sparta."

Today the most significant rising power is China. The world's oldest continuous civilization with a history rich in both creativity and tragedy, China stood largely outside the quantum leaps in wealth and power made possible by Western-centered advances in modern science, technology, and industrialization since the eighteenth century. From the mid-nineteenth to the mid-twentieth centuries, China endured its "century of humiliation," as the once grand but then defenseless country fell under the domination and exploitation of the West and of newly industrialized Japan.

Today, however, China is again on the rise economically, politically, and militarily. Though still much less economically advanced than nearby Japan or South Korea, for example, China's sheer mass—it accounts for fully one-fifth of the earth's population—means that already no Asian state can contemplate its own strategic requirements without taking China into account. Should its ascent continue, China will become a leading power of global, not merely regional, status.

China already possesses some of the trappings of superpower status: it has nuclear weapons and is one of the five permanent members of the United Nations Security Council. If its economy continues the robust growth of the past two decades, then China may truly arrive as a state capable of wielding power on a large scale. China's growth raises two questions about its future growth: Will China continue to grow to the point that it *can* upset the power balance? And will a newly robust China (if it emerges) accommodate itself to the existing international system or instead act in ways that defy international norms and threaten international stability and security? In other words, will China pose a threat to the emerging international order, or will it become another major, but orthodox, member of the international system? The purpose of the analysis of this case will be to examine these prospects. To do so, we will first look briefly at China's past as the context of its ascent, and then at the elements of China's assertion into the world's geopolitics.

BEFORE THE RISE: HUMILIATION, CHAOS, AND POVERTY

China's "century of humiliation" reduced it to a semicolony, a situation resulting from the loss of creativity, corruption, and resistance to reform within the imperial court, the obsolescence of its emperor-based political system which relied upon a corps of bureaucrats chosen for their mastery of Confucian classics rather than their command of modern ideas, and the numerous unequal treaties imposed upon it by foreign powers since its defeat in the Opium War with Great Britain in the 1840s. Westerners roamed throughout China. Merchants, adventurers, diplomats, and missionaries all enjoyed special privileges placing them beyond Chinese authority, which were simply humiliating to all Chinese. Those privileges included foreign spheres of influence and foreign concessions, foreign troops and police, foreign post offices and telegraph agencies, and consular jurisdiction that kept foreigners beyond the reach of Chinese justice.

As evidence mounted of the decline and weakness of this once mighty power, a cascade of disastrous events befell it. Domestic rebellions, including the Taiping Rebellion of the mid-nineteenth century and the Boxer Uprising of 1900, further bled an already anemic country and invited greater foreign domination. The collapse of China's last dynasty in 1911 plunged the country into even greater chaos, as regional warlords vied with one another for national supremacy.

Layered atop all of China's other discontents was a split between two centers of political and military power, each of which was determined to unify, govern, and strengthen China against the domestic and foreign ills that had befallen it. The Guomindang—or Nationalist—forces led by Chiang Kai-shek were generally supported by the United States. But beginning in the 1920s, an initially small upstart group of communists led by Mao Zedong made clear its own vision of mobilizing mass support to overthrow China's antiquated social order and to restore unity to the nation.

As the two forces began their titanic struggle in earnest, China endured yet another devastating blow, this time from Japan's exceptionally brutal aggression, first in its invasion of Manchuria in 1931 and then throughout its bloody drive through China proper from 1937 to 1945.

The defeat of Japanese forces by the United States in 1945 gave the people of China not a new era of peace but rather a renewal of the violent and conclusive phase of the titanic struggle between Chiang Kai-shek's Nationalist forces and Mao Zedong's communist followers. By the autumn of 1949, China's communists emerged victorious and drove Chiang's forces to the island refuge of Taiwan.

In October 1949 Mao could boast to the assembled mass in Beijing's Tiananmen Square that "China has stood up." He meant, of course, that China was at long last unified under a strong central authority and that foreign intervention in its internal affairs would no longer be tolerated. Beyond unification and the reclamation of China's sovereignty, it was Mao's abiding passion to create within China a radical, egalitarian society. But however one judges Mao's achievements, it remains the fact that, throughout his long rule (1949–1976), China remained largely outside the international community, terribly repressive within, and its people mired in poverty.

THE FOUNDATIONS OF CHINA'S RISE

Upon Mao's death, a scramble for power ensued among China's ruling elites. Within a year, Deng Xiaoping had effectively consolidated governing authority within his own hands. Purged three times during Mao's reign and standing less than five feet tall, Deng seemed at first glance to be an unlikely ruler of the world's most populous state. But more remarkable than his personal tenacity or physical diminutiveness was the boldness of his vision for China. Deng soon implemented his famous "Four Modernizations" campaign. Undaunted by the giant shadow cast by Mao, Deng announced an audacious series of reforms designed to advance China beyond the revolutionary dogma of Maoism and to create instead a stronger, more modern country by loosening the reins of state authority, more fully embracing economic globalization in search of foreign markets, technology, and investment, and frankly accepting income differentials in a society which had so recently been singularly animated by radical egalitarianism.

The Four Modernizations—agriculture, science and technology, industry, and military—began in the countryside, home to three-fourths of all Chinese. Gradually, socialist-style communal farming was phased out. Under the new "household responsibility system," peasants were now allowed individually to lease land from the state. Without quite admitting it, Deng's regime injected market—that is, *capitalist*—incentives by allowing peasants whose production surpassed their obligatory quotas (which were turned over to the state at fixed prices) to sell any surplus which they could produce for as much money as they could get for it. A system of rural markets and distribution systems sprang up to buy farm produce and sell it to independent urban vendors. As longer land leases gave peasants new incentives to undertake capital improvements, food production soared. With it, rural incomes rose sharply. And the most successful peasant families reaped the greatest awards.

The older norm of imposed egalitarianism was quietly shelved. In its place evolved what the regime today calls "Socialism with Chinese Characteristics." With the passage of time this slogan has simply become a euphemism for capitalism with state supervision, but with much less direct central control. Gradually the limited market system begun in the countryside spread to the cities. Individuals were allowed to open restaurants, shops, and factories. Workers could be hired and fired, something that had been utterly unthinkable under Mao's "people's" regime. The wheels of a more market-driven economy were thus set into motion. The second and third modernizations—industry plus science and technology—inherently required China's leaders to turn outward to the most advanced industrial countries for investment capital, markets for Chinese goods, scientific know-how, and the most modern production technology and management skills. Four Special Economic Zones (SEZs) were established in southeastern China in which foreign corporations were granted concessionary incentives to form joint ventures with Chinese partners and thus transfer their leading-edge technological, manufacturing process, and managerial expertise to initially quite limited enclaves of capitalist experimentation.

As local laboratories of industrial modernity, the SEZs were intended to, among other things, create a new leadership cohort of technologically sophisticated managers whose expertise, it was hoped, would in time fan out from the SEZs themselves and help jump-start China's obsolescent and inefficient state-owned enterprises. During Mao's era, "redness"—that is, communist ideological purity—was more highly prized than substantive expertise in filling leadership ranks. But Deng was much more of a pragmatist. In his famous aphorism, he said, "It doesn't matter if a cat is white or black, as long as it catches mice." Results, then, would be the new measure of the country's rising managers and leaders, not their ritual incantation of Marxist-Maoist dogma. The Deng program provided the launching pod for China's ascent into the realm of world powers. How far will it ascend? How will China use its new status? To answer these questions, we will assess China on three dimensions: economic growth, military strength, and diplomacy.

ECONOMIC GROWTH, BUT A LITANY OF WOES

The economic results have been the most dramatic. Riding a boom powered by foreign capital inflows and an aggressive export strategy, China's economy grew at an average annual rate of around 10 percent throughout the 1980s and 1990s. Not all the China specialists in the West accept these astounding government-promulgated growth statistics, and in any case the real nominal growth rate would have been eroded by inflation. But regardless of whose figures one accepts, there is no denying the fact—easily observable to any return visitor to the country—that China's economy has grown dramatically during the past two decades. It is today the third-largest economy in the world, ranking only behind the United States and Japan.

China's recent leaders—Deng Xiaoping and now Jiang Zemin—have realized that for their country to develop and modernize economically, they would have to thoroughly repudiate Mao's policies of economic self-sufficiency and instead fully embrace economic globalization. The international trend toward reducing barriers to the free movement of goods and capital has very much worked to China's advantage. In recognition of this, the current leadership's commitment to globalization has been most clearly demonstrated by its single-minded drive to gain membership in the World Trade Organization, a goal it achieved late in 2000. As a precursor to its accession to the WTO, China negotiated a complex commercial agreement with the United States. The agreement contains a number of key concessions on China's part. Especially notable among them are market-opening measures that place many of its state-owned industries at a competitive disadvantage, thus risking a substantial loss of jobs for Chinese workers. This process has produced both WTO membership and permanent trade relations for China with the United States, but at the cost of forcing China to accept international norms that tie the country more fully to the international community and limit its ability to act outside systemic rules.

Even as we sketch China's dramatic economic ascent over the past two decades, however, we must also note that it is a country beset by a litany of domestic woes which, taken together, raise the alarming possibility of widespread social unrest. Its internal preoccupations include a mounting political crisis of regime legitimacy as faith in communism has atrophied, severe environmental degradation, immense population pressures, almost daily revelations of official corruption, a growing gap in urban versus rural incomes, high unemployment, a steady loss of arable land, a diminished social safety net for the poor and displaced, and secessionist movements in Tibet and in the westernmost province of Zinjiang. The leaking of documents allegedly describing the communist party's debate over how to deal with the Tiananmen Square protesters in 1989 (the authenticity of which was denied by the party) is some indication of the kind of political turmoil that may be present in the future.

We must keep in mind, too, that China remains very much a developing country, with a per capita income only about one-tenth that of the United States, Germany, or Japan. But after beginning its economic ascent so recently and from such a low base, China's living standards are up—way up, in many instances—and the Beijing regime now has available to it far greater resources with which to enhance the historical *sine qua non* of international power: military strength.

THE "FOURTH MODERNIZATION": MILITARY ENHANCEMENT

In recent years China's leaders have introduced major equipment modernization, battlefield doctrine, and a slimming down of the old, low-technology People's Liberation Army (PLA). Originally configured to wage a defensive "people's war" on the ground, the PLA traditionally stressed massive numbers of light infantry and sought to compensate for China's low industrial and technological base by presenting to any would-be intruder the specter of a numerically overwhelming mass of ground forces.

More recently, the focal concept guiding China's battlefield doctrine, force structure, and weapons procurement policy is "local war under high-tech conditions." Three principal factors account for this altered strategy. The first was China's 1979 armed incursion into neighboring Vietnam (then a Soviet client state), an attempted reprisal for Vietnam's overthrow of Cambodia's Khmer Rouge regime (a Chinese client). But the attempt to "teach Vietnam a lesson" went very badly. Chinese forces were outmaneuvered and outfought by the battle-tested Vietnamese. So it was China, not Vietnam, which was dealt the harsh lesson that its war-fighting capabilities were in serious need of modernization.

Second, China's commanders and strategists were deeply affected by Operation Desert Storm, the rollback of Iraq's invasion and annexation of neighboring Kuwait led by the United States in 1991. Chinese military leaders could watch on CNN real-time demonstrations of America's advances in C^3I (command, control, communication, and intelligence) which allowed battlefield commanders to coordinate their technologically advanced, exceptionally mobile and lethal air, land, and sea forces. Though military modernization was planned in any case as the fourth and final initiative of the "Four Modernizations," the Gulf War created in China a heightened awareness of its own backwardness in weapons technology, unit coordination, and force mobility.

Third, China's strategic priority has shifted somewhat away from defending against receding threats of ground invasion of its core home territory. Today, its political-military strategy is more focused upon (1) defending its new industrial centers concentrated along its Pacific coast, (2) preventing the Chinese-claimed Taiwan from making a formal bid for independence, and (3) securing China's claim of sovereignty over all of the Spratly Islands in the South China Sea, a potentially oil-rich assortment of islets also claimed in whole or in part by Taiwan, Brunei, Malaysia, and the Philippines. With the end of the Cold War, China's potential military confrontation with traditional rivals like Russia, Japan, India, and even the United States have unquestionably receded, but the new environment is more fluid and unpredictable. Could, for instance, a revived Indonesia (see Chapter 9) pose a threat to Chinese commerce through the Straits of Malacca? Inherent in each of these new priorities is the requirement for substantially enhanced air and naval, rather than traditional ground, capabilities. Let us examine, then, recent and ongoing efforts by China to modernize its coercive capabilities in light of its altered concept of its strategic requirements.

Map 1.1 Map of China and surrounding areas, including Spratly Islands.

Elements of Modernization

China has clearly invested heavily in updating its military forces. Two measures of this commitment are changes in the size of the military and in the amount of military spending.

In terms of *size*, China's forces have recently shrunk from three million to two and one-half million men. Additional uniformed slots are currently being phased out. Prevailing doctrine has it that a leaner, better trained, and more technologically equipped force is better suited to meet the country's security requirements in light of the extraordinary advances made by other states, particularly the United States. As measured by *spending*, China has clearly made military modernization a leading priority. In 2000, for example, official on-the-books defense spending rose by 12.7 percent in an economy that grew by only 7 percent. But it is difficult to ascertain how much money China actually spends on the PLA. The formal defense budget does not cover such important components as weapons purchased and military research. At the same time, a dollar-for-dollar comparison between, for example, Chinese and American military spending tells us rather little, given the much lower salaries of the PLA and its lack of the elaborate overhead costs incurred by the United States to provide costly amenities such as modern housing, health care, travel, dependent care, and the like for its excellent but very high-priced armed forces. What we can say with confidence, however, is that China's budgetary allotments for the PLA have risen sharply in recent years.

What has that money bought? China's recent *weapons acquisition* program has proceeded along two tracks: (1) indigenous development and (2) foreign purchases. As noted earlier, Beijing's strategic focus has shifted toward potential clashes over disputed islands in the South China Sea, with Taiwan should it make a formal attempt at independence, and against any threat to its new industrial centers near the Pacific Ocean. Each emphasis requires modernization efforts in China's air and naval forces.

China's fleet of fighter aircraft is outmoded by today's standards. Its domestically produced F-8II (one of which crashed after colliding with an American "spy" plane off the Chinese coast in April 2001) is broadly comparable to a U.S. F-4, a 1960s aircraft. The J-10, a more advanced fighter, is now under development. Based in part on Israeli technology, the J-10 will enhance China's jet fighter capabilities, but a substantial amount of time is required to develop, test, manufacture, and deploy complex modern aircraft.

In order to close the technology gap of its fighter fleet while the J-10 is being developed, China has purchased 48 Su-27s from Russia and is now building that aircraft under a licensing agreement with Moscow. But its much-publicized acquisition of the SU-27 has been fraught with problems. In the first place, phasing out old F-8IIs and replacing them with SU-27s represents a technology leap from the 1960s squarely into the 1970s. That was the decade during which the former Soviet aircraft was originally designed and developed.

Worse, the purchased SU-27s sat unattended in Russia's harsh winter conditions while the two countries haggled over terms of payment. When the aircraft finally arrived in China, they did so without operating manuals. To add final insult to injury, they proved too heavy for Chinese runways, thus necessitating costly airfield construction. China's air force, then, remains a rather primitive war-fighting machine. Moreover, the Chinese air force lacks aircraft with sufficient range to menace enemies very far from its borders.

As to warships, China's "blue water" fleet—that is, its oceangoing ships as opposed to its "gray water" coastal vessels—is a relatively small and not terribly advanced one by contemporary standards. Its navy has equipped some of its fleet with radar-guided surface-to-surface missiles. In some ways, this represents a substantial enhancement of its naval might, but it must be noted that the missiles deployed—the old fashioned HY-2—are liquid-fueled, are inherently volatile, and could thus be quite dangerous to China's navy itself. Also, they can be reloaded only while the ships are in port. So what at first glance appears as a major addition to naval capability turns out to be a rather problematical development.

Four relatively modern submarines have been purchased from Russia, along with several destroyers. Both types of vessels somewhat improve China's ability to project a naval presence beyond its own shores. To date, however, China has been unable to acquire the one naval asset that represents true long-distance power-projection capability—a fleet of aircraft carriers. Attempts to negotiate foreign purchases have thus far been unsuccessful. And indigenous development seems quite unlikely for the near future due to the extraordinary cost involved, the specialized, highly advanced engineering skills required for carrier construction, and the logistical capacity needed to manage the substantial flotilla of supply ships necessary to support a carrier's operations. Moreover, there is growing agreement that carriers are increasingly vulnerable to missile attacks that will make them obsolescent in the future, making development questionable.

Assessing China's Military Strength

It is widely assumed among defense analysts that China possesses the military manpower and equipment needed to fend off any foreseeable land-based assault upon its core homeland. The sheer size of both the country and of the PLA make a "defense in depth" strategy both feasible for China and daunting to any would-be invader. Any currently imaginable scenario in which an aggressor sought to quash the Beijing regime through invasion would require it to penetrate deep into the country's heartland. Even should an invader seize portions of Chinese territory, it would face nightmarish contingencies. China's highly nationalistic populace would prove exceedingly difficult to neutralize and pacify, and the enemy's long lines of supply would be an obvious point of vulnerability. It is thus essentially a given that China is able to defend its home continental territory and population against ground invasion.

Similarly, on current evidence Chinese defense planners believe that the probability that the country will be attacked by nuclear weapons is rather low. Absent an extraordinary escalation of a regional conflict, the states which currently possess both proven warhead and missile delivery capability—the United States, Russia, Britain, France, India, and Pakistan—lack a rational incentive to launch a doomsday nuclear assault on China. Even amid rising tensions, China's small and defensively configured nuclear arsenal should accomplish its doctrinal purpose of "minimum deterrence," that is, ensure that it could deter a "first use" nuclear assault by maintaining the capacity to retaliate and inflict unacceptable damage upon its attacker. This confidence in their nuclear security would be undermined somewhat by a U.S. decision to deploy a national missile defense system, one aspect of which clearly would be to deflect a Chinese nuclear retaliation against the United States, a prime reason the Chinese have actively opposed such a deployment by the Bush administration (see Chapter 11).

So despite the considerable technological gap between Western and Chinese defense capabilities, its home territory is currently rather secure against either major ground-based penetration or wholesale destruction from nuclear assault. While China is by no means invulnerable to the severe punishment that could be delivered to its military structure, industrial assets, and population through foreign aerial and naval means, it currently faces little credible threat to its survival and independence as a sovereign state, except by an unlikely nuclear strike from a major nuclear power. This assessment is reinforced by a reasonably benign post–Cold War security environment of economic interdependence and the virtual absence of cross-border wars by states.

What, then, of China's power projection capabilities, that is, what is its ability to impose its will outside of its borders? Here we are principally interested in the broader question of China's ability to challenge the current balance of power and stability within the crucial East Asian region. For greater clarity, this issue is best divided into two distinct questions: its strategic position *vis-à-vis* nearby states within continental Asia, and its ability to project its power beyond its territory into the more distant continental and maritime states of East Asia.

As to its potential to coerce its continental neighbors, it is necessary to stress that China's *latent* strategic dominance of both the Korean peninsula in Northeast Asia and of Indochina (Laos, Cambodia, and Vietnam) in Southeast Asia is a widely accepted reality. The likelihood of it actually employing its coercive capabilities in either location will be discussed later. But its capacity to wield power in both theaters is simply a reality.

In order to be able to alter significantly the existing balance of power in the broader East Asian region, however, China would have to achieve the ability to project power beyond the mainland. Doing so would require attaining sufficient aerial and naval power projection capability both to operate in distant locales and to do so with capabilities that surpass those of other states in the region.

As Robert Ross has shown in his insightful "Beijing as a Conservative Power," China must contemplate the requirements of acting in three distinct maritime theaters in East Asia: (1) the East China Sea, (2) the northern portion of the South China Sea, and (3) the southern reaches of the South China Sea.

China would have to establish its clear dominance over the first—the East China Sea—in order to seize Taiwan or to reassert its historical primacy over Japan and South Korea. Acquiring and sustaining that primacy would require superior air power in support of naval operations against an adversary. In this theater, China could take advantage of its geographic proximity to utilize its land-based aircraft. But, as noted earlier, China's air force is technologically primitive and severely limited in range. Its outdated inventory of 1960s and 1970s aircraft would fare poorly against Japan's much more sophisticated F2 fighter jet. Also, Japan's aerial defenses are greatly enhanced by its possession of modern AWACS (airborne warning and control system) aircraft, and its fighters are being equipped with much more advanced air-to-air missiles than are China's.

In addition, Japan possesses a science, technology, and industrial base which far exceeds China's, and it must also be kept in mind that current Japanese policy places sharp voluntary curbs on defense spending, rarely allowing it officially to exceed 1 percent of GNP. Should it feel threatened by China, then Japan is exceedingly well poised to maintain or even extend its current air and naval superiority over China. Chinese military dominance of the East China Sea in ways menacing to Japan is thus highly unlikely in the foreseeable future.

Much the same could be said of Taiwan. More economically advanced than mainland China, Taiwan possesses the wealth, the technology base, and the manufacturing capability to maintain a sophisticated defense against a potential armed takeover by Beijing. Equipped with both an advanced navy and a highly sophisticated air force which includes U.S.–built F-16s, Taiwan can most likely repulse a military assault from the mainland. The important caveat for Taiwan, however, is China's current drive to acquire a growing arsenal of quite accurate cruise and ballistic missiles, virtually all of which are deployed in coastal southeast China and targeted at Taiwan. The warning time for launch of these modern missiles is brief, and in any case Taiwan is unable fully to defend itself against a missile barrage. This is the instrument of choice for Beijing to prevent Taiwan from carrying out a policy of formal independence from the mainland during the next decade or two while China lacks a credible air, sea, and land capability to hold the island against formal secession. Such a barrage could virtually destroy Taiwan, but the results would be a Pyrrhic victory, wiping out one of the largest sources of foreign investment in China. China can destroy Taiwan if it so chooses, but what would be the point?

China is similarly currently incapable of effectively projecting a great deal of armed might into the southern portion of the South China Sea, a region that includes Indonesia, the Philippines, Singapore, and Malaysia. Absent either aircraft carriers or difficult-to-master aerial refueling, the sheer distances involved buffer this region against any potential threat from China's land-based aircraft. Singapore, Malaysia, and Indonesia all have fleets of sophisticated American and British fighters capable of repulsing hostile intrusion by China's navy. So in two of the three East Asian theaters where a Chinese challenge to the current balance of power would carry both regional and even global consequence, China is currently incapable of presenting a credible threat, even if it had the desire to do so.

It is in the third regional theater—the northern portion of the South China Sea—where China's land-based aircraft could provide aerial support for both ground operations in Indochina and for operations in the waters near the Paracel Islands east of Vietnam and in the northernmost disputed Spratly Islands. Rightful ownership of the Paracels—which China seized from Vietnam in 1974—is a matter of dispute among Taiwan, Vietnam, and China. China's unyielding stance on the islands was captured in an interview with a Chinese official in Beijing in the summer of 1999. "We can discuss the Spratlys," he said, "but the Paracels are simply off the table. Period."

Perhaps more significantly, maritime dominance of the crucial shipping lanes in the region would confer upon China strategic leverage in the overall calculus of regional and global might. But such a scenario is essentially negated for the foreseeable future by the presence of the U.S. Seventh Fleet, an unrivaled armada of naval and aerial capability that is broadly perceived throughout the region as essential to the maintenance of a stable regional balance.

On current evidence, then, fears of a militarily predatory China both bent upon and capable of imposing its will across East Asia would appear to be minimal. It is true, of course, that China's "Fourth Modernizations" is an evolving phenomenon, and that with the passage of time the country's power-projection capabilities will become more potent than they are today. But it is equally the case that China's neighbors will not remain standing still, but will rather maintain a cautious eye upon any perceived security threat from its huge neighbor and will enhance their own coercive capabilities as needed in order to balance—and thus neutralize—that potential threat. If economic globalization continues in the region, military rivalry may well retreat as well.

Non-Coercive Influence: China's New Diplomacy

Well aware of its military backwardness and of its economy's growing dependence upon trade, China has in recent years adopted what for it is a new style of diplomacy. Until quite recently, the characteristic style of Beijing's envoys abroad was one of secrecy, aloofness, inaccessibility to host media and public organizations, and a pronounced rigidity in repeating abroad the "line" laid down by the Chinese government. Today, however, there is a growing awareness that the old-style diplomacy was an ineffective instrument for advancing China's interests abroad.

Increasingly, Chinese diplomacy reflects a growing sophistication about how best to get the country's message out, an appearance (at least) of sensitivity to the other state's apprehensions, and the appearance in prominent posts of a new generation of diplomats more skilled at the arts of gentle persuasion rather than the dogmatic assertion of unilateral pronouncements. Characteristic of this new breed of diplomats is Fu Yung, the 40-something ambassador to the Philippines. Her refreshing accessibility, sympathetic manner, and low-key presentation of Beijing's point of view has helped to dampen the atmosphere of crisis and mistrust between the two countries over their disputed claims to portions of the Spratly Islands. Unlike the older generation of Chinese diplomats, Miss Fu is highly educated—she graduated from China's premier Beijing University—and possesses a more cosmopolitan worldview.

Her task, of course, remains the same as that of all diplomats—to advance her country's interests abroad. But it is her style—highly visible, sympathetic towards the concerns of other states, receptive to continuous invitations to meet with local politicians, the media, and local civic and professional organizations—which has won her plaudits. She readily concedes that China's rise presents "a learning process both for China and its neighbors." And when questioned about the dispute between Beijing and Manila over the Spratly issue, she begins her remarks by conceding that "there's a difference in perception."

Soothing diplomatic personalities and expressions of pop-psychology empathy will not, of course, themselves neutralize Asian and global anxieties inherently created by a rising state. But they are certainly valuable noncoercive instruments that China is learning to utilize in order to smooth the path of its ascending stature as an international player.

Beyond mere style, Chinese diplomacy has recently focused upon (1) joining literally hundreds of international organizations from which it was previously aloof and (2) mending fences with its Asian neighbors. In Southeast Asia, for example, China has adroitly cultivated bilateral ties (its preferred method in international dealings) in order to dilute the political will of the region's states to adopt a common stance in opposing China's claims in the South China Sea. In initiatives as diverse as resolving its long-standing border dispute with Vietnam in 1999 or agreeing to import more of Thailand's goods in exchange for Thai diplomatic efforts on China's behalf in 1997, China's concerted drive to improve its bilateral ties throughout Asia are beginning to pay off.

The Philippines' dispute over China's construction of structures on Mischief Reef—one of the Spratlys claimed by both countries and, significantly, located far from China but quite close to the Philippines—is instructive. When Chinese construction on the reef first began in 1995, it set off alarm bells about Chinese expansionism throughout Southeast Asia. Presenting a united front through the Association of Southeast Asian Nations (ASEAN), the region's states loudly expressed their strong opposition and demanded that China engage them in multilateral diplomacy to resolve competing claims to the Spratlys. But only four years later, when China decided to test the region's united resolve by sharply reinforcing and expanding the structures, the Philippines found itself alone in its protests to Beijing. ASEAN unity had crumbled. China's newly adroit bilateral fence mending had paid off.

Diplomacy, then, has become an important foreign policy instrument for a developing China whose coercive and economic instruments of influence remain quite constrained. Unable to emulate Japan's generous foreign aid and—for now, at least—unable to present a credible military threat to most of Asia, it is learning how to employ age-old diplomatic arts in order to advance its strategic intentions. But this begs the question of what, precisely, are China's strategic intentions?

CONCLUSION

A recent study commissioned by the U.S. Air Force (Swaine and Tellis) argues that China's overarching strategy aims to advance three broad objectives: (1) maintain internal order and enhance the well-being, understood principally in economic terms, of the populace, (2) maintain the territorial integrity and sovereignty of the state, and (3) attain great-power status within the international system.

It is the first of these objectives—economic advancement—upon which the remaining two increasingly depend. Defending against ever-shifting external and secessionist threats to state sovereignty necessitates the maintenance of costly, constantly modernizing armed capabilities, which in turn requires a strong domestic economic foundation. And, in an increasingly interdependent world, international power itself is increasingly understood to be a compound both of its traditional coercive component and more modern modalities of influence, the prime one being economic stature. For Beijing's leaders, then, economic advancement is *the* overriding objective.

If the forces of globalization—reduced barriers to trade, foreign direct investment, and financial flows among them—create opportunities for China's economic aspirations, it is also the case that they impose constraints upon the permissible forms of international undertakings. Today over one-third of China's economy is accounted for by trade. Its global trade surplus is nearly $40 billion annually, and its trading surplus with the United States is an astounding $60 billion. Both the accrued wealth from its trade surplus and the domestic jobs that depend upon ready access to foreign markets are essential components of Beijing's drive for national economic development.

The past and present constrain as well as encourage Chinese economic growth. Although China's economy has grown rapidly, much of that growth has been in low-technology consumer manufactures (toys, clothing, etc.) rather than in the high-technology sectors in which the most advanced states operate. Moreover, much of the economy remains socialized under the jurisdiction of the state-owned enterprises (SOEs). Much of the power of the party and the military resides in the SOEs, which are economically unproductive but politically difficult to dissolve.

Yet even as opportunities enhance China's economic modernity, its growing dependence upon them means that in its international political and military undertakings, Beijing's freedom of action is inherently constrained. An unprovoked bid to take Taiwan by force, for example, would most certainly trigger broad economic sanctions that would deal a costly setback to China's development efforts. Likewise, an uncompromising insistence upon its unilateral declaration of sovereignty over *all* of the disputed Spratly Islands—backed by armed force or even threats of force—will alienate China's neighbors in Southeast Asia, raise alarms about the pacific inclinations of the emerging regional giant, and thus dampen growing trade and investment sources in the crucial East Asia region. On net, then, China's determination to ascend from poverty and attain the level of economic advancement which will both sustain social cohesion and confer upon it great power stature provides its leaders with powerful disincentives to threaten its neighbors and to otherwise become perceived as a problematic international citizen.

That being said, it would be unwise to conclude that a rising China presents only negligible challenges to existing international arrangements. Its immense size alone means that it will be a state of growing weight in the global system. And the ballast of that weight is in large part its collective memories of having been violated by foreign powers, memories kept very much alive by its current regime. While understandable, China's ritualized invocation of past injustices sometimes renders it an unusually prideful and nationalistic state. It is perhaps the single most reflexive champion of a rigidly traditional conception of state sovereignty, a conception that is gradually losing vitality in the developed states of Europe, North America, and East Asia. In those areas, notions of interdependence and the growing role played by non–state actors in foreign affairs are gradually leading to a modernist view that state sovereignty is no longer the alpha and the omega of the international system.

Beijing's almost daily denunciations of "hegemonism" must also be understood. When viewed from China, the United States often appears as towering, sometimes arrogant state bent upon imposing its own values and visions of global order upon others. Such "hegemonism" is perceived as inherently threatening to China's long-violated and now championed sovereignty. So it is axiomatic that Beijing will seek to reduce American influence, particularly in Asia.

That fear of American "hegemonism" is leading it into an increasingly close informal alliance with neighboring Russia. Should both states become so dissatisfied with the international *status quo* that their shared discontent transmutes into, at a minimum, obstreperous resistance to common major power efforts to maintain international comity or, worse, armed revisionism, then the latent anxiety created by the specter of a rising giant could give way to a new cold war.

Even without credible fears of foreign domination, it is likely that Beijing's leadership wishes to see China reclaim its historical role at the center of Asian geopolitics. Its location alone—adjacent at once to Northeast Asia, Russia, Central Asia, and Southeast Asia—places it at the symbolic as well as the geographic center of Asia. In 1999 Joseph Prueher—then a Navy admiral and now the American ambassador to China—made this assessment of China's strategic aspirations: "At some point in the future, they would like to have everyone in the region have to have China's approval for whatever they might want to do."

Certainly Prueher's interpretation is a widely shared one among foreign policy elites in both Northeast and Southeast Asia. It is the prime mover behind developments as diverse as Japan's 1997 strengthening of its security relationship with the United States, Philippines' decision to allow American forces back into their country after evicting them only several years earlier, Singapore's offer of its deep-water port facilities to the U.S. Seventh Fleet, and Vietnam's 1995 entry into the Association of Southeast Asian Nations (ASEAN), an organization which now includes every country in the region.

In addition to the national security concerns inherently sparked by a rising major power, there is also a broad interest in Asia in preventing China from gaining a chokehold over economically crucial shipping lanes. Each day, 114 ships (or 41,600 ships per year) transit the Strait of Malacca at the southern reach of the South China Sea. As then-Admiral Prueher put it, "It is not in our mutual interest for any state, including the United States, to become a Pacific hegemon."

The consequences of China's rise on regional and global stability and security will be closely monitored in the coming decades. As other states seek a better understanding of China's intentions, Chinese leaders would do well to keep in mind that their unique place in Asia means they must be especially sensitive to how others view both their ascent and what they plan to do with it.

So what kind of a rising power will China be? Clearly, historical experience suggests to the Chinese that their clear mission to become a central actor on the international scene and the dominant actor in East Asia. While China has some of the wherewithal (a huge population, a growing economy) to realize these goals, it has restraints as well. The Chinese military, despite efforts at modernization, is technologically behind, the economy is large but comparatively primitive, and the web of global interdependence constrains Chinese assertiveness. Being a rising power in the new global system may prove to be quite different than being a rising power in an earlier time.

STUDY/DISCUSSION QUESTIONS

1. Chinese-American relations are often made more complex by each side's *perceptions*—sometimes unconsciously held—of the other. Viewed from Beijing, why might the United States appear as simply the most recent in a long line of foreign powers who have imperiously ordered China about, viewed it in a condescending manner, failed to accord it the respect it feels that it deserves in light of its often brilliant history, and generally sought to contain its international influence? Conversely, what factors might well be at work in the thinking of those American officials, advisors, and policy analysts who believe that a rising China represents a "threat" to both regional and global security and stability? To what extent might race play a role? Or the broad ignorance in the West of Asian history, culture, and values?

2. In an interview with the author, a Japanese foreign policy official once described the Chinese as being uncommonly rigid, ethnocentric, self-regarding, and dogmatic in their worldview. If indeed this is so, (a) Why might this be the case? (b) How might this cultural trait affect China's aspiration to wield influence abroad on a larger scale? and (c) Is China's growing interaction with the community of nations likely to diminish Chinese intellectual rigidity, or is the country instead likely to spark growing conflict abroad by carrying its unyielding outlook into a growing number of international forums?

3. As a matter of practical statecraft, why does China almost always insist upon dealing with its Southeast Asian neighbors through *bilateral* talks rather than in the *multilateral* settings preferred by ASEAN's member states?

4. List, discuss, and evaluate several concrete, practical steps which China could undertake to lessen the anxieties among its regional neighbors occasioned by its rising strength?

5. Evaluate the implications for world order and major power comity of the recent emergence of an informal Sino-Russian alliance.

READING/RESEARCH MATERIAL

Bernstein, Richard, and Ross H. Munro. "The Coming Conflict with America." *Foreign Affairs,* March/April 1997, 18–32.

Campbell, Kurt M. and Derek J. Mitchell. "Crisis in the Taiwan Strait." *Foreign Affairs,* July/August 2001, 14–25.

Gilboy, George, and Eric Heginbotham. "China's Coming Transformation." *Foreign Affairs,* July/August 2001, 26–39.

Gurtov, Mel, and Byong-Moo Hwang. *China's Security: The New Roles of Military.* Boulder, CO: Lynne Rienner Publishers, 1998.

Khalilzad, Zalmay M., et al. *The United States and a Rising China: Strategic and Military Implications.* Santa Monica, CA: RAND, 1999.

Nathan, Andrew J., and Robert S. Ross. *The Great Wall and the Empty Fortress: China's Search for Security.* New York: W. W. Norton, 1997.

Ross, Robert S. "Beijing as a Conservative Power." *Foreign Affairs,* March/April 1997, 33–44.

Segal, Gerald. "Does China Matter?" *Foreign Affairs,* September/October 1999, 24–36.

Starr, John Bryan. *Understanding China: A Guide to China's Economy, History, and Political Structure.* New York: Hill and Wang, 1997.

Swaine, Michael D., and Ashley J. Tellis. *Interpreting China's Grand Strategy: Past, Present, and Future.* Santa Monica, CA: RAND, 2000.

WEB SITES

A compendium of online resources about Chinese military policy and capabilities
Chinese Military Power at http://www.comw.org/cmp

Index of web-based information sources relating to China's foreign relations
Chinese Foreign Policy Net at http://www.stanford.edu/~fravel/chinafp.htm

Compilation of resources concerning China's proliferation activities and agreements
Proliferation News and Resources: China at http://www.ceip.org/files/nonprolif/html

U.S. government profile of China, including its people, government, and economy
CIA World Fact Book: China at http://www.cia.gov/cia/publications/factbook/geos/ch.html

Comprehensive overview prepared by the Federal Research Division of the Library of Congress
China, a Country Study at http://memory.loc.gov/frd/cs/cntoc.html

Offers overview of Chinese nuclear systems and facilities
China Nuclear Forces Guide at http://fas.org/nuke/guide/china

CHAPTER TWO

The Growing Significance of NGOs:

MEDECINS SANS FRONTIERES AND PEACEKEEPING

PRÉCIS

The phenomenon of international activity being conducted by international organizations whose members are not the governments of states—referred to as nongovernmental organizations or NGOs—is not a unique attribute of the contemporary period. NGOs, in a number of guises, have been in operation for over a century, and some, such as the International Red Cross, have been prominent actors on the international scene.

In the contemporary world, NGOS have become more obvious in international discourse in at least two distinct ways. First, they have become increasingly activist in their pursuit of their interests, and this is especially true in the area of peacekeeping operations (PKOs) that forms the context of this case. Second, at least some of the more activist NGOs pose an open challenge to the principle of state sovereignty, snubbing the idea when it interferes with their work. The *Medecins sans Frontieres*, which is the NGO that is the subject of the case, is especially open in its disdain for trappings of sovereignty such as international frontiers, and it shows its lack of respect particularly in circumstances of great human suffering, which often accompanies the situations which become PKOs. The two factors in combination form the thrust of this new aspect of NGO activity in the contemporary environment.

Nongovernmental organizations (NGOs) are playing an increasingly important and in some cases controversial role in the international relations of the post–Cold War world. Much of this controversy arises from their independence from the controls of national governments, which frees them to engage in activities unconstrained by governmental concerns. One of the areas in which they have become particularly active and are playing a significant but controversial role is in their participation alongside governments in a variety of humanitarian efforts falling under the category of peace-keeping operations (PKOs). French-based *Medecins sans Frontieres* (MSF), whose title translates into Doctors without Borders, is one of the most prominent examples of this phenomenon and one of the best examples of NGOs not only ignoring but virtually flaunting their independence from national control.

International organizations (IOs) are generally divided into two groups for analytical purposes. The most prominent kind is *intergovernmental organizations* (IGOs). The defining characteristic of an IGO is that its members are the governments of states. The most obvious examples of IGOs are the United Nations and its specialized agencies such as the International Monetary Fund or the World Bank (discussed in Chapter 8, "The New Trinity of Globalization").

The other kind of international organization is the nongovernmental organization (NGO). The NGOs are also international in their membership, but unlike IGOs, their members are private individuals or groups from different countries rather than governments. NGOs are far more numerous than IGOs, and their numbers have swelled markedly in an Internet age where communications across borders is both easy and cheap. For instance, there were around 200 NGOs in 1909. Today, there are over 17,000. Most NGOs are narrow in their focus and operate well outside the public eye. Some, however, have very ambitious agendas and play a role in the most public areas of international relations. MSF is one of those prominent organizations.

One of the venues in which MSF and other high-profile activist NGOs are increasingly involved is peacekeeping operations (PKOs). The origin of these operations, normally created with at least a mandate from the United Nations and often kept under UN authority, goes back to the Cold War. In that environment, PKOs generally were mounted to keep two formerly warring states separated physically and to oversee either implementation of some form of peace agreement or, more minimally, to prevent formerly warring parties from resuming hostilities by providing a physical barricade of blue-helmeted soldiers that potential attackers would have to penetrate before reaching the foe. The prototype of this kind of operation was the United Nations Emergency Force (UNEF), which separated Israel and Egypt from the end of the Suez War in 1956 until the outbreak of the Six Days War in 1967 (the UNEF was asked to leave Egypt, where it was stationed, prior to that war). Other examples include the United Nations Force in Cyprus (UNFICYP), which has been in operation since 1973, and the United Nations Interim Force in Lebanon (UNIFIL), which operated between 1976 and 2000.

The nature and thrust of peacekeeping changed radically with the end of the Cold War. During the Cold War, most of the PKOs involved the outcomes of interstate wars, although a few (the Congo between 1960 and 1964, for instance) focused on internal (or civil) wars. Since the post–Cold War world began to emerge, however, interstate wars have virtually disappeared from the menu of world violence, and the vast majority of armed conflicts have been conducted inside the boundaries of existing states, normally fought exclusively (or nearly so) by nationals of that country. While it is true that the large majority of wars during the Cold War were also internal, there has been a shift in the kinds and qualities of wars being fought.

During the Cold War, most civil conflicts were fought between a recognizable government and an armed and organized insurgent movement. The clear purpose of the two sides was to gain (or maintain) control of the political system within the country in question. Although civilians were sometimes the victims of terrorist or other forms of suppression by one side or the other, the major form of combat was between armed units of the government and the insurgency. In most cases, the Soviets supported one side (usually the insurgents, until the Reagan Doctrine championed U.S. support of anticommunist insurgents in places like Nicaragua and Afghanistan) and the United States supported the beleaguered government. Among the effects of sponsorship was the ability to place some restraints on how the client group conducted hostilities.

All internal wars during the Cold War did not conform to this "model" of conduct. The most prominent exception was the genocide in Cambodia, where the infamous Khmer Rouge gained power after an internal struggle and engaged in the massive extermination of all Cambodians who opposed them between 1976 and 1979, when the country was invaded and conquered by Vietnam in an extension of the Sino-Soviet competition in Asia (the Khmer Rouge were aligned with the People's Republic of China, the Vietnamese with the Soviet Union). The massive slaughter by the Khmer Rouge of innocent civilians proved to be a chilling premonition of the kinds of violence that have shaken the post–Cold War world.

The new pattern, which I have called *new internal war* in *UnCivil Wars* and *When America Fights,* has become the distinctive, if not the exclusive, form of violence in the post–Cold War world. The list of places where these internal wars have occurred is familiar—Somalia, Bosnia, East Timor, Sierra Leone, Kosovo—and so is the aura of tragedy and savagery that has been a major characteristic of these conflicts. The countries where they have occurred generally have had governments in tatters where they existed at all, and the armed insurgents have been little more than armed thugs who roam the countryside, terrorizing, uprooting, or murdering innocent, unarmed civilians, usually for criminal or other less than exemplary purposes. One of the most shocking symbols has been the use of young teenagers—little more than boys—as "soldiers" by movements such as Sierra Leone's Revolutionary United Front. With the retreat of the former Cold War competitors from much of the developing world, there is little to restrain the participants in their reigns of terror. It is symbolically significant that the individuals who participate are more often called "fighters" than they are "soldiers."

The results of these "wars" are familiar as well: the starving children of Somalia with their distended bellies and pencil-thin extremities, the emaciated prisoners of war in Bosnian detention camps, the homeless natives of East Timor sitting outside their burned-down homes, the Sierra Leoneans with their multiple amputations, and the displaced Kosovars in refugee camps or attempting to return home after the ethnic cleansing ceased. The common thread in all these cases has been the extreme human suffering endured by the victim populations and the obviously compelling need for the international community to take actions somehow to alleviate the human tragedies being endured.

These tragedies raise multiple questions for the international system and its members. Some of these questions, such as the right to intervene (see Chapter 5) and the prosecution of war criminals (see Chapter 4), are dealt with elsewhere in this volume, and the question of whether involvement should be part of U.S. policy was one of the few foreign policy issues that dented the electoral agenda during the 2000 presidential campaign.

A major concern in all of these deliberations is also how to try to deal with and ameliorate the suffering of the victims. Part of the short-term question is how to stem the worst of the immediate effects of war; in the longer run, there is also the question of making the target societies whole and stable once again (if they ever were). MSF is a major part of the answer to the short-term question; increasingly, it is part of the longer-term solution as well.

The current case study thus has two related focuses. The major focus is on MSF as an example of a highly activist, dedicated, and visible NGO. Because it is a medical organization, there is a natural bridge to the second focus on civil conflicts, since the kinds of human medical suffering that MSF is dedicated to relieving is nowhere more obvious than in these conflicts.

MEDECINS SANS FRONTIERES

Although it has been active for nearly 28 years, MSF did not attract the broad public eye until 1999. Between its formation in December 1971 and its emergence in the public spotlight with the receipt of the Nobel Peace Prize in 1999, its relative anonymity was, to a large degree, a matter of choice; its mission is to provide relief to those suffering through natural and man-made disasters, and its methods are often highly unorthodox (some would argue occasionally controversial and even illegal). The doctors who work for MSF prefer to operate in the shadows of the international stage. These shadows were illuminated when the organization was awarded the Nobel Peace Prize, thereby making its low profile less possible to maintain.

Background and Evolution of MSF

MSF is largely the result of the experiences of a handful of young doctors attempting to relieve the hardships of the civilian population during the Nigerian-Biafran Civil War of 1967–1970. The "French doctors," as they are known, worked under the auspices of the International Red Cross, a highly respected but very conservative NGO, during that conflict. The Red Cross has a tradition of strict neutrality and deference to political and legal authorities that makes it respected and trusted by governments in matters such as the conformance of prisoner-of-war camps to international conventions on the treatment of military prisoners. In the eyes of the young, idealistic doctors who formed MSF, this conformance came at the expense of providing maximum relief and succor to those civilians suffering the kinds of indignities associated with modern new internal wars. The French doctors were frustrated by the impact of the International Red Cross's conservative approach and practices; MSF was their answer.

After the Biafran experience, a small group of doctors who had participated in the attempt to alleviate the worst civilian suffering by Nigerian soldiers against Ibo tribesmen in Biafra decided that the diplomatic, institutional approach practiced by the Red Cross had made the suffering worse than it would otherwise have been. They thus set out to form a more aggressive, interventionist organization. The result was MSF, whose first activity was to provide medical care for victims of flooding in Pakistan. MSF then gradually enlarged its activities to encompass both man-made and natural disasters that have carried them around the world to locations as diverse as Ethiopia, Honduras, El Salvador, Peru, Yemen, Mozambique, Liberia, and Sudan. Their goal is to find those suffering medical problems and to alleviate those problems; overt political and other concerns are excluded from their motivations.

The organization has grown dramatically. There were originally six founding members of MSF, the most prominent of whom has been Dr. Bernard Kouchner, who later became the French health minister and who until recently served as the special representative of the secretary-general (SRSG) of the United Nations effort in Kosovo. In this role, Kouchner was the operational leader of peacekeeping and state-building efforts in that bitterly torn land, the first time someone with a primary background in an NGO has ever occupied that kind of position.

From its modest beginning, the organization has increased in size. In 1999, for instance, MSF had 23 offices in various countries (the American chapter of MSF uses the English translation Doctors without Borders to designate itself). MSF has over 2,000 medical volunteers at work in 80 countries. Underlying its operation is a budget of over $167 million, almost four-fifths of which comes from private donations worldwide. Such an extensive operation with such a modest budget is possible because most of the medical personnel, including physicians and nurses, act voluntarily and do not receive remuneration beyond living and travel expenses.

Most of the medical activities in which MSF engages have been carried out far from the public eye. In 1980, for instance, MSF sent medical teams into Afghanistan to care for the wounded that resulted from the Soviet invasion and occupation of that country, in the process gaining some reputation as a human rights monitor, since MSF doctors witnessed and reported violations. In 1984, it instituted a nutrition program in Ethiopia, and ended up denouncing the misuse of humanitarian assistance to that country. In 1988, MSF had the only medical team to reach the Kurdish town of Halabja in Iraq after Saddam Hussein's forces had attacked the Kurdish stronghold with chemical weapons. When the Persian Gulf War broke out, it set up camps in the no-man's land between Iraq and Jordan to provide aid to refugees. When the Kurds fled Iraq at the end of the war to avoid the vengeance of Saddam Hussein, MSF was the first to arrive on the Turkish mountainsides to provide relief to the 70,000 refugees clinging to the most tenuous existence until global publicity, much of it created by MSF itself, resulted in the U.S. government intervening under the banner of Operation Provide Comfort (later renamed Northern Watch).

MSF has grown to be the world's largest nonprofit medical relief agency. In addition to its willingness to involve itself in conditions of man-made emergency, it has also been very active in other, less controversial activities such as programs of inoculation against deadly diseases and its Access to Essential Medicines Campaign, which seeks to raise awareness about and to bring relief to poor peoples who are routinely denied access to medical treatment.

But it is MSF's willingness to insert itself into highly political situations—notably war zones where civilians are subjected to grossly inhumane treatment—that has become its international claim to fame. No one argues that its basic mission, the alleviation of human suffering from whatever source, is not noble or praiseworthy. But MSF is also the subject of criticism, much of which follows from its origin. MSF was, after all, born out of a fairly scornful rejection of the means of international medical caregiving by the most establishment of caregiving organizations, the International Red Cross. MSF was born as something of a "maverick," and it is a reputation in which it takes satisfaction, even pride. And that does not always sit well with the organizations with which it must interact in providing its services.

Controversies Surrounding MSF

In some ways, MSF resembles another highly activist organization, Greenpeace. Although that organization was formed with a different substantive mission, they share the characteristic of being reasonably scornful "of governments and journalists," according to *The Economist*. MSF and Greenpeace share a level of devotion to their mission that borders, to some observers, on zealotry. It also leads to a set of controversies about what MSF does and how it carries out its mission that has an impact on its ability to work effectively within the framework of PKOs. Five interrelated sources of controversy are worth mentioning.

The first controversy surrounds the very core of the reason for MSF's existence, the notion of being "without borders." The idea that political boundaries cannot and should not be a barrier to the provision of medical attention is the basic reason MSF was created in the first place. As one of the cofounders, Rony Brauman, explained in an interview in *Time International* in 1999, "International relief agencies were too respectful of notions of non-interference and sovereignty. When we saw people dying on the other side of the frontiers, we asked ourselves, 'What is this border? It doesn't mean anything to us.'"

This statement summarizes a major source of irritation between MSF and other helping agencies and also governments in the countries where MSF operates. The organization Brauman accuses of being "too respectful" was, of course, the International Red Cross, suggesting a less than cordial relationship with that NGO. At the same time, MSF ignores the sovereignty of states where it operates; when officially denied permission to enter countries to provide medical relief, the response by MSF has been simply to sneak across borders, in effect illegally infiltrating the sovereign territory of states in an act of overt defiance of international norms. Aside from a firm belief in the righteousness of what it is doing, MSF understands that the nature of its mission and its willingness to publicize unfortunate conditions means governments are reluctant to arrest and deport MSF personnel (although this occasionally does happen), but that its methods are often annoying and even embarrassing to those governments.

This leads to the second controversy surrounding MSF, which is its explicitly political character and nature. Generally speaking, it is a hallmark of international organizations that they must remain fundamentally politically neutral in order to be effective. Certainly this is true of most IGOs, and in most cases, it is also true of NGOs as well. The constraints on NGOs in this regard are less than than those on IGOs, since they are not accountable to the national governments of their origin or where they do business.

MSF has never denied that it is political, at least in the impact it has on situations where it acts. As cofounder Kouchner (who split with MSF in 1980 to form a competitor, *Medecins du Monde*) puts it, "The movement was political from the start. The tradition was medical, the action was medical, but we had to convince people that borders should not protect disgraceful conduct and suffering." (Nolan, 1999) This frank admission, of course, puts MSF at direct odds with governments that are the source of suffering in their countries; as we shall see later in this chapter, their virtually monomaniacal devotion to their mission also puts them at odds with peacekeepers on occasion.

The role MSF has taken upon itself leads to a third controversial characteristic, its tendency to view itself and be viewed as a loner. The doctors who work for the organization have a mission, "a 'duty to interfere' in troubled areas and to speak out about what they saw," in the words of the *Time International* article. This notion of special mission sets MSF aside as something different from others around it. MSF volunteers are proud of the fact that they are often the first caregivers on the scene (e.g., such as ministering to the Kurds in the wake of the Persian Gulf War) and that when all the others have left, they will still be there. Being aloof is, indeed, part of MSF's effectiveness, as its Nobel citation observes: "By maintaining a high degree of independence, the organization has succeeded in living up to its ideals." It does so, of course, at the expense of being thought of as something less than a team player.

The tendency to be viewed as a loner reinforces the fourth characteristic, MSF's penchant for honesty and integrity, some would argue to a fault. The agency's single-minded concern (some would argue obsession) not only with treating but with publicizing the human causes of suffering clearly does not endear it with those organizations (which are often national governments) against whom it levels charges. The leaders of MSF are medical personnel, not diplomats, and while this may endow them with a refreshing degree of candor not usually present in complex international situations, it may also compromise their effectiveness in dealing with others.

Finally, MSF has particular disdain for peacekeeping operations. The basic reason for this feeling arises from the MSF perception that peacekeeping missions simply get in the way of their performance of their duties and that the peacekeepers rapidly adopt self-protection as their basic mission rather than the promotion of the well-being of the target population which MSF seeks to protect.

The attitude of MSF toward peacekeepers was made explicitly in a 1993 report dealing with the UN effort in Somalia and titled "Life, Death, and Aid." The report begins by criticizing governments for their selectivity in terms of which humanitarian disasters they deal with and which they ignore, such as mounting a major effort in Somalia but turning a blind eye toward the equally horrendous slaughter in nearby Sudan. Turning to the actual operation in Somalia, MSF argues additional points. On one hand, MSF maintains that UN PKOs often have imprecise mandates that tie their hands in providing needed assistance to those suffering the effects of war. Instead, the peacekeepers come to define their mission as self-protection rather than the promotion of agendas such as MSF's. Moreover, in their efforts to be fair and impartial, the peacekeepers may actually make it more difficult to conduct operations than it was before their arrival. In Somalia, for instance, the report alleges that UN efforts to provide protection to food supplies being convoyed to remote locations disrupted an informal arrangement MSF had with various warlords whereby the warlords would be allowed to plunder a share of humanitarian relief supplies in return for allowing the rest to get through. When the peacekeepers arrived and restored an open transportation system, this informal arrangement was interrupted, and the clans then began attacking the supply caravans, with the effect that delivery became more, rather than less, difficult than it had been under the clan-MSF arrangement.

Clearly, there are two sides to the story of the impact of PKOs on troubled areas, and those two things are as certain as the proverbial death and taxes. One, there will be additional situations in the world where humanitarian disasters befall countries, thus activating international relief concerns. Second, MSF will be one of the early arrivals on the scene, probably followed by peacekeepers under one banner or another. In these circumstances, the question arises about how they will get along. Answering that question requires looking at the nature of PKOs.

PEACEKEEPING OPERATIONS

As noted earlier, international involvement in the internal violence in a number of Third World countries has become an increasingly prominent component of contemporary international affairs. The frequently gory nature of these conflicts makes them difficult to ignore, especially if television's roving eye happens to capture the worst examples of the gross human suffering that accompanies them. While a few places, such as Sudan, have avoided scrutiny and thus attention by terrorizing the journalists who would otherwise be present so they avoid the country, in most cases suffering will be recorded, and there will be a great temptation to intercede to right the situation (I have elsewhere called this the "do-something syndrome").

The problem is that we have little systematic understanding about how to deal with these great human tragedies, and especially how to create or restore a stable peace in war-torn lands. The Cold War period offered very few counterparts to the ongoing dilemmas—the former Belgian Congo and Cambodia come as close as any—from which the system could learn how to cope, but they are imperfect analogies.

The problem is controversial and revolves around three questions. The first is what outcomes one expects from intervention. Is the goal a mere cessation of the hostilities? Is a return to the status quo ante from which the violence emerged in the first place enough? Or is a stable environment that will nurture a post-involvement peace the desired end we seek? The second question has to do with what must be done to accomplish whatever end one has in mind: the alternatives are interceding into the violence and forcefully making sure it does not resume (what I call conflict suppression) or building viable institutions and structures that will create an atmosphere in which peace will be built (what I call state building). The third question is who should engage in this process and how, which gets to the heart of the involvement of NGOs such as MSF.

Nature of the Problem

When a PKO is first considered, the situation into which it will likely be inserted is either an active war zone or a former war zone where some form of ceasefire (probably not very durable) is in place. In all likelihood, the violence that has occurred has largely been perpetrated against civilian groups within the country by other indigenous groups, leaving a strong residue of bitterness, hatred, and suspicion among the warring parties.

Peacekeepers will normally enter with an initial mandate to restore the order and to stop the killing. As the report by MSF cited in the last section indicates, they may have little mandate beyond that.

The initial conditions frame the sequential tasks that the peacekeepers may undertake. Their first duty, unless a peace of sorts is in place, is to stop the fighting, what I call *peace imposition* (PI). This is a combat job and requires well-equipped combat soldiers. Once peace has been imposed, the task moves to making sure the situation does not revert to fighting once again, or what I call *peace enforcement* (PE). This task requires combat soldiers to convince or intimidate the former fighters into remaining peaceful, but it also involves providing conditions conducive to a return to normalcy, such as reinstating some form of civil justice (police and courts) or instituting such structures if they did not exist before the violence. Providing health care and basic services such as power and water also fall unto this category. The development of institutions is a task for which military force may provide the necessary safety—or shield—to undertake, but the actual tasks are more clearly civilian in nature. If peace enforcement produces an atmosphere where animosities are overcome to the point that the former warring parties prefer continuing peace to the resumption of war, then the task can move to simply maintaining the peace, or *peacekeeping* (PK). Once peacekeeping has reached the point that peace will likely be maintained in the absence of the peacekeepers, then the mission is accomplished and the PKO can be terminated.

Two comments should be made about this continuum at this point. The first is that experience over the past decade has demonstrated that the international system has become reasonably proficient at imposing and even enforcing peace, where the criteria for success of the mission are preventing the resumption of fighting and avoiding casualties to the peacekeepers. The second is that no mission in the post–Cold War world has reached the point of successful peacekeeping, where the criterion of success is whether there is confidence the peace will hold after the mission has been withdrawn. Missions have been terminated, as they were in Somalia, but not with the assurance the peace would remain intact (and in that case, the peace did not hold).

Whether the failure to this point to achieve a stable peace is a critical shortcoming depends on the purposes for which a PKO is commissioned. Basically, such a mission can have one of two basic purposes. The first is *conflict suppression*, the act of forcing warring parties to cease the mayhem. The actions associated with conflict suppression consist of peace imposition and peace enforcement. In addition to ending the direct killing, a mission with this purpose may provide other benefits, such as alleviating hunger and starvation, as was the case in Somalia.

The danger of conflict suppression as the ultimate goal is that it may provide little more than a lull in the fighting. If the situation in a country has deteriorated to the point that a new internal war has raged, there must have been underlying reasons that must be addressed if there is to be a reasonable chance for a stable post-mission peace. In all likelihood, political institutions and processes are dysfunctional or nonexistent, economic conditions are either so wretched or so skewed toward a minority that most people have little stake in the ongoing system, and social, cultural, ethnic, or religious differences are so deep as to leave a thoroughly noncohesive social structure (these problems are also addressed in Chapter 7). When one adds the animosities generated by the war itself, it is clear that a simple cooling-off period provided by peace imposers and enforcers is not going to be sufficient to heal the wounds and scars that war has produced. Something more must be done.

To create at least the prospect that a stable peace will endure after a PKO is completed, these kinds of problems must be addressed and solved. To do so is the aim of the second possible purpose of a PKO, *state building* (the term "nation building" is sometimes used as a synonym, but that is technically incorrect, as the actions are aimed at changing the nature of the political unit, the state). Creating political, economic, social, and psychological conditions which the population prefers to war is the way that a PKO can move along the continuum from a war zone (PI) to a stable post-mission peace where war is unlikely to recur.

There are two basic problems with adopting state building as the purpose of a PKO. The first is, as suggested, that we have little experience with doing these kinds of missions, and thus there is very little concrete guidance based on prior successful experience on how to go about the various tasks that are needed to build a viable state (for that matter, there is no agreement on what the list of tasks is). If there was a "State Builder's Manual" that had proven reliable in the past, the task would be much more manageable. Such a manual does not exist, and if it did, its contents would be mostly conjecture.

The other problem is that the task is certain to be very complex, and that one of the complexities is the very large and varied number of tasks that must be performed and the variety of actors that must be involved in the enterprise. Among the actors who have a part in any operation are NGOs; and for the medical needs that are always one of the major byproducts of these wars, that means MSF.

The Structure of State Building

Outsiders entering a former internal war zone face one of two major political problems. They may enter a country that at one time was reasonably well ordered, although in all likelihood any form of political organization was authoritarian in one way or another. In these circumstances, the war has likely disrupted whatever organization there was (indeed, the political structure may well have been the major target of fighting), leaving behind a dysfunctional, disrupted set of institutions that can only be rebuilt with some effort and care to avoid replicating whatever it was about the old order that was a precipitant of violence in the first place. In addition, it is very likely that the economic and social systems, whatever their prior condition, have suffered similar disruptions. The situation in Kosovo is emblematic of this possibility; it was a reasonably coherent land the structure of which was shattered by war.

The other possibility is virtual chaos, where either there never was a viable political and economic system, or where whatever system may have preexisted has been so thoroughly destroyed that no semblance of order and authority can be identified. Most of the countries where this condition holds are deeply divided along ethnic, religious, or some other (e.g., clan) lines and can agree on no form of organization that is acceptable to all groups. These states are generally grouped together under a category name such as failed states; Sierra Leone is a current example.

In either case, the situation is bleak, and its alleviation is going to be difficult, if not impossible. Once the fighting is stopped, which is often the easier of the tasks faced by peacekeepers, outsiders are faced with a solid wall of problems, many of them life-threatening. The scourges of war have left many victims as refugees, living in squalid conditions without adequate shelter, sanitary conditions, medical help, or food. Others have had their homes destroyed and huddle in the ruins. Electrical power has long since gone out, as has water, garbage pickup and other services. Employment has ceased for many as factories have been destroyed and crops torched. Many are suspicious of neighbors as the sources of their suffering, which may include the violent loss of loved ones that leave physical and psychological wounds that need to be tended. And there is either no political authority to turn to or available officials are viewed as part of the problem.

The human needs to be tended fall into several categories. One is the simple restoration of order and safety, a task that intervening troops can perform for a time but must eventually be provided indigenously. A second is basic survival needs, including an adequate supply of food, potable water, shelter against the physical elements, cooking facilities, medical care for those who need it, inoculations against diseases that may increase in frequency and severity because of the wretchedness of conditions, and more. A third is the rebuilding of whatever structures have been destroyed, beginning with basic services and infrastructure. Finally, there is the need to begin to expand the preexisting structures to improve conditions so that there will be no incentives for a recurrence of the violence in the future.

The list of tasks to be performed is obviously extensive, and they all cannot be performed simultaneously. Fortunately, disasters attract those organizations and individuals who want to provide assistance in the specific areas of their expertise. The soldiers arrive to restore the order, and the Red Cross is there to coordinate aid and to provide things like warm clothing and blankets. CARE and other food providers are not likely to be far behind. And, of course, MSF will be among the first to arrive.

The problem is coordination of the overall effort. A welter of governmental and nongovernmental agencies will almost certainly descend on the scene, each with a specific agenda of assistance that it wants to provide but with no coordinated plan for the comprehensive provision of services in an ordered program. In fact, each aid giver is likely to view its own mission as supreme and to treat other priorities and providers whose missions conflict with theirs as detrimental or less important. Those who would help thus can become part of the problem as well as the solution.

Here is where the case of MSF, specifically in terms of its relations with military forces on the scene, becomes illustrative. As already noted, MSF is likely to be one of the first international agencies on the scene when disaster befalls a particular location.

In fact, they will probably be present before the problem reaches the level of suffering and atrocity that creates international awareness and the impetus necessary to authorize some form of PKOs. When the peacekeepers hit the beaches, in other words, MSF will be there to see them ashore, if not necessarily to greet them.

Part of the problem is perspective. For MSF, the central problem is medical, and alleviating the immediate medical suffering of the target population is by far the most important task it believes needs to be undertaken. Anything that other agencies do to make the provision of medical assistance easier is valued; anything that does not contribute to that end, and especially if it makes medical caregiving more difficult, is to be opposed.

Military forces entering a new internal war are likely to have a different perspective on the problem. Certainly they are aware of medical problems and want them dealt with; in Haiti, for instance, military doctors became an integral part of the health care system during the 1994–1998 operation there. But the military also realizes that medical attention is only one of a number of priorities within the general mandate of peace imposition and enforcement. Securing areas from military violence and restoring physical order are likely to be their highest priorities, followed closely by providing reasonable security for the peacekeepers themselves. Once these objectives are achieved, then more strictly humanitarian concerns can be undertaken. While the basic mission is being implemented, however, the caregivers like MSF who want to get out into the field—usually in unsecured areas—simply get in the way and make the accomplishment of their mission more difficult. At this point, the caregivers (MSF) and the soldiers may come into direct conflict. As an example, the news media reported on January 10, 2001 that an American MSF doctor being escorted by military forces in Chechnya was attacked and kidnapped along with his military escorts by Chechen separatists.

This was apparently the situation in Somalia in the early 1990s. Before the United Nations identified the suffering of the Somali people from a combination of drought-based starvation and civil war as a candidate for international assistance, MSF doctors were in the country dispensing medical aid and assisting in the distribution of food in those areas where it was most needed. In order to carry out their function, they were forced to compromise with the clan warlords who controlled various parts of Somali territory. As already noted, to ensure that enough food got to where it was needed, MSF worked out an arrangement whereby the clans were allowed to commandeer enough grain to feed their followers in return for allowing the rest of the supplies to go forward, a practice the UN peacekeepers ended. At the same time, MSF doctors working in war zones sometimes allowed themselves to be seconded into service to run military hospitals to treat soldiers wounded in battle.

Such compromises became unacceptable when the UN mission entered the country. The first and major mission of the UNISOM (United Nations in Somalia) was to reestablish the integrity of the food distribution system, which required securing the country's road network and convoying food supplies. As noted, these actions deprived the warlords of the ability to skim their previous shares, thereby interrupting their bargain with the MSF. To the United Nations forces, this was simply a matter of restoring order and integrity to the country; to MSF, it amounted to the disruption of a functional—if extralegal—means to ensure that people got the medical services they require.

MSF also believes that peacekeepers are likely to get in the way of solving problems the longer they stay. Partly, this is the case because, as the "Life, Death and Aid" report maintains, "humanitarian aid permits intervention by armed forces yet gives them no precise political programme." In some sense, this charge is true, but it may be misleading as well. The purely military aspect of PKOs is peace imposition and peace enforcement. During peace enforcement it has an ongoing role in maintaining the absence of a return to violence, but it has little other intrinsic role to play. It may be asked to perform other roles, such as constructing temporary housing facilities (tent cities and the like) but peace enforcers basically do exactly that, enforce the peace. This is largely a defensive, passive role, and it is likely that the orientation of the peace enforcers will gravitate toward their own protection, as well as that of the target population they are there to protect. It is not at all unnatural for them to seek to minimize personal dangers, as long as doing so does not endanger the basic structure of peace. This attitude is likely to be especially prevalent among forces from democratic countries where the support for peacekeeping is not very strong and where there is the fear that sustaining casualties will undermine what support there is.

The problems go beyond conflicts of mission definition, reflecting very different institutional and organizational cultures. MSF is, quite openly and proudly, antiestablishment and iconoclastic. It was, after all, born because the traditional, establishment providers of medical assistance, were, in its view, dysfunctional and hamstrung by conventions (in this case, honoring sovereign borders) from performing necessary medical tasks. In some ways, Doctors without Borders is Doctors *against* Borders, a way of thinking hardly likely to endear them to political authorities and their agents, notably the military. One result is that each group, and its members, tends to treat the other with suspicion, even disdain. From a military viewpoint, MSF personnel are likely to be viewed as impractical dreamers who obstruct orderly operations and who make demands that can put military forces in unnecessary danger, as in the Chechen example. From an MSF viewpoint, the military is likely to be seen as a reactionary barrier to mission accomplishment, a force to be avoided and circumvented, not a partner in a broader enterprise to build states and leave behind conditions of stable peace.

Yet, both military forces and organizations like MSF have roles throughout the various purposes for which PKOs may be mounted. When the mission is conflict suppression, the military has the job of bringing the fighting to an end, and MSF has the imperative of treating the wounded and suffering. When the mission turns to state building, their roles continue: the peacekeepers as shields behind which state building occurs, organizations like MSF helping to build or rebuild a medical infrastructure to leave behind when peace is ensured.

CONCLUSION

This case study is only a microcosm of the growing roles of NGOs in important international situations, in this case the provision of services in circumstances where PKOs are involved. Real situations, of course, are often far more complicated than has been portrayed. In any real PKO, for instance, there will be a wide variety of actors coming together; in addition to military forces and caregivers like MSF, there will be numerous IGOs (the UN and its representatives), the media, representatives of governments providing assistance, and a whole host of other NGOs with other specialized roles, responsibilities, and perspectives.

What this very narrow case seeks to illustrate is how difficult it is to coordinate the relations among emerging international actors in a new and largely uncharted environment. The MSF-peacekeeper relationship is no more than the tip of the iceberg in suggesting the multiple difficulties and opportunities that interaction may produce.

What can we draw from this experience? The question is worth exploring, both because peacekeeping opportunities are likely to continue, possibly even proliferate, in the international relations of the upcoming years, and because nongovernmental organizations like MSF will probably play an increasing part in the system generally and in PKOs in particular. The problem, in other words, is both prominent and difficult.

The 2000 presidential election in the United States featured, to a small degree, the debate over PKOs in areas of the world outside the most important interests of the major powers (where these are likely to occur in the future). In particular, the candidates debated the propriety of an ongoing commitment in the Balkans (Bosnia and Kosovo), two locations arguably closer to the important interests of the United States and other Western countries than similar potential operations in places like Sierra Leone.

What makes these situations controversial? Partly, it is the intractability of the circumstances in which PKOs are contemplated. By and large, these are very difficult, bitter situations, where it is unclear of how much assistance outsiders can be beyond stopping (or interrupting) the violence and tending to the immediate suffering of populations. Long-term solutions have remained elusive, at least in part because we have no reliable methods for moving situations toward positive outcomes. A good bit of our uncertainty in this regard is the absence of anything like a plan to integrate and coordinate the activities of a large number of individual organizations with differing and sometimes contradictory missions they seek to accomplish. Some of these actors will be NGOs like MSF, and some of them will be contentious and even contemptuous of other authorities, as MSF often proudly is. Dealing with programmatic elements that provide vital services but are likely to resist or refuse coordination is part of the PKO problem that needs to be addressed.

The blossoming of organizations like MSF also points to a more general international phenomenon, the privatization of international interactions. This trend has been most apparent in the area of economic globalization where, for many purposes, the interaction of states has become nearly irrelevant as a factor in economic and financial transactions. The 1980s trend toward privatization and deregulation of economic activity has included an assault on underlying dynamics of the international order, including the principle of state sovereignty that has underlaid the system for over 300 years.

The rise of NGOs may represent a similar assault from another direction. Certainly, MSF fits the bill: it was born explicitly as a reaction to the strictures placed on the provision of medical assistance that honoring sovereignty created for the medical caregivers. Its very name, Doctors without Borders, is indicative of exactly what it thinks about the underlying truisms of the international order. How much of a threat organizations like MSF represent to the conventional order is a question worth pondering.

STUDY/DISCUSSION QUESTIONS

1. What is a nongovernmental organization (NGO)? Contrast NGOs with intergovernmental organizations (IGOs).

2. Compare and contrast the pattern of internal wars in the Third World during the Cold War and post–Cold War periods.

3. How and why did *Medecins sans Frontieres* (MSF) come into being? What are its major self-proclaimed missions and purposes?

4. Why is MSF a controversial organization?

5. Discuss the nature of contemporary peacekeeping operations (PKOs), including the sequential military problems they have and the goals for which they may be commissioned.

6. What is state building? Why is it a controversial goal for a PKO? Where do organizations like MSF fit into state-building operations?

7. How is the relationship of an NGO like MSF and PKO military forces a microcosm of the kinds of difficulties that a complex PKO faces in the field? Explain.

8. Why are both PKOs and NGOs like MSF important to the future evolution of the international system?

READING/RESEARCH MATERIAL

Dorozynski, Alexander. "*Medecins sans Frontieres*: 20 Years Old." *British Medical Journal* 303, 6817 (December 21, 1991), 591.

Krasner, Stephen D. "Sovereignty." *Foreign Policy*, January/February 2001, 20–30.

Mawlawi, Farouk. "New Conflicts, New Challenges: The Evolving Role for Non-Governmental Actors." *Journal of International Affairs* 46, 2 (Winter 1993), 391–413.

Nolan, Hanna. "Learning to Express Dissent: *Medecins sans Frontieres*." *British Medical Journal* 319, 7207 (August 14, 1999), 446.

"No Thanks: Armed Protection for Aid." *The Economist* (U.S.) 329, 7839 (November 27, 1993), 43.

Rupesinghe, Kumar. "Non-Governmental Organizations and the Agenda for Peace." *The Ecumenical Review* 47, 3 (July 1995), 324–328.

Rufini, Giovanni. "Peacekeeping and the Coming Age of NGOs." *Peacekeeping and International Relations* 24, 2 (March/April 1995), 7–9.

Sancton, Thomas. "Distinguished Service: *Medecins sans Frontieres* Receives the Nobel Prize." *Time International*, October 25, 1999, 68.

Snow, Donald M. *UnCivil Wars: International Security and the New Internal Conflicts.* Boulder, CO: Lynne Rienner Publishers, 1996.

———. *When America Fights: The Uses of U.S. Military Force.* Washington, DC: CQ Press, 2000.

Spencer, Miranda. "The World is Their Emergency Room: *Doctors* Without *Borders.*" *Biography* 4, 6 (June 2000), 55–58.

WEB SITES

Contains alphabetic listing of NGOs affiliated with the United Nations
>   NGO Global Network at http://www.ngo.org

Directory of NGOs associated with the UN Department of Public Information
>   DPI/NGO at http://www.un.org/MoreInfo/ngolink/ngodir.htm

Database of international organizations, nongovernmental organizations and permanent missions based in Geneva
>   Geneva International at http://geneva-international.org/GVA/Directory/Welcome.E.html

Clearing house for information on over 40,000 international non-profit organizations and constituencies
>   Union of International Associations at http://www.uia.org/website.htm

International humanitarian aid organization providing emergency medical aid in more than 80 countries
>   Doctors Without Borders at http://www.doctorswithoutborders.org

Worldwide campaigning movement that works to promote human rights
>   Amnesty International at www.amnesty.org

NGO dedicated to protecting human rights around the world
>   Human Rights Watch at www.hrw.org

CHAPTER THREE

The Democratic Peace:

WHO WILL PREVAIL?

PRÉCIS

Almost no one would argue that the 1990s was not an expansive period for the growth of political democratization in the international system. With the collapse of the ideological opposition to political democracy as Marxism-Leninism disappeared operationally and philosophically, the "third wave of democracy," in Samuel Huntington's phrase, washed across the globe, resulting in a net increase in the number of politically democratic states in the world.

While hardly anyone would deny this trend, many wonder whether it will endure into the 2000s, and it is the major burden of this case study to examine arguments that are made about sources of failure of democracy in individual countries and even more widely. The question "Will democracy prevail?" is thus raised, and ways in which it might fail are grouped around five possible sources, ranging from antidemocratic reactions from traditional elites losing power as the result of democratic reform to the possibility of an economic crash like that of the 1930s, which sent the citizens of numerous countries scurrying for nondemocratic alternatives. The possibilities for the 2000s are raised in the conclusion that, in effect, asks whether the democratization of the 1990s is a permanent or transitory phenomenon.

In 1991, Harvard political scientist Samuel P. Huntington published a book titled *The Third Wave: Democratization in the Late Twentieth Century*. His basic thesis was that the end of the Cold War was ushering in a worldwide movement toward political democratization in a number of states around the globe. His concern was over the nature and durability of this phenomenon. In addition, he sought to place it in historical perspective within the twentieth century. He chose to call this trend as the "third wave" purposefully. It was the third wave because a similar phenomenon had occurred twice before in the twentieth century, after the triumphs of the Western democracies in the two world wars.

His choice of the analogy to a wave was both symbolic and controversial, because it suggested an underlying thesis that many others either denied or at least hoped was untrue. The symbolism arises from the actions of waves: they rise in the sea and crash onto the shore. And then they recede. In the cases of the first two twentieth-century waves of democracy that is exactly what happened, according to Huntington. First, there was a wave of democratization, as formerly authoritarian countries overthrew (or had overthrown for them by the victorious allies) their governments and replaced them with democratic forms. As time passed, however, a number of those states reverted to nondemocratic forms, in much the same way that a receding wave acts. The controversial aspect of Huntington's analysis was that he predicted the same thing would likely happen again this time: the euphoria of post–Cold War decommunization would produce a series of political democracies (especially in the formerly communist world), but some would revert to nondemocratic form.

We are now well over a decade removed from the beginning of the physical end of the Cold War (which, for practical purpose, can be dated to the revolutions of 1989 in Eastern Europe that overthrew communist regimes). The wave of democratization has continued to roll in; standard monitors of the process like the Freedom House and its Map of Freedom (frequently reproduced in international relations textbooks) show a steady increase in the number of countries where individual freedom is exercised and where political democracy is in place. The two lists are not, of course, identical. Citizens of China exercise a large number of individual freedoms in the day-to-day conduct of their private lives. These freedoms do not, however, extend to political participation. More to the point, there have been virtually no reversions, and where democracy has been suspended, that act itself has been reversible. (Peru, which had its constitution suspended in the 1990s but democracy reinstated, is a good example.) The wave apparently has not crested.

It is possible that the analogy does not hold this time. At the end of each of the world wars, the world situation was different than it was after the end of the Cold War. Most obviously, 1918 and 1945 were the ends of very hot wars, where countries were defeated and devastated, in some cases torn apart (the Ottoman and Austro-Hungarian Empires in 1918, for instance); not a shot was fired to end the Cold War. In 1918 and 1945, there were viable ideological alternatives to political democracy, most notably communism. With the collapse of communism, there were still a number of authoritarian governments, but there was no intellectual defense (as opposed to practice) of antidemocratic principles. Fundamentalist Islam is the closest thing to an intellectual rival, and it would be largely ignored but for its connection to international terrorism. One important question to ponder is whether circumstances are sufficiently different this time to invalidate Huntington's thesis.

There is little evidence that the trend toward greater democratization of the globe has crested. Certainly, the forces of democracy are having more success in some parts of the world than in others. Almost no Latin American expert, for instance, would have predicted fifteen years ago that there would only be one country in the Western Hemisphere that would greet the new millennium with a government that had not been elected (Cuba). At the same time, there is much less progress toward democracy in most of war-torn Africa, where grinding poverty and deprivation join violence as impediments to democratic growth. The process of democratization is also uneven in Asia. Having said that, there is no part of the globe that is showing systematic signs of reversion away from democratic norms. Such a contrary trend is, of course, possible; it is just that it is not yet evident.

Whether democracy will prevail and whether democratization will lead to greater peace in the future are the subjects of this case study. From the Western perspective shared by the author and most of those who will read this study, it is an assessment about which it is somewhat difficult to be entirely objective—a condition particularly pointed for Americans. The democratic peace, along with the spread of capitalist economics, is the symbol of the *pax Americana* that began with the end of the Cold War and continues into the new century (see related material in Part III). Moreover, we believe in the virtue of an international system dominated by political democracies—the reason people speak of a democratic *peace* is that they believe political democracies are more peaceful than other forms. While we will not analyze in detail the extensive, and familiar, debate on that subject, we will note it in passing as a major purported virtue of the trend toward greater democratization worldwide. At any rate, as Westerners we are not only observers of the process; because it is our system, we are also its proponents, and we must be mindful to separate advocacy from observation.

The subtitle suggests the thin line between our observations of trends and our preference for particular outcomes. Liberal political democracy is a distinctively Western value, and the uneven spread of democracy worldwide is, according to critics, due to the fact that it represents values and outcomes incompatible with the cultural norm of others. While people robustly disagree about the extent and effects of such incompatibility, we must remember that everyone does not necessarily want democracy to prevail.

The remainder of this study will be concerned with the post–Cold War experiences with two aspects of democratization, using case examples to illustrate points along the way. First, we will examine, in summary fashion, the dynamics of the third wave, including the relationship of democracy to the development of the globalizing economy and the advocacy of democracy as a means to induce change more generally, especially in the developing world. The analysis will then turn to potential threats, looking at a number of possible sources of contrary trends to the general movement toward more democracy. We will conclude with some assessment of the future prospects, and especially the impact of more or less democracy on the stability of the international system.

Because the process of democratization is an ongoing process the final outcome of which is somewhere in the future, using a single instance of the phenomenon as a case study is probably inappropriate, because the selection would suggest an outcome that may or may not be what eventually transpires and thus would suggest a groundless conclusion. Likewise, one of the dangers of studying an incomplete process is that whatever examples we use may in the end prove to have been the wrong ones. What is possible, however, is to lay out ways the democratization process—and the prospects for democratic peace—may turn out, and use smaller case examples to illustrate the possibilities. Thus, we will lay out some of the contrary arguments about the prospects, using the cases as examples.

THE DEMOCRATIZATION MOVEMENT

Few observers would dispute that the 1990s were very good years for advocates of political democracy. As the decade began, the single greatest intellectual and physical challenge to democracy, Soviet-led communism, disappeared with hardly a murmur, and the successor states to the old Second World spent the decade scrambling, with varying success, to adopt democratic forms. Combined with the spread of the globalizing economy, the advocates of democracy were on a roll. But will it last?

The road to democracy has not been easy, and different countries have had to travel it in their own distinctive ways. For some of the formerly communist countries like Poland and Hungary, the route has been fairly smooth; for others, especially parts of the former Soviet Union and notably Russia itself, the process has been very tense and uncertain. Especially for the Russians, there has been no shortage of doomsayers predicting the collapse of their democratic experiment and a Faustian descent back into the long history of Russian authoritarianism.

But the Russians continue to defy the doomsayers. No one would make the pretension that Russian democracy is a model for anyone to emulate, but despite the collapse of the Russian economy and most other institutions, the system endures. In 1991, the then Soviet Union endured a coup attempt by erstwhile communists that ended by propelling Russian president Boris Yeltsin into the world public limelight. Yeltsin was elected and reelected president of the Russian Republic, and Vladimir Putin succeeded Yeltsin in an orderly exercise of the ballot box in 2000. Some political scientists contend that a country that has successfully passed power along through the ballot box twice (the two-turnover test) provides an indication that democracy has taken root. In the face of widespread lawlessness and the collapse of the Russian economy in 1998 that has left as much as three-quarters of the Russian population living below the poverty line, the endurance of democracy is not unimpressive.

What explains this phenomenon in Russia and elsewhere? Why has the third wave of democracy appeared to be more successful and even resilient in places that do not seem particularly promising candidates for democratic systems in terms of their histories and national experiences? Is there something about this wave that is more powerful and thus enduring than the other waves of the last century?

TRANSPARENCY AND SOFT POWER

There is no real basic agreement on the answers to any of the questions posed above. The pages of scholarly and policy journals like *Foreign Affairs* and *Journal of Democracy* are filled with speculation on whether the new wave represents a future trend that will envelop the world or a passing phenomenon that will fade into a darker future.

The contending arguments are emotional and, in many cases, implicitly mask a prejudice about the place of the United States in the world. Analysts who see the twenty-first century as a continuation of American intellectual dominance tend to be optimistic about the future spread of Western-style democracy. What Joseph S. Nye, Jr., has called American soft power (the appeal of American ideals) has pointed the way for the present and will continue to do so in the future, which will see the gradual increase of democracy and a spreading global peace among democratic states. It is an optimistic view of the world that finds the United States at the center of the picture, as something like Ronald Reagan's depiction of the "shining house on the hill."

Not everyone agrees with his vision by any means. Some, for instance, argue that the trend toward democratization is exaggerated by using very generous definitions of democracy. In a number of the former republics of the Soviet Union, elections have been held for top leaders, but these have resulted in the same people in power as under communism. Belarus, the Ukraine, and a number of the central Asian republics are cited as examples. While 34 of the 35 states of the Western Hemisphere have governments that were elected, calling some of them democratic stretches credulity. Pakistan continues to elect governments, but unless the military approves the outcome, elected governments are overthrown and replaced by military juntas. As Thomas Carothers puts it, there exists "a profusion of hazy situations—countries with consistently stated democratic intentions but hazy political realities."

Skeptics also warn that the connection between the trend toward democracy and its chief advocate, the United States, may have a darker side. The general argument is that while the promotion of democracy is not a bad thing, the United States also ends up pushing its culture down the throats of others who may not be interested, and often acts as an arrogant upstart. If there is, as some predict, an anti-American reaction in the international system, the trend toward democracy could conceivably be both a cause and a victim of negative developments. The current wave of anti-Americanism in parts of the Middle East in the wake of the terrorist attacks against New York and Washington and the subsequent allied efforts against Afghanistan offers some support for this idea of a "clash of civilizations" (another Huntington construct).

A number of critics also contest the idea that a democratically dominated system will be more peaceful than a less democratic one. While acknowledging that stable, developed democracies do not go to war against one another, these critics contend that during the democratization process countries attempting to become democratic are more rather than less prone to go to war. Moreover, statistical tests demonstrate that democracies are no less likely to go to war (admittedly against nondemocratic opponents) than are authoritarian regimes.

The critics notwithstanding, the trend toward democratization has survived the 1990s and appears to be continuing as the 2000s unfold. This suggests that the trend has some tenacity that skeptics downplay or deny. To what can we attribute the longevity of the trend?

Clearly, there are numerous possible explanations. My personal response, while admittedly conjectural, centers on the idea of *the transparency of democratic practices*. The term transparency has gained considerable prominence in economic circles to describe the necessary conditions for financial institutions in countries seeking to join the globalizing economy (see Chapter 8, "The New Trinity of Globalization" for a discussion). In a political context, democracies are exceedingly open to inspection by those who do not possess political freedom. Overwhelmingly, people exposed to political democracy like what they see and aspire to a similar situation for themselves. Once again, Carothers captures the phenomenon: "what is notable about the recent democratic trend is the similarity of the political aspirations of such different societies." Why might this be the case?

There are several driving factors at work in spreading the democratic gospel, two of which stand out as examples of global political transparency. One is the role of the electronic media, including the Internet. Historically, one of the primary tools of repressive regimes was their ability to withhold and manage information, including comparisons of the political and economic living conditions of their citizens to those of others. The electronic revolution has completely destroyed what was left of that control (global television has also played a part). George Orwell was wrong; rather than aiding authoritarian ends, progress in telecommunications destroyed the ability to control information. There is no place poor or isolated enough in the world that it does not have access to global television (thanks in no small measure to the satellite dish). While some governments still attempt to restrict access to the World Wide Web with varying degrees of success, their attempts are increasingly forlorn and futile. The technology is surpassing the ability to control it, and withholding access leaves countries outside the global, information-based economic system—a situation that populations find progressively unacceptable.

There is also a prodemocratic elite in virtually every country of the world. Usually, the "democracy movement" (to borrow the phrase used by the Chinese students urging democracy in Tiananmen Square in Beijing in 1989) is composed mainly of young people in their twenties and thirties who are highly Westernized, often educated in the United States and other Western countries, and frustrated by conditions in their own countries. Normally, they are nonviolent, but they demand the introduction of freedom and democracy into their countries. And they often succeed, as in the case of the mass demonstrations in Indonesia in 1999 that led to the forced retirement of long-time dictator Suharto.

New York Times foreign affairs correspondent Thomas L. Friedman, writing in *The Lexus and the Olive Tree,* draws particular attention to the Indonesian case through a process he calls "globalution." The idea refers to the problem facing those who seek political and economic change in authoritarian regimes but lack the power to bring it about. If they reject violence as a change agent—in the Indonesian case because of the fear of violent repression by the Army—then the only method to induce change is from the outside. Thus, the "globalutionaries" enlist and encourage outside investment, knowing that outsiders will insist on economic and political reform before they will seriously consider investing in a country. Among the changes they will insist upon is democratization of political institutions, if for no other reason than to discourage corruption. The evolution of this progress in Indonesia since the fall of Suharto has been quite tentative, as explained in Chapter 9.

The effect of transparency is a kind of contagion effect that transcends political borders and which, according to Carothers, "have been a major factor in the proliferation of democratic transitions around the world." This contagion, in turn, has resulted in a parallel phenomenon, which comes in the form of an increasingly global expectation about democratization. Not only does this manifest itself as an expectation that democracy should spread, but also that the reversal of democracy is increasingly unacceptable behavior for states. The overthrow of an elected government by the military in a *coup d'etat*, a fairly common event in the 1960s and 1970s that was generally decried but tolerated, now brings massive amounts of international condemnation, even in places like Pakistan where the precedent is firmly entrenched. Although it remains a possibility, as discussed in the next major section, such an action can affect the economic status of a state, as other members of the global economy express their distaste at the prospects of working with tyrannical regimes. The great battle between China and the United States over issues of human rights and trade is only the most obvious example of this problem.

Democracy and Globalization

To many of its proponents, political democratization is part and parcel of the general trend toward the creation of the globalized economy, or what Friedman and others call the international system of globalization.

The assertion that democracy and capitalist economics go hand in hand has both philosophical and practical elements. Philosophically, the argument is made that the two phenomena are simply expressions of the same basic dynamic, which is freedom. Capitalism is the economic expression of freedom, because it is the system in which individuals have the ability (at least in theory) to make all their own economic choices. Similarly, democracy represents the ability for individuals to make political decisions for themselves.

Singer and Wildavsky make the practical side of the combination clear in their description of what constitutes "quality economies." In their description, the most advanced states in the world are market democracies, and this combination is not coincidental. They argue that political freedom of choice and the ability to make your own economic choices results in a highly motivated and productive work force, where the members can decide how hard they want to work and what their rewards will be. Since the possibility of very hard work and very large rewards are part of that mix, the result is the encouragement of innovative entrepreneurs who, in turn, produce goods, services, and ideas that become the cutting edge of the most advanced countries and keep them ahead of the rest. They emphasize that both forms of freedom are necessary to produce an adequately motivated and satisfied population to be a world-class economy. Thus, countries (like, for instance, China) that provide economic incentives but withhold political freedoms will ultimately either have to democratize or fail to become fully competitive at the cutting edge.

Friedman adds the element of transparency to this calculation. Part of the inherent strength of the most advanced economies is that most of the practices of the private firms, and especially financial institutions, are subject to effective oversight that both makes certain they are not engaged in corrupt practices and gives potential investors confidence in those institutions. Political systems that are not directly accountable to the general population through devices like elections find it very difficult to create and enforce the kinds of legal regimes that allow this oversight. Thus, democratic institutions become part of the necessary base for entry into the globalization system. This process is never entirely perfect, as the Enron scandal of 2002 demonstrated. In that case, democratic processes were used to promote barriers to accounting transparency that shielded economically corrupt practices.

This coincidence of democracy and the market is not universally accepted. Italian entrepreneur and political figure Jacques Attali, for one, believes that the two phenomena, rather than forming a "virtuous circle," are really competitive and contradictory. The logic of capitalism is acquisition, and if capitalist success runs afoul of democratic practices, one or the other must give—for instance, when government attempts to regulate economic expansion. It is his contention that economic forces are the more powerful of the two and thus most likely to prevail.

WHAT COULD GO WRONG?

A casual examination of the global trend toward democracy as it has been presented in the previous pages will almost certainly lead to an optimistic outlook, at least for the foreseeable future. But anyone reaching that conclusion must face a nagging possible reality that the trend is transitory and will somehow not last. History, of course, supports a measured conclusion: periods of peace have been followed by war, and periods of prosperity have been followed by periods of economic privation. Why should we believe that the current period of democratic ascendancy will not be followed by a period of democratic decline? The question of whether democracy will prevail remains lively.

The hopeful answer is that things are different now, but are they really? If we can conjure good reasons why the democratic peace will prevail, can we also not conceive reasons why it might not?

The following pages will examine a series of arguments about how democracy might be reversed. Although making no claim of exhaustiveness, I will examine five scenarios, each of which represents how political democracy might fail to take hold in different places, or how it might not take root but instead revert to some authoritarian form in the manner suggested by Huntington's wave analogy. Each is based in post–Cold War experience, and while it is methodologically questionable to extrapolate and suggest generalizations from a single instance, the examples do at least suggest the possibilities that may exist.

When we talk about threats to the spread of democracy, it is important to understand what we are and are not examining. The threats that exist or may emerge are not to the well-established democracies of the most economically advanced countries, where democratic traditions are firmly in place. Rather, we are talking about countries in the developing world, most of which are straining to join the globalizing economy that requires them to increase individual liberties and democratic participation in the process. Where this process is most problematical is in those parts of the world, principally in Africa, parts of Asia, and to a lesser degree, parts of Latin America. Regardless of how this process works out in particular countries, there will be a democratic peace among most of the most powerful (certainly in economic terms) states; the question is whether democracy will take hold and persist in those parts of the world currently outside the politicoeconomic mainstream. With that rejoinder in mind, we can begin to address the question, "what can go wrong?"

Each of the five examples presents a somewhat different challenge. The "Revenge of the Losers" explores the resistance of traditional elites and their reactions as democratic forces erode their power in places like Indonesia. The "Coming Anarchy" looks at the barriers to democratic emergence in the most chaotic, violent places in the world, such as central Africa. The "Clash of Cultures" examines the contention, heard most often in Asia, that some region's values are incompatible with democracy. The "Rocky Road to Freedom" examines the difficult path to democracy for countries nearly totally unprepared for the process; Russia is the prime example. Finally, "Economic Collapse" explores the more general question of what an economic implosion worldwide of the scale of the Great Depression of the 1930s could mean to democratization.

Revenge of the Losers

One of the clearest sources of resistance to democratization within traditionally organized societies comes from those classes and groups who enjoy privilege under whatever form of autocratic rule prevails and who will lose some of their power in a democratic society. This is a familiar problem that is well documented in the developmental literature that accompanied decolonization during the 1950s and 1960s, and it gains a new twist during the third wave, as the pressures of globalization demand the forfeiture of those elements of closure that are often manifested in corrupt practices.

Although it varies in detail from society to society, the traditional pattern has similarities. Normally, governance is the province of a narrow segment of society, usually hereditary, land owning, and wealthy by the standards of the society. The privileged group is often in league with the country's military, with which the elite forms a mutually supportive bond in which the military receives prestige and material support in return for buttressing the government's control. Haiti, discussed in Chapter 7, is a classic example.

Among the major characteristics of this form of political system is that it is *closed*. What this means is that governmental tasks are performed in secret, outside public purview and not subject to criticism by a free press or other critics. While the closed nature is often rationalized on cultural or historical grounds (especially in Asia), one of its main outgrowths is governmental corruption, and particularly the misallocation of revenues for the benefit of the privileged class at the expense of the rest of society. Friedman, for instance, refers to these political systems simply as "kleptocracies" (governments that operate to steal from their citizens)."

The globalization system does not tolerate these kinds of arrangements for reasons already discussed, and the onslaught of demands for democracy and entrance into the global economy leave the elite and its supporters in a bind. They face the devil's choices of relenting to democratic pressures (and thereby having to relinquish their power and privilege) or of resisting and thus coming under ever increasing pressure from both outside the country and internally to reform.

The ongoing crisis in Indonesia may best illustrate this problem. During more than thirty years in power, Indonesian President Suharto had fashioned one of the most closed, corrupt political systems in the world. Nepotism was rampant, with almost all power and privilege residing in Suharto's extended family and supporters. He remained in power largely because of his close alliance with the Indonesian military, an arrangement facilitated by the fact that Suharto was an army general before assuming the presidency in 1968.

Pressure for change began to build in the 1990s. Internally, the pressure came from two sources. One was a series of secessionary movements in parts of the world's largest archipelago, notably in East Timor, Aceh, and West Papua. While governmental support for suppressing these movements helped cement the relationship between the military and the government, the suppression brought considerable international criticism of the regime, culminating in the international effort to save East Timor from lawlessness and violence in 1999. At the same time, there was growing pressure from younger, reformist elements of the population to end the corruption, cronyism, and nepotism. Internationally, Indonesia was clearly being punished by the globalizing economy, as investors were reluctant to chance losing their investments to mismanagement and political chaos.

Growing domestic pressures associated with the East Asian economic crisis forced Suharto, who had been reelected to a seventh term on March 10, 1998, to resign on May 21 of that same year. The Indonesian military stood by as Suharto was replaced by his vice president, Bachanuddin Jusuf Habibe. Abdurrahman Wahid, leader of the largest Muslim organization in the country, was elected president on October 20, 1999, but was driven from power in 2001 by Megawati Sukarnoputri, the daughter of Achmed Sukarno, the first president of Indonesia.

While Indonesia is currently a tentative victory for democratization, it is also a candidate for reversion. The change of power clearly produced some losers, and they may seek their revenge. Suharto and his cronies amassed an enormous amount of wealth, and there is an ongoing movement to try to recapture it through the court system. It is not clear that Suharto and his supporters will accept judgments graciously. At the same time, the fall of the Suharto regime apparently emboldened secessionists in places like East Timor, Aceh, and elsewhere. While the military had no direct and official role in the situation in East Timor, it was forced to step aside and allow the imposition of an outside force to end the violence, a source of acute embarrassment for the Indonesian military. If similar movements emerge elsewhere in the island empire (which is certainly a good possibility) and the army is restrained in putting the sedition down, its continuing loyalty to the democratically elected government could become suspect. Indonesian democracy clearly remains a work in progress (see Chapter 9 for a more detailed discussion of the prospects).

The Coming Anarchy

Atlantic Monthly correspondent Robert D. Kaplan has suggested another threat to democratization, a phenomenon that he has termed, in a magazine article and book of the same name, "the coming anarchy." It is a horror scenario based on his travels in some of the poorest and most violent places on the globe. While his analysis is centered in the heart of central Africa, the condition he describes could occur in other places as well.

The dynamic that bothers Kaplan is the essential collapse of governance and even society in a number of countries undergoing particularly chaotic, vicious wars within their boundaries. These wars, which the author has elsewhere termed "uncivil wars" or "new internal wars," occur in some of the poorest parts of the world, where governance has always been problematical, where the fighting has appeared to be motivated by no more noble motive that creating chaos as a condition for organized criminality, where the participants are highly irregular fighters rather than trained and disciplined soldiers, and where it is not always clear that "leaders" in fact control their "followers."

The locus of these conflicts is often the so-called *failed states*, countries so desperately poor that they cannot sustain themselves and demonstrate over time an inability at self-governance. Somalia was the prototype for the failed state phenomenon, but it is a designation that is often applied to places like Liberia, Sierra Leone, and Haiti, to name a few of the more obvious candidates.

If there is a *leitmotif* (recurring theme) for these kinds of kinds of conflicts, it is criminally inspired anarchy. In the Andean region, organizations that argue they are revolutionary are in fact little more than agents of the narcotics producers and traffickers whose job is to destabilize the government enough that it cannot interrupt criminal activities (these are sometimes referred to as narco-insurgencies). In other places, roving bands with revolutionary titles do little more than terrorize the population and void the policing activities of the government in order to facilitate stealing natural resources. There are, for instance, currently parts of the armies of six to eight neighboring countries occupying parts of the Democratic Republic of Congo (formerly the Belgian Congo and Zaire) where precious commodities such as diamonds, gold, and copper are mined. Needless to say, the occupiers end up plundering the wealth of the areas they control.

Possibly the most vicious example of this phenomenon is in Sierra Leone. An organization known as the Revolutionary United Front (RUF) has been waging a "war" against the government for some years. Occasionally, there are lulls in the fighting, but the general purpose of the RUF is to weaken the government to the point that it cannot counteract the RUF's other agenda, which is exploiting the diamond-rich region of the country. The RUF is probably best known in the West for its campaign of amputation of the hands and feet of members of the population for reasons beyond physical intimidation or pure cruelty that are not apparent. An internationally imposed and enforced peace has existed in the country since 2001. Its stability, especially were the peacekeepers to withdraw, is problematical (see further discussion in Chapter 14).

Clearly, it is impossible to talk about the emergence of political democracy in the short term in places such as Sierra Leone. The United States attempted to buttress the movement of Haiti toward political democracy in 1994 when it sent troops to the island country to reinstall its elected president, Jean-Bertrand Aristide, who had been overthrown by a military coup. The Americans stayed for almost five years before withdrawing; no one would argue they left much of a democracy behind.

Kaplan paints a more ominous picture for the future. His fear is that conditions in many of these countries will become so wretched that large numbers of refugees will flee their countries, with the developed states as their destination. He fears that they will also bring with them the criminal habits and animosities that destabilized their countries. The worst-case scenario for the coming anarchy is the stable democracies being flooded with the least stable world's problems and being swamped by them.

The Clash of Cultures

An allegation is put forward in some parts of the world, notably in Asia, that political democratization is simply culturally incompatible with long-held values. In such cases, the attempt to transpose democratic values and practices is said to be culturally disruptive, even destructive, and thus should be resisted. It is a variant on the argument of the cultural destructiveness of the American model of economic and political organization.

What should we make of this argument? One point is that it does have an historical basis. In most Asian countries, there is a long-standing practice of nondemocratic rule that dates back at least to the imposition of the Mandarin system in China several thousand years ago. The tradition includes a greater degree of communalism than is present in many western cultures (e.g., the idea that the common good transcends the interests of individuals) and a belief in the veneration of elders, the most conservative element in society but also the element thought to have accumulated the most wisdom. This leads to a deferential element of the culture that facilitates political control by a small group within society. Many Asian societies, but especially those that were influenced by China, contain these cultural elements and also defenders of the sanctity of these values.

There is, of course, a flip side to the culture argument that is increasingly heard in the societies where it is defended. Most of the defenders of the culture argument, whether it is Singapore's Lee Kwan Yew, Malaysia's Datuk Mahathir bin Mohammad, or the current Chinese leadership, are parts of authoritarian regimes where defense of cultural uniqueness is part of the basis for avoiding widening the political base. The deference attaching to this traditional society has also promoted the opacity of financial and other economic institutions that is a barrier to full participation in the global economy (with the exception of Singapore, where strict laws effectively prevent corruption). Moreover, all of the societies defending cultural uniqueness are under some level of siege from elements of their societies—normally the young, Westernized, and highly educated rising elite—who demand democratization.

Which force will prevail? Will it be the defenders of traditional cultural differences? Or will it be the Westernizers who seek to bring their countries into the emerging globalization system? It is too early to say in any comprehensive manner, but there are lightning rods that can be watched to see. As noted in Chapter 1, China is a rising power, but there are questions about how far and how fast it can or will rise among the world's powers. If hypotheses about the nature of the globalization system described above have any validity, a barometer of Chinese success will be the extent to which China adopts Western economic and political norms. The embrace of capitalism is part of the bargain made between the Chinese regime and its people when the four modernizations were announced: "We let you become rich, and you will let us remain in power." If the Chinese regime is ultimately forced to widen the bargain to include political democracy, one of the inevitable victims will be the guise of cultural difference.

Rocky Roads to Freedom

The Russian experience provides another possibility. While it has already been noted that Russian democracy, at least at the federal level, has become more stable than its detractors have warned, the road has indeed been a rocky one, and the end result is by no means assured. The ultimate success or failure of democracy in Russia will play a major part in whether the third wave of democracy is ultimately deemed to have succeeded. Will Russia be part of the wave or the wake?

Russian democracy got off to a chaotic start in the late 1980s under former Soviet leader Mikhail S. Gorbachev. When Gorbachev and his followers realized that the Soviet Union was becoming increasingly uncompetitive with the West, he faced unpleasant choices. A devout Marxist, he could not bring himself to believe the underlying flaw was Marxist economics; instead he blamed flaws in the Stalinist system that administered the economy.

His program of reform, what became known as *perestroika*, attempted to open Soviet society and to induce change by encouraging criticism of the operation of the economy (notably the lethargic large state-run enterprises) that would lead to reform and a more competitive system. This was the cutting edge of democratization, and as it grew into increasingly public criticism of the whole system, its consequences were almost totally unexpected, because they had not been anticipated.

When the Soviet Union became Russia on January 1, 1992, it was officially a democratic state—in name if not in operation. The problem was that Russia was not prepared for such a radical departure from its authoritarian past. There was essentially no democratic tradition anywhere in the country, for instance, and the communist system of the Soviet Union did nothing to prepare politicians to work in a democratic atmosphere. The process of democratization also occurred in a politically tempestuous period where political boundaries between the republics of the former union were being redrawn and where separatist movements were emerging in places like Chechnya. Moreover, democracy was instituted with none of the necessary underlying institutions in place to support and nurture it. Two examples demonstrate the consequences.

One hallmark of a democratic system is a free, fair, and impartial criminal justice system—honest police and courts that apply the law in a manner that is accepted by the population as equitable. No such system existed in the Soviet Union, and it could not be created overnight. Much of the lawlessness that undermines the Russian system and threatens its democracy is directly attributable to a deficient criminal justice system that citizens do not trust and criminals do not fear.

A second hallmark of a democratic system is the ability to levy and collect taxes and to distribute the revenues resulting from taxation. The willingness to be taxed is a basic indicator of the amount of legitimacy the people place in the system. In Russia today, tax collection is at best spotty. At the local and provincial levels, there are places where the taxation system works fairly efficiently; at the federal level, however, the central government has had a very difficult time detecting and suppressing tax evasion, which is often aided and abetted by lower levels of government.

Will democracy ultimately succeed in Russia? It is an important question both because Russia, while diminished as a global power from its Soviet past, is still a major power, and because there are other states in the system not unlike Russia. Certainly the Russian influence can have a positive or negative influence on a number of the other successor states of the former Soviet Union. At the same time, whether Russia can hold together in the face of centrifugal influences and remain democratic will have implications for other large countries with similar problems—like India.

Economic Collapse

The fifth prospect is slightly more abstract and general, but with an historic precedent the possibility of which causes a major concern. That is the possibility of a worldwide economic collapse on the scale of the Great Depression of the 1930s that could conceivably send states scurrying their separate ways, including succumbing to the Faustian bargains that helped grease the path to World War II.

No two historic situations are exactly the same, so it is not possible to make a direct analogy with 1929, when the stock market crash in the United States helped trigger the onset of the economic maelstrom that became the Great Depression. The depression of the 1930s was, in some ways, an outgrowth of the settlement of World War I's punitive peace against Germany, which contributed to hyperinflation in Germany, the rise of Hitler, extreme economic nationalism in the form of prohibitively high trade barriers, and ultimately the slide toward World War II. This level of political turbulence is not found anywhere today except possibly in those areas included in Kaplan's coming anarchy, and those areas probably lack the economic power or political clout to destabilize the entire system. Moreover, the collapse of the 1930s occurred in an absolutely unregulated international economic environment. Safeguards and rules described in the case study on globalism (Chapter 8) suggest that there are now mechanisms that can soften the impact of economic downturns if not eliminate them altogether.

The fact that we think we have learned from our economic past does not mean we will necessarily avoid that past in the future. It has been nearly a decade since the last major global recession, much less depression, and it is not clear how countries will handle a return to bad times if or when they occur. In terms of democracy and the democratic peace, the great fear is of economically based panic that turns populations toward authoritarian demagogues, as happened in the 1930s. Such a fear has been associated with Russia and the possible rise of an ultranationalist like Vladimir Zhirinovsky when the Russian economy collapsed in 1998. Even more traumatic would be a systemwide failure of the globalization system that recreated the panic and economic nationalism of the 1930s. We do not know how such a downturn might happen, but we also do not know that it could not. The same optimism that suggests we have had a very good decade for democracy in the 1990s contains the nagging realization that history has rarely been linear and that bad times have generally followed good times. Will it be that way again?

CONCLUSION

Will democracy and peace prevail? An analysis of the prospects of democratization and a subsequent democratic peace reveals a mixed bag. For the most part, the 1990s witnessed a positive third wave that has not clearly crested and left recidivists to authoritarian rule in its wake. At the same time, the wave has not washed ashore uniformly; there are clearly parts of the world that have not enjoyed the phenomenon of democratization. It is probably not coincidental that these areas have also enjoyed the least of the benefits of anything like a democratic peace.

What is the environment like in which the progress of democratization will compete? On one hand, there are clearly positive aspects. The most notable of these are the continuing progress of economic globalization and the absence of ideological divide among competing governmental forms. Political democracy and economic prosperity are the norm in large parts of the world and the aspiration of many not currently enjoying the benefits of the system. In most of the areas that are part of the globalization system, there is also peace.

But the world that Kaplan describes is present as well. Most of Africa remains outside the prosperity, and it remains politically chaotic as well. Add the disaster of AIDS and other infectious diseases (see Chapter 15), and the situation is bleak indeed. Is Africa just a part of the world that the international system will simply write off out of despair for the future? Will the poorest and politically most divided places in Asia suffer the same fate?

What, then, are the possibilities for the third wave of democracy? There are three broad categories of possible outcome that can be sketched in no particular order of probability.

The first is that the wave will continue to rise, with no crest in the foreseeable future. That is, of course, the most optimistic outcome, and its prospects are clearly tied closely to the continuing vitality of economic globalization. If the global economy continues to spread and bring democratization in its wake, then one would expect the peace to extend as well. Admitting there may be political instability and even violence in some of the places attempting to make the political transformation from authoritarian to democratic rule, the overall prospect should be for growing tranquillity.

There is an objection one can make to this rosy projection. It may well be that the positive economic and political process of the 1990s has largely exhausted itself, because democratization and globalization have succeeded in all the manageable places to implement them, leaving only the hard or impossible places left for the wave to wash over. If that is true and, say, the Great Lakes area of Africa is simply impossible to bring into the democratic peace, then the second possibility is that the wave may indeed spend itself, as Huntington implies, and that there will indeed be a wake where some converts to democracy may fall by the wayside.

How damaging to the overall democratically induced tranquillity this second scenario is depends on where reversion occurs. Clearly, the outcome of the democratizing process in two countries is most critical. Russia remains the system's work in progress; a Russia that becomes a stable democracy (and which finds a way to join the global economy) could provide great stability to the global system. A Russia that reverts to its authoritarian, xenophobic past could do more than just about any other country to upset any notion of a democratic peace. The other crucial country is China. While the PRC is an active member of the global economy, its regime resists democratization that would undermine its power, instead granting its citizens personal but not political freedoms. China contains one-fifth of mankind; its addition to the democratic ranks would go a long way toward universalizing the democratic movement.

The third possibility is a continuation of the present, which includes essentially two parallel subsystems. In such an outcome, one could expect what President Clinton liked to call the "circle of market democracies" to continue slowly to expand, but never meaningfully to penetrate some parts of the world. It is the scenario, alluded to above, where some places in the developing world are quietly written off because of the inability to do anything about within the resources we are willing to commit to bring them into Clinton's ring. Then, the question is whether Kaplan's prediction that the wretched will overflow borders and infect the rest of us, and thereby change our order of priorities about their fate is true or not.

We finish where we began, with a question: Will democracy and the democratic peace prevail? The 1990s provided mostly positive evidence, as globalization and democratization washed progressively distant shores. Whether that trend can be sustained in the third millennium will play a major role in determining how tranquil or stormy the next century will be.

🌐 STUDY/DISCUSSION QUESTIONS

1. Obtain the latest Map of Freedom or online copy of *Freedom in he World* from the Freedom House (http://freedomhouse.org/). What changes does it report from previous years? Which of the various interpretations about trends in democratization are supported by its findings?

2. Much of the optimism that surrounds evolving notions about the spread of democracy derives from the supposed relationship between economic globalization and democratization. Assess that relationship.

3. As noted in the text, there is disagreement about whether there *is* a democratic peace, and if so, exactly what that means. Do you think democracies are most peaceful than other systems? Would a world of democracies be a more peaceful place?

4. The text describes several scenarios that could arrest or reverse the trend toward democratization. Can you add to the list? If so, what other "horror scenarios" can you think of?

5. The text describes three broad outcomes of the democratization process. Which do you think are most and least likely to occur? Why?

READING/RESEARCH MATERIAL

Attali, Jacques. "The Crash of Western Civilization: The Limits of the Market and Democracy." *Foreign Policy*, 107 (Summer 1997), 54–64

Carothers, Thomas. "Think Again: Democracy." *Foreign Policy*, 107 (Summer 1997), 11–18.

Freedom House. *Freedom in the World, 1999–2000*. New York: Freedom House, 2000. Available online at http://freedomhouse.org/.

Friedman, Thomas L. *The Lexus and the Olive Tree: Understanding Globalization*. New York: Farrar, Straus, Giroux, 1999.

Huntington, Samuel P. *The Third Wave: Democratization in the Late Twentieth Century.* Norman, OK: University of Oklahoma Press, 1991.

Kaplan, Robert D. *The Coming Anarchy: Shattering the Dreams of the Post Cold War World.* New York: Random House, 2000.

Nye, Joseph S., Jr. *Bound to Lead: The Changing Nature of American Power.* New York: Basic Books, 1990.

Singer, Max, and the Estate of Aaron Wildavsky. *The Real World Order: Zones of Peace. Zones of Turmoil.* Chatham, NJ: Chatham House, 1996.

Snow, Donald M. *UnCivil Wars: International Security and the New Internal Conflicts.* Boulder, CO: Lynne Rienner Publishers, 1996.

WEB SITES

Global coalition devoted to combating corruption

Transparency International at http://www.transparency.org

Organization working to advance the worldwide expansion of political and economic freedom

Freedom House at www.freedomhouse.org

Contains information about a wide range of groups and organizations working to strengthen democracy around the world

Democracy Resource Center at http://www.ned.org/research/research.html

Project analyzes efforts by the United States and other international actors to promote democracy worldwide

Democracy and Rule of Law Project at http://www.ceip.org/files/projects/drl/drl_home.ASP

Center aims to provide better understanding of the democratic process

Center for the Study of Democracy (CSD) at www.democ.uci.edu/democ

Research database created by the National Democratic Institute for International Affairs

Access Democracy at http://www.accessdemocracy.org

PART 2

Evolving Dynamics of International Relations

The cases in this part of the book deal, directly or indirectly, with the question of sovereignty within the international system, a major area of concern both to practitioners and students of international relations. Two of the studies deal with areas that represent direct challenges to the total supremacy of the territorial state in specific areas of state practice; the third deals with adjustments of sovereign boundaries within one of the traditionally most volatile parts of the world, the Middle East.

Challenges to sovereignty certainly are not a unique characteristic of the post–Cold War world. The concept has evolved over time from a justification for the ruling monarchs of Europe to hold total sway over their kingdoms (and to treat their citizens however they wanted) to a more restrained version of what constitutes sovereignty authority and how it can be exercised consistent with international norms. Many of the challenges have their genesis in the Cold War period and have continued with the breakdown of the Cold War competition. The two direct challenges in this part are of that general nature.

Chapter 4, "War Crimes," examines the evolution of international consideration of criminal actions occurring during wartime. The case traces the emergence of the idea of "crimes against humanity," which is used more or less synonymously with war crimes in contemporary usage, from the war crimes trials against the Axis powers at the end of World War II through the ad hoc tribunals set up in the 1990s in places like Bosnia and Rwanda to the present. The case culminates with the controversy over the creation of a permanent war crimes tribunal, the International Criminal Court, emphasizing the challenge to sovereignty the court represents.

Chapter 5, "Sovereignty and the 'Right' of Intervention in Internal Wars," is connected to the war crimes chapter, in two ways. First, many war crimes occur during contemporary internal wars, and it is these atrocities that cause members of the international system to consider intrusion into a country's internal affairs. Second, the assertion that there is an international right to intervene is a direct assault on the territorial sovereignty of states where it is invoked. The consequences for sovereignty and international norms come in direct conflict in these cases.

The third chapter, "Camp David I and II," examines the attempts of the disputing parties assisted by outsiders like the United States to negotiate a peace settlement between Israel and its Muslim neighbors. It argues that the enormously successful Camp David meeting of 1978 was a success in part because it did not deal with the most fundamental issues, which have to do with sovereign control of territories that were once Palestinian and are now Israeli, notably Jerusalem and the former home sites of Palestinians that are now Israeli (the question of Palestinian repatriation). Sovereign control of disputed territories ties this case to the others.

CHAPTER FOUR

War Crimes:
THE PAST IN THE PRESENT
IN THE FUTURE

PRÉCIS

Although events in the 1990s in places such as Bosnia and Rwanda have made the idea of war crimes and their prosecution a widely recognized part of international relations, the notion is relatively recent in its derivation. There have always been more or less well-accepted rules for conducting war, the violation of which was deemed criminal, but the ideas of crimes against peace and, especially, crimes against humanity are largely the result of the prosecution against German and Japanese officials after World War II. The 1990s revived this interest, which receded from prominence during the Cold War.

Two major aspects of the war crimes issue are highlighted in this case. Following an introduction that lays out basic history and concepts, the case concentrates on two related aspects, both of which have placed the United States in a controversial situation in the international community. One aspect is the proposal for an International Criminal Court (ICC), a permanent tribunal with jurisdiction over alleged war crimes. The other aspect is the assault on sovereignty implicit in the ICC statute; by granting jurisdiction to the court over war crimes, the sovereign control of a country over its citizens who may be accused of committing war crimes is compromised. For this reason of lost sovereignty, the United States is one of a handful of states that has rejected the ICC's jurisdiction. This theme is further amplified in Chapter 5.

In the middle of the 1986 movie *Platoon*, the group of American soldiers who are the subject of this Vietnam War story are on patrol and discover one of their fellows killed, presumably by the Viet Cong, searching for whom is the purpose of the patrol. The incident occurs near a small Vietnamese village. This raises the suspicion that it was Viet Cong (VC) from the village that perpetrated the killing, although members of the patrol have no direct evidence linking the village to the death of their comrade.

The patrol enters the village, which is apparently populated by innocent civilians, mostly older men and women and children. The patrol discovers food supplies clearly excessive to the needs of the villagers and concludes this is a VC food stash, providing "evidence" of VC presence. Members of the patrol attempt to coerce admissions from village residents that they are VC. When the villagers refuse to confess, the soldiers become physically abusive: an old woman is executed with a pistol, a young man is beaten to death with a rifle butt, a young girl is raped, and ultimately the village is set on fire as the remaining villagers flee in a panic.

Did the platoon engage in war crimes for which they might—or should—have been punished? At the time the film was released, the major purpose of the scene was to demonstrate the brutality of the Vietnam War, including the outrageous acts committed by both sides, in this case by American soldiers, and the psychological effects committing these acts had on them and the war.

Although the scene draws upon the facts of the Vietnam War incidents that occurred in My Lai, almost no one at the time raised the question of whether the scene depicted war crimes; had the movie been released in 1996, that would have been one of the first questions asked. What had changed in the interim?

The answer is that one of the important phenomena to reenter the international dialogue during the 1990s has been the subject of war crimes. The immediate precipitant has been a rash of so-called humanitarian disasters, in which intolerable acts against groups within states, often grouped under the name "ethnic cleansing," occurred during the decade. The worst of these occurred in Bosnia during the early 1990s and in Rwanda in 1994. A somewhat more limited case occurred in Kosovo in 1998–1999. The result, according to Richard Goldstone (in Gutman and Reiff), is a paradox: "Humanitarian law and international human rights has never been more developed, yet never before have human rights been violated more frequently. This state of affairs will not improve absent a mechanism to enforce those laws and the norms they embody."

This quote suggests that the contemporary concern with war crimes stems from two parallel developments. One is the assertion that there are universal human rights to which people and groups are entitled and which, when they are violated, are subject to penalty. The second is an interest in some form of *international* mechanism for dealing with violators of these norms.

While the ideas of defining criminal behavior and enforcement of laws in international and thus universal terms may not seem extraordinary, both are in fact of recent origin in international affairs. The idea of universal human rights transcending state boundaries, which is a recurrent theme in several of the studies in this volume, is really a phenomenon of the post–World War II period; the primary crime that has been identified in war crimes, genocide, was not identified until the word was coined by Richard Lemkin in 1944, and the United Nations Convention on Genocide, which bans the commission of genocide, was not passed until 1948. Similarly, the term war crimes, which now refers to a broad range of activities associated with war, was basically associated with violations of the so-called laws of war (actions permissible and impermissible during wartime) until war crimes trials were convened in Nuremburg and Tokyo to prosecute accused Nazi and Japanese violators after World War II. Following those trials, the subject remained fallow until it was revived in the 1990s.

The subject of war crimes is unlikely to disappear from international discourse any time soon, for at least four reasons. First, acts now defined as war crimes continue to be committed in many of the savage internal wars that plague the developing world. Exclusionary nationalism (where national groups persecute nonmembers) in some developing world states may increase the number of savage acts that are now considered war crimes. Second, the war crimes trials over Bosnia and Rwanda that were impaneled in the early 1990s have only begun their work, and the international legal community fully recognizes that the outcomes of those trials will influence the subject in the future. Third, definitions are rapidly evolving. (Rape, for instance, has only recently been added to the list of punishable crimes against humanity.) As suggested in Chapter 16, terrorist mass murders almost certainly qualify. Fourth, one outcome of the concern for war crimes has been the negotiation of a permanent International Criminal Court with mandatory jurisdiction over war crimes. This proposal is controversial, primarily because the United States is one of a handful of states that opposes granting universal jurisdiction to the tribunal, specifically over American service members.

This statement of the problem suggests the direction this case study will take. We will begin with a brief historical overview of war crimes, making the major point that while the idea of crimes of war have long been part of international concerns, war crimes as we now think of them are of recent vintage. We will then look at the various categories of war crimes that arose from the experience of the war crimes trials at the end of World War II. Since concern for war crimes was dormant during the Cold War, the discussion will move forward to the contemporary period, when the existence of well-documented atrocities in places like Bosnia and Rwanda rekindled interest in the subject. The Bosnian and Rwandan cases have, in turn, sparked renewed interest in a permanent war crimes tribunal, the International Criminal Court (ICC). The major opponent of the ICC as proposed at the Rome Conference of 1998 has been the United States, for a variety of reasons. The case concludes with an assessment of the problem of war crimes and the barriers to creating a permanent tribunal, the key elements of which revolve around the concept of sovereignty.

BACKGROUND OF THE PROBLEM

The idea of war crimes is both very old and very new. Throughout most of history, the term has been associated with conformity to the so-called laws of war. This usage can be traced back as far as 200 B.C., when a code of the permissible behavior in war was formulated in the Hindu Code of Manu. Enumeration of codes of warfare was part of Roman law and practice throughout Europe. These rules began to be codified into international law following the Thirty Years War between 1618 and 1648, when most of Europe was swept in very brutal religiously based warfare. The first definitive international law text, Hugo Grotius' *Concerning the Law of War and Peace*, was published in

1625 and included the admonition that "war ought not to be undertaken except for the enforcement of rights; when once undertaken, it should be carried on only within the bounds of law and good faith." Definitions of the laws of war, and hence violations of those laws, developed gradually during the eighteenth and nineteenth centuries, culminating in the Geneva and Hague Conventions of 1899 and 1907.

While the concerns expressed in the laws of war continue to be an important part of international concern, the idea of war crimes has been expanded to cover other areas of the conduct in war in the twentieth century. The precipitant for this expansion was World War II and wartime atrocities committed by the Axis powers (notably Germany and Japan). Some of the crimes fit traditional definitions of war crimes, such as the mistreatment of American and other prisoners of war (POWs) by the Japanese in instances such as the infamous Bataan death march. Many actions went well beyond the conduct of war per se, however, as in the systematic extermination of Jews, Gypsies, and others by Germany in the Holocaust, and the so-called Rape of Nanking, where Japanese soldiers went on a rampage and reportedly slaughtered nearly 300,000 citizens (some Japanese sources dispute the numbers) on the pretext that some of them were soldiers hiding among the civilians.

The laws of war as they had evolved to that point were inadequate to deal with this expansion in the use of military force to systematically brutalize civilian populations. There had been discussion about limitations on fighting and the treatment of noncombatants prior to World War I, but there were no real enforcement mechanisms to deal with transgressions, a recurring problem in enforcing war crimes violations that the ICC seeks to rectify.

The Impact of World War II

As noted, World War II provided the impetus for change. It was a truly global and brutal war, and one of its major "innovations" was to extend what the American General William Tecumseh Sherman called the "hard hand of war" during the Civil War to civilian populations. The Allies discussed the problem throughout the war. The first formal statement on the subject was the Moscow declaration of 1943, which stated that Nazi officials guilty of "atrocities, massacres, and executions" would be sent to the countries in which they committed their crimes for trial and appropriate punishment.

The document that defined modern war crimes precedent was the London Agreement of August 8, 1945. That document did two major things. First, it established the International Military Tribunal as the court that would try alleged war crimes and thereby set the precedent for a formal, permanent body later on. At the time, it specifically set the groundwork for the Nuremberg and Tokyo tribunals. Second, the agreement established the boundaries of its jurisdiction, which have become the standard means for defining war crimes.

The London Agreement defines three kinds of war crimes. The first is *crimes against peace*, "namely, planning, preparation, initiation, or waging of a war of aggression, or a war in violation of international treaties, agreements or assurances, or participation in a common plan or conspiracy for the accomplishment of any of the foregoing." This admonition was reinforced that same year by the United Nations Charter, in which the signatories relinquished the "right" to initiate war. Under this definition, the North Korean invasion of South Korea in 1950, or the invasion and conquest of Kuwait by Saddam Hussein's Iraq in 1990 both qualify as crimes against peace. What should be clearly noted is that this definition applies most obviously and directly to wars between independent states, due to the emphasis on territorial aggression, and it is not so clearly applicable in the kinds of internal wars that form such a predominant part of the fabric of contemporary violence—Bosnia, Rwanda, and Kosovo, for instance.

The second category is a reiteration of the traditional usage of the concept. *War crimes* are defined as "violations of the laws or customs of war. Such violations shall include, but not be limited to, murder, ill-treatment or deportation to slave labor or for any other purpose of civilian population of or in occupied territory, murder or ill-treatment of prisoners of war or persons on the seas, killing of hostages, plunder of public or private property, wanton destruction of cities, towns or villages, or devastation not justified by military necessity." This enumeration, of course, was a virtual "laundry list" of accusations against the Germans and the Japanese (although the Allies arguably committed some of the same acts). While acts against civilians are mentioned in the listing, the crimes enumerated are limited to mistreatment of general civilian populations rather than their systematic extension to segments of the population.

A true incident from World War II, recorded by W.E.B. Griffin in *The Corps: Call to Arms*, illustrates the point with regard to the fate of U.S. Marine Raiders captured on Makin Island in the South Pacific and held as prisoners of war. He wrote, "On October 16, [1942] the Marine prisoners were blindfolded and their hands tied behind them. The Marine prisoners were led one at a time to the edge of a pit dug for the purpose, and placed in a kneeling position. Then they were beheaded by one or another of the three [Japanese] warrant officers—using swords." This act was among those tried at the Tokyo tribunal; those ordering the executions were tried, found guilty, and themselves executed for their deeds.

The third category was the most innovative and controversial. It is also the type of war crimes with which the concept is most closely associated in the current debate over war crimes. *Crimes against humanity* are defined as "murder, extermination, enslavement, deportation, and other inhumane acts committed against any civilian population, before or during the war; or persecutions on political, racial or religious grounds in execution of or in connection with any crime...whether or not in violation of the domestic law where perpetuated." The statute goes further, establishing the basis of responsibility and thus vulnerability to prosecution. "Leaders, organizers, instigators, or accomplices participating in the formulation or execution of a common plan or conspiracy to commit any of the foregoing crimes are responsible for all acts performed by any persons in execution of such plan." This latter enumeration of responsibility justified the indictment of former Yugoslav President Slobodan Milosevic, who has never been accused of physically carrying out acts qualifying as war crimes.

To someone whose experience is limited to the latter part of the twentieth century, this notion of crimes against humanity may not seem radical, or possibly even unusual in content. At the time, however, it clearly was, for several reasons. First, it criminalized actions by states (or groups within states) that, while not exactly common in human history, were certainly not unknown but previously not thought of as criminal. Imagine, for instance, any of the following being accused as criminals and placed on trial: Genghis Khan and the leaders of the Golden Horde; the Ottoman Turks, executors of the genocidal campaign against the Armenians early in the twentieth century; or, for that matter, the U.S. government, who instigated the post–Civil War campaigns against the western Indian tribes (e.g., Wounded Knee).

The second radical idea contained in the definition is that of jurisdiction. By stating that crimes against humanity are enforceable "whether or not in violation of the domestic law" of the places they occur, the definition creates a certain universality to its delineation which, among other things, seems to transcend the sovereign rights of states to order events as they choose within their territory. That assertion remains at the base of controversy about the institutionalization of war crimes, because it entwines war criminal behavior (the reprehensibility of which is agreed upon) with the controversy over sovereignty (about which there is considerable disagreement). Third, the statute seeks to remove the defense that crimes against humanity can be justified on the basis that they were committed on orders from a superior. Thus, anyone with any part in crimes against humanity is equally vulnerable under the law, and this provision creates the flexibility of the tribunal to delve as deeply as it wishes into the offending hierarchy.

The statute does not address one element about war crimes prosecution that is almost always raised. It is the problem of "victor's law," which is the charge that war crimes are always defined by the winning side in a war, and those tried are always those from the losing side. While the Nuremberg and Tokyo tribunals labored hard and long to make the proceedings as judicially fair as they could, it is nonetheless true that it was Germans and Japanese in the dock, not Americans or Britons. It is possible, but not very likely, that no one on the Allied side ever committed a war crime or a crime against humanity during the events surrounding World War II. It is arguable, for instance, that the officials who ordered and carried out the fire bombing of Tokyo or the leveling of Dresden, in which many innocent civilians were killed, were guilty of crimes against humanity, but none of these officials came before the war crimes tribunal. The recognition of the potential charge that any trial applies victor's law has been an ongoing concern in the further development of the concept of war crimes, and is reflected in the jurisdiction of the International Criminal Court.

Clearly, the major form of activity that a definition of crimes against humanity seeks to outlaw is that involving the systematic suppression or elimination of parts or all of a population, what we conventionally call genocide. In the context of 1945, as mentioned earlier, the German Holocaust against the Jews, Gypsies, and others and Japanese atrocities in China and elsewhere formed the spotlight of such concern

Post–World War II Efforts

This concern carried over into the postwar world. In 1948, the General Assembly of the United Nations passed the International Convention on the Prevention and Punishment of the Crime of Genocide, known more compactly as the Convention on Genocide. Building upon the assertion of crimes against humanity, the Convention on Genocide provided clarification and codification of what constituted acts of genocide.

According to the convention, any of the following actions, when committed with the intent of eliminating a particular national, ethnic, racial, or religious group, constitutes genocide: (1) killing members of the group; (2) causing serious bodily or mental harm to members of the group; (3) deliberately inflicting on the group conditions of life calculated to kill; (4) imposing measures intended to prevent births within a group; and (5) forcibly transferring children out of a group.

In important ways, enunciating the Convention on Genocide (and the parallel UN Declaration on Human Rights) was a form of international atonement for Axis excesses, and especially for the Holocaust. Most countries signed and ratified the Convention, which then went into force—without, one might quickly add, any real form of enforcement. A few countries, notably the United States, refused to ratify the document for reasons based in infringement of sovereignty discussed later.

EVOLUTION OF THE PROBLEM

With the completion of the war crimes tribunals after World War II and the flurry of activity that produced the Convention on Genocide, the subject of war crimes dropped from the public eye, not to reemerge publicly until the 1990s. Well beneath the surface of public concern, attempts were indeed made to create some sort of enforcement mechanism for dealing with these issues, but they never received very much public attention, nor did they generate enough political support to gain serious consideration in the international political debate.

Why was this the case? It is not because crimes against humanity became less unacceptable, although those acts and traditional war crimes certainly continued to occur, at least on a smaller scale than had happened during World War II. Rather, the more likely explanation is that the subject matter became a victim of the Cold War, as did other phenomena such as the aggressive promotion of human rights.

It is almost certainly not a coincidence that the emergence of a broad international interest in war crimes emerged at a time of United States–Soviet cooperation, that concern and progress ground to an effective halt during the ideological and geopolitical confrontation between them, and that the subject has resurfaced and been revitalized since the cessation of that competition.

Why would the Cold War competition hamstring progress on a subject that would, on the face of it, seem noncontroversial? No one, after all, officially condones acts that we have described as war crimes, and yet, in the Cold War context, neither the clarification nor the codification was aggressively pursued internationally.

The problem was similar to, and had the same roots as, the advocacy of human rights, which also lay fallow on the international agenda through most of the Cold War period. In a sense, war crimes are one of the flip sides of human rights: the crimes against humanity clearly violate the most basic of human rights, and traditional war crimes violate those rights in times of combat.

In the Cold War context, issues like human rights tended to get caught up in the propaganda war between the superpowers. The Soviets would assume that American advocacy of certain principles (for instance, free speech) was championed to embarrass the Soviet Union, where such rights were certainly not inviolate, an assumption with at least some validity. Had the Soviets decided to push for greater progress on war crimes during the American participation in the Vietnam War between 1965 and 1973, the United States would, with some justification, have assumed the purpose was to embarrass American servicemen and discredit the American military effort. The incident depicted in *Platoon* and the reality of what occurred at My Lai both illustrate the extension of this dynamic to war crimes. Innocent civilians were slaughtered at My Lai in what was a clear crime against humanity, but dispassionate consideration was drowned by wartime propaganda duels over Cold War issues. In such circumstances, little if any progress could be expected on issues with a Cold War veneer; by and large, there was little attempt to pursue agreements in areas where one side or the other might impose a formal veto (in the United Nations Security Council) or informal veto (by convincing its friends and allies not to take part).

There was a second problem with extending the idea of war crimes, and especially the codification of the idea into some enforcement regime, and that problem has been a particular sticking point for the United States government: the issue of sovereignty. Among the major states in the international system, the United States (as well as nondemocratic states like China) has been among the staunchest supporters of the doctrine of state sovereignty, the idea that supreme authority to act (in other words, sovereignty) resides exclusively with states and that any dilution of that status is unacceptable and thus actively to be opposed.

Because the Convention on Genocide is universally applicable to all states which have signed and ratified the Convention and thus have acceded to its provisions, it can be viewed, and was by powerful political elements in the United States, as an infringement of the authority of the U.S. government to regulate its own affairs. This argument may seem strained in the area of genocide: one way of looking at the objection is that it preserves the right of the United States to commit genocide without breaking agreements of which it is part. Nonetheless, the argument against diluting American national sovereignty was sufficiently politically powerful to prevent the U.S. Senate from ratifying the Convention until 1993, when it was submitted to the Senate by President Clinton and approved by the necessary two-thirds majority. As we shall see, this same basic objection has caused the United States to be one of a handful of countries, and the only prominent political democracy, to refuse to sign or ratify the statute of the International Criminal Court.

BOSNIA AND RWANDA: THE PROBLEM REVIVED

The problem of war crimes remained a moot point until the 1990s. As suggested, there undoubtedly were instances where questions of war crimes, and especially crimes against humanity, could have been raised previously but, due to their entanglement in the Cold War, were not. The extermination of well over a million citizens by the Khmer Rouge in Cambodia between 1976 and 1979 is a good example. Because the struggle in Cambodia was between rival communist forces, one supported by the Soviets and the other (the Khmer Rouge) supported by the People's Republic of China, it was viewed as an intramural struggle in which the West had little direct interest. China's Great Cultural Revolution between 1966 and 1976 probably qualifies as well.

Two other things that changed between the 1970s and the outbreak of concern about crimes against humanity in the 1990s help explain international indifference to war crimes in the 1970s and international activism in the 1990s. The first change was the emergence of a much more aggressive electronic media infrastructure, which had the physical capability to probe much more widely around the globe and thus to expose and publicize apparent violations. In 1976, one must remember, there was no such thing as global television; Cable News Network (CNN), with which we tend to associate the globalization of world news, was not launched until 1980 and did not become a prominent force for some time thereafter. Moreover, media tools such as handheld camcorders and satellite uplinks were theoretical ideas, not the everyday equipment of the reporter. As a result, there was much less coverage of the slaughter in Cambodia than there typically is today of similar events. There were lots of rumors and verbal accounts by escaping refugees and reporters (the gist of the 1980s movie *The Killing Fields*) but little graphic visual accounting of the tragedy. The stacks of skulls of the victims that are our lasting memory of what happened are products of the latter 1980s and early 1990s, well after the fighting and killing were over. Moreover, the death of Pol Pot, the leader of the Khmer Rouge, in 1999 has removed much of the focus on the event.

The other change has been the growing *de facto* (in practice) if not *de jure* (in law) acceptance of the permissibility of international intervention in the internal affairs of states when states (or factions within states) grossly abuse other people or groups—in other words, commit crimes against humanity and especially genocide. Without an elaborate statement of the principle of *humanitarian intervention*, this is what the United Nations authorized when it sent UN forces into Somalia in1992. This action was widely touted by then UN Secretary-General Boutros Boutros-Ghali as a precedent-setting exercise for the future—the establishment of international enforcement of universal codes of behavior.

Thus, by the early 1990s, three dynamics affecting international politics had changed sufficiently to raise the prospects of dealing with war crimes onto the international agenda. The end of the Cold War meant atrocities would not be hidden or accusations about them suppressed on ideological grounds or based on the charge that such expressions were mere propaganda. A more aggressive and technologically empowered electronic media with global reach was available to report and publicize atrocities wherever they could reach (which was not universal; government intimidation has kept the media from reporting effectively the slaughter over the last decade in the Sudan). At the same time, the UN operation in Somalia had established something like a precedent about the notion of humanitarian intervention. The only issue that was not resolved was the question of the implications of all this for state sovereignty, a problem that remained latent until the formal call for a permanent war crimes tribunal was issued by the Rome Conference of 1998.

The Bosnian "Ethnic Cleansing"

The first test of this new environment came in Bosnia and Herzegovina (hereafter Bosnia). As part of the general dismemberment of Yugoslavia in 1991 and 1992 (an event itself made possible by the end of the Cold War, since the Yugoslav state had been communist), the multiethnic state of Bosnia joined several other former Yugoslav states like Croatia and Slovenia and declared its independence from Yugoslavia in 1991. Because of its ethnic composition (with sizable Serb, Croat, and Muslim minorities) and its geographical location (bordering both Serbia and Croatia), the result was the bloodiest civil fighting anywhere within the old Yugoslav boundaries. Part of this fighting involved the displacement of ethnic minorities by groups with claims to different parts of Bosnian territory, a process that became known as ethnic cleansing. One of the outgrowths of ethnic cleansing was the allegation of atrocities against different ethnic groups—crimes against humanity, or war crimes.

While this is not the place for a detailed description of the Bosnian war, it was (and could easily become again) a triangular affair. The three principal antagonists were Bosnian Serbs, who wished either for a Bosnian state they controlled or reunion with Serb-controlled Yugoslavia (effectively reduced to Serbia—including Kosovo—and Montenegro); Bosnian Croats, who wanted either an independent state or, in most cases, union with Croatia (one of the other states that had seceded); and the Bosnian Muslims, who desired full independence and who had declared the Bosnian state.

The war, such as it was, was primarily a land grab, where one of the three sides would seek to occupy territory in which the other ethnic groups resided, thereby creating a claim to territorial possession when partition inevitably occurred. Although there was some traditional combat in places like the Krajina region between Croatia and Serbia, a great deal of the "action" consisted of "militia" units attacking basically defenseless members of the other groups to force them from territory the attackers desired. In some cases, large numbers of civilians were killed and interred in mass graves, forming one of the strongest bases for later war crimes indictments. All three groups participated in this action at one time and to one extent or another. The Bosnian Serbs, backed physically and politically by the Yugoslav government in Belgrade, were the best armed and most brutal and successful, and their efforts thus attracted the most—negative—attention.

The nature of this decidedly unmilitary conflict inevitably raised the likelihood that its conduct could be described in terms of war crimes, as defined nearly a half-century earlier. Although the chaotic beginning of the conflict made it difficult to apportion crimes against peace, the fact that much of the "fighting" involved attacks on civilians meant traditional war crimes probably occurred, and that crimes against humanity were likely committed. This constellation of dynamics had occurred before, and no one had cried "war crimes." Why was this case different?

Two factors stood out. The first was the role of the media, which, accurately or not, portrayed the slaughter largely in terms of Serb responsibility but, more importantly, in ways that raised the worst memories of World War II and its war crimes. The first and most vivid depiction of the Bosnian war was the publication of still photographs and television footage of Bosnian Muslim prisoners of war in Serb detention camps. The

Map 4.1 Map of Yugoslavia (featuring Bosnia).

images were explosive: gaunt, sunken-eyed prisoners staring through the wire fences, who looked eerily like Jewish prisoners in the Nazi death camps a half-century earlier. The analogy was impossible to ignore, whether it was accurate or not (a matter of some controversy); the implication that something had to be done to rectify the situation was equally difficulty to resist.

The second factor was the physical presence of the United Nations on the scene. During a lull in the fighting between Croatia and Serbia over contested territory in 1992, a UN peacekeeping mission, the UN Protection Force (UNPROFOR), was put in place to monitor the cease-fire. While the cease-fire quickly (and predictably) broke down and UNPROFOR was incapable of reinstating it, the UN presence had two impacts that helped frame the situation in war crimes terms. First, UN inspectors associated with UNPROFOR investigated allegations of atrocities against civilians and unearthed evidence of atrocity that could not be dismissed by the contestants as mere propaganda. UN presence thus unearthed (in some cases literally) evidence of crimes against humanity in forms like the mass graves in which the bodies of executed civilians had been unceremoniously dumped.

Second, these revelations meant that the parent organization, the UN itself, was involved; in 1993, the UN Security Council passed a resolution setting up a temporary, ad hoc war crimes tribunal. The location would be at the International Court of Justice (ICJ), which is itself affiliated with the UN. On November 29, 1996, the tribunal handed down its first sentence against Serb leader Drazen Erdemovic. It was the first conviction of an individual charged with war crimes since Nuremberg and Tokyo. The Bosnian tribunal remains in session, and in February 2002 the trial of its most famous defendant, former Yugoslav president Slobodan Milosevic, began. Its greatest problem has been the ability to capture indicted violators who remain in Yugoslavia, where the government refuses to allow them to be extradited.

The Rwandan Rampage

War crimes in Bosnia were soon followed by even more spectacular, gruesome events in Rwanda, a small country in eastern Africa. On May 8, 1994, members of the Hutu majority encouraged by Hutu politicians of that country began a systematic, countrywide campaign of genocide against their fellow countrymen, the Tutsi. By the time the slaughter was finally halted, over a half million people had been brutally slaughtered.

Although it received less initial publicity than Bosnia, the rampage in Rwanda was a crime against humanity on a scale that dwarfed what had happened in the Balkans. Ethnic cleansing in Bosnia had largely had the purpose of displacing, not systematically eliminating, rival groups. Crimes against humanity undoubtedly occurred; systematic genocide with the intent of extinguishing part of the population probably did not.

The campaign in Rwanda was a clear case of genocide. The purpose of the "fighting" was to kill all Tutsi who could be identified and murdered, often hacking them with machetes. Given the scale of the slaughter and the number of people who took part in the atrocities (and one must recall that the standards indicate that there are no limits about how low in the decision-making chain one can go to prosecute offenders), the potential task of sorting out and prosecuting the war criminals was daunting.

Rwanda raised a quandary for the international community. Who should investigate and administer war crimes trials? The UN system offered the best hope for legitimacy and fairness, but it clearly lacked the resources to conduct a comprehensive investigation and trial, given the number of Rwandan Hutu undoubtedly vulnerable to prosecution (the UN initially assigned 12 investigators to the task). The Rwandans themselves (notably the surviving Tutsi who took control of the government) promised swift and comprehensive justice, but that alternative was fraught with the chance that justice would turn into retribution—victor's law at its worst. Ultimately, an ad hoc war crimes tribunal was created at the Hague on the model of the Bosnian panel. Like that panel, it remains in session, with little prospect of an early disbanding.

The impaneling of the Bosnian and Rwandan war crimes tribunals inevitably created momentum for the idea of a permanent court. There was very little objection in principle to the idea of a war crimes court to deal with these two instances. Moreover, it was increasingly clear from atrocities being committed in other countries that there would be no shortage of situations where allegations of crimes against humanity would be commonplace. Internal conflicts in places as widely separated as Sierra Leone in Africa, Kosovo nearly on the Bosnian border, and East Timor on the Indonesian archipelago provided evidence of both geographic diversity and numerous opportunities to enforce sanctions against a new breed of war criminals whose war crimes consisted of gross crimes against humanity perpetrated against their fellow citizens. Beyond the anticipated amount of demand for a permanent structure was the hope that the existence of a court and the knowledge it could bring criminals to justice might deter some future crimes against humanity. But, how should the international community react?

PROPOSALS FOR A PERMANENT WAR CRIMES TRIBUNAL

Advocacy of a permanent court to adjudicate war crimes accompanied the flurry of activity surrounding Nuremberg and Tokyo and the adoption of the Convention on Genocide. In 1948, the UN General Assembly commissioned the International Law Commission (a private body) to study the possibility of establishing an International Criminal Court (ICC). The Commission worked on this problem until 1954 and produced a draft statute for the ICC. Unfortunately, this document appeared during the darkest days of the Cold War; there were objections from both sides of the Iron Curtain, and the UN dropped the proposal.

The idea of an ICC lay dormant until 1989, when the tiny island country of Trinidad and Tobago revived the proposal within the UN. Their motive, oddly enough, was to provide an instrument in their struggle against drug traffickers from South America. Nonetheless, the events in Bosnia and Rwanda revived broader interest. The early experience of trying to mount an ad hoc effort also suggested the wisdom of creating a permanent body to provide a more effective, timely approach to war crimes.

The proposal has been controversial. The matter of jurisdiction has been at the heart of the contention. Champions of the ICC contend that the court must have mandatory jurisdiction over all accused instances of war crimes and that its jurisdiction must supersede national sovereignty to be effective. Opponents object that this infringement on national sovereignty is unwarranted and could form the basis for future abuses of sovereignty. The ICC statute contains provisions for mandatory jurisdiction.

The Case for the ICC

The idea of an ICC has several advantages over impaneling tribunals as the need arises. First, it would avoid having to start essentially from scratch each time suspected war crimes are uncovered. A permanent ICC would have, among other things, a permanent staff of investigators and prosecutors, and it would have vested in its staff the authority and jurisdiction to ascertain when crimes against humanity have indeed occurred.

Second, and related to the first point, a permanent ICC could be much more responsive to the occurrence—or even possibly the likelihood—that war crimes had occurred or were about to occur. Not only would a permanent staff have or develop the expertise for efficient intervention in war crimes situations, they could be rapidly mobilized and applied to the problem.

Third, it was hoped that a permanent ICC would act as a deterrent to future potential war criminals. Would, for instance, the Bosnian Serb leaders who have been indicted (mostly in absentia) for authorizing ethnic cleansing in Bosnia have been dissuaded from doing so if they knew there was an international criminal authority that could bring them to justice for their deeds? What influence would a permanent ICC have had on the planners and implementers of the slaughter in Rwanda? While no one can know the answers to these questions, the chorus that the existence of the ICC might have made a difference continued to grow, particularly as evidence mounted of potential and actual war crimes being contemplated or committed in Kosovo.

Pressure to negotiate a treaty to create an ICC grew during the 1990s. As early as 1995, the Clinton administration in the United States became an activist in the movement in support of the tribunal. The movement culminated with the Rome Conference of 1998 (technically the United Nations Diplomatic Conference on the Establishment of a Permanent International Criminal Court). The conference produced a draft treaty that would establish the ICC as a permanent court for trying individuals accused of committing genocide, war crimes, or crimes against humanity and gave the court the jurisdiction over individuals accused of these crimes. When the draft came to a vote, it passed by a vote of 120 states in favor, 7 opposed, and 21 abstentions. In order for the treaty to come into force, at least 60 states must ratify the treaty. As of February 2002, it had been signed by over 100 states and ratified by 52. The court will come into full being when it is ratified by 60 states.

The United States government was one of the seven states to vote against the treaty in Rome and has neither signed nor ratified the document, despite the Clinton administration's involvement in promoting and drafting the ICC statute. In one of his final acts in office, President Clinton signed the statute in December 2000. In February 2001, Secretary of State Colin S. Powell announced that President George W. Bush had no intention of submitting it to the Senate for ratification.

Objections to the ICC

While the United States advocating and then opposing the ICC statute may seem anomalous, it is not entirely unusual. The apparent schizophrenia represents different views of America's place in the world, the American attitude toward the world, and especially the question of sovereignty. The Clinton administration, broadly internationalist and seeing the ICC statute as a way both to demonstrate responsible U.S. leadership and to improve the quality of the international environment, became a champion of the idea of dealing with war crimes, and a war crimes court with "teeth." Other powerful political forces, however, summoned the specter of the loss of sovereignty that joining the treaty possibly entailed. Within the minds of many conservative elements in the country, the problem came to focus on the potential loss of control of the United States government over its own forces in the field. Whether converted to this position or accepting the inevitability that it would prevail, the Clinton administration came to accept the critics of the treaty.

David Sheffer, head of the American delegation, delivered the U.S. objection at the end of the Rome Conference. He began his objection by pointing out that the ICC would only have jurisdiction in countries that were parties to the treaty, and he noted that a number of the countries in which the internal wars that were producing accusations of war crimes could and would evade prosecution by simply not joining the treaty. The qualifying point of this objection was that a UN Security Council Resolution (UNSCR) can extend that jurisdiction in a given case, and that these are common in these circumstances.

The heart of the objection was that the treaty forces countries to relinquish their sovereign jurisdiction over their forces and leave those forces vulnerable to international prosecution with no U.S. ability to come to their aid when the United States participates in UN–sponsored peacekeeping operations, such as those in Bosnia and Kosovo. As Sheffer put it, "Thus, the treaty purports to establish an arrangement whereby U.S. armed forces operating overseas could be conceivably prosecuted by the international court even if the U.S. has not agreed to be bound by the treaty. Not only is this contrary to the most fundamental principles of treaty law, it could inhibit the ability of the U.S. to use its military to meet alliance obligations and participate in multinational operations, including humanitarian interventions to save civilian lives."

The sovereign control of American forces potentially accused of war crimes thus stands at the base of the U.S. refusal to sign off on the ICC statute. The same fear of diluting the ability of the United States to maintain total control over its citizens and territory have left the United States in anomalous situations before: the failure to ratify either the Convention on Genocide or the Universal Declaration of Human Rights for over forty years, for instance. More recently, the same logic has put the United States in the virtually singular situation of opposing an international treaty on land mines that was largely the creation of a private American citizen.

In order to get around the problem of sovereignty forfeiture, the United States has dredged up a tactic it used after World War II to ensure Senate ratification of the statute of the International Court of Justice (ICJ or World Court), to which the ICC would be affiliated. In the case of the ICJ, the United States insisted that the statute state the Court would only have jurisdiction in individual cases if *both* (or all) parties granted jurisdiction for that action only. In other words, countries, including the United States, can only be sued and have judgments made against them in situations where they have given their permission: sovereign control is only abrogated by explicit consent. This so-called Connally Amendment (named after the Texas senator who proposed it) has been used on numerous occasions by the U.S. government (for instance, in 1986, when Nicaragua tried to sue the United States for mining the harbor at Managua, the United States simply refused the jurisdiction).

The same approach is incorporated in the American approach to the question of the jurisdiction of the ICC. The proposed "supplement" to the Rome Treaty reads: "The United Nations and the International Criminal Court agree that the Court may seek the surrender or accept custody of a national who acts within the overall direction of a U.N. Member State, and such directing State has so acknowledged *only in the event (a) the directing State is a State Party to the Statute or the Court obtains the consent of the directing State, or (b) measures have been authorized pursuant to Chapter VII of the U.N. Charter against the directing State in relation to the situation or actions giving rise to alleged crime or crimes."* [emphasis added]

This amendment, if approved, would effectively exempt American citizens (or the citizens of any other country, should the supplement be generally accepted) from being tried by the ICC without the explicit permission of the United States government. The first exception asserts that the United States can avoid the jurisdiction of the Court either by not joining the Court (its current status) or by refusing jurisdiction in individual instances. The second exception requires an action of the UN Security Council (acting under Chapter VII, by which force is authorized). The United States, of course, has a veto in the Security Council.

Is the American position realistic? The U.S. government, and especially the military, argues that the United States, as the remaining superpower, is uniquely vulnerable to international harassment in the absence of this kind of protection. More specifically, there are usually American forces involved in major peacekeeping missions globally, where accusations of war crimes are commonplace. The military fears that unfounded accusations against Americans can become a means of harassment of the United States against which they should guard and which the American amendment seeks to protect. Opponents of this position counter that the widespread international acceptance of this limitation would create such a large loophole for states with personnel accused of war crimes as to render the court powerless.

The concern is neither abstract nor academic. During the early stages of American participation in the Kosovo Force (KFOR) peacekeeping mission, American Army Staff Sergeant Frank J. Ronghi was arrested for sodomizing and murdering an 11-year-old Albanian Kosovar girl, whose body was found on January 13, 2000. Under terms of the ICC, Ronghi should have been arrested and tried by the international body for crimes against humanity. Instead, he was tried by an American military tribunal in Germany, before which he pleaded guilty and received a life sentence without parole on August 2, 2000. He will serve his sentence in a U.S. military prison. International criticism of this U.S. evasion of the ICC's jurisdiction was muted by the swift prosecution of Ronghi and by a sentence as severe as the ICC would likely have handed down.

What must the international community which, by and large, rejects the American objection, do to gain acceptance—including American—of the ICC? First, it must acknowledge that the absence of the world's most powerful state from the regime greatly undercuts its legitimacy and physical clout. As the Clinton administration's Secretary of State Madeleine Albright put it, the ICC without the United States is "dead upon arrival." Thus, some way must be found to overcome the objections of the Americans and others who find fault with the statute as written. These objections will almost certainly be redoubled by the Bush administration. Clearly, the issue of intrusion into state sovereignty must be resolved satisfactorily. Leaving war crimes an ad hoc problem where decisions are made politically in individual instances allows individual states the ability to assert their sovereignty more effectively than if the ICC independently can determine jurisdiction. The Russian government certainly would not have wanted the ICC independently to rule on whether war crimes have occurred in Chechnya and then to prosecute violators (who might have been found very high into the Russian regime). On the other hand, sovereignty can be used as a screen behind which those who have committed atrocities can hide. The other major problem with an ad hoc system is that it will always be subject to accusations of victor's law.

There is another objection that takes us back to the beginning of this study and provides a point of conclusion. It is the question of how to treat past instances of war crimes, situations that either predate the assertion of crimes against humanity or that were ignored previously in war crimes terms. If, for instance, the scene from *Platoon* with which we began is really an allegory for the My Lai massacre during the Vietnam War, should those who perpetrated the atrocities, in which a large number of entirely innocent Vietnamese were executed in violation of traditional war crimes and crimes against humanity, be tried over thirty years later? The current statute does not specify the question of what amounts to a statute of limitations, but in its absence, there is almost certainly a very long list of potential defendants.

CONCLUSION

Now that it has been raised and publicly entered the international agenda, the question of war crimes is not likely to go away. In a gradually democratizing world in which authoritarianism is still practiced but rarely extolled, there is no longer any organized, principled objection to the notion that there are limits on the conduct of war and the limits on how individuals and groups can be treated. Although the development of something like a consensus on this matter is really quite recent in historical terms (particularly the idea of crimes against peace and humanity), it nonetheless seems well on its way to being established as an international norm.

The major remaining question is institutionalization of war crimes enforcement. As noted in a quote at the beginning of this study, the emergence of a consensus has coincided with a spate of war crimes, principally in the bloody, brutal internal wars in a number of developing world states. The practical implication of this situation is that there are almost certainly going to be places where war crimes tribunals will need to be formed if there is not a permanent court. In the present environment, Kosovo and East Timor would seem to be candidates, and undoubtedly there will be others.

Is some form of the ICC the answer? Clearly, it would solve some problems and have some advantages, as already noted. It would certainly be more responsive when problems arise, it would maximize whatever deterrent value a potential violator would experience knowing the court was waiting for him or her, and it would insulate the system from accusations of victor's law in future cases. Moreover, it would contribute to the general promotion of lawfulness in the international system. To its proponents, these are powerful and compelling justifications for the ICC.

Then there is the American position. The U.S. objection to the ICC is not a defense of war crimes nor is it an explicit defense of international disorder. Rather, it stems from a long-standing American fixation on state sovereignty and the need for the American government to have sole jurisdiction over its citizens. In practice, this policy puts the United States at cross-purposes with most of the international community, including most of its closest allies, and on the same side as some rogue states on this and similar issues. Within the United States, there is division on the position we should take: the Clinton administration did, after all, both champion and subsequently back down into opposition about the ICC, and the Bush administration is highly unlikely to reverse that opposition. Given the American status as the remaining superpower, the American decision on ratifying the ICC statute or an amended version is probably critical. If the United States remains opposed, Secretary Albright could well be correct in her assessment about the ICC.

In the end, the international debate pitting the United States against most of the rest of the world (and especially its principal allies) is not about war crimes or the establishment of a court. No one is *for* war crimes or *against* a tribunal to prosecute offenders. The debate is over the nature of the court's jurisdiction. Should that jurisdiction be mandatory, automatic, and supreme? Or should that jurisdiction be tempered by a filter that allows states to maintain primary control over their own citizens accused of war crimes? Ultimately, the issue all boils down to the question of sovereignty.

STUDY/DISCUSSION QUESTIONS

1. Assuming that the definitions of war crimes arising from the post–World War II experience are acceptable, should their application be retroactive, either before the standards were adopted or in cases where violations may have occurred since 1947 but where prosecution did not occur at the time? If so, what criteria can you think of to choose among instances?

2. Why do you suppose that war crimes tribunals were authorized for Bosnia and Rwanda but not for Chechnya? Does this suggest a double standard where the weak are vulnerable but the powerful are not? Since the United States is clearly a powerful country, should we also be exempt?

3. Are the arguments in favor of the International Criminal Court compelling? How much of the American objection to the question of automatic, overriding jurisdiction should be accommodated?

4. Is the participation of the United States necessary for the success of the permanent war crimes tribunal? Assess the American objection. Is it reasonable, arrogant, or possibly both? If you were the representative of another government, how would you feel about the American position?

5. The trial of Sgt. Ronghi by an American military court avoids the precedent of American acquiescence to the ICC statute, and his sentence is as severe as it could have been under ICC jurisdiction. Is such an outcome an adequate and justifiable alternative to full U.S. participation in the ICC?

6. Since most of the situations where allegations of war crimes are likely to occur are internal wars in the developing world, how does this affect the value of having a permanent court rather than ad hoc tribunals, as we have done up to now? Would a permanent ICC be more effective in deterring or investigating and bringing to justice violators?

7. Should some measure of national sovereignty be surrendered to make the ICC effective? Which value is more important: national control over a country's citizens, or justice for the victims and perpetrators of war crimes when those two values come into conflict?

READING/RESEARCH MATERIAL

Bassiouni, Cherif. "Policy Perspectives Favoring the Establishment of an International Criminal Court." *Journal of International Affairs* 52, 2 (Spring 1999), 795–800.

Casey, Lee A., and David B. Rivkin. "Against an International Criminal Court." *Commentary* 105, 5 (May 1998), 56–59.

Dempsey, Gary. *Reasonable Doubt: The Case Against the Proposed International Criminal Court.* Cato Policy Analysis No. 311. Washington, DC: Cato Institute, 1998.

Griffin, W.E.B. *The Corps: Call to Arms.* New York: Jove Books, 1995.

Gutman, Roy, and David Rieff, eds. *Crimes of War.* New York: W. W. Norton, 1999.

Kahn, Leo. *Nuremberg Trials.* New York: Ballantine Books, 1972.

Neier, Aryeh. *War Crimes: Brutality, Genocide, Terror, and the Struggle for Justice.* New York: Random House, 1998.

Reiff, David. "Court of Dreams: A Nice Idea That Won't Work." *The New Republic* 219, 10 (September 7, 1998), 16–17.

Rubin, Alfred P. "Challenging the Conventional Wisdom: Another View of the International Criminal Court." *Journal of International Affairs* 52, 2 (Spring 1999), 783–794.

Tucker, Robert W. "The International Criminal Court Controversy." *World Policy Journal* 18, 2 (Summer 2001), 71–82.

Tusa, Ann and John Tusa. *The Nuremberg Trial.* New York: Atheneum Publishing, 1983.

WEB SITES

Provides access to documents relating to the Nuremberg Trials

The Avalon Project at http://www.yale.edu/lawweb/avalon/imt/imt.htm

Collaboration of journalists, lawyers, and scholars that seeks to raise awareness of the laws of war and war crimes

Crimes of War Project at http://www.crimesofwar.org

Overview of documents and events leading up to the adoption of the Rome Statute
    Rome Statute of the International Criminal Court at
    http://www.un.org/law/icc/index.html

Extensive collection of relevant resources in print and electronic format
    ICC Resource Links at http://www.lib.uchicago.edu/%7Ellou/icc.html

Focuses on international criminal law and criminal justice topics, including all
    criminal law information generated by the United Nations
    ASIL Electronic Resource Guide to International Criminal Law at
    http://www.asil.org/resource/crim1.htm

Study examining the relationship between the proposed International Criminal Court
    and US national security interests
    The United States and the ICC at http://www.amacad.org/projects/icc.htm

CHAPTER FIVE

Sovereignty and the Right of Intervention in Internal Wars:

A STUDY OF THE ASSAULT ON STATE SOVEREIGNTY

PRÉCIS

The principle of sovereignty, or supreme authority, has been the bedrock principle of operation of the international political system since it began to take on its contemporary shape in the wake of the settlements ending the Thirty Years War of 1648, a process known as the Peace of Westphalia. Over time, sovereignty has come to reside in the governments of the states, where it is generally conceded to exist today. Because war is a primary result of the international system that has evolved around the principle of sovereignty, it has never been without its critics, who would prefer an order based on something other than sovereignty. The movement to "internationalize" war crimes, the topic of the last chapter, is one aspect of that criticism.

This case study looks at the assault on sovereignty through a prominent and very important problem of contemporary international relations—the very bloody, anarchical internal wars raging in some of the poorest countries of the developing world. A common phenomenon in many of these conflicts is the inability of any faction to end them and reestablish a peaceful order, leaving the population in a state of enormous, perpetual misery. In places like Bosnia and Kosovo, the frustration has led to calls for and the implementation of interventions by outside states to stop the fighting. Such missions, usually undertaken under the auspices of the United Nations, represent direct violations of the sovereignty of the countries where they are launched. Examining the effects on eroding the overall quality of sovereignty in the system is a major purpose of the case.

For the past 350 years, the bedrock principle of international relations has been the evolving concept of sovereignty, and more specifically the idea of state sovereignty. This concept was first formulated formally in a book written in the sixteenth century as the philosophical underpinning for the consolidation of power by Europe's monarchs, most specifically the authority of the king of France. With the settlement of the extraordinarily brutal, religiously based Thirty Years War in 1648, the triumphant secular monarchs of northern Europe adopted the concept as part of asserting their independence of papal authority.

State sovereignty, the idea that state governments have supreme authority in the international system and that there can be no authority superior to the state, has been around ever since as a first principle by which international relations is organized. The primacy of sovereignty has never lacked its critics, either in terms of the validity of the concept or its philosophical and practical implications. Nevertheless, the principle has endured, and governments cling tenaciously to their possession of sovereignty.

Sovereignty has always done more than provide the philosophical underpinning of international relations. The idea—even the necessity—of possessing and protecting sovereignty has formed much of the basis of state action, and particularly the geopolitical task of protecting the state from its enemies. The idea of a "national security state" that was a popular depiction during the Cold War was based in the need to protect the state's supreme authority over its territory from predators which threatened that authority. Among the defenders of this notion, the United States has stood out for its staunch defense of the sanctity of state sovereignty.

As we have moved into the post–Cold War period, the sacrosanct status of unfettered sovereignty has been increasingly questioned. Part of the assault has come from the traditional opponents of sovereignty such as the opponents of war, who argue that armed conflict is an integral and inevitable consequence of a world in which sovereignty reigns. From this view, the dismantling of sovereignty is the necessary prerequisite for world peace. At the same time, the rise of other concerns such as human rights creates collision points with state sovereignty. Why? Because a major historical justification for mistreatment of individuals and groups within states is that sovereign states possess absolute authority over their citizens, and how states act within their sovereign jurisdiction is their own business, not the concern of the international order. This is roughly the position that the Russian government has taken with regard to its treatment of Chechnya during the attempted Chechen secession during the 1990s and into the 2000s. During the Cold War and before, the argument that states could treat their citizens however they liked was hardly ever assaulted; today it routinely is.

There is one area in particular where state sovereignty collides most directly with the realities of the post–Cold War world. The major source of violence in the contemporary system is internal war in the developing world, and that violence is often chaotic, brutal, and bloody. Often, gross violations of human rights occur and instances of war crimes (the subject of Chapter 4 in this volume) abound. When these kinds of tragedies occurred in the past, the vast majority of the world simply averted its gaze from, for instance, the slaughter of Cambodians by their countrymen, the extermination of Armenians by the Ottoman Turks, or even the Holocaust against European Jews, Gypsies, and others. The reason for ignoring these events was that they were acts of sovereign governments regarding their own citizens, over whom they had total authority. No matter how badly a government treated its citizens within its own boundaries, that was its own problem and prerogative, not the business of outsiders.

This indifference may seem incredible in contemporary terms, but it is an idea that was virtually unchallenged as little as a half-century ago. Take a real example. When the war crimes trials at Nuremberg were being organized, there were questions about what crimes the Nazi defendants could be charged with committing. The leading U.S. jurist at the trials, a member of the U.S. Supreme Court, offered the official view that the Nazis could be charged with killing non–German citizens on German soil, but not with exterminating German Jews, because, as German citizens, they could treat them any way they saw fit. The position was not particularly controversial at the time (partly, of course, because as a practical matter, there were plenty of other war crimes with which to charge them).

The bloody internal conflicts in places like the Balkans and parts of Africa have challenged the idea that state sovereignty provides an unfettered license for governments to do as they please to their citizens or, where governments are incapable or nonexistent, not to protect portions of their populations from ravage. Using the United Nations as a vehicle to justify actions, the international system has, upon numerous occasions which will almost certainly continue into the future, intruded itself into these situations in order to prevent further abuse and to protect citizens.

The collision of traditional conceptualizations of sovereignty with the evolution of the post–Cold War world generally is thus a major question in international relations, a question of whether the world and its values are changing so much that the principle of sovereignty must be modified or abandoned to adjust to a new reality. One aspect of that reality is the collision between sovereignty and the assertion of an international right or need to intervene in civil wars within states, or more recently to pursue international terrorists. The outcome of that collision will help answer the broader question of the role of sovereignty in the twenty-first century and is thus the focus of this case study. Among the world forces that will have a major impact on the debate is the Bush administration in the United States, because of the centrality of the U.S. position on both elements of the problem.

Does the international system have a right to violate the sovereignty of states when the state is at war with itself—with hideous consequences for its population? In order to examine the problem, we will begin with a brief overview of the content and evolution of the concept of sovereignty, followed by some of the major criticisms of the concept and its implications for international relations. We will then look at the problem of internal wars and the justifications that are used when interventions are contemplated and implemented. We will conclude by examining the consequences of multiple interventions on the underpinning of sovereignty in the system, with special emphasis on the United States as one of the strongest defenders of the idea of state sovereignty.

THE CONCEPT OF SOVEREIGNTY

The basic concept of sovereignty has three distinct elements, which collectively define what it means to possess sovereignty. The first element is legitimate authority. Authority is simply the ability to enforce an order; the qualifier "legitimate" means that authority is invested with some of legal, consensual basis. Put another way, sovereignty is more than the exercise of pure force.

The second element of sovereignty is that it is supreme. What this means is that there is no authority superior to that of the possessor of sovereignty; the sovereign is the highest possible authority wherever the sovereign holds sway. The third and related element is that of territory; sovereignty is supreme authority within a defined physical territory. Since the Peace of Westphalia, the political state came to be the territorial definition of sovereignty. Thus states (or countries) have supreme authority over what occurs within their territorial boundaries, and no other source of authority can claim superior jurisdiction to the sovereign.

Before looking at why sovereignty has developed the way it has as a concept, it is worthwhile briefly to look at the consequences of these characteristics politically. In the *internal* workings of states, sovereignty is the basis of the political authority of state governments; the idea of supreme authority provides the state with the power to order its own affairs and the government to create and enforce that order. When the concept of sovereignty was first developed, this internal application was the emphasis. *Externally*, in the relations between states, this same sovereignty creates disorder, because there can be no superior authority to the sovereign within the defined territory of states. The result is *anarchy*, or the absence of government (political authority) in the relations among states. Thus, sovereignty has the schizophrenic effects of creating order and disorder, depending on the venue in which it is applied.

Early Origins and Evolution

This consequence was not so clear when Jean Bodin formally enunciated the concept of sovereignty in his 1576 book *De Republica*. Bodin, who was French, decried the inability of the French monarchy to establish its authority throughout the country, since lower feudal lords instead claimed what amounted to sovereignty over their realms—especially through charging taxes (tolls) to cross their realms. Bodin countered with the idea of sovereignty, which he defined as "supreme authority over citizens and subjects, *unrestrained by law*" [emphasis added]. The added and italicized element, Bodin felt, was necessary to avoid the unifying monarch being hamstrung by parochial laws in his quest for establishing the power of the French monarchy. While this part of the definition has fallen from common conceptions of sovereignty, its implications remain and are part of the ongoing controversy central to this case: if the sovereign is above the law, then nothing he or she does can possibly be illegal, at least when committed within the sovereign jurisdiction over which the sovereign reigns. It can be seen, among other places, in the determination that Nazi officials could only be tried for crimes committed outside Germany against non–citizens of Germany, as mentioned earlier.

When Bodin enunciated his principle of sovereignty, he was unconcerned about it as a maxim for international relations. This is not surprising in that the period of its gestation was a period when the monarchs of Europe were consolidating their holds on what became the modern states of Europe and the modern state system. Given that all these states were absolute monarchies, it is further not terribly surprising that another presumption quickly evolved (aided by philosophical publicists like Thomas Hobbes): sovereignty resided with the monarch (which, among other things, helps explain why monarchs are often referred to as sovereigns).

The concept of sovereignty was extended to international relations as the state system evolved and the structure of the modern state emerged and solidified. Hugo Grotius, the Dutch scholar generally agreed to have been the father of international law, first proclaimed state sovereignty as a fundamental principle of international relations in his 1625 book *On the Law of War and Peace.* By the eighteenth century, the principle was well on its way to being in place, and by the nineteenth it was an accepted part of international relations. Only in the second half of the twentieth century and now the twenty-first would it become controversial.

By the nineteenth century, the content of sovereignty had evolved from its context. Because virtually all countries were still ruled by more or less absolute monarchies (the fledgling, and not very important, United States, revolutionary France, and slightly democratizing Great Britain being the exceptions), the idea of absolute state sovereignty was the rule, and this principle governed both domestic and international relations. From the view of the international system, a prevailing way to describe international politics was in terms of something called the *billiard ball* theory. The idea, never to be taken entirely literally, was that state authority resembled a billiard ball, and that international relations consisted of these objects bouncing against one another, causing them to change course in their international behavior from time to time. Important to the theory, however, was that the balls were also impermeable, which meant that nothing in international interactions could affect what went on within the balls, such as how states treated their citizens. Under this principle, it was simply impermissible for states to interfere in the internal affairs of other states, no matter how distasteful or disgusting domestic practices might be.

Even during its heyday, this conceptualization was not universally accepted. In fact, conceptual challenges tended to be grouped around two related questions that continue to be important in the contemporary debate. How much authority does the sovereign have in the territorial realm it controls? Within whom, or what body, does sovereignty reside? Different answers have decidedly different implications for what sovereignty means in the relations among states.

As sovereignty was originally formulated and implemented, the answer to the first question was that sovereignty is absolute, that the possessor has total authority over his or her realm. This interpretation flows from, among other places, the idea that the sovereign is "unrestrained by law," to repeat Bodin's term. The contrary view emerged during the eighteenth and nineteenth centuries and reflected the growing notion of political rights asserted in the American and French Revolutions, each of which claimed the sovereign's powers were limited and could be abridged. Among the primary publicists of this view were the English political philosopher John Locke and his French counterpart, Jean-Jacques Rousseau.

The assertion that there are limits on sovereignty reflects the second question: Where does sovereignty reside? It was a question (at least at the time) not so much about whether states as opposed to some other entity possessed authority. Rather, it *was* a question about the basis on which authority can be legitimately claimed by those who seek to wield power within their political jurisdictions.

The traditional view, extrapolated from the gestation ground of applying the concept, was that sovereignty resides in the state. In the sixteenth and seventeenth centuries, when sovereignty was taking hold as an organizational principle, this meant the king or queen had sovereignty, since the monarch was the unchallenged head of government. It was what we would now call a "top-down" concept; the government exercised sovereignty over the population, whose duty it was to submit to that authority.

Beyond the philosophical positions taken by Locke and Rousseau, the contrary argument had its base in, among other places, the American Revolution. A major theme of the American complaint against the British monarch was his denial that the colonists had *rights* in addition to obligations. From that assertion, it was a reasonably short intellectual odyssey to the assertion that the *people*, not the state (or monarch), were the possessors of sovereignty. Under the notion of what became known as *popular sovereignty*, the idea was that the people, as possessors of sovereignty, ceded some of that authority to the state in order to provide the basic legitimacy for the social and political order. Ultimately, however, sovereignty resides with individual citizens, who can grant, withhold, or even, in some interpretations, rescind the bestowing of authority to the state.

These distinctions are more than abstract academic constructs. Their practical meanings and implications become particularly clear if one combines the two ideas in matrix form.

Sources and Extent of Sovereignty

		Extent of Sovereignty	
		Absolute	Limited
Source	State	(Cell 1)	(Cell 3)
	Individuals	(Cell 2)	(Cell 4)

The idea that sovereignty is absolute can be associated with authoritarian governance of one sort or the other. Traditional authoritarian regimes derive their claim to authority on the combination of absolute sovereignty and the state locus of authority (Cell 1). The populist/fascist regimes in Italy and Germany that arose between the world wars combine absolutism with some popular, individual base, and would be placed in Cell 2 (both regimes originally came to power popularly). On the other side of the ledger, the idea that sovereignty is limited is associated with democratic regimes. The idea of state sovereignty derived from the people is the backbone of traditional Western democracy (Cell 3). Where the conferral of sovereignty to the state is denied and maintained by subnational individuals or groups, the result can be the kinds of instability one associates with many of the unstable regimes in the developing world (Cell 4). These regimes, in turn, are the source of many of the problems in the system that forms our concern here.

Much of the debate about intervention in the internal affairs of states derives from the situation depicted in Cell 4. If one accepts the notion of absolute state sovereignty, there are no conditions under which it would be legitimate to interfere in the internal affairs of states, regardless of what was going on (as argued in the billiard ball theory, for instance). If one counters that sovereignty resides with individuals, then the possibility of legitimate interference on behalf of those sovereign individuals can be argued to override the sovereignty of the state. Before looking at this particular philosophical and practical debate and its relevance to the case of intervention in internal wars, it is worthwhile to look briefly at other objections to sovereignty that have developed across time.

Objections to Sovereignty

The idea and consequences of sovereignty have come under increasing assault as the twentieth century evolved toward the twenty-first century. Some of the objections are largely technical and academic and as such go beyond present purposes, as do generalized, overall critiques (which can, at any rate, be found in most textbooks on international relations). Two broad categories of criticism, however, relate directly to the question of international intervention in the internal affairs of states and thus have direct relevance to our task of examining the impact of intervention on sovereignty. Both are attacks on the implementation of the concept.

The first critique is aimed at absolutist conceptions of sovereignty. Critics of this argument maintain that sovereignty in application has never been as absolute as sovereignty in theory. The myth of the impenetrability of states by outside forces, including other states, is no more than a fiction to buttress the principle. States have always interfered in the internal affairs of other states in one way or another. The billiard ball theory is not, in the scientific sense, a theory at all, but instead a false hypothesis.

According to this argument, sovereignty not only has never been as absolute as its champions would assert, but it is becoming increasingly less so. A major reason for this dilution derives from the scientific revolution in telecommunications, which is making national borders entirely more penetrable from the outside, a trend anticipated more than a half-century ago by Sir Anthony Eden in a speech before the British House of Commons on November 22, 1945: "Every succeeding scientific discovery makes greater nonsense of old-time conceptions of sovereignty."

Those "old-time" conceptualizations refer, of course, to state-centered, absolutist interpretations of sovereignty. Forces such as the spread of the Internet, the trend toward economic globalization, the emergence of a homogenized commercial and popular culture around the world, and the more or less global desire to embrace the globalized world system all make the factual content of total sovereign control by governments over territory increasingly suspect. From our vantage point, however, we must ask whether this factual dilution of sovereign control extends to the "right" of the international system to infringe on the sovereign ability of the state to treat its citizens in ways that the international community disapproves? Is the spread of popular global culture, for instance, any kind of precedent to assert the rightfulness of forceful interposition by foreign troops into civil strife?

The other objection to absolute sovereignty has to do directly with the consequences of a system based in state sovereignty. Once again, a number of assertions are made about the pernicious effects of this form of organization on the operation of the international system. Two will be explored here.

The first, and most commonly asserted, objection to state sovereignty is its legitimization and, in some constructs, even glorification of war as a means to settle disputes between states. In a system of sovereign states, after all, there is no authority to enforce international norms on states nor to adjudicate or enforce judgments resolving the disputes that arise between states, except to the extent states voluntarily agree to be bound by international norms or, ironically, can be forced to accept international judgments. If states cannot agree amicably on how to settle their differences, then they can only rely on their own ability to solve favorably those disagreements they have.

The principle involved is known as *self-help*, the ability to bring about favorable outcomes to differences, often at the expense of the other state. This resolution becomes an exercise in *power* (the ability to get someone to do what they would not otherwise do), and one of the forms of power available to states is military force. In situations that states deem to be of sufficient importance to settle with armed force, then war may be the conflict resolution means of choice. In a system of self-help, there is thus no alternative to possessing and in some instances using armed force to get your way.

Despite the fact that all member states of the United Nations have renounced the waging of war as a means to resolve conflict (we simply do not call them "wars" anymore), the resort to force is understood and accepted in international practice (with some reservations). A fairly large number of analysts, including many scholars and practitioners of international relations, however, decry this situation, because they abhor war and would like to see it end. Because sovereignty is the cornerstone concept to organizing a system in which war is an integral part, therefore, they welcome the dilution and replacement of sovereignty as an international principle.

The other, more contemporary, objection to the principle of sovereignty is the power it gives governments over their people. In an international sense, governments still are, after all, legally "unrestrained" by international norms in dealing with their own populations, except, once again, to the extent that states have voluntarily limited their rights by signing international agreements. Historically, many in the international community abhorred the notion that governments could do horrible things to their citizens, but the right to such behavior was unchallenged on the basis of sovereignty. The phrase "patriotism is the last refuge of a scoundrel," first uttered by the English author Samuel Johnson in 1775, could easily be paraphrased , in international terms, as "sovereignty is the last refuge of a scoundrel."

Whether this is good or bad is not easy to determine. Governments strongly support sovereignty because it preserves the ability to conducts affairs without undue interference from outside. Unfortunately, the greater the protection of internal actions, the greater is the potential for abuse. In those cases where abuse results in atrocity and human suffering, the calls for outside intervention arise as a challenge to that sovereign authority.

The sanctity of this concept of sovereignty began to erode with the global reaction to the reality of the Holocaust that surfaced after World War II. The extermination of Jews, Gypsies, and others by Germany (and to a lesser extent, some German allies) both dwarfed historically known atrocities in history and was made exceedingly public and undeniable. When the defense of sovereignty was made to justify the "right" to carry on such programs, the legitimacy of the concept inevitably suffered.

The active revival of this objection came at the end of the Cold War. Scoundrel-like behavior did not, of course, go into hibernation during the Cold War (Pol Pot and the Khmer Rouge guaranteed that), but its condemnation—and especially proposing action to combat it—tended to get entangled in Cold War politics. Could, for instance, the United Nations have proposed a peacekeeping mission to Cambodia in 1975 (when the Khmer Rouge seized power and began their slaughter), when the fighting and killing involved two communist factions, each aligned with a different communist superpower (China and the Soviet Union), each of which had a veto in the Security Council? Of course not!

The end of the Cold War lifted that veil and coincided with the outbreak of a number of instances of atrocious behavior offensive to an international community no longer concerned about whether intervention would precipitate a Cold War crisis, or even World War III (the parallel with the evolution of concern with war crimes is not coincidental). Moreover, the trend also coincided with the emergence of a more activist leadership within a United Nations reinvigorated by its role in the successful Persian Gulf War campaign to remove Iraq from Kuwait. The UN was poised as a willing conduit for the mounting assault on the abuses of human rights that included an attack on state sovereignty.

The Assault on Sovereignty Through the UN

To borrow a term from military tactics, the attack on sovereignty emanating from actions from the United Nations during the 1990s was not a "frontal assault." None of the actions authorized by the UN Security Council has directly challenged the concept of state sovereignty nor aligned itself explicitly with a particular interpretation of the concept, such as limited sovereignty residing in individuals. Rather, they have been justified under Chapter VII of the UN Charter, which gives the Council the authority to determine threats to or breaches of the peace and to authorize responses, including the use of military force.

The assault on sovereignty has thus been conducted indirectly and inductively. It began when the Security Council authorized a peacekeeping force (UNOSOM I) to go to Somalia on December 3, 1992. The official reason for the mission was to alleviate human suffering (the threat of massive starvation) due to a five-year-long drought and a civil war, one of the consequences of which was that international relief efforts to get food to the afflicted were being interrupted by the combating factions. The motivation for the mission was hence a humanitarian one, to alleviate suffering in what would subsequently be referred to as a major humanitarian disaster.

The UN action was a major precedent in at least two ways, and one influenced by the unique circumstances in Somalia at the time. First and possibly most importantly, it was a mission authorized and implemented without any consultation with the government of the country to which it was dispatched. The idea that the UN would in effect invade a member state presumably for its own good was a major change of policy for the international community working through the world body.

Circumstances on the ground in Somalia made this an easy course to take. The government of Somalia was not consulted before the intervention because *there was no legal government to consult.* Since the overthrow of Siad Barre the previous year, Somalia had been in a state of anarchy, and the overall objective of the civil war was to install one clan leader or another to form a new government capable of rule. The United Nations could not negotiate with one leader or another, because intervention in a civil war at the invitation of any party is illegal under international law. The UN in effect skirted the issue by invoking Chapter VII and using its provisions to determine a breach of the peace and to take appropriate action to restore the peace. One could argue, but no one did publicly at the time, that the absence of a government meant there was no sovereign territory involved; that issue was officially ignored.

The second precedent was that this was the first occasion where the Security Council interpreted its jurisdiction to include purely humanitarian crises. Without going into the legislative history of the Charter, it is clear that the framers meant for Chapter VII to be invoked primarily in the case of cross-border invasions by states (interstate wars). The Persian Gulf War effort was the prototype the framers had in mind. While the UN had (rather unhappily) intervened in a civil war in the former Belgian Congo (later Zaire, now the Democratic Republic of Congo), the decision to engage in humanitarian intervention in a civil war in a country for which the term "failed state" was later coined represented a major change of direction. The involvement raised the question of what it meant to the overall nature of the international system if a world body like the UN could simply be used to ignore the sovereignty of its members. It did so by deed, not by explicit acknowledgement that this was its intent or its effect. It was the beginning of an inductive process, because the 1990s witnessed more situations with similar sources and arguably similar precedents.

INTERNATIONAL INTERVENTION IN INTERNAL WARS

The Somali case was not the last instance in the 1990s where a developing country would experience a chaotic, bloody civil war that the citizens of that country would prove incapable of resolving and where there would be gross instances of individual and collective human rights abuses. The list of places where these situations have occurred has become familiar and is a litany of the world's trouble spots: Bosnia, Haiti, Rwanda, Liberia, Kosovo, Sierra Leone, and East Timor, to name the most obvious. All are fragile states, where full sovereign control by governments is tenuous and where breakdowns of control nearly invite interference from outside. Not all have evoked the same kind of international responses, but each raises the same kinds of questions about international rights and obligations in situations where humanitarian issues arise and the degree to which traditional views of sovereignty are applicable or require amending. In other words, these are the kinds of situations where the sovereign control of states collides with the temptation to engage in sovereignty-violating interventions, the subject of our case study.

The Problem: New Internal Wars

The existence of organized armed violence within countries for the purpose of displacing a government and replacing it with some alternative is certainly not a unique characteristic of the period since the end of the Cold War. Largely connected to the unraveling of the European colonial empires that began shortly after the end of World War II, internal—or civil—war has been the dominant form of political violence for a half century. Most of it has occurred, of course, in the developing world of Africa, Asia, and in parts of Latin America.

This pattern has continued since the end of the Cold War, although with some changes. During the Cold War, civil conflicts generally took on a Cold War ideological flavor, with one side (usually the insurgents) "sponsored" by the major communist states and the other (usually the government under siege) aligned with the West. This provided a surrogate battleground for the superpowers, and it also meant that the sponsoring states could (and usually did) impose some constraints on how their proxies conducted themselves. Moreover, these wars were clearly for the political purpose of gaining or maintaining political control in order to govern the state.

The new internal wars that have become a troublesome part of the post–Cold War international environment often do not follow this traditional pattern. The end of the Cold War was accompanied by the retreat first of the dying Soviet Union and then of the United States from active participation in much of the developing world where these conflicts occur. The restraint they imposed on their clients left with them. While it goes beyond present purposes to describe these new internal wars in detail, several characteristics relevant to understanding how they contribute to the crisis of sovereignty need to be mentioned.

These wars have tended to be especially brutal and chaotic, accompanied by large-scale accusations and evidences of atrocities that have, among other things, resuscitated interest in war crimes. Part of the bestial, bloody conduct of these conflicts (for instance, the systematic amputation of hands and feet by Sierra Leone's Revolutionary United Front and the genocide in Rwanda) reflects the absence of outsider influence on the "rebels." At the same time, many of the participants, rather than being trained and disciplined soldiers, are instead untrained "fighters" who are only nominally under anyone's control. Especially in African variants of new internal war, the forces are often little more than children (the 10- to 12-year-old "child soldiers" of the Liberian civil war, for instance). Moreover, beyond pure criminality (much of the war in Sierra Leone is about who will control the diamond-rich area of the country), it is often difficult to discern the purposes of the wars.

These wars are generally occurring in the poorest, most destitute parts of the world. Somalia was, as mentioned, the prototype of the so-called "failed state" (countries that have historically shown an inability to govern themselves in a stable manner), and a number of other conflicts have been in similar countries (Haiti and East Timor, for instance). The failed states also tend to be very poor, meaning there is little materially to fight over but also meaning that ending them and restoring a stable order is difficult, because there is little material base on which to build. Moreover, most of the countries and regions where these wars occur are clearly outside the areas of important interests of the major powers (the Balkans are an arguable exception); as a result, it is difficult to argue that any outcome would much discomfort major countries like the United States and thus generate great enthusiasm for involvement.

In a growing number of instances, the internal parties seem totally incapable of resolving their differences, either by one side prevailing militarily or through negotiations. What has become a familiar pattern is for some third party to convene the combatant groups, arrange a cease-fire and tentative peace settlement, which more or less instantly fails (this has been particularly true in Africa; the ongoing instability in the Democratic Republic of Congo is a particularly vivid example). In these situations, the only solutions may appear to be either ignoring the situation and letting the slaughter continue or intervening and imposing a peace.

Ignoring the problem is, however, made difficult by the very public nature of the conflicts. Modern electronic media are able to penetrate, cover, and report on the tragedy in a Rwanda in a manner that would have been quite impossible two decades earlier in Cambodia. The world knew of the rampage by the Khmer Rouge as they decimated their own population, but the accounts were in the print media, not on television as the slaughter of the Tutsi by the Hutu was in Rwanda. The steady flow of wretched refugees in Kosovo was a daily CNN story that could only be avoided by not watching the news. The result is to activate a desire to alleviate the problem (what I call the "do something syndrome"). The question is, do what?

The Response: Intervention (?)

In an international environment that has embraced human rights as a primary value, the new internal wars are the system's black eye, its not-so-well-kept dirty little secret. We are embarrassed at the slaughter of the innocents wherever the carnage occurs, although we feel more impelled to act in some cases than in others.

The pattern of international response has not been uniform. The international community, and especially the major powers, has been willing to act forcefully in places like the Balkans, but not in Africa, for instance, where we have sought regional solutions that are probably a chimera. Similarly, the major powers heaved a sigh of relief when nearby Australia agreed to provide the bulk of the resources for the International Force in East Timor (INTERFET) in 1999. Differing levels of response are often explained in terms of how important the interests of states are in various outcomes.

In the intractable situations described in the last section, possible international solutions often boil down to figuratively averting our eyes and doing nothing, or physically intervening with armed force to stop the carnage. When some sort of response is deemed unavoidable, the common mechanism for authorizing an international response has been to take it to the Security Council of the UN for a United Nations Security Council Resolution (UNSCR). The precedent for this route was Somalia, which in turn was the outgrowth of the successful use of UNSCRs in the Persian Gulf War. Although the Somali operation was less than a success, the precedent was set for using UNSCRs to legitimize intervention in civil wars.

The use of the UN in this way serves two broad purposes. First, since most of the world's countries are members of the world body, passing a resolution serves as a statement of world opinion, a kind of legitimizing event that says that an action has the support of the international community. This avenue was not available to deal with civil conflicts during the Cold War, of course, since the parties were normally aligned with one superpower or the other, one of which would veto any proposed action that harmed its client's interests.

The second, and more controversial, purpose of the use of UNSCRs is to create a kind of legal basis for intervention in civil wars. As noted earlier, intervention in civil wars violates international law and, especially when done without invitation, is clearly a violation of the sovereignty of the country where the intervention occurs. The UN Charter, however, does authorize the United Nations to act in the name of peace. Articles 39 and 42 (both part of Chapter VII) create the authority. Article 39 states, "The Security Council shall determine the existence of any threat to the peace, breach of the peace, or act of aggression and shall make recommendations or decide what measures shall be taken...to maintain or restore international peace or security." Article 42 makes the military option explicit: "the Security Council...may take such action by air, sea or land forces as may be necessary to maintain or restore to maintain or restore international peace and security." These provisions appear to refer to *international* rather than internal disputes. Earlier in the Charter, Article 2 (7) makes an ambivalent statement to that effect: "Nothing contained in the present Charter shall authorize the United Nations to intervene in matters which are essentially within the domestic jurisdiction of any state or shall require the members to submit such matters to settlement under the present Charter; but this principle shall not prejudice the application of enforcement measures under Chapter VII." One can use this language to justify intervening in a country's civil strife under two apparent circumstances: if there is a question about whether there is a domestic institution with jurisdiction (anarchical Somalia in 1992, for example); or if one determines that whatever is happening within a given country constitutes a threat to or breach of "international peace and security."

Why would the members of the United Nations go to all this trouble to justify interfering in internal violence? Beyond the motivation of ending humanitarian disasters, at least part of the answer has to be that it is a way to avoid the direct assault on national sovereignty that such actions involve. The UN Charter is quite explicit in its defense of the "territorial integrity or political independence of any state" (Article 2 (4)), or in other words, its sovereignty. The organization cannot directly admit that it is violating sovereignty without violating its own constitution, and its members, by signing the Charter, have also agreed to the sanctity of sovereignty. And yet that is exactly what the members do when they pass UNSCRs favoring intervention in internal wars and then dispatch their troops to foreign shores to enforce those decrees. (In some cases, such as the Balkans, a different agency such as the North Atlantic Treaty Organization may be in effect "deputized" to carry out the actual military mission.) Manipulating the Charter effectively finesses the underlying issue of the violation of sovereignty.

How long can the sovereignty issue effectively be skirted? As postwar experience with these interventions mounts, the answer would appear to be not indefinitely. The reason for this assertion is the length of the missions and the conflicts they produce with native populations, who over time may see the UN peacekeeping missions as an increasingly unwelcome intrusion rather than as helpful.

What a decade's experience has shown is that interventions are more complicated and their success more difficult to attain than was believed when American and other UN forces waded ashore in Somalia. We have learned that it is relatively easy to end the violence by inserting well-armed peacekeepers into situations such as Bosnia, Kosovo, and East Timor and to keep the peace as long as the peacekeepers remain. We have also learned, however, that the presence of an intervening force in and of itself does not cause the formerly warring parties to settle their differences, so that the peacekeepers can pack their bags and leave behind a tranquility that will result in continuing peace. To the contrary, it is generally agreed that if foreign troops leave, the situation will likely revert.

The effect is to create open-ended commitments where foreign troops are in place for a long time and eventually may be viewed as occupiers, even neocolonialists, rather than saviors or protectors. In extreme situations like Kosovo, the UN operation (including the deputized NATO military force) is dedicated to an outcome—Kosovo returning to the status of an autonomous region within the Yugoslav federation—that the vast majority of Albanian Kosovars oppose. When (or if) the hosts come publicly to oppose the continued presence of the outsiders, then it will become increasingly difficult to maintain the fiction that the intervening forces are not directly violating the sovereignty of their hosts.

CONCLUSION

The desirability of outside intervention has come into question in the United States and elsewhere in the past year or so. In the United States, the primary reasons for questioning have been both political and practical. The 2000 election campaign of Republican George W. Bush, for instance, came out strongly against the use of American forces in peacekeeping operations. The reason was practical: these deployments have become numerous and have placed a strain on declining manpower and financial resources that should be devoted to more traditional military priorities. At the same time, the Bush foreign policy team, notably National Security Advisor Dr. Condoleeza Rice, argued that these deployments occurred in places well outside the important, vital interests of the United States and thus represented a misapplication of American power. The new president had been in office for less than nine months before the terrorist attacks of September 11, 2001, opened the window for intervention—possibly protracted—in Afghanistan to get at the terrorist roots harbored by the Taliban regime that provided sanctuary for the Al Qaeda terrorists. President Bush even embraced state building in postwar Afghanistan, an idea he had previously rejected for other places like Kosovo. Questions of Afghan sovereignty were not raised in the deliberations.

The major European countries have also become more ambivalent on the subject. While it was possible to get their united support for multilateral missions in the Balkans (Bosnia and Kosovo), there has been growing apprehension about the apparently endless, open-ended nature of these missions. At the same time, there is little agreement about so-called out-of-area missions (the use of forces outside Europe), where former colonial relationships may create interests for one or two countries in a given situation, but not others.

In all these discussions, the sovereignty question has never been raised publicly as part of the decision process. Does this mean there is a reluctance to open a Pandora's box of problems if the relationship is addressed directly? Are we afraid to raise a position that comes at odds with the more politically correct notion of humanitarian rights? Or is the question simply unimportant?

Whether we admit it openly or not, international intrusion into the domestic politics of states, no matter how objectionable or horrific the behavior of states may be, reflects a far different conceptualization of sovereignty than the one that reigned for the first 300 years of the modern state system (from the Thirty Years War through World War II). Had one asked in 1946 whether it was permissible to mount Operation Restore Hope in Somalia without the permission of the Somali government, the answer would have been overwhelmingly negative. The explanation would have been that such a mission would have been a direct violation of Somalia's sovereignty. The conception of sovereignty reflected in that argument, of course, would have been the traditional definition based in state sovereignty as an absolute and exclusive possession.

The situation has clearly changed in the interim. What we have witnessed is a de facto, indirect assault on the idea of absolute state sovereignty as a consequence of the rise in legitimacy of the idea of human rights. As noted elsewhere in this text, the idea that all human beings have certain inalienable rights simply because of their humanity is a surprisingly recent development, one whose international expression can be dated to the post–World War II enunciation of the Convention on Genocide and the Universal Declaration of Human Rights in the latter 1940s. The end of the Cold War rekindled interest in the subject. With the Cold War competition ended, the United Nations sponsored a series of 1990s conferences on various aspects of human rights (women's rights and children's rights, for instance), and the former UN Secretary-General, Boutros Boutros-Ghali, added the idea of "humanitarian interest" to those reasons for which force might be authorized.

Since all the instances where outside intervention has occurred were the results of often gross violations of human rights, the two movements in effect fused. Without putting the matter in terms of the historic debate about the nature of sovereignty, the effect has been to move the rationale for outside interference into alignment with the conceptualization of sovereignty based in the individual and the limited grant of individual sovereignty to the state. In terms of the meaning of sovereignty, there can be no other rationale for violating state sovereignty other than saying that state sovereignty *is no longer an inviolable principle of international relations*. To make that assertion, in turn, it is necessary to locate sovereignty somewhere else, as in individuals and groups whose rights are being violated and to whose rescue international efforts are directed.

No state makes the justification of their participation in UN or other peacekeeping activities in these terms. Why not? The answer is simple and straightforward: no state is willing to admit the dilution of the concept of state sovereignty because to do so admits its own sovereignty is potentially diminished in the process; sovereignty is too much a bedrock of national jurisdiction to make such an admission. And no state will admit that its ability to control absolutely what occurs within its territory is not entirely its own but may be subject to internationally imposed limits. Nowhere is that sentiment more fiercely felt than in the United States.

Among the most jealous guardians of the doctrine of absolute sovereignty is the government of the United States, as already noted. The idea that no outside force should have the ability to interfere in internal American affairs can be dated back certainly to the revolutionary period and the very negative view of governmental power that most of the supporters of the American Revolution held, and it remains an untouchable first principle which, if breached, brings howls of protest. As the study of war crimes (Chapter 4) notes, this often places the United States in strange positions, such as opposing a permanent war crimes tribunal because the statute for that tribunal gives it automatic jurisdiction over accused war criminals, thereby taking from the U.S. government total control of its citizens who might be so charged.

The result is schizophrenic but long-standing. The United States asserts the absolute nature of American national sovereignty, but has for a long time been willing in effect to ignore the sovereignty of others when it served our purposes. The numerous U.S. interventions in Central America and the Caribbean in the nineteenth and early twentieth centuries were nothing more than gross violations of the sovereignty of countries like Nicaragua, Panama, and Haiti. In some ways, the United States was simply acting as a large power in its "domain," the Western Hemisphere. Its profession of principles about sovereignty and its actions were, however, hardly consistent with one another.

The United States, of course, is not alone in this schizophrenia. The Russians (as Soviets), after all, invaded and occupied Afghanistan during the 1980s, a clear violation of Afghan sovereignty, and then turned around during the 1990s and used the absolutist rationale for sovereignty to argue that it was nobody's business but theirs how they dealt with the uprising in Chechnya while concurring in UNSCRs that violated the sovereignty of several other countries.

If American actions are not unique, why do they matter? The answer lies in the fact that the United States is the remaining superpower, what former Secretary of State Madeline Albright liked to refer to as the "indispensable nation," an argument similar to that made about U.S. accession to the International Criminal Court in Chapter 4. In terms of international actions like interventions in the internal affairs of countries, this means that whether such efforts are mounted often will depend on the American position.

The United States may decide to forego future interventions on pragmatic bases such as interests or costs, thereby making the erosive effect of such actions on sovereignty a moot point. The general international trend toward asserting the legitimacy of human rights and the need to punish violators, however, makes abstinence on these grounds unlikely. The alternate justification for abstinence is based in the effects on sovereignty. If international interference in the new internal wars occurs, eventually the question of the impact on sovereignty will have to be confronted directly and decisions will need to be made by the international community about generally how much of the principle of state sovereignty it is willing to jettison in the name of humanity. The outcome is yet to be determined.

⊕ STUDY/DISCUSSION QUESTIONS

1. Is the idea of outside intervention in the civil wars of countries a viable, justifiable action by the United Nations or the international community more generally? Can you think of circumstance where such interference is or is not wise?

2. With which conception of sovereignty do you agree? Are, in other words, the rights of state more important that the rights of individuals and groups within states? How would the international system be different without the supremacy of state sovereignty?

3. Does American participation in peacekeeping operations in countries torn by civil war violate American principles, such as our position on sovereignty? Or should the question of our participation be made on pragmatic grounds rather than principles? If you were in a position to do so, how would you advise President Bush when the next humanitarian intervention is proposed at the UN or elsewhere?

4. What would be worse for the relations among countries, a situation where sovereignty is overridden in cases of large-scale abuse of human rights, or a situation where such abuses are ignored and the sovereign rights of states upheld?

5. The American intervention in Afghanistan in 2001 to assist rebels in overthrowing the Taliban regime represented a direct violation of Afghan sovereignty, since it was uninvited. Do the circumstances (the terrorist attacks) justify this action? Do we have to add destroying terrorism to the list of permissible violations of state sovereignty?

READING/RESEARCH MATERIAL

Boutros-Ghali, Boutros. *An Agenda for Peace: Preventive Diplomacy, Peacemaking, and Peace-Keeping*. New York: United Nations, 1992.

Cusimano, Mary Ann, ed. *Beyond Sovereignty*. Boston: Bedford St. Martins, 1999.

Hashmi, Sohail H., ed. *State Sovereignty: Change and Persistence in International Relations*. University Park: Pennsylvania State University Press, 1997.

Kantor, Arnold and Linton F. Brooks, eds. *U.S. Intervention Policy for the Post-Cold War World*. New York: The American Assembly, 1994.

Lyons, Gene M and Michael Mastanduno, eds. *Beyond Westphalia: State Sovereignty and International Intervention*. Baltimore: Johns Hopkins University Press, 1995.

Mills, Kurt. *Human Rights in the Emerging Global Order: A New Sovereignty?* New York: St. Martin's Press, 1998.

Snow, Donald M. *UnCivil Wars: International Security and the New Internal Conflicts*. Boulder: Lynne Rienner Publishers, 1996.

———. *When America Fights: The Uses of American Force*. Washington: CQ Press, 2001.

———, and Eugene Brown. *International Relations: The Changing Contours of Power*. New York: Longman, 2000.

WEB SITES

Organization promoting a comprehensive global debate on the relationship between intervention and state sovereignty

> International Commission on Intervention and State Sovereignty at http://www.iciss.gc.ca

Compendium of authoritative viewpoints on the 1999 crisis and on recommended follow-up steps

> Kosovo and the Challenge of Humanitarian Intervention at http://www.unu.edu/p&g/kosovo_full.htm

Comprehensive collection of resources addressing the moral dilemmas raised by humanitarian intervention

> Human Rights Initiative at http://www.cceia.org/themes/hrdwinter2001.html

Report by the Stanley Foundation on the problems and prospects of humanitarian intervention

> Using "Any Means Necessary" for Humanitarian Response at http://reports.stanleyfdn.org/UNND01.pdf

Contains collection of conference reports and statements on intervention, sovereignty, and international security

> Pugwash Regional Conflict and Global Security Reports at http://www.pugwash.org/reports/rc/rclist.htm

Project analyzing how the international community can more effectively respond to threats of ethnic strife, civil war, and genocide

> Emerging Norms of Justified Intervention at http://www.amacad.org/projects/norms.htm

CHAPTER SIX

Camp David I and II:

IT'S ALWAYS JERUSALEM, OR IS IT?

PRÉCIS

The ongoing conflict between Israel and its Islamic neighbors has remained a central feature and irritant in the international system for well over a half-century, and it does not appear to be moving toward any rapid conclusion today. In 1978, major progress was made in settling parts of this dispute when President Jimmy Carter brokered an agreement between Israel and Egypt to defuse the state of war between the two countries at the presidential retreat at Camp David, Maryland (Camp David I). In 2000, President Bill Clinton took the Israelis and Palestinians to the same place and attempted to complete the process. Camp David II was unsuccessful, and its failure led to widespread violence between the Israelis and Palestinians.

This case study looks at this process through two lenses. The first lens is a comparison between the two Camp David processes and why one succeeded and one failed. It basically concludes that the issues the first time, while difficult, were resolvable, whereas the issues the second time could not be resolved to the satisfaction of both sides. The second lens is the structure of current differences that make peace elusive: the issue of Jerusalem, the size and nature of a Palestinian state, and whether the Palestinians have the right to be repatriated to their former homes in Israel from which they fled when the Israeli state was born. The positions of the two sides on these issues have proven too far apart to allow a solution.

The meetings occurred twenty-two years apart, in 1978 and 2000. Each was convened by an American president at the presidential retreat of Camp David (named after Dwight Eisenhower's grandson) in Maryland's Catoctin Mountains, not far from

Washington. In both cases, the presidents, who happened both to be Democrats, locked away the participants and spent a considerable amount of time attempting to jaw-bone and cajole an agreement of enormous importance to the Middle East and world peace. The meeting in 1978 produced a groundbreaking peace agreement between Egypt and Israel that ended the cycle of war that had plagued the region for 30 years and began the peace process in the region that the 2000 meeting between Israel and the Palestinians was supposed to bring close to fruition. Because Camp David I suc-ceeded in producing a groundbreaking accord, it was widely touted as Jimmy Carter's finest hour. Because Camp David II failed to produce a comprehensive agreement between Israel and the Palestinians over the Palestinian state and ended with the two sides still significantly at odds, the contribution of Camp David II to the legacy of Bill Clinton is more constrained.

No two negotiations are ever identical, although there were clear similarities between the events that we will explore in the pages that follow. Both centered on the Middle East and the reconciliation of Israel with its Islamic neighbors, for instance, and convening the second meeting at the site of the original was a conscious choice made with its con-siderable symbolic value in mind. At the same time, Camp David I was negotiated in the atmosphere of the Cold War, the nature of which contributed to the purpose and urgency of the meeting, while Camp David II was conducted in a very different geopolitical atmosphere. The participants and issues were also not the same, despite the participation of Israel in both. The Islamic side was represented by the president of Egypt, Anwar el-Sadat, in 1978 and by the chairman of the Palestinian Liberation Organization (PLO), Yasir Arafat, in 2000. As a result, the motivations and aspirations of both the parties and the American mediators were not identical in the two cases.

Looming over both sets of meetings was the issue of Jerusalem, or more precisely, the Old City of Jerusalem. (In addition to the Old City, there is Israeli West Jerusalem and Islamic East Jerusalem outside the Old City's walls.) Because it is the site of some of the most significant holy shrines of each of the world's three largest monotheistic religions (Judaism, Christianity, and Islam), the dispensation of the fate of political control of Jerusalem has always been the most nettlesome and difficult problem divid-ing the principals in the region. The bottom line is simple: the Muslim neighbors of Israel will never accept total Israeli sovereignty over all of East Jerusalem and especially Mus-lim holy sites; and Israel will never accept total Muslim (in this case Palestinian) sover-eignty over the Old City either. Tensions and emotions are high because Israelis were denied access to the Wailing Wall between 1948 and 1967, when East Jerusalem was part of Jordan, and because Muslims have effectively been denied access to shrines such as the Haram al Sharif ever since. Resolving this problem has so far proven elusive.

The Jerusalem issue also has great symbolic significance that provides a mask for other fundamental issues that divide Israel and the Palestinians and remain barriers to peace. As the two sides stumbled toward negotiations in January 2001 without Ameri-can intermediation, for instance, the fate of the Palestinians who fled Israel in 1948 and now seek repatriation and the shape of Palestinian economic and political devel-opment were as nettlesome as the fate of Jerusalem.

The Jerusalem quandary demonstrates a major principle of diplomacy: that you negotiate the issues on which you are least divided first, and leave the hardest ques-

tions for last. At Camp David I, Jerusalem was addressed and a general position was negotiated, but for political reasons the resolution never made its way into the final accords
(discussed below). At Camp David II, the rest of the agenda was negotiated and basically
resolved; the meeting foundered on the hard rock of East Jerusalem, leaving other issues
unresolved as well.

    This case study will examine the two meetings at Camp David. The focus will not
be on the meetings themselves: in the case of Camp David I, there is a reasonably complete record of the proceedings in the memoirs of participants like President Carter;
but in the case of Camp David II, there is not yet an adequate public record to consult. With no record other than a few journalistic snippets about Camp David II to work
from, any attempt to compare the two meetings as diplomatic events or negotiations
would be purely speculative and of limited interest or value.

    What is possible is to compare the two meetings in terms of the contexts in which
they occurred and what they accomplished or failed to accomplish. As already stated, the
most obvious contextual difference is the presence or absence of the Cold War influence. What difference does it make that the Middle East was a major focal point of the
Cold War competition in 1978, but not today? The actors and issues were different as
well. In 1978, Anwar el-Sadat was forced to show enormous courage in recognizing Israel's
right to exist in the face of almost universal rejection of that position in the rest of the
Islamic Middle East. Was that different than the pressures on Yasir Arafat as the chief representative of the Palestinians in their quest for a sovereign state carved out of the West
Bank of the Jordan River?

    These are the kinds of questions we will explore in the pages that follow. The com-
parison is valuable in its own right: how things have changed and remained the same
in that part of the world helps us understand the direction in which the future of the
Middle East is heading. At the same time, the fact that the two meetings bridge the
end of the Cold War provides some instruction on how international politics and diplomacy compare in those two geopolitical contexts.

    We will proceed first by looking briefly at the two events, focusing on the issues that
brought the parties together and how, in a general sense, they were resolved. With that
factual base established, we will then turn to the main thrust of the case study, which
is a comparison of the contexts in which the two meetings occurred and how those influences may have affected the outcomes. We will conclude with some extrapolation from
the two meetings at Camp David on outstanding issues and their resolution—the
prospects for a literal or figurative Camp David III.

ISSUES AND OUTCOMES, 1978 AND 2000

The two negotiations were conducted in considerably different atmospheres that manifested themselves in very different issues and proposed outcomes. Camp David I was
the beginning of formal discussions between Israel and any of the surrounding Islamic
states, and much of its significance came from the fact that it occurred at all. The discussions did, however, produce a landmark agreement that formed the foundation for
the reconciliation of Israel with all of its neighboring states except Syria by 2000, when
Camp David II was convened with the high hopes of bringing the Middle East peace

process to a virtual close by creating the conditions for the Israelis and the Palestinians to resolve their remaining differences.

Camp David I

That there even *was* a first meeting at Camp David between the prime minister of Israel and the president of Egypt is one of the true miracles of twentieth-century diplomacy. The context in the region was about as unpromising for peace as any place in the world. During the 30 years since the creation of the state of Israel in 1948, the Jewish state and its neighboring Islamic states (Egypt, Syria, Jordan, and even Iraq) had fought four wars (in 1948, 1956, 1967, and 1973). All had resulted in Israeli victories, but that fact had done little to diffuse the stated Islamic purpose of destroying the Israeli state and returning the territory known as Israel to their Islamic brethren and former occupants, the Palestinians. An absolute and intractable hatred for Israel and its people was the only acceptable stance for the so-called Arab states (technically, a state is Arab only if its people can trace their ancestry back to the Arabian Peninsula). No state in the region recognized the Jewish state diplomatically or accepted its continuing right to exist.

The map of the region fanned these animosities. In the Six-Day War of 1967, Israel seized and occupied territory from each of its contiguous antagonists: the Golan Heights from Syria, the West Bank of the Jordan River from Jordan, and the Sinai peninsula and Gaza Strip from Egypt. Arab demands for the return of each piece of real estate were loud and unceasing; Israeli insistence that they must be retained on security and other grounds were equally adamant.

There was, however, incentive to change matters. In the wake of the 1973 Yom Kippur War, Egypt had expelled the Soviets and ridded themselves of their influence, thereby altering the geopolitical context. One of President Jimmy Carter's earliest initiatives toward the Soviet Union was to encourage discussions with them about a Middle East peace settlement. Although neither Egypt nor Israel liked the American-Soviet proposal, at least it got the matter on the table. In 1977, President Sadat made the bold move of flying to Jerusalem and meeting with Israeli Prime Minister Menachem Begin, thereby establishing a direct connection that led to bilateral meetings between the two countries. When those talks failed, the stage was set for Carter to bring the two leaders to Camp David.

The prospects for Camp David I were decidedly mixed, and the political stakes for Carter were very high. On the negative side was opposition to negotiations of any kind both within the Islamic world and in Israel. The fact that Sadat even met with the Israelis appeared a sign of the recognition of the Israeli state and thus met the uniform, unremitting opposition of leaderships and publics throughout the Islamic world. Israeli opposition came from the religious right in Israel but was moderated by the fact that Begin was the leader of the rightist Likud party, where the greatest opposition to any accommodation with the Arab states resided (and still does). Opponents could hardly attack their own leader on the issues. On the positive side, both sides had something to offer that the other wanted, so that a basis for a negotiated agreement was possible. Carter, in calling the meeting, took a large political gamble, because if the talks failed, his already low public opinion ratings would go even lower.

The talks succeeded because the leaders rose above the negatives and because they had points on which they could bargain and reach accommodation. In Israel, there was considerable ambivalence to dealing with Egypt. The 1973 Yom Kippur War, in which the Egyptians had made some military progress for the first time before their ultimate defeat, was still fresh on Israeli minds, and many Israelis were reluctant to discuss giving back the Sinai Peninsula to Egypt, since that desert area provided a buffer against a new invasion by Egypt. On the other hand, Egypt was becoming militarily dependent on the United States, which would oppose another attack, and a growing number of Israelis were concluding that ending the state of siege imposed on Israel by its hostile neighbors might require exceptional efforts. Moreover, the Israelis recognized American pressure to negotiate an end to a military confrontation that had brought them to the brink of war in 1973.

Sadat faced similar ambivalence. The Islamic world uniformly opposed any dealings with the Israelis, and when an accord was reached, the Egyptians were isolated from the rest of the region and even had economic assistance cut off by Saudi Arabia. At the same time, having the Sinai and Gaza in Israeli possession was humiliating for the proud Egyptians, and Sadat reasoned that if he could negotiate a deal that also included movement toward a Palestinian state, a sort of talisman within the Islamic world, that misgivings would evaporate.

Thus, both sides had something the other wanted, and there was consequently the basis for negotiation. Israel badly wanted recognition of its legal existence and its *right* to exist, which Egypt could offer. The Egyptians wanted the Sinai Peninsula (including the small but significant oil industry that Israel had established there during the occupation) and the Gaza Strip back. To avoid or minimize the overwhelming backlash in the Islamic world, Egypt also required some guarantees regarding the status of Palestine and the Palestinians and Israeli willingness to address the Palestinian issue.

As has been well documented in places such as Jimmy Carter's memoirs, the negotiations were long, difficult, and, on several occasions, nearly failed. In the end, the historical enemies found enough common ground to agree on three basic matters that constitute the so-called Camp David Accord:

1. the withdrawal of Israel from the Sinai Peninsula;

2. a peace treaty between Israel and Egypt that included recognition of Israel;

3. a promise to resolve the Palestinian question in the form of autonomy for the West Bank and Gaza Strip, to become the basis for a Palestinian state.

The first two provisions were implemented routinely. The Israelis withdrew from Sinai in two steps, in 1979 and 1982, returning control to Egypt. The peace treaty between the two countries was signed in 1979.

The Palestinian question, which includes the fate of East Jerusalem as its thorniest issue, remained contentious. While the Israelis agreed to enter into negotiations with representatives of the Palestinians and gradually have increased the degree of Palestinian autonomy in the West Bank and Gaza, the translation of that effort into a full-fledged sovereign Palestinian state lagged throughout the 1980s and 1990s. The failure to resolve the Palestinian question produced much frustration among Palestinians and other Muslims. It also provided the reason for something like Camp David II.

Camp David I did not go beyond these issues, and left the remaining divisive problems as the subject for negotiations between the Israelis and the Palestinians. The fate of Jerusalem was omitted from the final declaration, even though it was discussed and the principles for a settlement privately reached. The problem was, and still is, the mutually exclusive claims both sides have on East Jerusalem, positions inflamed by the religious shrines in the Old City. As Jimmy Carter explained the 1978 situation in a *New York Times* op-ed piece in 2000, shortly after the conclusion of Camp David II, "We knew that Israel had declared sovereignty over the entire city but that the international community considered East Jerusalem to be legally part of the occupied West Bank. We realized that no Israeli leader could renounce Israel's position, and that it would be politically suicidal for Sadat or any other Arab leader to surrender any of their people's claims regarding the Islamic and Christian holy places." Because the only possible solution involved compromises that one or both principals would have to renounce, language suggesting a solution was simply omitted rather than create political firestorms in Israel and Egypt that might singe both Begin and Sadat. Palestinian independence and self-determination and the fate of Jerusalem were deferred for another day.

Camp David II

Less is publicly known about the negotiations between Israeli Prime Minister Ehud Barak (even though many of the compromises proposed by Barak were printed in the Israeli press shortly after the meetings ended, and both sides leaked invidious comments about the other) and Palestinian Authority President Yasir Arafat convened by President Bill Clinton in July 2000. The talks lasted over two weeks, a considerably longer period than the original negotiations; both sides brought larger negotiating teams to the Catoctin resort than had been the case in 1978; and there was even a break in the proceedings to allow both sides to regroup. Considerable progress toward a comprehensive agreement was apparently made, but in the end the efforts fell short. The public stumbling block in 2000 was Jerusalem, just as it had been in 1978. As the situation deteriorated in late 2000 and early 2001, the less public but in some ways more fundamental issues like the question of Palestinians' "right" to return to Israel came to the fore.

In important ways, the agenda for Camp David II was comprised of the outstanding issues from Camp David I. The major point of contention was the third point in the 1978 accords, the dispensation of the West Bank and Gaza and the fate of the Palestinians. In the minds of the Islamic states (and especially Egypt), the Israelis had agreed to a process that would lead systematically toward a fully sovereign Palestine located on the West Bank and in Gaza. For them, the "autonomy" contained in the 1978 agreement was only a stepping-stone on the way to independence. Israeli administrations, on the other hand, debated whether autonomy (giving the Palestinians control over, for instance, schools and local police matters) was not the end state, rather than a movement toward independence. Moreover, the Arab world viewed the process—whatever its purpose—as unduly slow, suggesting less than full Israeli adherence to the spirit of Camp David. The construction of Israeli settlements in the occupied West Bank added to tensions. A very rancorous political debate within

Israel about whether there should be *any* concessions toward the Palestinians added to Muslim doubts about Israeli sincerity.

A breakthrough had occurred in September 1993. Meeting clandestinely under the auspices of the Norwegian government, representatives of Israel and the PLO agreed to mutual recognition in what became known as the Oslo framework. The PLO agreed to end its call for the destruction of Israel and to renounce terrorism. In return, Israel agreed to withdraw its authority from Gaza and the West Bank town of Jericho, turning both over to the Palestinians for self-governance. The deadline for a final agreement on Palestine was set for September 12, 2000. In 1994, Israel and Jordan agreed to a peace treaty that included a permanent border between them from which the Palestinian state would be forged. The peace process seemed to be moving toward a successful conclusion.

There remained a significant political problem on both sides. While polls indicated that the majority of Israelis and Palestinians favored a permanent settlement of the long conflict that included a Palestinian state, there were extremist elements on both sides who so hated and distrusted the other that they would go to any ends to subvert the process. In 1995, for instance, a Jewish extremist shot and killed Israeli Prime Minister Yitzhak Rabin for the avowed purpose of stopping the process. Although there were no instances of equal drama on the Palestinian side, terrorist acts by extreme groups have accompanied progress toward peace as well. Neither side demonstrated the political will or ability to suppress these elements dedicated to preventing a final accord.

By the time Clinton invited Barak and Arafat to Camp David, there were four major remaining outstanding issues facing the conferees. The largest and most public issue was the pace and extent of transfer of the West Bank from Israel to the Palestinian Authority. Both sides had their own formulas for both acts; as might be guessed, the Palestinians consistently maintained that more territory should be transferred faster than Israel proposed. The problem was exacerbated by the Israeli settlements on the West Bank; although they do not occupy a large amount of territory, Israel insists on maintaining control, and the settlers themselves fear being abandoned by Israel to what they assume will be the not so tender care of the Palestinians. The differences in concept were not so enormous as to be nonnegotiable, and considerable progress toward agreement was made during the talks.

The second issue was the timing of the declaration of Palestinian sovereignty and total independence. This issue was related to land transfer by the question of sovereignty over what. Arafat wanted to declare the Palestinian state as early as September 2000 (the expiration of the Oslo interim agreement), and threatened to do so unilaterally when the conference failed to reach an overall agreement. Although the September 2000 date was allowed to pass, the possibility that it might be invoked remained a potential threat for the Palestinian leader. Barak wanted to delay the declaration to avoid criticism from political elements in Israel that opposed *any* Palestinian independence.

The third issue that could not be surmounted was the status of East Jerusalem. It remained as immutable a problem as it had been at Camp David I, the only major difference being that it became an open point of contention in the second meeting. The issues remained the same: both Israel and Palestine declared their sovereignty over the

Old City. Israel claims all of Jerusalem as its capital, and Arafat insisted upon East Jerusalem as the Palestinian capital. The positions were mutually exclusive, which meant all parties would have to compromise to bring about a reconciliation and solution. The emotional significance of the holy sites—the Western Wall of the Second Temple (the Wailing Wall and Little Wall) to Jews, the place where legend has it Muhammad ascended to Heaven (the Temple Mount) to Muslims, the sites where Jesus was betrayed and resurrected (Gethsemane and the Church of the Holy Sepulchre) to Christians—made and continues to make compromise difficult.

Various proposals have been made across time to resolve the difficulty. The major principle that must be agreed to is guaranteed free access to all parts of the Old City by people of all faiths. In 1978, the proposal to accomplish that included acknowledging that the city is holy to all three faiths, permitting holy places to be controlled by religious representatives, and creating some governing body in which all three religions were represented to administer the city. At Camp David II, the United States argued for Palestinian sovereignty over the Islamic and Christian Quarters of the Old City, and Israeli control over the Jewish and Armenian Quarters. A second idea included giving the Palestinians sovereign control over several of the neighborhoods surrounding the Old City and administrative autonomy within the walls of the Old City. A third approach deferred the issue of Jerusalem for several years. None proved acceptable, and without an agreement on Jerusalem, no comprehensive agreement was possible.

The fourth issue, easily as difficult as Jerusalem, is the question of whether Palestinians who fled Israel in 1948 have a right to be repatriated into Israel. There are approximately 4 million Palestinians who might seek repatriation to an Israel that has a population of about 5.75 million, of whom slightly over a million are already Muslim. In addition to the problems of absorbing such a large influx in a limited amount of space, repatriation threatens Israel's status as a Jewish state, an absolutely unacceptable possibility to the majority of Israeli citizens. As a result, Barak captured Israeli opinion when he declared in January 2001, "I will not accept under any circumstances the right of return of [Palestinian] refugees." Arafat has been equally adamant that no final agreement is possible that does not include repatriation, because many Palestinians have long clung to the dream of returning to their former homes. As he put it in a *New York Times* op-ed column on February 3, 2002, "Left unresolved, the refugee issue has the potential to undermine any permanent peace agreement between Palestinians and Israelis." Negotiating away that dream would be political suicide for Arafat.

INFLUENCES ON THE PROCESS

Why did the Camp David meetings of 1978 produce a major agreement promoting the peace in one of the world's most volatile regions, whereas the effort in 2000 failed ultimately to reach such an accord? It may have been a human problem: Jimmy Carter may have been a more persuasive arbitrator than Bill Clinton, and Barak and Arafat may not have been able to reach the same level of statesmanship as Sadat and Begin. Lacking direct access to what went on in 2000 allows us only to speculate on the human factor, although it was undoubtedly present in some manner.

The circumstances surrounding the two meetings are more public and thus easier to assess. What was similar and what was different about the context in 1978 and 2000 that may have influenced the outcomes? To answer that question, we will look at a series of factors, including three broad categories: the global geopolitical setting, the regional situation in the Middle East, and the ubiquitous problem of Jerusalem. The first two sets of factors had changed dramatically between the two meetings; Jerusalem was the same problem, but with a different centrality to a settlement.

Geopolitical Setting

The impact of the Cold War in 1978, and its absence in 2000, is the most fundamental and obvious geopolitical difference in the two settings. Camp David I was, in a very real sense, the final scene of a Middle Eastern geopolitical play that had reached its most dangerous moment during the Yom Kippur War of 1973, at a time when the Arab-Israeli continuing conflict was also part of the Cold War geopolitical competition. The outcome of Camp David I itself contributed to a changed geopolitical setting for the future, and Camp David II was intended to put the crowning touch on the transformation of the geopolitics of the region.

Although the point is not always made with great force, the Yom Kippur War of 1973 was a traumatic experience both for the region and the global system. Locally, it was the first time the Egyptians had military success against the Israelis, to the point that early in the fighting Israel reportedly armed its small nuclear arsenal in the anticipation of the need to attack its neighbors with those warheads. While the Israelis regained the initiative and dealt Egypt its customary crushing defeat in the long run, Egypt's early success suggested a change in the geopolitical balance in the region that would have to be considered a factor in the future.

Although it was not widely acknowledged at the time, the Yom Kippur War also traumatized the Cold War international system. After the Israelis turned the tables on their enemies, they drove the Egyptians back to the Suez Canal, where the Egyptians were trapped with no way to get back across into Egypt; at the same time, Israeli forces were poised 80 miles from Cairo with no opposition in their way. As the Israelis sat and contemplated whether to destroy the Egyptian forces trapped against Suez "in detail," the Soviets announced their intention to drop Soviet paratroopers into the Egyptian lines to aid in their defense. While such an action made little military sense (lightly armed airborne forces not being of much utility against Israeli tanks and heavy artillery), it did have symbolic value and precipitated a major confrontation between the United States and the Soviet Union.

With the Soviet announcement of intent, the United States signaled its resolve by going to highest alert status and prepared to counter intervene if necessary. During an incredibly tense 24 hours or so, U.S. Secretary of State Henry Kissinger shuttled back and forth between Moscow and Tel Aviv, gaining assurances that the Israelis would let the Egyptians back into Egypt if the Soviets did not physically intervene. Ultimately Kissinger succeeded and the crisis passed.

In reviewing what almost happened, the conclusion was that the United States and the Soviet Union nearly confronted one another in a manner that could have escalated to nuclear war between them. Indeed, many analysts came to believe that the world may have come closer to nuclear war in 1973 than it had been during the Cuban missile crisis of 1962. The Cuban crisis led to a major effort to avoid a repeat through arms control. Yom Kippur convinced the superpowers, and especially the United States, that another Arab-Israeli war that could lead to another nuclear confrontation was similarly intolerable, and that the possibility of such a future conflict had to be ended.

Between 1973 and 1978, the United States placed itself in a position to help broker peace in the region. In 1975, Egypt broke entirely with the Soviets (mostly over the slow pace of Soviet resupply and refitting of the Egyptian armed forces both during the war and afterward). The United States quickly moved to replace Soviet presence and influence through bilateral economic and military assistance. The stage was thus set for the process that began with Sadat's visit to Jerusalem and ended in the Maryland mountains.

Geopolitics thus congealed to encourage the first Camp David meeting. The perceived need to defuse the Arab-Israeli conflict as a potential precipitant of World War III combined with President Carter's natural instincts as a peacemaker to give the United States considerable incentives to engage and encourage the process. Egypt's success in 1973 meant that Sadat operated with a stronger hand than would have been possible earlier, and that same experience reduced an overwhelming self-confidence among Israeli officials that any military confrontation with its neighbors would be a walkover.

The geopolitical situation had greatly changed by 2000. The Cold War was over, of course, and thus the danger that the Middle East could provide the tinder for nuclear war was largely gone. At the same time, the peace process begun in 1978 had spread throughout the region. Egyptian-Israeli relations had totally normalized to the point that Israelis and Egyptians regularly flew back and forth between their capitals (a prospect impossible to imagine in 1978), and the peace process had spread to other countries in the region as well (as we will discuss in the next section). Because progress was being made toward turning over parts of the West Bank to Palestinian control (although at a slower pace than the Palestinians wanted and faster than some Israelis wanted), there was not the same sense of urgency emanating from the geopolitical situation as had been the case before, although the formal expiration of the Oslo agreement on September 12, 2000 and the need for a permanent replacement agreement created a sense of some urgency. Arafat's threat simply to declare the Palestinian state in the absence of any agreement simply added to the concern (see below).

Camp David II was meant to accelerate and complete an ongoing process; Camp David I broke entirely new ground. Jimmy Carter was making peace to lessen the likelihood the region could trigger Armageddon; Bill Clinton sought to bring closure to a process in which he had been an active participant and to burnish his presidential legacy. The motivations of the two presidents, as well as the principals, were not quite the same.

The geopolitical situation had changed in another way as well. In 1978, Israel and its neighbors stood as intransigent enemies with virtually no dealings among them. By 2000, not only had normalization occurred, there was a growing realization, especially in some of the Islamic states, that their future prosperity was linked to becoming part of the globalizing economy. In order to join the growing prosperity, many of the more progressive leaders such as Jordan's King Abdullah had concluded that change, including democratization *and* better relations with an Israel that was already part of the global system, made more sense than continued intransigence. This attitude, according to many observers, extended to the Palestinians and Israelis, the majority of whom wanted to put their differences behind them and to turn their attention toward the global system. This change in attitude made cries of potential violence and even war if an accord was not reached seem hollow and far-fetched, decreasing the sense of urgency in ways that may have been illusory. As the breakdown in relations in the wake of the failure of Camp David II demonstrated, highly emotional, deep-seated hatred still exists not far beneath more rational calculations.

Regional Situation

A major part of the changed geopolitical situation in which the two Camp David meetings occurred was the result of change in the region itself. As already noted, the situation in 1978 was bleak indeed. No Islamic state in the region (except Iran, which is not Arab at any rate) recognized Israel or its right to exist; all were, at least rhetorically, committed to the destruction of the Jewish state; and they all championed, once again at the rhetorical level, the cause of Palestinian statehood. Pan-Arabism, the drive to unify all Islamic peoples, was effectively defined as opposition to Israel.

In this situation, Israel was virtually totally isolated, a "Jewish state in an Arab Sea," as the saying went. Israel was, and still is, the only fully functioning democracy in the Middle East, and it also possesses the most advanced, diversified economy in the region. Petroleum wealth made some Persian Gulf states richer than Israel, but the diversity of the Israeli economy made it the only state in the region that was economically competitive with the most advanced powers. Israel also possessed by far the most powerful military machine in the region, which explained how a country of—at the time of the major wars—about three million had managed to hold off and defeat numerically much superior countries four times in its relatively brief existence as an independent state.

The Israelis were, however, basically on their own in the region and the world. Most of the advanced countries kept Israel at arm's length, because their dependence on Middle Eastern oil made them reluctant potentially to alienate the oil-producing Islamic states. This demeaning situation was demonstrated most completely in 1973. At the end of the Yom Kippur War, the Islamic oil-producing states called upon the world to condemn what they dubiously called Israeli aggression and threatened an oil boycott against any countries that did not join them in their repudiation of the Israelis. Of the major powers, only the United States and the Netherlands refused and were thus subjected to a cutoff of Middle Eastern oil.

The depth of the animosity between Israel and its neighbors cannot be overemphasized, because it created an enormous chasm for President Sadat to leap when he went to Jerusalem and started the dialogue that led to Camp David I. Sadat broke ranks in what had theretofore been a solid front against Israel; indeed, as the largest country in the coalition that had militarily opposed Israel, Egypt had *led* the opposition for much of the period of confrontation. It took enormous courage on his part to take the leadership for change, and he paid the price in terms of vilification and isolation within the Islamic world for having done so. Arguably, the Muslim militants who assassinated him in 1981 were at least partially motivated by his initiative to Israel.

The situation had clearly changed by 2000. Israel had made peace with all of its historical opponents except Syria, and the change in regime in Damascus (the death of Syrian strongman Hafez al-Assad and his replacement by his son Bashar) in the summer of 2000 raised the prospects of progress there at some future point. Egypt's Hosni Mubarak and Jordan's new King Abdullah had established good relations with Israeli Prime Minister Ehud Barak, and the process of handing over jurisdiction on the West Bank and Gaza from Israel to the Palestinian Authority had become an accepted and expected practice.

The emotional, adversarial nature of the situation thus clearly appeared to have abated a great deal. Except at the political extremes in both Israel and elsewhere in the region, expectations for continuation of the peace process was an accepted fact of life of the region, if one to which all Israelis were not equally devoted. As already noted, those extremists who opposed progress had proven capable of slowing progress, and incidents occurred while the leading parties were sequestered in the sylvan confines of the presidential retreat and thereafter.

The regional situation in 1978 meant that Egypt and Israel agreeing to meet with one another took an act of considerable political courage on the part of both President Sadat and Prime Minister Begin. Since Egypt was less than a democracy at the time, the primary (but certainly not sole) political pressures on Sadat came from his counterparts in the capitals of the other Islamic states, and those pressures were severe, as noted. For Begin, the pressures were primarily internal. After 30 years and four wars, a substantial portion of the Israelis so hated and distrusted the Muslims that they could not bring themselves to imagine that any negotiation was meaningful or any positive outcome possible. At the same time, a large number of Israelis believed that the perpetual state of military preparedness and war would eventually wear down Israel and that accommodation leading to peace should be pursued.

Nearly all observers have noted that Menachem Begin was in a uniquely advantageous position to engage in the process. Begin had been a freedom fighter (some would say terrorist) during Israel's fight for independence, he had fought against the Arabs, and he was the leader of the Likud Party, the most conservative, hard-line party in the Israeli Knesset (Parliament). Any other Israeli leader could have been accused of being somehow "soft" on the Arabs; Begin could not. (The analogy between Begin and the Arabs and Richard Nixon, the staunch anti-communist who opened relations with China, is often drawn in this regard.)

The situation in 2000 did not require equivalent leaders or leadership. Although there remains some residual animosity in places like Damascus, the idea of a Muslim leader entering into negotiations with Israel has certainly lost its uniqueness or even controversy. One of the more notable visual images of the 1990s was Yasir Arafat reaching across the table and grabbing the hand of Israeli Prime Minister Yitzhak Rabin at a ceremony on the White House lawn on September 13, 1993, and Camp David II began with the videotape of Barak and Arafat jostling playfully to see who would enter the lodge at the retreat first. Like Begin before him, the fact that Barak is a retired military hero insulated him from charges of being "soft" on the other side. At the same time, Arafat, who has been reported to be in poor health, clearly had the incentive to want a deal that would allow him to see the fruition of a state for the Palestinians within his lifetime.

The problem for both leaders was the political extremes. In 1978, distrust and suspicion of the motives of the other side was a mainstream emotion on both sides that made bold agreements all the more politically risky. By 2000, on the other hand, the majority of Israelis and Palestinians had embraced the idea of peace and had come to realize that sacrifices would be necessary to complete the peace process. Intractable opposition on both sides had been reduced to the fringes, the highly sectarian Orthodox right in Israel and their equivalent in Palestine. Unfortunately, neither Barak nor Arafat could control the irreconcilable opponents, and they remained the major barrier, other than Jerusalem and associated issues, to a comprehensive agreement.

Jerusalem

Jerusalem is the lightning rod that energizes all the worst fears both sides have about cooperation with the other. It is almost exclusively an emotional problem in the sense that there are, and have for some time, been reasonable and rational solutions to the underlying situation that could solve the problem. The underlying principle has to be the unfettered ability of members of each religion to worship at its most holy places with no fear of interruption or harassment. Unfortunately, in the period since Israeli independence, Jews have been excluded from their holiest shrines by Muslims, and followers of Islam have been denied free access to their holy places by Israelis. There is no reservoir of trust or good feelings from which to begin negotiations. The distrust and emotionalism blends with the other intractable issues like Palestinian repatriation to serve as a solid barrier to a final peace.

As already noted, various solutions, including turning the Old City into an international city, either on the model of Vatican City or possibly administered by an organization like the United Nations, have been put forward from time to time. These proposals have always failed because they meant that someone other than members of the affected religions would have control, a situation that is intolerable to all groups.

A physical solution is possible, if the will to implement it is present. Several of the more promising—or less unpromising—suggestions propose a physical division of the Old City and environs along sectarian lines. Under one proposal, Israel would have sovereignty over "the Jewish Quarter of the Old City, the entire Western Wall, and all the Jewish neighborhoods, new and old." (New and old refers to neighborhoods both inside and surrounding the Old City.) The Palestinians, on the other hand, would "be given sovereignty over all outer Arab neighborhoods, virtually all the inner neighborhoods, and the Muslim, Christian and Armenian Quarters of the Old City." That leaves one holy site common to both Judaism and Islam, and a compromise solution proposes that "what the Muslims call the Haram (al Sharif) and what the Jews call the Temple Mount must be shared, with joint sovereignty." In trying to move the process forward in its waning days, it was reported that the Clinton administration made a similar proposal, except it gave the Armenian Quarter to Israel.

As the accompanying map indicates, the effect is to partition the Old City: Israel maintains control of the Jewish population and sacred sites for Judaism, and the Palestinians get most of the rest. An important aspect, and one of enormous emotional importance for both sides, is that Jews can go to their shrines like the Wailing Wall and Muslims can approach shrines like the Haram al Sharif *without passing through a checkpoint controlled by the other religion.*

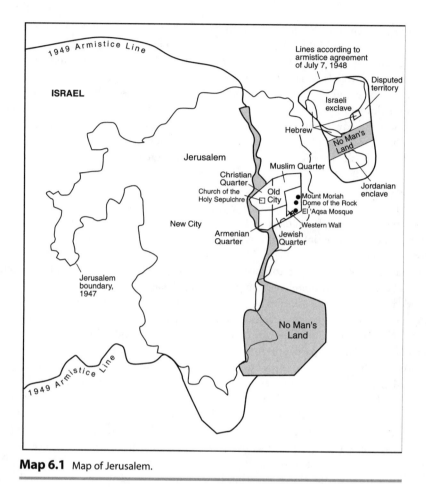

Map 6.1 Map of Jerusalem.

There are clearly details to be settled, if there is a remaining will to reach accord. How do you resolve the insistence of both parties that East Jerusalem is its capital, and that the issue is not negotiable? A division could certainly establish separate Palestinian and Israeli legal and police jurisdictions, but what about common services such as water and sewer? Would Jewish police have the authority to pursue a criminal who commits a crime in the Jewish Quarter and attempts to flee into the Armenian Quarter? These are details that can be worked out if, for instance, Palestinian and Israeli police can learn to cooperate, as they have been doing in parts of the West Bank where land has been ceded back to the Palestinians.

The tricky part is the proposal for joint sovereignty over the Temple Mount/Haram al Sharif. As the site of the first and second Jewish Temples and the site from which Muhammad ascended to Heaven, it clearly has enormous religious value to each side, and neither is going to accept any outcome that does not absolutely guarantee its continuing access. Finding common ground that will produce a trustworthy regime to meet the demands of both Jews and Muslims will require the utmost political acumen and courage in the entire Camp David 2000 set of issues.

The End of the Camp David Process?

Palestinian violence beginning in 2000 (the so-called Intifada II) and the Israeli election that brought Likud leader Ariel Sharon to power in February 2001 ended the Camp David process for now. Within days of Sharon's victory, a spokesman declared "everything in Camp David is null and void unless it was signed, and nothing was signed."

All three elements that had blocked progress have been addressed in ways that broaden the gulf between the parties wider and make renewed progress more difficult—or impossible. On Jerusalem, Sharon declared, the Old City is "the united and indivisible capital of Israel—with the Temple Mount as its center—for all eternity." On repatriation, he announced a renewal of the Zionist goal of Jewish immigration to Israel, a position that precludes the return of Palestinians to their former homes. On the Palestinian state, he says this is negotiable, but only on the basis of the 42 percent of the West Bank the Palestinian Authority currently administers, not the 95 percent offered by Barak. Arafat and the Palestinians cannot possibly accept any of these terms, leaving the situation at a stalemate that may be the only possible outcome until positions soften on one side or the other (see Chapter 12 for a comparison with the situation in Kashmir).

CONCLUSION

At the outset, it was suggested that one of the most salient differences between the two Camp David meetings was that one produced a dramatic agreement, while the other failed to do so. Viewed in that light, it is possible to conclude that Camp David I was a success, whereas Camp David II was something less than successful, even an abject failure.

Is such a conclusion warranted? Or, for that matter, is it a fair assessment of the meetings and the people involved? If the two meetings were replications of one another, as calling them Camp David I and II may seem to imply, then the conclusion that the 1978 conferees did a "better" job than their 2000 counterparts would most certainly be warranted.

But the meetings were different. As we have argued, they occurred in very different international settings and greatly altered regional contexts. Jerusalem hung over each deliberation like the Sword of Damocles—suspended over the rest of the proceeding by a slender thread—but in 1978 it was ignored as too hard to solve. In 2000, it at least made the final agenda. Moreover, the two meetings had very different emphases— 1978 broke dramatic new ground; 2000 was intended to tie the pieces together at the end of a long process that had been ongoing for a decade or more. Camp David II addressed the most difficult issues left over from Camp David I.

A comparative assessment must recognize these differences, because they affect the urgency of the negotiations and the expectations of the participants and the world at large. The international system was very different in 1978 than it was in 2000. The end of the Cold War had two major impacts on the settings in which the two meetings would be held. The first, as noted in the text, was the legacy of the Yom Kippur War and the consequent fear that another major Arab-Israeli confrontation could somehow draw in the superpowers on opposite sides in ways that might inexorably lead to war between them. The intolerability of that prospect gave the first Camp David meeting urgency and importance to the world system that was missing the second time.

The other geopolitical difference was that in 2000 it was more difficult to avoid the influence of the United States than it had been during the Cold War. When the Soviet Union existed and sought to compete with the United States for influence in the region, an unwanted American initiative could be countered by going to the Soviets for aid and succor, as various Islamic states and the PLO had done in the past. Such cover was clearly no longer available in 2000; when President Clinton issued the call for Camp David II, there was little choice but to respond with a packed suitcase. On the other hand, one of the evolving realities of the American status as sole remaining superpower is that while the United States is likely to be involved and influential most of the time, it is not a hegemon the advice of which must be taken. As evidence, it was clearly President Clinton's ambition to have a Camp David II accord as dramatic as Jimmy Carter had achieved, and that did not transpire.

The Middle East is also a very different place than it was in 1978. The idea of a united pan-Arab world is clearly a thing of the past, especially an Islamic world united in the cause of destroying Israel. Internecine wars like that between Iran and Iraq, a nearly united Arab opposition to Saddam Hussein's invasion and annexation of Kuwait, openly cordial relations between Jordan and Israel and Egypt and Israel, and joint cooperation between Turkey and Israel are only a few manifestations of the ways things have changed in the Middle East. With peace between Israel and all its neighbors a near reality and pressure mounting on the more militant states like Syria to join the general global system, the atmosphere is not forbidding, as it was then. Sadat dramatically broke ranks in 1978 to go to Maryland; Yasir Arafat's decision did not have to weigh whether he would become a pariah among his co-religionists because he negotiated with the Jewish state.

The fate of Jerusalem is the visible but not only common link, and the way the Jerusalem issue was treated demonstrates as well how things have changed in the intervening period between 1978 and 2000. As noted, Carter, Begin, and Sadat discussed Jerusalem and even reached some agreement on the issues in 1978, but no mention of the holy city made it into the final, public accord. Certainly part of the reason was that Jerusalem was not really an Israeli-Egyptian issue beyond the fact that Muslims in Egypt as elsewhere wanted access to the Old City. The heart of the matter, according to Carter, was that Jerusalem was too volatile to lay on the table politically because its potential domestic explosiveness in Israel had the potential to undermine the success of the entire enterprise.

That the fate of Jerusalem became part of the public debate in 2000 shows how much the circumstances had changed. The peace process between the major claimants to the territory the Jews call Israel and the Muslims call Palestine had progressed far enough that the last, and toughest, part of the final equation was now out on the table. The majority on both sides were now willing to talk and negotiate about Jerusalem, because they had learned to negotiate about other parts of their mutually claimed territory. The trust they built may not be enough for the most suspicious extremists, and overcoming their objections remained a major barrier. But at least they were talking.

But talking has not proved enough on the highly visible issue of Jerusalem and the less visible but equally intractable issue of Palestinian repatriation. These are the end game issues, the final problems that must be resolved before the deal can be made.

If the expectations and consequences of failing were higher in 1978, there were potential costs for both sides that militated for a second round of Camp David II before the Oslo accord expired in September 2000. Arafat had declared that he might declare the Palestinian state unilaterally on September 13, 2000, but that would stop the process and mean he would only get the territory he already has, which is about 40 percent of the West Bank and which Sharon has consistently stated is all he is willing to discuss ceding. Dire predictions of war were almost certainly overblown, but this outcome would certainly have been a blow to regional stability. At the same time, a breakdown of the process also threatened Barak's tenure as prime minister, since it provided ammunition for the Likud Party's charge of the prime minister's weakness and resulted in early Knesset elections in February 2001 to determine if Barak or Likud leader Ariel Sharon would lead future negotiations. Sharon, of course, prevailed.

Finally, there is the matter of expectation. Calling the summer 2000 meeting "Camp David" and holding it at the same place where the dramatic events of 1978 transpired may, in retrospect, prove to have been an unfortunate choice, because it drew obvious parallels. Among those parallels was the expectation of a dramatic breakthrough in the peace process equivalent to what was achieved then. The problem is that there probably was no parallel outcome that could have occurred. In 1978, almost *any* agreement represented a dramatic change. It does not diminish the accomplishment of Carter, Begin, and Sadat to say that, because reaching an accord of any kind was much more difficult in the poisonous setting that existed. Conversely, reaching an agreement of some sort of agreement in the year 2000 was not all that difficult to imagine, and in fact many of the remaining issues were resolved. What may have been more difficult, or even impossible, was to reach a dramatic breakthrough of the kind Clinton hoped for as a crown jewel in his presidential legacy. Probably the only possible parallel would have been an agreement on Jerusalem, which has been elusive throughout the peace process.

The new Bush administration inherited these frustrations and reacted initially by backing away from the situation. The terrorist attacks of September 2001 and terrorist instigator Usama bin Laden's championing of the Palestinian cause in October 2001 ended this respite. Realizing the cause of a Palestinian state resonated positively with many Muslims, Bush adopted the goal of a Palestinian state as his own, but stood shoulder-to-shoulder with Sharon as the violence continued. The problem is now his.

And so a final peace remains elusive. Both sides talk periodically, amid a new rock-throwing *intifada* (uprising) by the Palestinians and gunfire by Israeli troops. The fate of Jerusalem stands at the center of the controversy, as it has in the past, and one is tempted to conclude that resolving Jerusalem's fate is the magic key to success: "it's always Jerusalem." But there is more—repatriation, West Bank settlements, Palestinian development, a legacy of hatred and mistrust, to name a few. "It's always Jerusalem!" Or is it?

🌐 STUDY/DISCUSSION QUESTIONS

1. How and why did the existence of the Cold War create a different atmosphere in the Middle East in 1978 than in 2000? Assess the effects of the differences.

2. What did Camp David I accomplish and fail to accomplish? How is it linked to Camp David II?

3. Why is the final status of Jerusalem so critical to any territorial settlement involving Israel and Palestine?

4. Look at the map of Jerusalem and the various proposals to divide it. Which do you find most and least viable? Why?

5. Is a comprehensive peace settlement in the Middle East possible without resolving the Jerusalem problem to the satisfaction of all parties? Is such a solution adequate to end the problem between Israel and the Palestinians?

6. How can (or should) the Palestinian repatriation issue be resolved to the satisfaction of all parties? Why do both sides feel as strongly as they do on this issue? Can there be peace without resolving the issue?

READING/RESEARCH MATERIAL

Arafat, Yasir. "The Palestinian Vision of Peace." *New York Times* (national edition), February 3, 2002, A28.

Carter, Jimmy. "A Jerusalem Settlement Everyone Can Live With." *New York Times* (electronic edition), August 6, 2000.

———. *Keeping Faith: The Memoirs of a President.* Fayetteville, AR: University of Arkansas Press, 1995.

Friedman, Thomas L. "Uniting Jerusalem." *New York Times* (national edition), August 11, 2000, A21.

Hedges, Chris. "The New Palestinian Revolt." *Foreign Affairs* 80, 1 (January-February 2001), 124–138.

Hertzberg, Arthur. "A Small Peace for the Middle East." *Foreign Affairs* 80, 1 (January/February 2001), 139–147.

Lacey, Marc, and David E. Sanger. "With Legacy in Mind, Clinton Tried, Tried, and Tried Again, to Bitter End." *New York Times* (electronic edition), July 26, 2000.

Perlez, Jane. "Clinton Ends Peace Summit Saying It Is Deadlocked." *New York Times* (electronic edition), July 26, 2000.

Sadat, Anwar. *In Search of an Identity: An Autobiography.* New York: Harper and Row, 1978.

Sontag, Deborah. "Down from the Summit, Into Vale of Uncertainty." *New York Times* (electronic edition), July 26, 2000.

Viorst, Milton. "Middle East Peace: Mirage on the Horizon?" *Washington Quarterly* 23, 1 (Winter 2000), 41–54.

WEB SITES

Contains selected statements and background material relevant to the Israeli-Palestinian negotiations in general, and the Camp David 2000 Summit in particular

The Middle East Peace Summit at Camp David at
http://www.mfa.gov.il/mfa/go.asp?MFAH0hls0

A collection of official U.S. State Department materials, including briefings, background information, and a photo gallery

The Middle East Peace Summit Homepage at
http://www.state.gov/www/regions/nea/cdavid_summit.html

Compilation of UN documents and actions on the Palestinian question and the Arab-Israeli conflict

The Question of Palestine at http://www.un.org/Depts/dpa/qpal

An in-depth look at the conflict in the Middle East, including political, historical, and cultural issues

The Mideast Struggle for Peace at http://www.cnn.com/SPECIALS/2001/mideast

Details U.S. government policy on the Mideast

Bureau of Near Eastern Affairs at http://www.state.gov/p/nea

Site offers extensive information on the state of Israel and updates users on current events in the Middle East

The Israel Ministry of Foreign Affairs at http://www.mfa.gov.il

Site has press updates, a history of the Palestinians, and a variety of other documents relating to the Palestinian cause

The Palestinian Ministry of Information at http://www.minfo.gov.ps

PART 3

Economic Globalization

The spread of the international economy through increased world trade, commonly known as globalization, has been one of the distinctive characteristics of the 1990s, and it continues to be a dominant force in the new century. Globalization, often combined with political democratization, provided much of the optimism of the early and middle 1990s, an optimism only partly dampened by the Asian financial crisis of 1997–1998 and the virtual collapse of the Russian economy in 1998.

Optimism about the future evolution of the world economy remains high among many observers, but that optimism is now more tempered than it was in the 1990s. The sources of restraint about the future tend to focus on places and issues surrounding globalization that seem to counsel caution. The three case studies in this part all look at aspects of the globalization process that are troublesome, at least to some.

Two of the cases deal with the impact of globalization on very different kinds of countries. Chapter 7, "Saving Failed States," examines the case of Haiti, a classic "failed state" (a country that has consistently been unable to engage in peaceful governance or provide adequately for their people). As such, the case is a hybrid, looking at two issues.

115

One is the nature of state failure and what can conceivably be done about it. The second is the extent to which the forces of globalization can have an impact on countries like Haiti, and what the preconditions to such a contribution are.

Chapter 8, "The New Trinity of Globalization," examines, among other things, one of the sources of developing world concern about the onslaught of the global economy. The "rules" for participation in the globalization system heavily involve accepting the American "model" of economic operation, which includes greater transparency in financial transactions than are customary in many areas, especially Asia. The instrument for enforcing this American-centered system has been the International Monetary Fund (IMF), and much of the focus of the case is on the dynamics of the triangular relationship between the United States, the IMF, and individual countries facing demands for American-style reform in order to participate fully in the global economy.

The next case, "Debating Globalization" (Chapter 9) looks at the impact of globalization—among other factors—on the world's fourth most populous country, Indonesia. Prior to the East Asian crisis of 1997, Indonesia was one of the most active Asian participants in globalization, despite having one of the world's most corrupt regimes. When the crisis hit Indonesia in 1997, the corrupt practices came to the fore and made the impact even more severe, including forcing the Suharto regime to resign. In the wake of that experience and related phenomena such as separatist movements in parts of the far-flung archipelago, Indonesia ponders its future. A major element in those deliberations is the relationship between Indonesia and the globalizing economy.

CHAPTER SEVEN

Saving Failed States:

THE PROBLEM OF HAITI

PRÉCIS

Economic and politicoeconomic problems are prominent issues in the post–Cold War world. While the 1990s produced a broad and growing prosperity for many of the world's countries, that bounty was not universally experienced. In fact, the gap between the richest and poorest states grew during that decade and continues to widen. This disparity is particularly glaring in some of the poorest and most chaotic states, the so-called failed states that seem capable of providing neither political order nor economic prosperity. In the worst cases, the result has been political disorder and violence as well as grinding poverty for the masses.

No country, especially in the Western Hemisphere, exemplifies the phenomenon and problems of failed states better than Haiti. The second oldest political democracy in the hemisphere, Haiti has suffered through political authoritarianism and anarchy and is the hemisphere's poorest country. In addition to examining the structure of Haitian failure, the case raises the question of what, if anything, can be done to alleviate Haitian misery. Because the process of economic globalization has provided the engine of prosperity and stability elsewhere, the question is posed particularly in terms of whether globalization is the answer to Haiti's problems and whether the international system has the will to make the kind of investment that would give Haiti the chance to join the global prosperity of the twenty-first century.

One of the major international problems of the post–Cold War world is what to do with states that seem incapable of peaceful self-governance and cannot meet the minimum needs of their peoples. The most dramatic instances of this problem have been in countries that either have experienced often hideous internal wars or have undergone chaotic political change, or in some cases both. Collectively, states which can neither govern themselves effectively nor provide for their citizens have become known as the failed states, a term originally coined to describe the situation in Somalia in the early 1990s but extended to describe other destitute countries as the millennium approached as well.

It is difficult to typify the failed states, because the sources and nature of their failure differ from country to country and from region to region. The prototype, Somalia, displayed both of the major interrelated characteristics which are normally ascribed: total governmental failure, to the point of literal anarchy, accompanied by grinding poverty, the effects of which had been exacerbated by a long draught that shrank food supplies and threatened massive starvation in the population. Appalled by conditions and energized by globally distributed images of starving children with distended bellies, a United Nations peacekeeping force was sent into the country to allay the misery and to end the fighting between warring parties that only made the human suffering all the more acute.

The international mission to Somalia both succeeded and failed. On the positive side, the relief effort was able to reestablish the flow of donated food to those who most badly needed it and thus managed to staunch the worst of the starvation (generally accepted estimates are that between 150,000 and 250,000 lives were saved in the process). On the negative side, the international community was unable to solve the underlying causes of misery in this desolate part of the Horn of Africa. As of early 2002, there was still no national government that had the loyalty of the population or controlled more than a small portion of Somali territory, and Somalia remains one of the most destitute countries in the world. Short-term success has not translated into long-term stability and prosperity.

Not all failed states share Somalia's tale. A number of candidates for failed state status in Africa (Sierra Leone, Liberia, and the Democratic Republic of Congo, for instance) have failed because of chaotic new internal wars (discussed particularly in Chapter 5) that are either ethnically based or criminally inspired (disrupting government to facilitate the looting of Sierra Leone's diamond fields, for instance). Bangladesh in southern Asia has no particular political turmoil, but its geography (mostly the flood plain of the Ganges River) leaves it perpetually poor and the helpless victim of endemic flooding. Colombia has become dysfunctional because of the battle between the government and the drug manufacturers and traffickers (the *narcotraficantes*).

While each failed state is in some ways unique, they all share common characteristics that are derived from their prototype. First and foremost, all share some combination of political turmoil and economic misfortune. The result is a condition of misery for the people (a variant of the so-called misery index) that makes stability and prosperity difficult to achieve and to sustain. Political and economic misery are interactive: political elites cannot gain (where they try to) legitimacy because they cannot produce prosperity and a stake in the system for the average citizen. In many cases, these countries are extremely poor because they lack the physical wherewithal to achieve prosperity, and venal or incompetent governments cannot or will not do anything about the problem, instead concentrating whatever meager wealth that may exist in the country in the hands of the few.

State failure becomes an international problem when conditions in a country become intolerable to the international community, usually because something particularly tragic or atrocious occurs and is publicized through the global media. Not all human misery, of course, receives international attention. The East Timorese suffered anonymously in their small part of the Indonesian archipelago (see Chapter 9) for nearly a quarter-century before their plight became publicly intolerable enough to merit international attention, for instance. But when something happens that attracts attention, the question becomes what to do about it.

International responses to failed states are the important international concern in the present context. During the Cold War, there were very poor states whose citizens endured enormous privations that did not energize international efforts. The idea of "humanitarian intervention," already introduced in this volume in Chapter 5, has achieved a level of prominence (in some circles notoriety) since the early 1990s that it had not previously had.

Saving failed states is highly controversial. There is disagreement within and among governments about whether scarce governmental resources should be invested in trying to stabilize and uplift some of the world's most difficult countries. More to the point, there is major disagreement about *what*, if anything, can be done to save the failed state. Most would agree that the noteworthy goal of any efforts that are undertaken ought to be to leave the failed state in a condition of political stability and some improved level of economic status (two changes which, as already noted, should reinforce one another). The disagreement is not on ends but means: What does it take to uplift a failed state into the community of states? Afghanistan is the most recent example of this problem and disagreement.

Global response to the plight of the failed states takes place in the broader context of the globalizing economy, which is improving the economic lot of states in the developing world that are taking part in the globalizing process. The failed states stand uniformly outside the global economy, looking in. Generally, the political and economic conditions in the failed states are so wretched or uncertain as to make them unattractive to the flow of private investment capital that fuels globalization. Entering the global economy, however, is one potential way to redeem the failed states, and exploring strategies that may achieve that end is part of both saving failed states and extending the globalization system.

The broad problem, however, is that we do not know how to save a failed state and thus how the globalization process can contribute to that end. The first step in answering the question is to find out exactly what the problems are that must be overcome, and then workable solutions can be fashioned accordingly.

For better or worse, there is a test case in the Western Hemisphere. Haiti, which lies about 500 miles from the tip of Florida on the western end of the island of Hispaniola in the Caribbean Sea, is an almost classic failed state. It has a long history of governmental failures and misdeeds that combine with grinding levels of poverty for the masses of the population. The misery has resulted in waves of political discord and violence, and in the 1990s the problem spilled over into American politics as thousands of Haitian "boat people" attempted to land in south Florida on flimsy craft. Moreover, Haiti has been the recipient of international (admittedly mostly American) efforts to deal with its conditions. As in other cases of trying to assist failed states, those efforts have been largely unsuccessful in producing a better, more stable country.

Haiti thus emerges as a kind of laboratory for assessing the problems and prospects of trying to transform the failed states, including the prospects for drawing Haiti into the global economy, in which it barely participates today. This case will focus on the Haitian example and how it may apply to other international efforts. The assessment is important. If, on the one hand, trying to save failed states is to become an international priority, then we need to learn how to accomplish the task, and that begins by determining why states fail and what can be done to arrest or reverse that process. On the other hand, if such an assessment concludes that efforts are doomed to be feckless and unsuccessful, then it is useful to know that to avoid future frustrations resulting from championing lost and impossible causes.

HAITI: PORTRAIT OF A FAILED STATE

Haiti, a state slightly smaller physically than Maryland but with a population of nearly seven million that the land is hard pressed to sustain, has all the markings of a classic failed state. Although it has a much longer history of independence than most of its counterpart failed states in Africa and Asia, it nonetheless has a consistent history of political struggle, authoritarianism, and general instability that have been particularly highlighted during the last decade. Its economy has always been weak and underdeveloped, with considerable skewing of what little wealth existed toward a small elite that has lived in splendor while the majority exist in squalor. Wretched and uneven conditions of life have in turn produced political discontent that reinforces the misery of the population.

The prospects for changing these conditions are not, on the surface, very promising. Political reform—notably curbing the power of the Haitian army—has been attempted, but the emergence of the political democracy that the United States intervention in 1994 (under the euphemistic code name Operation Uphold Democracy) promised has been problematical at best. Weakened by an economic boycott on Haiti imposed in 1987 after the overthrow of a civilian government and lifted after the 1994 intervention, the Haitian economy continues to wobble, resisting the kinds of reforms the international community seeks to impose as a condition for reinstating needed economic assistance and as a prerequisite to entering the globalizing economy. Each of these factors help to frame the Haitian predicament.

The Political Legacy

Haiti (the name is Indian for "high land") had a remarkable beginning. It was the first land mass on which Columbus established a permanent settlement when he arrived on his historic voyage (thanks to the *Santa Maria* running aground on its shores), and it

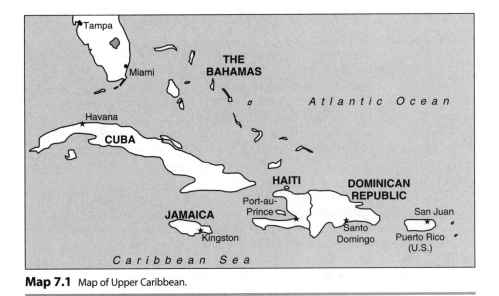

Map 7.1 Map of Upper Caribbean.

became the first Spanish settlement in the New World. Over the next two centuries, it was a colony of Spain and France, and the influence of those two European countries, in addition to that of the native Indians and imported African slaves, resulted in a unique Haitian culture and language that endures to this day.

Haiti achieved its independence in 1804 as the result of a series of revolutions that were begun by an ex-slave named Francois-Dominique Toussaint (also known as Toussaint Louverture) and completed by his chief lieutenant Jean-Jacques Dessalines after Toussaint was arrested and taken to prison in France, where he died. This revolution was notable for two reasons. First, it represented the only totally successful slave revolution in modern history; second, it established Haiti as the second state in the Western Hemisphere (after the United States) to achieve political independence. On the darker side, the aftermath of the revolution also established some unfortunate political legacies, including the intrusion of military force into politics, divisiveness within the population, and inefficient administration, all of which continue to plague the country in the contemporary environment.

Haiti's political history has been rocky throughout its existence, and especially so in the twentieth century, during which, among other things, the United States and others undertook two interventions when Haitian politics spun out of control. The first intrusion occurred in 1915, at the end of a particularly chaotic period of Haitian political history. Between 1888 and 1915, eleven men held the presidency of Haiti, but none served a complete term of seven years. Of the eleven, one died peacefully in office, while the other ten were either assassinated or overthrown. In the four years immediately preceding the intervention and occupation, there were seven occupants of the presidential palace, and the murder and mutilation of the last one, Vilbrun Guillaume, provided part of the official rationale for sending in the Marines to restore order to the chaotic political situation.

This first U.S. intervention was officially justified on largely humanitarian grounds, such as restoring order and improving the lot of the Haitian people. Lurking slightly behind the noble reasons were geopolitical considerations. With the completion of the Panama Canal in 1914, protection of access to it became a major U.S. security interest. By 1915, there was suspicion that the Germans were casting covetous eyes on several Caribbean islands, including Hispaniola, a situation exacerbated by the condition of virtual anarchy in Haiti. Hispaniola under German occupation would have been intolerable to American commerce heading back and forth from the canal to the east coast of the United States.

The occupation lasted until 1934, when the Americans withdrew from Haiti. During their stay, they succeeded in developing a professional army to deal with the lawlessness of roaming militias that had plagued the past, and in reforming the government's financial practices. There were few long-term salutary effects of the experience, however. The army became an ally of the political elite and a frequent participant in government actions; when the Americans returned in 1994, one of their first chores would be to disband this institution they had created. When the United States departed in 1934, they left behind an overpopulated and poverty-stricken Haiti; things had not changed noticeably for the better during the 20 years of American overlordship.

The period between interventions was most noteworthy for the extremely brutal, corrupt 30-year rule of the Duvalier family. Francois (Papa Doc) Duvalier seized power in 1957 as the leader of a black nationalist movement and, unlike dictators before him, he was able to consolidate and successfully hold onto power. His power base was a ruthless armed militia, the Tontons Macoutes (although the derivation of the name is obscure, some sources trace it back to a *kreyol* root meaning "uncle boogeyman"), who managed to terrorize the population into conformance with Duvalier rule. Papa Doc declared himself president for life in 1964. When he died in 1971, the title was passed on to his 19-year old son, Jean-Claude (Baby Doc), who held power until 1986, when he fled into exile in France.

The downfall of the Duvaliers issued in another era of chaos reminiscent of the period that led to the first U.S. intervention. During the five years between 1986 and 1991, Haiti had no less than five presidents, including military leaders who seized power from one another. Of some note for the future, the influence of drug money entered the Haitian equation during this time period, an influence discussed later in the chapter. While General Henri Namphy was in power, it has been reported that $700 million worth of cocaine, mostly headed north to the United States, flowed through Haiti each month, and that senior military officers skimmed off 10 percent of that amount for their own profit according to published reports.

In June 1990, one of the interim Haitian governments requested UN assistance in holding fair elections. The United Nations Observer Group for the Verification of Elections in Haiti (UNUVEH) was dispatched to oversee this task, and on December 16, 1990, successful elections were conducted. The winner was Jean-Bertrand Aristide, a Roman Catholic priest who had been expelled from the Salesian order for revolutionary activities. Aristide was inaugurated on February 7, 1991, and immediately set out on a massive program of reform that negatively affected large parts of the elite, including the army. The effects of the reforms were made worse by Aristide's uncompromising, righteous style, and on September 30, 1991, the army carried out yet another successful coup that sent the president into exile in the United States seven and a half months after he had assumed office.

International condemnation of the coup was rapid. The Organization of American States (OAS), led by the United States, imposed an economic embargo on Haiti, an action joined by the European Union (the largest source of trade and assistance for Haiti other than the United States). The embargo only added to the misery of life for the average Haitian, who suffered increasingly while the generals continued to life sumptuously. The result of Haitian misery, however, was to create another geopolitical basis for U.S. intervention. That result of worsening conditions in Haiti was the flow of large numbers of Haitian boat people across the Windward Straits to the American military base at Guantanamo Bay in Cuba and to south Florida. The unpopularity of the boat people in south Florida (and the prospect that their numbers would continue to swell unless something was done at the source to stop them) and pressure from Aristide to return to Haiti caused the United States to advocate further UN action.

On July 31, 1994, the United Nations Security Council passed Resolution 940, authorizing the use of force by its members in Haiti. The Council approved a U.S. plan to "use all necessary means to facilitate the departure from Haiti of the military dictatorship" and to "establish and maintain a secure and stable environment on the understanding that the cost of implementing this temporary operation will be borne by the member states." In order to carry out this mission, the United Nations Mission in Haiti (UNMIH) would dispatch 6,000 peacekeeping forces to the island country and that among their tasks would be to professionalize the armed forces and to organize and train a national police force free of corruption and political activity.

The American deployment to Haiti began on September 19, 1994, and President Aristide returned to the country and resumed the presidency on October 15 of that year. The American contingent was replaced by a UN force during 1995, and the final UN forces began their departure in November 1997. Except for some American police trainers, all foreign forces were gone by 1998.

On December 17, 1995, an unprecedented political act occurred when a presidential election was held. The winner was Rene Preval, a close aide of Aristide, and for the first time in Haitian history, one elected president of the country transferred power peacefully to another elected president on February 7, 1996. In 2000, Aristide was returned to power in an election widely boycotted by the Haitian electorate on the grounds of election rigging. Nonetheless, it did represent a second consecutive transfer of governments for Haiti.

The Economic Burden

If Haitian politics has been unsettled and sometimes chaotic, the economic condition has been fairly consistent, a legacy of misery and poverty for the vast mass of the population contrasted with the opulence and conspicuous consumption for the small, racially distinct elite that has historically dominated the Haitian economy and political system. Physical conditions (only one-third of the island's land, which is mostly mountainous, is considered arable, for instance) and the lack of a developed infrastructure have combined to assure the continuation of harsh economic conditions and hence retard the prospects for either economic or political development or to make the country attractive to outside investment.

By nearly any measure, Haiti is the poorest country in the Western Hemisphere and among the poorest in the world. The economy is severely underdeveloped, and the misery compounds itself. As one flies over the island of Hispaniola, one of the more striking features is the physical contrast between the western end of the island on which Haiti is located and the eastern part of the island, which is the Dominican Republic. The DR, as it is known, is green and verdant, typical of the tropical vegetation of the Caribbean. By contrast, Haiti is almost entirely brown, because vegetation has been systematically stripped to provide the wood for charcoal, the single largest source of fuel (about 70 percent) for the country. This deforestation has caused enormous erosion problems, as the already thin soil is washed away, where, among other things, it covers beaches—a potential source of tourist dollars—with dirt.

The agricultural sector mirrors the general economic malaise. Agriculture provides about 32 percent of the country's gross domestic product while employing about 70 percent of the work force, according to the 2000 *CIA World Factbook.* Coffee is the main cash crop, especially for export. The two other main crops that have historically been grown commercially reflect Haiti's predicament. Sugar cane export to Europe and elsewhere has virtually vanished in the face of a European shift in consumption to beet sugar. Similarly, the production of sisal has essentially disappeared as world markets have gone from natural rope to stronger and cheaper plastic rope.

The economic infrastructure—or more properly, its absence—offers little hope for a turnaround of Haiti's plight. In the transportation sector, for instance, the country has a total of three airports with paved runways, slightly more than 600 miles of paved roads, and one privately owned industrial rail line that travels 40 kilometers. In the area of communications, there were 60,000 telephones in use in 1995, and as of 1997, there were a total of 37,000 television sets in use in the country. (All figures are from the 2000 *CIA World Factbook.*)

Other segments of the economy suffer as well. The manufacturing sector is limited to the processing of agricultural items and a light-assembly industry based on imported parts, such as textiles. Energy use, a major indicator of industrial development, is among the lowest in the hemisphere, and more than two-thirds of the work force did not have what the CIA calls "formal jobs" in 1999. The CIA summarizes the situation by saying, "About 80% of the population lives in abject poverty." While other sources may dispute these depictions at the margins, they do not seriously question the general nature of the conclusions.

Haiti would have a difficult time achieving anything like economic prosperity under the best of circumstances given its natural situation. There is very little upon which one could base hope for development. The agricultural sector is in shambles due to the loss of markets for exportable goods, soil erosion, and the need for most farmers to concentrate on subsistence farming practices. There is essentially no industrial sector (which employs only 9 percent of Haiti's workers), infrastructure is basically nonexistent, and Haiti even lacks exploitable mineral resources. Only about 45 percent of the population over age 15 could read as of 1995, and the 2000 estimate was that life expectancy was slightly over 49 years.

To make matters worse, what little wealth the country possesses is very poorly distributed. Historically, a small elite of mostly light-skinned mulattos has controlled the economy, living opulently while the masses suffered. The elite's control has been linked to their alliance with the military, whose backing has kept the elite in political power in return for preferential treatment.

The rise of Aristide and Preval was, in some measure, a movement to bring economic change, although it is proving difficult. The trade embargo has been lifted with the return of Aristide, the "Paris Club" of lending countries has cancelled $75 million of bilateral debt, and international lending agencies has pledged upward of $2.1 billion to assist the resuscitation of the economy. These new sources of funding are all contingent on Haiti's acceptance and implementation of economic and financial reforms negotiated with the International Monetary Fund in 1996. Progress has been slow in this area.

The upshot of both the political and economic condition of the country is to make Haiti unattractive for foreign direct investment (FDI), the "mother's milk" of participation in the global economy. A history of political instability and corruption makes the prospect of investing a risky business, and the structure of the economy provides few opportunities for outside business ventures. Either problem alone would make Haiti uncompetitive in the global investment competition among developing countries, and the combination makes Haiti doubly so. Unfortunately for the Haitians, that is not even the entirety of their disadvantage.

Other Sources of Misery

As if Haiti did not have enough problems economically and politically, two additional burdens have popped up in recent years to further bedevil the country. One of these problems, which goes back to the 1980s, is the intrusion of drug transit from South America to the United States, with all the criminal and corrupting baggage that phenomenon brings with it. The other problem is the emergence of HIV-AIDS as the island's major health problem, and Haiti simply lacks the physical capital to deal with this challenge. At this point the AIDS problem has not reached the proportions it has assumed in Africa (see Chapter 15, "Worse Than the Bubonic Plague" case study), but it is already placing great stress on a very fragile health care system.

Drugs.   The spread of the drug trade has become a major criminal justice system problem in Haiti. Drug use by Haitians themselves is not a major internal problem, because the price of drugs is so far beyond the means of most Haitians as to make even the contemplation of drug use ludicrous. The drug trade, on the other hand, has some appeal in such a poor country, because it is the source of a great deal of money in a country where funds for any purpose are in extremely short supply. Since drug money has as its source illegal activity and is used to protect and promote that illegal activity, it has a corrosive effect on the Haitian political, and especially criminal justice, systems, adding to incentives for engagement in corrupt practices.

Why is Haiti vulnerable to the influence of the narcotics—and especially the cocaine—trade between South and North America? The answer has to do with the vulnerability of such a poor state to any source of capital, including illicit sources. At the same time, Haiti sits astride the means of transshipment of the product from the Andean producing countries to consumers in the United States and efforts by the United States and other governments to disrupt and staunch the flow.

One of the media for transporting cocaine from South America to market is by sea. Supplies of drugs are typically transported on small but very fast boats whose goal is to evade U.S. Coast Guard cutters and to dart into the many harbors along the thousand-mile Florida coastline, where comrades await. The boats used are generally small enough that making a voyage directly from Colombia to Florida is impractical, if for no other reason than that they might be detected crossing the Caribbean Sea and intercepted. Rather, the preferred method is to use a Caribbean island as the embarkation point, darting from behind the protective cover of an island and dashing for Florida in an attempt to evade detection or outrun law enforcement. It has long been alleged that Fidel Castro allowed Cuba to be used for this purpose. Haiti, only one major island down the Greater Antilles island chain from Cuba, has become a popular alternative.

The attraction of Haiti to the drug lords is understandable. In addition to location and the ability to use Cuba as a screen, Haiti is particularly vulnerable to the blandishments of the drug lords. As noted repeatedly, Haiti is desperately poor, and the *narcotraficantes* bring with them big money. Poverty, and access to foreign capital, was very strongly restricted during the boycott of the latter 1980s, and this put a particular bind on the elite and their military allies. Cooperation with the narcotics dealers provided an alternate means to generate wealth in a way not inconsistent with practice in an already corrupt society. The absence of an effective, impartial criminal justice system, a tradition of lawlessness and terrorism by various groups against one another, and a general cynicism and sense of hopelessness among many members of the general population made Haiti and the drug lords a natural match.

As noted, one of the major problems in Haiti historically has been the absence of a reliable, honest constabulary and court system on which the average citizen could depend for justice, and the recruitment and training of police and judicial officers was a major objective of the 1994 intervention into the country. While some progress was made in developing that vital part of the infrastructure, the process was neither perfect nor complete. At one level, there have been accusations that the U.S. and UN officials, in their efforts to create a constabulary rapidly, unknowingly recruited a number of new police who were in fact Tontons Macoutes veterans who had been dispossessed with the fall of the Duvaliers. At the same time, the amounts of money that the drug dealers bring with them have the significant potential for corrupting a delicate justice system just being taught how to perform in an honest way.

The problems are, of course, interactive. Although the military and organizations like the Tontons had officially ceased to exist, they had instead gone underground and saw gaining control of the newly emerging criminal justice system as a means both to return to power via the back door and, through positions in the police and court system, as a way to get in on the monies dispensed by the drug elements. Already adept at corrupt activities, the introduction of the drug trade fit the Haitian situation neatly.

What impact will drugs have on Haiti? It is an impossible question to answer directly, because of the dangers of direct analogies between the past experience of other countries and the future experience of countries like Haiti. If the experience in other countries in the Western Hemisphere is any indication, the prospects of corrosion are not inconsiderable. The influence of narcotics has greatly destabilized Colombia and has had an enormously negative impact on Mexico. The comparison with Mexico is potentially instructive. Like Haiti, Mexico has become a transshipment point where the narcotics traffickers have used their resources to align themselves with those charged with suppressing them, to the ultimate corruption and detriment of the Mexican political system. The electoral defeat of the Institutional Revolutionary Party (PRI) was to some extent the result of public revulsion with the degree to which the PRI had been corrupted by its association with drug elements, and the election of an avowed reformer, Vincente Fox, was seen by many as a referendum to excise the cancer. Whether Fox will succeed and whether there is an equivalent figure in Haiti to mount a similar campaign remains to be seen.

AIDS. The problem of HIV-AIDS has not yet reached the same level of public disaster in Haiti as has the pandemic in Africa, reported in Chapter 15 of this volume. AIDS is on the rise in the Caribbean, however, just as it is in other parts of the developing world. A recent estimate, reported by Peggy McEvoy in the *Washington Quarterly*, suggests that two percent of the population of the Caribbean region (about 500,000 people) have the disease. Nine of the twelve Latin American countries with the highest rates of infection are in the Caribbean, and residents of the island of Hispaniola, where Haiti and the Dominican Republic are located, reportedly account for three-quarters of that total.

To say that the Haitian health system is unequipped to deal with the epidemic would be a vast understatement. For one thing, there is a strong resistance to admitting the existence of the disease (a problem in other developing world areas such as Africa as well). According to McEvoy, part of the problem is cultural, "a labyrinth of stigma, taboo, denial, discrimination, and secrecy" that impedes open discussion of the existence of the problem. Sexual practices add to the difficulty of education and control, and, McEvoy adds, "the fact that realistically there is no treatment available for many people leads to a fatalistic attitude." Moreover, governments in the region are often reluctant to take on the problem frontally and admit its existence, because they "fear that the HIV-AIDS epidemic will hinder the development of their tourist industries."

As in Africa, much of the problem in dealing with the disease is economic. Even if the facilities and personnel were available to meet the problem aggressively (which, of course, they are not) there would simply not be the funds available to make even a token effort at a national program of treatment. As in Africa, the only ways to develop the economic capacity to treat AIDS victims are either through outside assistance or by sharp reductions in the costs of the drugs that are available in the developed countries (the current annual cost is over $10,000 a year per patient). Haiti simply is too poor even to begin to attack this problem, and its developmental needs are so numerous that assistance in dealing with AIDS must compete with a large number of worthy objects.

Left untreated, the consequences of the epidemic are predictable, since the African pandemic has already demonstrated what can happen. Already, AIDS has emerged as the largest cause of death in the region among both men and women between the ages of 17 and 45, with several consequences similar to those already witnessed in Africa. Among these are a shortening of life expectancy as large parts of the population die before their "natural" life spans have occurred; a rising number of orphans whose parents have died of the disease; and the loss of a generation of productive workers and leaders who might otherwise have contributed to the improvement of the human condition in Haiti. HIV-AIDS has not yet reached the same level of severity as it has in Africa, but it has the potential to add significantly to Haiti's misery.

SAVING HAITI

Can Haiti be uplifted from its status as a failed state to that of a successful country? As the foregoing analysis strongly suggests, the Haitian condition is sufficiently miserable that the task is not going to be an easy one, if it is possible at all. The answer is made more difficult because the international system is very new at trying to resolve this type of problem, and there are not positive examples of success in raising the status of failed states. Kosovo may provide the first true test case of an explicit international commitment to produce a stable state out of the ashes of state failure (an argument I have made more fully in *When America Fights*), and the jury is decidedly out on that experiment. Afghanistan will likely be the second "laboratory." Thus, the question of saving Haiti must begin by asking what is required to save it, and how do we go about it? The answers to both questions are open.

If there is no consensus about how to save failed states, there is some agreement that, whatever is involved, it will be expensive. That realization raises a second, and in some ways more fundamental, question: Are we committed to saving Haiti (or any other failed state)? At the purely abstract level, the desirability of helping raise the wretched out of their misery is apparently unassailable, even though some would question whether it is appropriate to become involved in the business of others. The real question is whether there is sufficient will among the members of the international community to allocate the resources necessary to underwrite the process in an atmosphere where there will always be competing claims on the resources that might be used.

The two basic questions are obviously related to one another and must be viewed sequentially. Whether one *should* engage in saving failed states like Haiti depends to a large degree on whether it is possible to do so, and at what costs. If we cannot figure out how to transform a society like Haiti's, or if it is simply not possible to do so, then the effort would prove futile, likely frustrating, and thus probably not an option to be pursued. That, of course, is an empirical question to which we do not know the answer. If it *is* possible to transform a place like Haiti, then the question of whether we should try becomes a lively one.

There is also a philosophical question even if one accepts the worthiness of trying to transform failed states like Haiti, and that is what do we want Haiti to be like at the end of the process? Clearly, the Haitians have something to say about that, and if asked, they are likely to reply that they want to be free and prosperous. Within the international values that emerged during the 1990s, that would suggest moving toward participation in the globalizing economy, with its political and economic benefits. Thus, the question of saving Haiti has, as a core component, whether or how countries like Haiti can be prepared for globalization.

What Are the Problems?

Before one can try to assess the prospects for transforming Haiti into a more prosperous, stable member of the international community, it is necessary to systematize the nature of Haitian misery and what must be done to create "eligibility" to join the prosperity of globalization. Our understanding of exactly what is entailed in the process is less than perfect, but we can look at the question in terms of the categories of tasks to be performed and the possible institutional arrangements by which these problems might be approached. We do have an example of where the effort to build a viable state capable of joining the globalizing system has been undertaken: the UN mission in Kosovo (UNMIK) will thus serve as an example.

In *When America Fights*, I have suggested there are four dimensions that must be addressed when seeking to engage in state building. These dimensions are the principal purposes of an effort to save a failed state and are prerequisite to becoming attractive to the forces of the globalizing economy. In the particular context of Kosovo, the categories were devised to address the aftermath of tragic civil wars, but they apply in situations where there has not been major systemic violence, like Haiti. The dimensions are political, economic, social, and psychological. Haiti has major difficulties in each area. Although we cannot address these dimensions in depth, we can suggest major components of each.

Political. The political dimension deals with the level of support for the political system, and thus its legitimacy and stability. By definition, a failed state fares poorly on this dimension, and it thus becomes a major objective of any state-saving enterprise to address and solve what it is about a place that has made it ungovernable in any predictable, stable way.

Haiti clearly fails the test of political stability. As the thumbnail history of the country revealed, Haiti's political history has been one of tyranny and instability, accentuated by political favoritism, corruption, and political violence as the principal tool by which regimes have risen and fallen. Attempts at political democracy have been generally short-lived, and whether the current democratic transition can be sustained is an open question. Moreover, it remains an interesting question whether the tender democratic roots will be destroyed if the country becomes more involved in the drug trade or more consumed by a growing HIV-AIDS epidemic, to cite the two potential sources of destabilization already raised.

Dealing with the political dimension was the large purpose of the American-led intervention in 1994. In addition to reinstalling the elected but overthrown and exiled President Aristide to office, the mission also addressed two of the major political problems associated with failed states: the existence and operation of political institutions in which the people could have faith, and the development and nurturing of competent, incorruptible public servants to operate those institutions. The major emphasis of this effort during the occupation period was the police and court system. The criminal justice system is generally the starting point in these kinds of efforts, because public order and safety are the fundamental base for developing public trust and support—especially when they have been fractured. The notion that the people had to have their faith in the justice system restored before they would come to support the new political order was also a key underlying assumption in the Kosovo mission.

As noted earlier, the effort has proven less than a total success. While order was restored by the occupying powers and efforts were undertaken to develop the infrastructure for a competent and fair criminal justice system, allegations that the police have been infiltrated by members of the former ruling groups like the Tontons Macoutes—at least partially to benefit from the drug trade—suggest the effort has been compromised. Since the last UN forces left the country, there have been growing reports of lawlessness and police misconduct to the point that the U.S. Consular Information Sheet of November 16, 2000, reports "There are no 'safe areas' in Haiti. Crime, always a problem, is growing….The police are poorly equipped and unable to respond quickly to calls for assistance." The lawlessness of the past is apparently returning, with negative implications for citizen support for the fledgling Haitian democracy. As evidence of this absence of support (or as evidence of cynicism), barely 15 percent of eligible Haitians cast votes in the November 2000 presidential election, because of the widespread belief that the election was rigged.

Should we be surprised that four years of foreign intervention could produce no more progress toward political stability than it has? Probably not. As noted throughout, there is no tradition of participatory democracy in the country on which to build, just a history of repression and corruption that has left the Haitian people cynical and distrustful of the political process. While the majority of the Haitian population undoubtedly would prefer political democracy to the alternatives, it is almost certainly unrealistic to expect change to occur so rapidly.

Economic. The transition would almost certainly be easier and enjoy greater support if it were accompanied by economic improvement, the second dimension of change. Haitians are desperately poor, and that condition has not changed since 1994. Building a more prosperous Haiti is a daunting task, and one that might be impossible or beyond the realistic levels of support that can be expected to try to nurture it. As the previous discussion suggested, there is little basis on which to develop Haiti economically. It is not at all clear what kind of blueprint would fit the country. Where, for instance, would public developmental assistance be directed? Toward the physical infrastructure of transportation and communications? Toward educating a population where almost half the people are illiterate? Toward strengthening a public health system to relieve the debilitating effects of the HIV-AIDS epidemic? All of these issues (and more) must be addressed before useful progress is possible. Hardly any of these questions were fully investigated during the 1994–1998 occupation.

Three related comments should be made about the economic dimension. First, until economic conditions improve for the average Haitian, he or she will have very little incentive to support the regime. The political and economic dimensions are thus clearly related. Second, the process of developing the basic building blocks for economic progress are expensive, the funding will have to come from outside sources (since the resources are unavailable in Haiti itself) and will almost certainly have to come from public sources. Although there is a small amount of outside aid available from public sources, it is not clear that it is adequate to the task. Moreover, the Haitian tradition of economic corruption makes many public sources like the World Bank wary of loaning money unless Haiti agrees to extensive, and painful, economic reforms (negotiations for which are currently underway).

Third, until the human and physical infrastructure are improved, there is little prospect for Haiti to attract outside private investment (foreign direct investment) either in the form of capital or establishing job-producing businesses, both of which are necessary for the Haitian economy to produce progress. There is clearly an element of circularity here, and the question is at what point in the circle does one intrude. The economic task of state building suggests a strategy of political institution building and economic infrastructure development, both of which are prerequisite to attracting the attention of the global economy.

Social. The third dimension is social. There is a very deep cleavage within the Haitian population between the vast majority of the population, which is mostly black, and the mulatto population that, with the exception of the Duvalier era, has ruled most of the time. This cleavage is social, but it is also economic, since the mulatto population also controls most of the economic wealth of the country which, as already noted, is very badly skewed toward the wealthy few. The infusion of large amounts of drug money will likely only worsen this condition, since most of it is likely to end up in the pockets of the elite.

Psychological. The psychological dimension is not as dramatic in Haiti as it is in countries that have suffered through grotesque civil conflicts where people, and especially children, have been subjected to the physical horrors of war, experiences with which they cannot cope. In Haiti, the long culture of lawlessness and violence has undoubtedly produced more subtle psychological afflictions such as hopelessness and resignation. At the same time, the experience of the African AIDS pandemic suggests a newer form of distress in the form of AIDS-created orphans and the massive and apparently unavoidable loss of loved ones in what should be the prime of life. The psychological victim in Haiti is hope.

Can Haiti Be Saved?

The short answer, of course, is that we do not truly know. In Kosovo, where the most systematic attempt to engage in state building to date is underway, the effort is four-pronged under the auspices of the United Nations. At least three of the emphases are relevant to Haiti (the fourth deals with refugees from the "war"). The UN itself is in charge of general administration, which includes tasks such as reestablishing and maintaining order through devices like the recruitment of a police force that can recreate order and trust in the system, a task not dissimilar to that undertaken during the 1994–1998 occupation of Haiti. The Office of Security and Cooperation in Europe (OSCE) is charged with helping the Kosovars develop political institutions, including writing a new constitution, and the European Union (EU) has been given the task of aiding in economic development.

Saving Kosovo should be easier than saving Haiti. Kosovo was more developed phys-ically than Haiti before the civil conflict broke out, it has more natural resources (coal, for instance) than Haiti, and, as a part of Europe, it attracts more positive attention—and presumably commitment—than Haiti. And yet, two years after the state-building enter-prise began, Kosovo remains the victim of sporadic violence that makes it impossible to contemplate removing foreign troops or to attract outside capital to build the economy.

As the dismal assessment of Haiti suggests, the problem there is more complex and the outcome more problematical. We have learned (or should have) that attacking the political dimension alone will fail to save Haiti from itself, and that only an effort that combines an aggressive economic development program with political reform has any realistic chance of success. A Haiti where the political situation and the economic dimen-sion is improving may be able to address the social and psychological dimensions and withdraw itself from the ranks of failed states.

Will it work? Can Haiti be saved? Once again, we really do not know and can only find out by trying. Since we cannot accurately predict the outcome of whatever efforts we may undertake, the possibility exists that we will fail miserably, that our efforts will be wasted. Are we willing to take the chance? Or put another way, do we *really* care if Haiti can be saved?

CONCLUSION

As the new Bush administration in the United States was in its transition stage in Decem-ber 2000, it was the recipient of all sorts of advice from various parties. In the area of for-eign policy, one of the most frequently heard pieces of advice was that the United States had as a major interest bolstering the stability and prosperity of Russia, which contin-ues to flounder in the post-communist era.

Although their situations are quite similar in some ways, there was no equivalent advocacy of bolstering Haiti. Both countries are, after all, fledgling political democracies, and both face challenges from other, less than democratic, forces within their borders. Each has experienced considerable lawlessness (the Russian mafia, the drug dealers in Haiti) that threatens the political system, and each is desperately poor (recently released figures suggest that 75 percent of Russians now live in poverty, compared to 80 per-cent of Haitians). Moreover, both are arguably neighbors of the United States: Russia across the Bering Strait, Haiti across the Caribbean Sea and Atlantic Ocean.

There are, of course, considerable and important differences that speak to the remaining question, which is about motivation to undertake the possible saving of Haiti. Despite similarities in the nature of their internal problems, Russia is still one of the largest countries in the world (the largest in land mass), it still maintains powerful armed forces, it has been a superpower, and, most importantly, it still maintains the major trapping of a Cold War superpower, an arsenal of thermonuclear weapons capable of destroying the United States and most of Europe. By contrast, the major importance of Haiti to the United States is that it is nearby and that it has been the source of an illegal immigrant problem. What happens in Russia obviously has a lot more bearing on the international order than anything that may occur in Haiti.

So where does one invest resources for trying to save failed states, assuming one is going to invest at all? If there is some moral, humane, or other basis for interfering in the internal affairs of states to improve their conditions—a proposition that would be denied by some on geopolitical or moral grounds—how do we decide who to help and who to ignore (assuming we have neither the resources nor the will to help everyone who could use our help)? Who gets saved, and who doesn't?

In some ways, the question is the equivalent of triage, where the fate of countries rather than which wounded soldiers will or will not be treated is the bottom line. How do we decide? One way would be to look at those states most and least likely to succeed and help those with a chance and leave the others to their fate. A recent article by Ricardo Hausmann in the journal *Foreign Policy*, for instance, revived the old economic geography argument that states are, in its title, the "prisoners of geography." The argument is that tropical countries (those located between the tropics of Cancer and Capricorn) have such built-in disadvantages related to location, climate, and the like that even the most enlightened public policies (of the kind associated with state building) will almost certainly fail. Haiti is, of course, located squarely in the tropics. If the proposition that location determines status is accepted, then one way to decide who to help and who not to could be made on the basis of where states are located. In that case, Haiti loses.

An alternate method for deciding would be on the basis of how important countries are in the global system. Such a criterion would dictate an international effort to aid Russia but probably not Haiti. It would also represent a very limiting criterion, since most of the failed states are on the geopolitical periphery, and their failure would have few international political consequences in the way the collapse of Russia would. Interestingly, most are also located in the tropics.

In the end, saving Haiti or any other failed state comes down to two debatable propositions. The first is whether it is possible to accomplish the task of uplifting the status of the world's poorest, most wretched places. The second is whether we want to do anything to assist these states. Is there some humanitarian imperative to help our fellow humans? Or is this a Darwinian global environment where the strong survive and prosper and the weak are left to fend on their own? Or is the answer somewhere in between?

One thing is certain. As long as there is great human misery and the ability through global telecommunications to publicize that misery, there will be suffering and inequality, and we will know about it. Thanks to that same telecommunications technology, the citizens of the failed states also understand their privation and will demand our help. Will we give it?

STUDY/DISCUSSION QUESTIONS

1. What is a failed state? What characteristics do failed states share, and how are they different? Why have they become a concern in the post–Cold War world?

2. Why does Haiti qualify as a failed state? What are the political and economic dimensions of its failure? How are they related to one another?

3. How and why do the problems of drug trafficking and HIV-AIDS exacerbate the problems that already face Haiti? How do they relate to the economic and political problems faced by the country?

4. What are the major categories of problems that must be overcome in Haiti before it has any realistic chance of improving its situation?

5. Can Haiti be saved? If it is uncertain whether it can or not, is it worth the effort to try? Why or why not?

6. If it comes down to saving Haiti or some other failed state, should we try in Haiti? By what criteria do you reach your judgment? Justify your decision.

7. Is the whole idea of rescuing failed states an important national or international concern worth expending scarce resources on when there are other national and international priorities which need attention? In other words, how important is the effort?

8. Do we have a moral, humanitarian, or other obligation to try to improve the lot of the world's poorest countries? Justify your position.

RESEARCH/READING MATERIAL

Ballard, J. R. *Upholding Democracy: The United States Military Campaign in Haiti, 1994–1997*. Westport, CT: Greenwood Publishing, 1998.

Hausmann, Ricardo. "Prisoners of Geography." *Foreign Policy*, January–February 2001, 44–55.

McEvoy, Peggy. "Caribbean Crossroads." *Washington Quarterly* 24, 1 (Winter 2001), 227–237.

Morrison, A. and C. Dodge. "Haiti: The Work Has Just Begun." *Peacekeeping and International Relations* 26, 6 (1997), 1–2.

Orenstein, Catherine. "Haiti Undone." *NACLA Report on the Americas* 33, 3 (November 1999), 10–14.

Perusse, R. I. *Haitian Democracy Restored: 1991–1995*. Lanham, MD: University Press of America, 1995.

Schmidt, H. *The United States Occupation of Haiti, 1915–1934*. New Brunswick: Rutgers University Press, 1971.

Snow, Donald M. *When America Fights: The Uses of U.S. Military Force*. Washington: CQ Press, 2000.

WEB SITES

U.S. government profile of Haiti, including its people, government, and economy
> The CIA World Fact Book: Haiti at
> http://www.cia.gov/cia/publications/factbook/geos/ha.html

Comprehensive overview prepared by the Federal Research Division of the Library of Congress

Haiti: A Country Study at http://memory.loc.gov/frd/cs/httoc.html

Organization seeks to raise awareness of Haitian issues in the United States and links users to a wide variety of relevant information

National Coalition for Haitian Rights at http://www.nchr.org

Site contains archive and updates users on currents events in Haiti

Center for International Policy: Haiti at http://www.ciponline.org/Haiti/Main/main.htm

Official informational site on U.S. policy in the Caribbean

The U.S. and the Caribbean at http://usinfo.state.gov/regional/ar/islands

Offers a report made by Ambassador James F. Dobbins, Special Advisor on Haiti, U.S. Dept. of State in September 1995 at the Institute for the Study of Diplomacy Conference

Haiti: A Case Study in Post-Cold War Peacekeeping at http://sfswww.georgetown.edu/sfs/programs/isd/files/haiti.htm

CHAPTER EIGHT

The New Trinity of Globalism:
GEOPOLITICS FOR A NEW AGE?

PRÉCIS

The growing prosperity of the early and middle 1990s masked structural difficulties in the ways in which the global economy was evolving and even produced competing "models" of integration into the so-called (principally by Thomas L. Friedman) system of globalization. The euphoria of emerging political democracies in many of the countries joining the global economy was given a sharp jolt in 1997, however, when a financial crisis emerged in Thailand and rapidly spread throughout the region, even infecting Japan and driving down values on Wall Street before the crisis was overcome. One major result was the triumph of the so-called American model of economic development over its chief conceptual rival, the so-called Asian model.

This case examines the consequences of the ascendancy of the American model from two aspects. The first aspect is the structure of the American model and the difficulties that acceptance of the American "rules" of economic activity creates for many countries seeking to join the system (a phenomenon examined in more depth in Chapter 9). The second aspect of the case is the process by which the American regime is imposed and enforced. This process is conceptualized as a "trinity" in which American ideas are, to a large extent, enforced by the International Monetary Fund on the target countries that comprise the third element in the trinity.

The nineteenth-century Prussian military strategist and chronicler of the Napoleonic Wars, Carl von Clausewitz, described the preconditions for military success in terms of the relationship between three groups without whose mutual support a successful war effort could not be mounted. The three societal groups were the government, the military (in his time, the army), and the people. Unless all three were of like mind in terms of support for a military effort, such an effort was doomed to fail. He referred to the necessary synergy between the government, army, and the people as a trinity (sometimes called the "Clausewitzian trinity").

The term languished through the nineteenth and much of the twentieth century, during which there were few instances where the elements of the trinity came into cross-purposes. Clausewitz generally, and the trinity in particular, were revived after the Vietnam War, and especially by the U.S. military. The military concluded, quite correctly, that one of the principal reasons (although by no means the only one) why the United States did not prevail in that conflict was that the military effort lost the support of the American people. The Clausewitzian trinity provided a rationale for the failure—the link between the people and its army had been severed, and this break eventually infected the other sides of the triangle as well.

The idea of a trinity may well be appropriate to describe another relationship that underlies some of the economic dynamics of international relations for a new century. That dynamic is the spread of the globalizing economy around the world and the desire of increasing parts of the world to join the emerging global system. This phenomenon is also known as globalism or globalization. The trinity, in this case, consists of the major elements of and aspirants into the system: the United States, the International Monetary Fund (IMF), and those countries of the developing world which have either joined the global economy and want to expand their position in it or those who aspire to "membership."

The relationships within the new trinity have significant elements of power involved in them, hence the reference in the subtitle to geopolitics. In essence, the United States, as the predominant economic power in the new economic order, wields considerable influence over global participation in the world economy through the enforcement of what has become known as the "American model" (or Washington consensus) of economic activity: countries that accept and embrace the American way of doing business (in a literal sense) have much greater success in joining the general prosperity than those countries that resist the American model. The nature of this power relationship became particularly apparent in 1997–1998 as the global economy responded to the East Asian financial crisis. The existence and severity of that crisis was, especially in the United States, attributed to economic and business practices that were at odds with the American model and which, as a result, the United States insisted must be reformed to avoid a repeat performance.

The IMF enters the equation largely as the enforcers of the Washington consensus. The IMF is one of the charter members of the international economic organization created after World War II to restructure the international economic system in such a way as to avoid the economic crises that contributed to the war. The IMF's original role, and still one of its primary tasks, is as a currency stabilizer. Over time, and especially in the 1990s, it has expanded its duties to include being an evaluator of the health of the economies of various countries. In essence, the IMF rates the economic and financial practices of countries and their governments and provides them with ratings in terms of stability and thus attractiveness of a country for investment purposes. A good rating usually means investment will follow; a bad rating means it often will not. The criteria by which these evaluations are made resemble remarkably closely the values underlying the American model. Countries on whom the burden of conforming to IMF standards falls know full well that this is not a coincidence. Rather, they believe the system effectively reflects American control of the IMF and that the United States uses the IMF rating system to enforce its values in the international arena.

This evolving relationship represents an ongoing systemic problem that is not going away soon. To the extent that the coincidence of interests of the United States and the IMF produce burdens that developing countries must endure if they are to become active participants in the global economy, it will also remain a source of controversy and of resentment about the heavy-handedness of the United States in its role as the remaining superpower in the world.

The rest of this chapter will be devoted to exploring this new trinity, including the impact of IMF-enforced policies on developing countries that have evolved through the experience of the 1990s. We will begin by examining the nature of the problem, looking briefly at the evolution of globalism, the crisis in East Asia that brought the problem to a head in the late 1990s, and the competing American and Asian models of financial affairs. The evolution of the case to this point will serve as context for assessing the current status of the problem, focusing on the ways in which the American model influences the current problem and the controversy surrounding the role of the IMF. We will conclude with some assessment of how the controversy will likely evolve.

NATURE OF THE PROBLEM

The current condition of the globalizing economy is a product of forces that, for the most part, emerged in the 1980s and 1990s, although they can be traced back even further to the 1970s. There have been two primary lines of development that have combined to create this emergence. Technological advances have made possible a much more integrated and interactive economic condition than was heretofore possible, thereby making globalization physically possible. The adoption of policy emphases by the major economic powers has allowed the technological advances to be exploited in a global manner consistent with an underlying economic philosophy that has become the driving economic force in the world. All of this development has been remarkably rapid, changing, and fluid, resulting in global activity without a detailed framework within which to monitor the resulting floods of economic interaction. This amorphous nature of the system, in turn, came to a very public head with the economic crisis that centered itself in East Asia and created the perceived need for creating a uniformity in the global system that would minimize these kinds of problems in the future. How the international economic system evolved to the point of crisis and how the crisis stimulated the operation of the globalism trinity provides the heart of the case.

Technological and Policy Roots

The process of creating what is widely recognized as an integrating world economy is not a unique occurrence of the contemporary period. A century ago, there was the widespread belief in the emergence of economic interdependence among the major powers (principally in Europe and North America), which would produce a prosperity and economic interconnectedness that would, among other things, make war between them impossible or unthinkable. That vision, of course, was dashed by World War I, and many analysts who counsel caution about the current globalization point to the similarity between optimistic predictions about the salutary effects of global economic integration in 1900 and 2000.

No two periods of history are ever identical, and so the analogy between 1900 and 2000 would not be perfect under any circumstances. Beyond that observation, there are several significant ways in which twenty-first century globalization is different from its 1900 variant. First, economic integration in 1900 was limited to the most advanced parts of the world, notably the European countries that controlled much of the rest of the world through their colonial empires. Noncolonized but developing regions like Latin America were largely excluded from the process. The current round of globalization, on the other hand, is truly global; while some parts of the world are not as deeply involved as others (Africa, for instance), there are countries participating in and benefiting from the process in all parts of the world. Among other things this broadens the desire of other countries outside the prosperity to join it.

Second, the spread of the global economy today is proceeding in the absence of ideological division in the system. In 1900, Europe was still divided between authoritarian monarchies and empires and democratic states. This produced less similarity of outlook among countries, and eventually gave them enough to disagree about to engage in world war. Today, there are still remaining authoritarian regimes, but their number is dwindling and most are outside the globalizing economy (China, of course, is the notable exception). Instead, the overwhelmingly preponderant political ideology today is democracy, and democracy and economic advancement seem to be related to one another and to result in more peace and stability (a proposition discussed in Chapter 3 on the democratic peace). The fact that so many of the participants are political democracies, of course, also means they rely on popular consent in decision making on economic matters. Third, there was very little institutional coordination of economic activity in 1900, whereas today a robust nexus of international organizations like the IMF provides a stabilizing force unavailable a century ago. Fourth, this round of globalization is occurring as part of the technological revolution that began in the 1960s and beyond and without which the globalizing economy as we know it would be impossible.

The Role of Technology. The great advances in technology that have emerged over the past one-third century or so have been the necessary preconditions for developing a truly global economic structure. While a discussion of the nature and dynamics of the telecommunications revolution that is at the heart of this development goes well beyond present purposes, some suggestions about the impact and the possibilities it has produced are not.

Consider two economic possibilities present in the contemporary environment that were impossible as little as twenty years ago. The first is the globalization of financial markets. It is now possible for investors around the world to buy and sell stocks 24 hours a day by virtue of electronic access to stock markets around the globe. These transactions can involve the electronic movement of enormous amounts of capital instantaneously and without the ability of sovereign governments to interfere with, or in some cases even monitor, the volume and nature of transactions. This ability, in turn, creates an increased level of interest and concern about the quality of economic activity that is occurring worldwide. The interest of potential investors translates into a desire for accurate information about what is going on in national economies, and that desire in turn creates much of the need for monitoring by impartial experts like the IMF. The fact that many investors rely on the IMF's assessment of a country's economic soundness provides much of the leverage the IMF enjoys, and it makes developing countries fearful that a negative rating will cost them investment capital. It also means that private penetration of national economies by governments and especially private firms can occur routinely and create internationalization quite unthinkable before the electronic revolution.

The other example is the internationalization of production. This occurs in two ways. One is the movement of firms into countries with a favorable economic climate (low wages, favorable tax structures, etc.) to manufacture goods at lower prices than would be possible domestically. Apparel and toys are notably active industries for this phenomenon globally at the lower end of the production chain. The other method of internationalization occurs in the manufacture of complex products like automobiles and electronics. In this case, it is commonplace for multinational firms to contract for components of their products in several countries, which are then assembled elsewhere and sold at yet other locations. (Many automobile factories are now routinely referred to as assembly or production rather than manufacturing plants. The reason is that they do not manufacture any of the materials they put together. Rather, they take parts manufactured elsewhere and assemble them to produce automobiles.)

These examples are no more than the tip of the iceberg. What they share is that they represent phenomena that would have been quite impossible to imagine or implement before the telecommunications revolution. Buying stock in Tokyo requires instantaneous electronic access to the Tokyo stock exchange, subcontracting the sewing of shirts in China requires oversight and transportation capabilities that would have been quite inconceivable at the turn of the last century, and coordinating the manufacture and transport of the parts necessary to build a sport-utility vehicle requires enormous electronic computing and communications capacity to ensure all the parts are at the right places at the right times.

The Policy Element. The technological revolution made the emergence of the globalizing economy physically possible, but it by no means made it inevitable. Harnessing economic forces to technological possibility required an additional element, the adoption of a policy framework wherein those possibilities could be maximized. The major elements of that policy framework turned out to be the removal of major restrictions on capitalist entrepreneurship within the major countries of the world, and the adoption of a global economic system that facilitated the interactions of economies of the world's countries.

These two developments are sequential results of the 1980s and 1990s, although they have philosophical and policy antecedents in the 1970s and before. While the distinctions that will follow will be stated more simply than the complicated descriptions it would take to reflect the actual messiness of real world interactions, they are broadly illustrative of forces at work in the globalizing economy.

The 1980s was the decade when capitalist empowerment blossomed. With the battle between socialist and capitalist economics moving toward the total victory of capitalism with the collapse of communism at the decade's end, the unleashing of capitalist dynamics had two principal and influential proponents on either side of the Atlantic Ocean. While the messages they advocated were by no means original, their ceaseless advocacy was influential in promoting change. In the United States, President Ronald W. Reagan campaigned on the slogan of "getting government off the people's back," and took steps to do so in the area of economic activity. In Great Britain, Prime Minister Margaret Thatcher led the charge, arguing the need for promoting capitalist activity through the TINA (There Is No Alternative) principle.

The initiative associated with Reagan and Thatcher had two major thrusts. One of these was *deregulation*, the systematic removal of restrictions on the way private companies did business. A chief target of deregulation was something called "industrial policy," the idea that the private sector and government should cooperate in setting economic priorities (some of which would be financed by government through things like research contracts). To the Reaganites, industrial policy was just the kind of governmental monkey to remove from private enterprise's back. Other examples include removing restrictions on the price of airline tickets and deregulating long-distance telephone rates. This thrust was sharply at odds with the Japanese policy of extensive government intrusion in the economy that was widely credited with fueling the "economic miracle" of the 1950s–1980s but which came under fire in the 1990s.

The other emphasis was *privatization*, removing the government from performing certain economic tasks and turning these over to private enterprise. The idea behind this initiative was that private enterprises would provide the same goods and services at better quality and for lower prices than could government monopolies or regulated industries. Removing things like TV cable monopolies from local vendors and thus creating a competitive television provision industry made up of private companies is one example.

At the time, these trends were controversial, and as these principles are applied around the world to other national economies as part of the prerequisites for joining the global economy, they have met with varying degrees of resistance. When generally applied in Britain and especially the United States, they had an apparently dramatic effect on economies that had been suffering. During the early 1980s, the American economy was broadly believed to be in decline, but as the capitalist reforms went into place, the economy revived dramatically. While one can (and economists do) debate how much the Reagan-inspired reforms had to do with this resurgence, the two phenomena certainly did coincide. What was left was to wed the fruits of technological possibility to policies that would allow the new system to go global.

If the 1980s witnessed the victory of the major elements of the economic philosophy of Adam Smith (whose *The Wealth of Nations* is considered the "bible" of capitalism), the 1990s was the decade when the basic ideas of David Ricardo, who in 1817 wrote

Principles of Political Economy and Taxation, became relevant. The heart of Ricardo's theory of economics was the principle of *comparative advantage,* upon which he based his advocacy of free trade. The idea of comparative advantage was that producers should be encouraged to produce whatever they could produce at the lowest price and highest quality. On a global scale, interpretations of the Ricardian philosophy reasoning argue that the result would be production and distribution to the maximum benefit of all.

While Ricardo's ideas may have been abstract and incapable of implementation in the early nineteenth century, the implications and applications of something like comparative advantage could occur in the 1990s. The technological revolution had made global commerce possible, and President William J. Clinton arose as the oracle of free trade, an idea with a long history in the United States (and an idea that has competed with isolationism as a dominant economic philosophy). The heart of free trade is the progressive elimination of barriers to trade between countries, thereby allowing, at least in theory, for goods produced globally with the highest quality and lowest cost to move freely to market. Free trade advocacy became an international movement through mechanisms like the Asia-Pacific Economic Cooperation (APEC), an association of Pacific Rim countries, and the World Trade Organization (WTO). As developing countries in particular adopted the banner of free trade and began making their economies attractive to the form of capitalism advocated in the West, the globalizing economy took off.

The road to a global economy has not been without its dangers and pitfalls. To become a full-fledged "member" of the movement has required countries to adopt both capitalist principles and free trade and to adapt their economies to the dictates of both principles. This has been easier for some countries than others, depending on how closely the structures of their economies resembled those of the capitalist developed world (especially that of the United States), how willing they were to make the associated changes, and how well equipped they were physically and philosophically to undergo Westernization. The amount and trauma of change was masked by the sheer momentum of change and prosperity associated with the first half of the "go-go-1990s." The bubble burst (literally!) in 1997 with the emergence of an economic crisis that began in Asia and threatened to spread worldwide.

The East Asian Crisis of 1997–1998

The East Asian financial crisis was a very complex phenomenon—or really set of phenomena—that began in 1997 and spread throughout the region. It is difficult to generalize what caused it to occur and run its course, because it affected countries of greatly varying size and economic structure differently. This complexity means we can only speak generally about the crisis within the constraints of this book. Having said that, the financial crisis in Asia was basically the result of the globalizing economy growing too rapidly without an agreed framework of operating principles and rules to regulate its growth and to ensure that the system would remain stable. It began in Thailand, where the local currency, the *baht,* collapsed on both the local and world markets. The resulting steep devaluation of the currency meant that savings were worth much less than before and the number of *bahts* necessary to purchase goods rose sharply, all with negative impacts on the Thai population. The ensuing panic quickly spread regionally to Indonesia, Malaysia, and on to Hong Kong, South Korea, and even Japan. Much of the original crisis has been attributed to runaway current account deficits (the sum of trade deficits and the interest payments on foreign loans) that either could not be serviced or which could only be met with devalued currency that was worth only a fraction of its former value. It stopped when the contagion reached Wall Street, which experienced a 25 percent drop in the Dow-Jones, but quickly rebounded and stabilized within months.

It was not the first time in memory that the international economic system had gone into convulsions, and the lessons of the previous crises would be applied to correcting those aspects of the system that had contributed to the Asian problem. In 1982, a crisis had occurred in a number of Latin American countries. The problem was insolvency caused by excessive and often imprudent international borrowing that left several states on the verge of defaulting on their loans, mostly to private banks. After rescheduling and forgiving some of the loans, the lesson for the international economic system was to tighten criteria for foreign lending in the future. In 1994, the "peso crisis" in Mexico created the precedent for international intervention in the form of a massive bailout (American loan guarantees) tied to internal reform in Mexico. Although not international in nature, the American savings and loan (S&L) crisis of 1985, when a number of these savings institutions collapsed (mostly because of imprudent lending not open to public scrutiny), resulted in calls for more effective government regulation of the financial sector and improved means to protect investors. All these lessons would be applied in Asia and form part of the evolving system of which the IMF is a prominent part of the enforcement mechanism.

Whose fault was the crisis? As one might imagine in a situation where multiple billions of dollars were lost in a variety of countries, there was no shortage of finger pointing. The international financial community placed the blame primarily on the countries of East Asia for mismanagement of their economies. The governments of the affected countries, in turn, pointed the finger back at the West, arguing the real problem was the provision of foreign direct investment (FDI) in quantities excessive to needs and abilities to absorb it, what is known as overheating. Needless to say, both sides had a point.

The countries of East Asia clearly contributed to the problem. During the 1990s, there had been a debate of sorts about the virtues of the so-called Asian model of development versus the so-called American model. One of the central differences between the two was that in several of the Asian countries, financial dealings were carried out in private, beyond the purview of the public and, for that matter, independent government regulators. This opacity, as it is known, was justified by traditional Asian cultural practices such as deference to elders, but its effect was to promote practices that are viewed in the West as corruption. Part of the fallout of the crisis was the demand for more public access to the financial sector, what is known as transparency.

One of the most blatant practices arising from opacity was "crony capitalism." In this arrangement, government officials would collaborate with bankers and entrepreneurs to decide how investment capital should be used, usually to the personal advantage of the groups making the decisions. One of the areas where this happened most blatantly was in real estate development. With a seemingly endless supply of foreign investment flowing in, large amounts were spent developing real estate, notably building huge, glittering office buildings that are a staple part of the skylines of many Asian cities. In the process, the government officials authorizing the construction, the bankers making the loans, and the entrepreneurs doing the building would skim a little off the top for themselves. If one were a member of such an operation, the benefits were enormous; if one were outside, there were no opportunities.

The consequences in a number of places were so-called real estate "bubbles." Large office buildings would be commissioned and constructed, providing jobs and prosperity during the building stage but with little concern with who would occupy them, pay rent, and thus provide the revenue to repay the loans made to build them. The result has been a number of virtually unoccupied high-rise buildings in the region, where there are insufficient renters who can afford the rents necessary to pay off the loans and the builders are forced to default on their loans or the loans become nonperforming (which means that loan payments have not been made for a long period of time), thereby bursting the bubble. Those who made profits during construction generally keep the money they received, and it is the financial institutions and their customers who are left holding the bag.

Western countries and their own financial institutions have their share of the blame as well, mainly because of their contribution to the overheating of Asian economies that inflated the bubbles that eventually burst. Convinced of the growth potential in the region, lenders convinced themselves that there was a virtually endless amount of investment that could be absorbed, and that investors would reap substantial returns on their investments. The problem was that this created an excess amount of capital in some places, and in their zeal to utilize it, some honest (as well as some dishonest) mistakes in investing the money were made. There was simply more money available than there were productive uses for it. To make matters worse, when the crisis began to become evident, a number of foreign investors panicked and withdrew their investments, making the subsequent crashes of national economies worse than they probably would have been anyway.

The Clash of Models

The Asian crisis brought to a head a debate that had been going on for a decade or more about which model of development was most appropriate in the new globalizing economy, the Western (which is to say American) model or the Asian (largely Japanese) model. As long as the global economy was growing positively and the prosperity was general, the debate was academic and did not seem to require resolving. When the crash occurred, one of its victims was the viability of the Asian model.

At its heart, the debate between advocates of the two models was about how to do business. Advocates of the Asian model pointed to the Japanese economic "miracle" and the derivative economic booms in other Asian countries (South Korea, Taiwan, China, Hong Kong, for instance) as evidence of the superiority of their way of doing business, *at least for them.* The heart of their contention was based in the opacity of economic activity, which was justified by cultural practices in many Asian countries. This collaboration among the principal actors in the economic system could result in substantial cooperation between government, industry, and the financial system. At its worst, the result could be the kind of corruption suggested already; but at its best, it had apparently fueled the Japanese economic miracle, reason enough to emulate and advocate the model.

In the Japanese case, the chief symbol of this collaboration was the Japanese Ministry of International Trade and Industry (MITI). The major mission of MITI was to coordinate the efforts of the major industrial sectors of the Japanese economy (electronics and automobiles, for instance) in order to maximize the trade potential of Japanese manufacturers in a manner remarkably similar to what was called industrial policy in the United States. This system appeared to be highly successful in the 1970s and 1980s and particularly in contrast to the situation in the United States, whose economy was stagnating during the same period. The MITI-led system was so successful that, early in his first term, President Reagan suggested the creation of a Department of International Trade and Industry (DITI) for the United States, an idea he quickly jettisoned when he was told by aides that promoting industrial policy hardly constituted getting government off the people's backs.

In retrospect, the Japanese model probably received more credit than it deserved. MITI direction was fine as long as the economy was growing anyway and as long as Japan's chief competitor, the United States, was not yet making the structural adjustments to regain primacy. MITI direction stifled inter-firm competition within Japan and made mistakes, notably directing the Japanese electronic giants to adopt the wrong technology (analog rather than digital) for high definition television (HDTV).

By the early 1990s, reform in the United States was producing a new and more robust American model. Part of the new model was based on the American experience in the S&L crisis, the outgrowth of which were reforms in the laws governing financial institutions, principally intended to make financial dealings more transparent and thus available to potential private investors, as well as guarantees to protect investor funds. The United States economy was booming under the new model, at a time when the Japanese economy, for a variety of reasons that go beyond present purposes, was stagnating and even approaching decline.

When the crisis broke in 1997 and spread through 1998, it became evident that a primary difference between the two models was that the Asian variant permitted, even encouraged, corruption and the misuse of investment funds. Since the Japanese system was no longer the "poster child" of economic efficiency and prosperity, cultural arguments were the remaining pillar of the Asian model, and the argument that Asians were simply different was insufficient.

APPLYING THE PAST TO THE FUTURE

The outcome of the Asian crisis provides a kind of case experience about how the evolving international economic system will evolve in the future. Two primary lessons appear to have been learned. One is that a set of values must uniformly underlie the system and ensure financial honesty (the American model). At the same time, the model must be enforced to ensure investor confidence, a role largely assigned to the IMF in the developing world. The result is the globalization trinity. This emergence represents an advancement of sorts because it will make international economic activity more uniform and predictable in those places that choose to accept the rules and become part of the system. Potential providers of foreign direct investment, for instance, can assume that certain rules and procedures are in place that will provide protection for their investments, making states that have adopted the model attractive. Conversely, countries that reject the model, or, more often, want to adopt some but not all the rules will find themselves less attractive in the competition for foreign investment, either of funds or the location of industries in their countries.

The triumph of the American model provides the United States with considerable leverage in shaping the evolution of the evolving economic order. As might be expected, this manifestation of American leadership and power is embraced in some quarters and opposed in others on grounds as emotional as American cultural imperialism and arrogance. Globalism itself is not a universally accepted value. Some people (and countries) do not benefit directly and have manifested their opposition through large, intense demonstrations such as the disruption of the World Trade Organization (WTO) meeting in Seattle in 1999. At the same time, what Harvard political scientist Joseph S. Nye, Jr., has called American "soft power" (the appeal and attractiveness of American ideals) is a powerful force worldwide, and especially in many of the countries seeking to join the general prosperity. Inevitably, some of the animus that resides in developing countries about the imposition of the American model is directed at the third side of the trinity, the IMF, which helps impose the American model.

The American Model Applied

What we call the American model or Washington consensus is the composite of a set of economic practices that reflect both the positive and negative American experience. Most particularly, they reflect the experience of the 1980s and 1990s, specifically privatization and deregulation of economic activity and the internationalization of those ideas in free trade.

While there is no public, official list of requirements or practices a country must adopt to conform to the model, *New York Times* foreign affairs writer Thomas L. Friedman, in his 1999 book, *The Lexus and the Olive Tree*, describes in detail a representative list of the evolving rules of the system. Using the rhetorical device of putting on the "golden straitjacket" to depict conformance to these rules, he lays out the requirements for participation in the globalization system that arise from the American model.

The golden straitjacket is a list of criteria that countries must meet to make themselves attractive to outside investors who provide the capital that is the necessary underpinning for prosperity and thus participation in the global economy. This "electronic herd" of investors, as Friedman calls them, is composed of the "faceless stock, bond, and commodity traders" who, by controlling large amounts of investment capital, can make or break the developmental prospects for target countries. The electronic herd does not, by and large, have detailed expertise on the workings of the economies of all the countries of the world, but they do know what makes an economy attractive or unattractive to them. To make assessments about whether to invest their clients' funds, the herd must rely on the ratings of economies by private and public firms that specialize in rating economies. Amongst those organizations with the most prestige and access to information, of course, is the IMF.

While the IMF does not necessarily use the literal criteria of the golden straitjacket in its assessments of countries, the sixteen criteria on the list is representative and provides a good glimpse at the character of the economic conditions that are demanded. As suggested, the criteria can be linked to the dual emphases of deregulation/privatization and free trade.

Ten of the criteria flow directly from deregulation and privatization. According to Friedman, they are:

1. "Making the private sector the primary engine of its economic growth" (e.g., reducing practices such as industrial policy);

2. "Maintaining a low rate of inflation and price stability" (e.g., creating a stable macroeconomic environment);

3. "Shrinking the size of its state bureaucracy" (e.g., reducing the cost of government);

4. "Maintaining as close to a balanced budget as possible" (e.g., reducing competition between government and the private sector over capital to borrow);

5. "Privatizing state-owned industries and utilities" (e.g., making these sectors competitive);

6. "Deregulating capital markets" (e.g., facilitating the unfettered flow of capital);

7. "Deregulating its economy to promote as much domestic competition as possible" (e.g., removing subsidies for state-owned enterprises or eliminating them altogether);

8. "Eliminating government corruption, subsidies, and kickbacks as much as possible" (e.g., making the system more honest and above board);

9. "Opening its banking and telecommunications systems to private ownership and competition" (e.g., promoting transparency); and

10. "Allowing its citizens to choose from an array of competing pension options and foreign-run pension and mutual funds" (e.g., reducing reliance on archaic government or privately run pension systems that stifle flexibility and limit individual investment choices).

The straitjacket also contains six criteria that are associated with the promotion of free trade, according to Friedman. They are:

1. "Eliminating or lowering tariffs on imported goods" (e.g., reducing barriers to free trade);

2. "Removing restrictions on foreign investment" (e.g., cutting down barriers of foreign direct investment);

3. "Getting rid of quotas and domestic monopolies" (e.g., reducing artificial barriers to trade);

4. "Increasing exports" (e.g., specializing in goods produced at comparative advantage);

5. "Making its currency convertible" (e.g., removing restrictions on currency exchange to promote capital movement); and

6. "Opening its industries, stock, and bond markets to direct foreign ownership and investment" (e.g., ending economic isolationism).

Adoption of all these policies (or at least movement toward adoption) constitutes what amounts to acceptance of the rules of the global economy.

Accepting the rules of the golden straitjacket is easier for some countries than for others, which helps explain why some countries are more enthusiastic about globalization. Friedman, however, maintains that for full participation a country must accept the whole package; as he puts it, "one size fits all." Some countries prefer to adopt parts of the package but to ignore others, and limit their participation in and attractiveness to outside investors in the process.

Adopting the straitjacket in its entirety can be difficult, even traumatic, for countries whose traditional practices—such as high levels of secretiveness in business transactions that breed what Westerners regard as corruption—vary most from the rules. Some of these changes, moreover, have political or social bases that make necessary reform unpopular and thus difficult for governments to enact, in which case they resist, usually with negative economic effects.

The trauma is not limited to poor states outside the global economy. Take two prominent examples. China's booming economy has a giant albatross hanging around its neck in the form of a large number of *state-owned enterprises* (SOEs) that are holdovers from the Maoist period. These SOEs, mostly very large enterprises, employ about two-thirds of the Chinese industrial work force but only contribute about one-third of Chinese productivity. For China to put on the entire straitjacket, the SOEs clearly should be jettisoned and replaced by more efficient private enterprises. But the government, which has been reasonably economically enlightened on most issues and recognizes the economic liability the SOEs represent, continues to balk at dismantling the inefficient SOEs. Why? The answer is the SOEs serve other purposes. For one thing, a number of them are owned by the Chinese military, which uses receipts from the SOEs to pay for part of the defense budget and to buy prestige for ranking officers. The regime needs the support of the military, which insists on maintaining the SOEs. At the same time, the SOEs provide pensions for their workers. Since China has no real social security system, putting the SOEs out of business would require creating a "social net" or leaving a large number of pensioners without support, a politically unsustainable idea. So the SOEs remain, to the detriment of China's participation in the global economy and particularly to an expanding role in that economy.

Japan has a parallel problem. It has been a hallmark of the Japanese system that the bond between employees and companies is a lifelong proposition, where employee loyalty is rewarded by "cradle-to-grave" support by the company. The bond has been credited with contributing to superior Japanese productivity. As the Japanese work force grows older and the need for flexibility has become a characteristic of modern economies, this virtue is becoming a vice. The lifelong bond means companies have considerable sunk costs and obligations that cut into productivity, and it also means that "downsizing" segments of the work force in certain declining industries (which has been argued as one of the reasons for American resurgence) is made very difficult by the commitments firms have made to their employees. Japan also needs to adopt a different approach to pensions and is exploring the possibilities; it is not easy.

As Friedman and others note, there are other dangers inherent in the spread of the globalized economy to areas not fully participating already. Some countries, which he calls the "turtles," simply cannot compete; much of sub-Saharan Africa fits into this category. Some groups within countries—especially traditional elites—lose power and prestige and can be expected to resist the application of standards that undermine their positions. In still other countries, there is considerable resistance to the homogenization of societies that adoption of the straitjacket seems inevitably to entail.

The IMF as Enforcer

The International Monetary Fund has a central role in enforcing the system that is represented by the rules of the golden straitjacket. As already noted, the relationship between the U.S. government and the IMF, while informal beyond U.S. leadership as a member, is close, if for no other reason than that the economic philosophies of both are similar. This should be relatively unsurprising; the IMF (and World Bank) are located in downtown Washington, a short walk from the White House, and many of the same U.S. investors move back and forth between Wall Street and either the U.S. government or the IMF.

Because of these connections, the IMF is the victim of some of the criticism leveled at the United States and the Washington consensus. As the post–Cold War world has evolved and the American economic system has come to predominate the global economy, the United States has become the target of those countries unhappy with the global system for one of the reasons cited above or for other reasons that may or may not have an economic base.

The IMF influences the evolving system in two basic ways. First, it loans money to countries that are caught in economic crises. As analyst David Hale puts it, the IMF is "the global lender of last resort during liquidity crunches." Thus, when insolvency is threatened, the IMF can make loans that will recreate some underpinning of support for a currency until the crisis passes. This is a major role it played in the East Asian crisis and represents its traditional role in stabilizing the international economic system. Second, the IMF dispenses economic advice to distressed countries. The advice it renders is often less than palatable, but it can be offered more candidly than could, say, the U.S. government, because as an international organization, the IMF is more independent and nonpartisan. Countries that ignore IMF advice, however, are likely to get low ratings on their economic situation from the organization, which can scare away investors who rely on the IMF ranking. In effect, the IMF has money to lend and can influence the lending of others. It is a potent combination. The fact that the criteria it uses to rate economies closely parallels the American-based straitjacket adds to the controversy it raises when it seeks to influence governments to change their financial policies.

As anyone who remembers the news photographs from South Korea showing demonstrators carrying anti-IMF banners during the East Asian crisis can well recall, the wielding of IMF power has led to criticism of the organization. Although different critics draw different lists, the major criticisms can be condensed into three complaints.

The most fundamental criticism of the IMF is that it has outstripped its mandate and assumed a role for which it was not designed. When the organization was created as part of the Bretton Woods system of international economic organizations after World War II, its major purpose was currency stabilization by promoting and supporting a system of fixed exchange rates pegged to the U.S. dollar. When the dollar was floated in 1971, that rationale faded, and the IMF turned to helping countries cope with temporary shortages of foreign exchange and more sustained trade deficits through granting IMF credits to shaky systems. In the 1990s, that role has expanded even further, leading to the second criticism.

The second critique of IMF operations is that they have now extended into major intrusions into national economies, a role that far supersedes its original mandate and brings it into direct conflict with some of its members. The IMF now places more emphasis on imposing major structural and institutional reforms with very strict adherence policies that must be followed if a country is to get help from the IMF, including its "seal of approval" for lending by private investors, and this has been particularly true since the East Asian crisis. Critics such as Feldstein go a step further, accusing the organization of a kind of "cookie cutter" approach in its reviews. He maintains the IMF makes essentially the same kind of recommendations in all countries regardless of their individual situations: a macroeconomic policy of higher taxes, reduced spending, and high interest rates, for instance. These austerity policies often create short-term hardships for the populations on which they are imposed that make bad situations politically worse for regimes already under some political siege from the crises that brought the IMF to their door in the first place. These adverse effects have made some countries wary of the globalization process, as Chapter 9 points out.

The austerity policies imposed by the IMF have a number of purposes, one of which forms the third criticism. One reason for imposing burdens is to assist foreign lenders in recovering their investments when the domestic economy undergoes trauma (sometimes at the expense of domestic investors being able to recover their own assets from failed financial institutions, one might add). The IMF's rationale for placing emphasis on recovering investor funds is that if investors run a great risk of losing their money if they invest it in developing economies, those funds will dry up or be diverted to less risky prospects.

The critics see it differently. Beyond the fact that the emphasis creates additional suffering in the target country is the matter of what is known as *moral hazard*. What this means is that if investors know they will be compensated regardless of the quality of their investments, they are in effect encouraged to make investments they might not make if their chances of losing their money was greater. Although it clearly is not the IMF's intent to encourage risky investments, the very generous safety net provided by the IMF creates this moral hazard that could lead to even worse investments with even more tragic economic consequences. Moreover, the practice clearly aligns the IMF with the "fat cat" investors of the developed world—and especially the United States—thereby reinforcing the suspicion that the IMF in operation is little more than an appendage of the American government.

CONCLUSION

The subtitle of this chapter raises the question of whether the process of expanding participation in the globalizing economy represents a new form of geopolitics for the post–Cold War world. In a sense, of course, using economic might and incentives to gain what countries want has always been one of the geopolitical tools that states have employed. The "economic instrument of power" has always been part of the foreign policy "quiver" of those states with powerful economies. Are things any different now?

In some ways, they clearly are. For one thing, the globalizing economy *is* a more pervasive phenomenon than was the older system of international economics. More countries participate in the global system, levels of trade are up everywhere, the number of nonparticipants that desire "membership" is on the increase, and foreign investment is increasing worldwide. What is also different is that much of the dynamic for this increased penetration of world economies is by private investors and firms. If one of the characteristics of geopolitics is its association with promoting the policies of states (which has traditionally been the case), then a major geopolitical question surrounds whether states can control economic matters sufficiently to harness them to national ends. The promotion of the American model through IMF assistance in fashioning the rules of which the golden straitjacket is one depiction is a geopolitical application of American economic power, but its beneficiaries are more likely to be American firms than the U.S. government directly. What the case has sought to demonstrate is that the underlying rules of the system have evolved and changed in response to experiences like the East Asian crisis and that the direction of change has been toward the Washington consensus, of which the U.S. government and the IMF are leading symbols.

A second evidence of the greater difference of this round of globalization is its universality. Thanks to influences as diverse as global television and student exchange programs, there are advocates of joining the globalization system in virtually every corner of the world, and this creates in all countries a level of demand for the fruits of the system—political democracy and economic prosperity. In many places, there are also opponents, who mostly want to cling to the virtues of an earlier era or who are frightened by the prospect of change. But there is also a growing class, usually relatively young and well educated, wearing Western-style clothes and equipped with cell phones and laptop computers, eager to lace up the straitjacket and join the prosperity. This group has already been a factor in the overthrow of Suharto in Indonesia, and their influence is likely to increase other places as well.

A third difference is the greater impact that the globalization system has on the behavior of countries in other policy areas. In 1999, for instance, China began saber rattling against Taiwan when its elections threatened to produce a new president committed to total political independence of the island from the mainland. Before globalization, this might have become an important military crisis, but the concern quickly dissipated. The likelihood of Chinese military action was dismissed on decidedly nonmilitary bases: the fear such action would interrupt the considerable level of Taiwanese private investment in the Chinese economy (estimated in the $30–40 billion range), and fear that there would be economic repercussions, especially the suspension of trade with the United States that is a vital part of the Chinese economy. What Edward Luttwak called "geo-economics" more than a decade ago collided with traditional geopolitics, and economic concerns prevailed.

Finally, there is the unique position of the United States in the evolving system. The enormous economic strength of the United States, the fact that the new system is based heavily on American economic and political values, and the open desire of many to emulate the United States (at least materially) all place the United States in the central position in the new system. The fact that the United States is able, at least informally, to enforce its values and to "force" other countries to adopt its rules as imposed by instruments like the IMF produce an enormous responsibility and geopolitical presence. As noted, that position also creates resentment in some quarters as the new trinity permeates more and more of the global system. The major question is whether a new geopolitics based on this new trinity is a permanent or transient phenomenon. The terrorist attacks against the United States on September 11, 2001, have at least temporarily pushed globalization to the back burner, and the Enron scandal of 2002 raises questions about the virtues of the American model on which globalization is based, for example. The final point of the case illustrates that the evolving system is a work in progress.

STUDY/DISCUSSION QUESTIONS

1. The technological revolution was a necessary but not sufficient condition to produce the global economy. What political phenomena were necessary to create that economy? How do they create a changed environment?

2. The East Asian crisis had a major part in the evolution of the globalizing economy toward the model represented by the Washington consensus. Explain that contribution and the direction in which it helped impel the evolving system.

3. Thomas L. Friedman's golden straitjacket creates a kind of operational checklist of what states and regions must do to join the globalization system. What are the principal elements of the straitjacket? Does adoption create a homogenized system where all members are essentially the same? Is that good or bad?

4. Some countries and areas resist parts of the straitjacket, as the Chinese and Japanese examples suggested. Apply the criteria of the straitjacket to a region (e.g., Latin America) or country (e.g., Indonesia) and see what elements are most likely to be resisted.

5. The case is based on the relationship between the parts of the globalization trinity (the U.S. government, the IMF, and developing countries). Explain and assess how this relationship works, and especially the relationship between the U.S. government and the IMF and why this creates some level of resentment within countries that aspire to joining the global economy.

6. A major characteristic of the new global system is the extent to which it is "privatized" and not controlled by governments. What are the consequences of privatization? Are they good or bad? How does the Enron scandal affect your assessment?

7. Is the globalization system the geopolitics of the post–Cold War world? Or is it just a further element in the calculation of geopolitics? What are the consequences of your conclusions for international relations?

READING/RESEARCH MATERIAL

Feldstein, Martin S. "Refocusing the IMF." *Foreign Affairs* 77, 2 (March–April 1998), 20–33.

Friedman, Thomas L. *The Lexus and the Olive Tree: Understanding Globalization.* New York: Farrar, Straus, Giroux, 1999.

Hale, David D. "The IMF, More Than Ever." *Foreign Affairs* 77, 6 (November–December 1998), 7–13.

Kapur, Devesh. "The IMF: A Cure or a Curse?" *Foreign Policy,* 111 (Summer 1998), 114–131.

Keohane, Robert O., and Joseph S. Nye Jr. "Globalism: What's New? *Foreign Policy* 118 (Spring 2000), 104–119.

———. *Power and Interdependence.* 2nd ed. Glenview, IL: Scott Foresman/Little Brown, 1989.

Luttwak, Edward. "From Geopolitics to Geo-Economics: Logic of Conflict, Grammar of Commerce." *National Interest* 20 (1990), 17–24.

Snow, Donald M. *The Shape of the Future: World Politics in a New Century.* 3rd ed. Armonk, NY: M. E. Sharpe, 1999.

Spero, Joan Edelman. *The Politics of International Economic Relations.* 4th ed. New York: St. Martin's Press, 1990.

WEB SITES

Overview of the IMF's role in the financial crisis that erupted in Asia in mid-1997

Factsheet: The IMF's Response to the Asian Crisis at
http://www.imf.org/external/np/exr/facts/asia.htm

Archive of New York Times articles outlining the causes and the course of the global economic crisis that originated in Asia

The World Financial Crisis at http://www.nytimes.com/library/financial/index-global-fin-crisis.html

Think tank that seeks to broaden the public debate on economic issues, including the downsides of globalization and trade

Economic Policy Institute at http://www.epinet.org

Organization working to increase public understanding of the benefits of free trade and the costs of protectionism

The CATO Institute Center for Trade Policy Issues at http://www.freetrade.org

Official website for America's chief trade negotiator and principal advisor to the president

Office of the United States Trade Representative at http://www.ustr.gov

Presents the arguments of both those who support as well as oppose globalization

The Globalisation Guide at http://www.globalisationguide.org

CHAPTER NINE

Debating Globalization:

THE CASE OF INDONESIA

PRÉCIS

In the new century, some of the enthusiasm for the globalization of the world's economy that was such a prominent aspect of the "go-go 1990s" has faded. Part of the reason for this is that the world's economy has slowed since the latter part of the 1990s and especially in the wake of the East Asian financial crisis of 1997, introduced in Chapter 8. At the same time, the results of adopting globalization as a value have had mixed results in some states. As a consequence, some states are viewing the phenomenon of globalization and their part in it with more caution than they did a decade or more ago.

No state represents more fully the mixed impact of globalization than Indonesia, the world's fourth most populous state. Indonesia was an enthusiastic recruit to globalization in the early 1990s, but when the impact of the East Asian crisis washed onto its shores, it set into motion a political and economic crisis from which the archipelago continues to reel. Although all of Indonesia's problems cannot be blamed on globalization, the global economy contributed to the spiral that led to the resignation of the country's 32-year dictator on charges of corruption, a chaotic political democratization that shows little prospect of stabilizing, and even the emergence of open secessionist movements on a number of islands. A good deal of this might have happened without globalization, but the coincidence has made many Indonesians more wary of the consequences of economic globalization.

ntil the East Asian economic crisis of 1997 (described in Chapter 8), the spread of
the global economy worldwide seemed an inexorable process, a bandwagon leading to prosperity and political freedom onto which virtually every country in the world
sought to climb. When economies that turned out to be much more fragile than was realized before the crisis hit were devastated, enthusiasm dampened somewhat, especially
as the International Monetary Fund (IMF) imposed tough conditions on the affected
economies to guarantee their long-term recovery and viability. In some instances, the
IMF's political and economic requirements added to the woes caused by the crisis itself.
As a result, unbridled, nearly blind adherence to globalization has given way to somewhat greater restraint about participation in the world economy, which was suddenly
revealed to have a downside not seen during the great boom of the 1990s. The result,
at least in some places, has been a debate over globalization and the extent to which countries will participate in the global economy.

No country was more greatly affected by the Asian economic crisis of 1997 than
Indonesia. In addition to the economic ruination that accompanied the crisis itself,
the country has experienced the fall of a long-standing authoritarian regime that
was widely considered one of the most corrupt in the world, and has been hounded
by charges of excesses by the military in the face of secessionary movements on several islands. Indonesia is thus in the midst of a period of national trauma. It is the
world's fourth most populous country and one that is blessed with great natural
resources, but the archipelago was hit hard by the collapse of the currencies of most
of the states of Southeast Asia in 1997. The economic chaos surrounding the crisis
in turn energized a latent opposition to the Suharto regime that had ruled since 1966,
leading to Suharto's resignation in 1998. Shortly thereafter, the country was further
rocked by the uprising in East Timor, which was accompanied by allegations of widespread atrocities against East Timorese separatists allegedly abetted and supported
by elements in the Indonesian military. The seeds of separatism have spread to other
parts of the island country. The result has been great questioning about the future
of the Indonesian state.

Indonesia is thus in a state of deep national reexamination about the future of
the Indonesian people and state. Prior to the events unleashed in 1997, Indonesia
had been part of the network of prosperous states of East Asia that had enthusiastically
entered the globalizing economy through membership in organizations such as the
Asia-Pacific Economic Cooperation (APEC) and the Association of Southeast Asian
Nations (ASEAN). Like many of its neighbors, Indonesia seemed a "poster child" for
the virtues of globalization and a model for other states that aspired to participation in
the globalizing system.

And then the economic crisis of 1997 burst the bubble and revealed a very different, and far less happy, reality about Indonesian (as well as other regional) prosperity. The
crisis, as is well known, had its genesis in Thailand, where the *baht* (the Thai currency
unit) collapsed precipitously in 1997. In the resulting economic panic, almost all the
countries near Thailand and connected to it economically felt the backlash. Indonesia,
the largest and most populous country in the region, was not exempt from the trauma
that gripped the region.

The economic crash revealed, or highlighted, other sources of tension and instability that had been glossed over during the prosperity that washed over Indonesia during the early 1990s. During that period, Indonesia embraced globalization and the world
embraced Indonesia. The signs of trouble were there to be seen, but they tended to be
ignored or downplayed in light of what appeared to be perpetual expansion and prosperity. And then the crisis hit. During 1998, the Indonesian economy was traumatized,
with sharp contractions in economic growth accompanied by high inflation rates, massive bank failures, and extremely high interest rates. The economic bad times, in turn,
resulted in finger pointing against the regime of President Suharto, and the massive
corruption for which it was infamous. Amidst massive criticism of the cronyism and
the accumulation of great personal wealth for the benefit of his family, Suharto, who had
been elected to a fifth six-year term in 1996, resigned on May 21, 1998.

Even though the economy began to stabilize by the end of the year, Indonesia's woes
were by no means over. The province of East Timor, occupying roughly half the island of
Timor in the southern part of the archipelago, held a referendum on independence on August
30, 1999, and the citizens voted overwhelmingly (78.5 percent) for secession from the
Indonesian state. The vote prompted vicious attacks against East Timorese by pro-Indone-
sian "militias," marauding armed bands that, at a minimum, the Indonesian military was
unable to suppress. At worst, it was widely believed that elements in the Army supported the
actions and had helped organize, equip, and encourage the offenders. In the end, fighting
was ended only when an Australian-led UN peacekeeping force (the International Force
in East Timor or INTERFET) landed in East Timor and established order.

This jackhammer sequence of events has caused a basic reassessment of the future
within Indonesia that centers on Indonesia's place in the economic globalization system. During the 1990s, Indonesia embraced globalization with something of a vengeance.
During the first half of the decade, the result was great prosperity and even the hope
among some younger Indonesians, whom *New York Times* correspondent Thomas L.
Friedman calls the "globalutionaries," that involvement in the global economy could provide the engine for political and other reform. Moreover, the prosperity glossed over
the other very real problems that beset the country. Indonesia's good times proved to
be ephemeral indeed.

Post-crisis Indonesia is reassessing itself, and the outcome is uncertain. The economic
crisis, followed by the imposition of tough standards by the IMF to correct the situation (see Chapter 8, "The New Trinity of Globalization," for a discussion of the IMF's
role generally) have left some Indonesians wary of the country's place in the global
economy and anxious to place their participation in a more distinctly Indonesian context. The fall of Suharto has ended the long reign of corrupt, authoritarian rule. The political system is in a transition to something else, but the outcome is unclear. The fall of
Suharto and the extremely adverse publicity the Indonesian military received over the
East Timor situation has also raised questions about the military's heretofore privileged
position in Indonesia, including its role in keeping the island country together amid considerable centrifugal tendencies.

What happens in Indonesia is important both within its own boundaries and
beyond. As the world's fourth most populous country (with a population estimated in

July 2000 at slightly less than 225 million living on a land mass slightly less than three times the state of Texas), Indonesia is a tremendous potential market for the region and globally and, as by far the largest country in Southeast Asia, it is a regional power of importance. Moreover, the archipelago sits astride the Indian and Pacific Oceans, and the Straits of Malacca that flow between the Indonesian island of Sumatra and Malaysia carries more than 40 percent of the world's ship-borne commerce, making a stable Indonesia desirable for global commercial activity. Moreover, the outcome of how Indonesia deals with the future will almost certainly have a ripple effect in other, smaller countries in the region facing similar economic and political situations.

This construction of the problem suggests the method by which the case will proceed. We will begin with a sketch of the Indonesian past in a general sense, but will also focus on the three dimensions of the current crisis—economics and the relationship to globalization, the political transition, and the geopolitics of the military's role in holding the country together or allowing parts of it to break away. With the past as background, we will then examine the post–1997 choices available to Indonesia, which they may choose, and what difference those choices make for Indonesia and the region.

INDONESIA: A THUMBNAIL SKETCH

Indonesia is the largest archipelago in the world. It is comprised of over 13,600 individual islands, about 6,000 of which are inhabited. The major islands include Sumatra, Java (one of the most densely populated land masses in the world, at over 2,000 people per square mile), parts of Borneo and New Guinea, and the Maluccas, among others. The capital, Jakarta, is on Java, where the majority of the Indonesian population resides.

The archipelago has a very long history. Anthropologists have found human remains (Java man) that are amongst the oldest in the world. The country, which is approximately 85 percent Muslim, attracted the attention of Islamic traders in the 1400s, and they were followed by the Portuguese, British, and the Dutch in the sixteenth century. After a period of posturing, the Netherlands established domain over the heart of what became known as the Dutch East Indies (which had formerly been called the Spice Islands) through the Dutch East Indies Company. Dutch colonial rule remained until World War II, when Japan invaded and occupied the country following their defeat of an Allied fleet in the Battle of the Java Sea in 1942. During the war, the Dutch helped organize a resistance to Japanese rule in Indonesia that became the basis of the independence movement against the Netherlands after the Japanese surrendered in 1945. Under the leadership of the man who would become the first president of Indonesia, Achmed Sukarno, the Indonesians fought the reimposition of colonial rule until they prevailed and the Dutch granted independence.

Indonesia achieved its independence on December 27, 1949. After a period of transition, Sukarno gained and gradually consolidated power in the country, ultimately dissolving the country's parliament in 1960, euphemistically declaring the Indonesian system a *guided democracy*, and having himself declared president for life in 1963. Sukarno's rule was marked by general mismanagement of the economy, as he devoted great resources to meaningless projects that served as monuments to himself but did little for the economy (for instance, he had a world-class soccer stadium built, but the access roads turned to dirt ruts within blocks of the site and the average Indonesian could not afford tickets to see a match), and he gradually moved away from the West, seeking closer relations with the People's Republic of China.

Opposition to Sukarno gradually grew over time, particularly as the Indonesian Communist Party came to gain greater influence within institutions such as the country's labor unions. In 1965, a cabal of Army officers accused of links to the communists staged an attempted coup that was put down by a countercoup led by General Suharto. In 1966, Sukarno was forced to relinquish much of his authority to Suharto, and in 1968, Suharto was named president for the first of his terms that ended with his resignation in 1998. Interestingly, although Sukarno himself faded from prominence after his removal from office, his name remains sufficiently powerful that his daughter, Megawati Sukarnoputri, emerged as a major candidate for president in 1999, was named vice president by President Abdurrahman Wahid, who defeated her, and has since succeeded Wahid in the presidency after Wahid was driven from power by the Indonesian Parliament on charges of corruption.

The reign of Suharto lasted for three decades, and may have continued beyond that had it not been for the East Asian financial crisis of 1997. His rule will be remembered more for its longevity than for its quality. His government was certainly less than democratic or even democratizing, supported and sustained primarily by an alliance between the Indonesia military and supporters and cronies of the president. Economically and politically, Indonesia has had the reputation of being one of the most corrupt countries in the world. The Berlin-based independent agency Transparency International Inc. (founded by former World Bank official Peter Eigen) ranked Indonesia the fourth most corrupt country in the world in its 1999 Corruption Perceptions Index. The index, which asks respondents what countries they believe to be the most corrupt states, rated only Cameroon, Nigeria, and Azerbaijan as being more corrupt than Indonesia.

The Suharto regime was, however, very much a Cold War artifact. When Suharto replaced Sukarno, he did turn the country solidly anticommunist. He outlawed the Indonesian Communist Party, suppressed communists throughout the country, and brought Indonesia into the Western security and economic system. During the height of the Cold War, this reorientation of Indonesian foreign policy was adequate to win favor in the West (after 1975, the Federation of American Scientists, for instance, reports the United States sold $1.25 billion in arms to the Indonesian armed forces) and to cause the West to look the other way at Indonesian governmental malfeasance and expansionism. Among the more egregious examples of ignoring Suharto's excesses was the implied American acceptance of the violent annexation of East Timor in 1975.

The Suharto regime began to lose favor, as did a number of others around the world (Mobutu Sese Seku's Zaire, for instance), with the end of the Cold War. With no communist threat against which to be an apparent bulwark, there was a more critical, less accepting view of authoritarian regimes generally and the Indonesian regime more specifically in the world at large. When the economic bubble burst in 1997, the Suharto regime found itself with few friends internally or externally in much the same way the world treated Mobutu when his regime began to crumble.

The result has been the debate over the future of Indonesia. It is an illustrative case because of the size and importance of the country, and also because other states have or will attempt to make the transition from twentieth-century authoritarianism to some different form of twenty-first century arrangement, all within the framework of a relationship with the globalizing economy. To see how this may occur in the Indonesian case, we will thus look at each of the three dimensions of the crisis identified earlier—economic, political, and geopolitical—as preface to the ongoing debate and its possible outcomes.

The Economic Legacy

The economic and political legacies of the half-century of Indonesian independence can only be separated artificially, because what are now viewed as problems in both areas fed upon and reinforced one another. The "Chinese-dominated business class," as the *CIA Factbook* describes it, operated a classic form of *crony capitalism* (where economic collusion among economic entities were carried out for personal advantage and at the expense of public goods) that could only have flourished with governmental blessing or at least implicit approval. At the same time, rampant *nepotism* at the highest governmental levels allowed the Suharto family to own major segments of and to benefit from the civilian economy. In turn, this activity required the assistance or at least the indulgence of the private business sector.

The result was that Suharto's *new order* produced what has been described as one of the most corrupt regimes that East Asia has yet produced. Due to Indonesia's considerable natural resource abundance (the country produces between one-third and two-fifths of the world's supply of liquefied natural gas, for instance), the result of corruption was not necessarily the systematic impoverishment of the population. Rather, the underlying governmental and economic rot was obscured by Indonesia's participation in the global economy and the general prosperity that attached to that economy in the 1980s and 1990s. Indeed, during the 1990s Indonesia had one of the fastest growing economies in the world, with an average growth in GDP per capita around 7.5 percent. With this appearance of economic dynamism, the outside world looked the other way at the signs of gross corruption and malfeasance, emphasizing economic growth and ignoring institutional and other sources of weakness.

The East Asian crisis revealed that Indonesia's prosperity, like that of many of its neighbors, was a classic economic bubble ready to explode when pricked. High rates of foreign direct investment (FDI) were revealed to have been spent on unproductive projects, overextended banks collapsed as the *rupiah* plunged, and economic chaos ensued as panicky foreign and domestic investors removed their assets from Indonesia as rapidly as possible. The result was economic stagnation reflected in a flat economic growth rate and high inflation marked by exorbitantly high interest rates in 1998 that only began to come down in 1999.

The corruption of the system both allowed the bubble to form and made matters worse when it finally burst. In a manner reminiscent of the other East Asian countries, the chief culprits were in the financial sector, and encompassed both private entrepreneurs and governmental officials. Indonesia lacked a strong banking system, and had no regulation of the activities of banks to ensure the soundness of lending decisions and the accountability of financial officials to investors. The financial regulatory system, which one analyst has described simply as "decrepit," could thus not provide protection for the savings of average citizens who counted on the banks to protect them. Further, Indonesia lacked a bond market that could serve as an alternative conduit for savings by average Indonesians, who did not have access to overseas outlets to invest their money. The result was an opacity in the financial sector (transactions could be conducted secretly, with little or no accountability to savers) that encouraged crony capitalist networks of bankers, businessmen, and supposed governmental regulators to flourish, making decisions from which they benefited but those whose money was spent did not.

The Suharto family was in the middle of this system. In order to gain protection from government regulation and access to funds, members of the extended Suharto family became prominent entrepreneurs in the system, effectively wedding crony capitalism and nepotism. When a project was approved to develop an Indonesian-made automobile (a project that never reached fruition), the exclusive franchise was awarded to a Suharto family member, and support for developing the project was funneled through the financial system, with significant amounts of money ending up in Suharto family pockets. Although reliable estimates are difficult to find, the post-Suharto government has decided that the family looted the national treasury of at least $500 million. The government has attempted to sue Suharto for restitution, but as of late 2000, it seemed questionable whether any of it would be recovered. Although Suharto himself remained outside the criminal justice system through the end of 2000 by pleading his health was too poor for court appearances, his youngest son, Hutomo Mandala Putra (known as Tommy Suharto) was found guilty of corruption in a land deal in September and sentenced to 18 months in jail.

All of this activity did not go unnoticed, but until 1997 little was done to stop it. There was little desire among those outside the country to embarrass a long-time ally, even if economic rating services warned about the dangers of investing in the Indonesian economy. Similarly, there were Indonesians, mainly younger and better educated (often in the West), who recognized the corruption and wanted to see something done about it. The problem for them was how to bring about reform in a self-contained and self-reinforcing system that could reform itself only at the personal expense of the reformers themselves—an unlikely prospect. Moreover, the Indonesian economic system was grounded in an authoritarian state that supported the status quo. In addition, the Indonesian Army had shown little reluctance to squash dissent against the regime, leaving political dissent a physically risky form of enterprise. Indonesian politics thus reinforced the economic system.

Indonesian Politics

The combination of cronyism and nepotism in the Indonesian economy could only be sustained in a political atmosphere where criticism and exposure of corrupt—and ultimately economically debilitating—practices could be suppressed. In Indonesia, the development and continuation of these practices was made possible by an authoritarian political system originally devised by Sukarno and his followers that was refined by

Suharto and his supporters after he seized power. In the post-Suharto Indonesia, charges of corruption in early 2001 against President Wahid, the first democratically elected Indonesian leader in 45 years, suggested the practice was continuing (and ultimately led to his removal from office). While the symbols of representative government were present—an elected parliament and the periodic reelection of Suharto as president—the system rested on political repression enforced by the national police and, when necessary in the face of major disturbances, the Indonesian military. Such actions were generally justified under Suharto as means to deal with subversives (especially communists) and later separatists seeking to detach parts of Indonesia from the federation.

Corrupt government reinforced a corrupt political system. With government officials part of "iron triangles" with financiers and businessmen from which all three profited, the result was a system of purposely weak regulation and oversight, where policymakers and policy implementers protected rather than exposed practices that would ultimately be ruinous when the economic bubble burst. The practices were known both inside and outside Indonesia, but any attempt to expose them would bring the system down upon the head of the exposer.

Younger, more Westernized, Indonesians were particularly frustrated by the system, but did not know how to reform it. Thomas L. Friedman describes this group as "educated 20- and 30-year-olds…(who) wanted to get rich, but without having to be corrupt, and they wanted democracy, but they didn't want to go into the streets to fight for it." Seeing that the chances for reform from within the country were negligible and unwilling to engage in violent revolution from below, their solution was *revolution from beyond*, integrating Indonesia into the global economy, which would force the Indonesian economy to adopt the noncorrupt practices of the global economy as a way to force reform of the domestic economy and political system. Although their approach has been compromised by domestic reaction to Western demands in the post–1997 environment, it remains one possible route for the country to travel if it seeks full integration into the global system.

Authoritarian rule is on the wane in Indonesia, although one observer, Patrick Smith, warns, "A working democracy is still distant in Indonesia." One of the remaining vestiges of authoritarianism in the country is an Indonesian military that has always played an active part in the country's politics and that retains the ability to affect the outcomes of reform efforts. Much of the military's remaining claim to a part of the post-Suharto political action is the effort to keep parts of Indonesia from leaving the federation.

The Geopolitics of Separatism

Although the core of Indonesia is the Dutch East Indies, and the vast majority of the population practice the religion of Islam, not all of the Indonesian state shares these unifying characteristics. Rather, there are areas that either have been forcefully added to the Indonesian state over time or which have specific grievances against the government in Jakarta. As a result, there have been several active separatist movements within the archipelago that remained latent during the Suharto period but surfaced publicly during the latter 1990s. For most of Indonesian history (certainly during the Cold War), the outside world ignored these rebellions, because good relations with the Suharto regime was deemed more important than support for secessionists. The organized violence that sought to intimidate the East Timorese so they would not vote for secession and the successful, internationally supervised removal of Indonesian forces from East Timor raised international awareness of the other claims against Jakarta.

The situation in East Timor is both exemplary of the other claims and unique in its own right. East Timor was not a part of the Dutch East Indies nor was it an original part of the Indonesian state. Rather, the half of the island of Timor (located about midway between Java and New Guinea and several hundred miles north of Australia) that constitutes East Timor is a former colony of Portugal. When Portugal relinquished the last of its colonial empire in 1975, East Timor was among the former possessions to receive its independence from the mother country.

Freedom did not last long. Indonesian troops forcefully entered the country in December 1975 with the tacit approval of the West (and notably the United States), and Suharto declared it a province of Indonesia. Indonesia forcefully annexed the overwhelmingly Catholic country in 1976 (an action condemned and not recognized by the United Nations) and began a brutal campaign of assimilation of the East Timorese people into Indonesia. Amnesty International, among other organizations, estimates that as many as 100,000 East Timorese (of a total population of about 700,000) were killed by security forces during this period, and a "transmigration" program brought tens of thousands of Muslims from West Timor and other parts of the country into East Timor.

A low-level campaign for independence sprang up in East Timor—the Revolutionary Front for an Independent East Timor (Fretilin)—but the Indonesian Army managed to keep the lid on the problem until the 1990s. In 1991, East Timor returned to international attention when Western journalists witnessed Indonesian troops killing up to 270 unarmed East Timorese civilians in the capital of Dili. In 1996, two East Timorese (Bishop Carlos Filipe Ximenes Belo and exiled political spokesman Jose Ramos

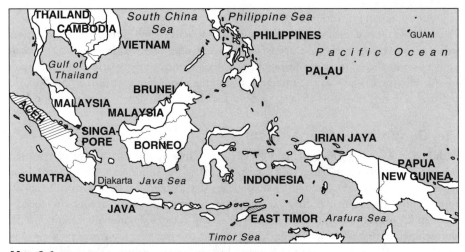

Map 9.1 Map of Indonesia, featuring East Timor and Aceh.

Horta) received the Nobel Peace Prize, and they added to publicity about the plight of the beleaguered East Timorese.

Bowing to international pressures, President B. J. Habibie, Suharto's immediate successor, agreed to a referendum on the future of East Timor in January 1999. Despite harassment and violence led by "militias" suspected of being aligned with the army, 98 percent of East Timorese voted in the referendum, which was monitored by the UN and global television, and 78.5 percent of those voting cast their ballots for independence. When Jakarta could or would not suppress the militias, the Australian-led UN force (INTERFET) intervened to restore order as the Indonesian Army sat idly by in West Timor. The United Nations Transitional Authority in East Timor (UNTAET) has been charged with preparing East Timor for independence, although reports in late 2000 indicated that little assistance needed to end the suffering of the population had arrived or been distributed. In January 2001, the provisional authorities announced the formation of a 1,700-man East Timor Defense Force made up primarily of former guerrillas who had fought for East Timorese independence during the 1990s.

The other currently active separatist movement is located in Aceh under the leadership of the Free Aceh Movement (GAM), which has been fighting the government since 1989. Unlike East Timor, Aceh is a Muslim province located in the northwest corner of Sumatra. Located closer to the Middle East than any of the other parts of the archipelago, Acehnese consider their territory "the front porch of Mecca."

The Acehnese complaints with Jakarta are economic and political. Economically, Aceh contributes more to the central government than it receives in return, prompting a demand for economic parity in the form either of lower taxes or greater services. The lopsided economic balance arises because 40 percent of the liquefied natural gas to which allusion has already been made comes from off the coast of Aceh. Considering themselves to be more pious than most Indonesians, the Acehnese demand greater religious freedom and also want to see an end to military suppression in their region by the Indonesian army. President Wahid has suggested that the East Timor referendum precedent may well apply to Aceh as well. Tensions increased in late 2000 when a popular Acehnese nationalist, Tengku Safwan Idris, was assassinated in Banda Aceh, the provisional capital. Indris had been appointed by former President Habibe to investigate unrest in Aceh. Other uprisings include Papua (Irian Jaya), which has been ongoing since 1969, and several potential conflicts in the Molucca Islands and on Borneo, where native Dayaks went on a rampage against Madurese immigrants who had been forcefully relocated into traditional Dayak lands.

WHERE IS INDONESIA GOING?

The events of the latter 1990s—the financial crisis, the downfall of the authoritarian Suharto regime, and the emergence of secessionary movements— have broken old patterns and left decisions to be reached about the direction that Indonesia will take in the new century. The first and most central concern will be the relationship of the country to the global economy, since the recovery of the Indonesian economy would probably moderate the other problems. Indonesia was one of the most enthusiastic converts to globalization during the early 1990s, and the results included great prosperity for many Indonesians and a muting of criticism of the corrupt and authoritarian Suharto regime as the good times unfolded. The financial crisis hit Indonesia hard, collapsing banks and other financial institutions and sending many Indonesians (there are estimates of as many as 40 percent of the population) below the official poverty line. As Indonesia faces stringent International Monetary Fund (IMF) requirements for recovery and read-mission into the globalization system, Indonesians, once having been stung, are more cautious in their enthusiasm for globalism this time around.

What may prove in the long run to have been a benefit of the 1997 crisis is that it swept from power the 30-year long Suharto dictatorship. Opposition to the regime and its corruption had been simmering below the surface of Indonesian politics for a long time, but the Army's alliance with Suharto and its consequent willingness to suppress dissent violently, even ruthlessly, had kept that opposition out of view and on the fringes. When it became clear that the depth of the 1997 crisis was in large measure the fault of the government—or at least made worse by corrupt practices—and Indonesian soldiers showed a great reluctance to attack student-led demonstrations, the days of Suharto were numbered. The problem, of course, was that a half-century of despotic rule has left Indonesia with neither democratic, participatory institutions nor traditions, and it is not entirely clear what kind of political future holds for the country. The old ways were so pervasive that they have continued to infect the post-Suharto transition.

Finally, there is the question of the territorial integrity of the country, an issue also integrally related to the future of the Indonesian armed forces that have been the violent glue of Indonesian unity in the past. Whether East Timorese independence will act as a significant lightning rod for others in the far-flung archipelago or as a fairly isolated incident has yet to be determined. When President Wahid said that East Timor did create a precedent that others could follow if they chose, he was rapidly beseeched to qualify his statement out of fear the Acehnese or others might take him up on the offer. Whether Indonesia will be held together by force or will splinter further remains a choice both for the Javanese-dominated majority and the various minorities.

Reevaluating Globalization

There are two contradictory positions with regard to Indonesia's future participation in the globalizing economy that stand out and, given Indonesia's immediate past, both of them are understandable. Neither argument calls for outright rejection of the world economy, although there are probably those who would favor total isolationism from the world system, at least for a time. Rather, there is disagreement about the degree of enthusiasm Indonesia should show toward taking its place in the world economy. In its most pure sense, it is a debate between the globalutionaries/Westernizers and a group known in Indonesia as the *reformasi*.

Those elements in Indonesia committed to transforming Indonesia into a full participant in the global economy (and for most of them, into a fully functioning political democracy as well) view the events since 1997 as an opportunity of sorts. Certainly, no one advocates more of the economic pain that has been inflicted on the country by the crash and subsequent restructuring that is being forced on the country. Having said that, the crash did cause the autocratic Suharto regime to collapse, thereby creating the possibility for reform that would have been served by the "revolution from below" that the globalutionaries, as described earlier by Friedman, could not bring themselves to carry out. The subsequent imposition of IMF reforms to restructure the economy also brings with it the possibility of further "revolution from beyond," which also serves their interests. From this vantage point, the crash and fall of Suharto represents an opening and opportunity to be seized.

Not all Indonesians are quite so certain about the virtue of a headlong flight into the embrace of globalization. The more conservative *reformasi*, rather, see the fall of Suharto's New Order as an opportunity for a process that Patrick Smith calls "national reinvention" that includes questioning "the very ideals the West urges upon the world—democracy, liberty, equality, self-determination, modernization, progress." Instead, many Indonesians who are less Westernized than the globalutionaries see the need to assert Indonesian autonomy as more desirable than the homogenization of the Indonesian culture with the Western world that appears to be part and parcel of joining the globalization system.

The imposition of stringent requirements for financial reform by the IMF energizes the debate over the future. The gist of the IMF's program has been to grant large credits (up to $5 billion, according to the *Economist* Intelligence Unit) to Indonesia in return for reform of the country's financial sector. In addition to rules to create greater transparency in the banking sector and corporate restructuring, it also emphasizes measures to enhance the power of Indonesian financial regulatory agencies such as the Indonesian Bank Restructuring Agency (IBRA), the Jakarta Initiative Task Force, the attorney general's office, and the bankruptcy court. If all the proposed reforms are instituted, the hoped-for result will be an Indonesian financial sector from which much of the endemic corruption has been removed and a high level both of transparency and standardized banking procedures that will make Indonesia once again attractive to outside investors who took their money and left during the 1997–1998 crisis.

This intrusion of Western economic values into Indonesian affairs is the source of controversy within the country. Many Indonesians believe they uncritically embraced globalization in the early 1990s, only to get burned in 1997. The counter argument to this belief is the assertion by the globalutionaries that the reason Indonesia suffered was because it adopted the trappings of globalization but not the essential underpinnings of a truly globalizing country, notably openness and honesty in the financial sector. The veneer of globalization covered the rotten core of an essentially corrupted economic system; when the veneer was cracked by the reverberations from the *baht* crisis, the effect swept across the region and engulfed Indonesia, revealing how rotten the core was.

Which side of the argument one finds compelling is a matter of perspective that reflects the ambivalence many developing states have about globalization. Essentially, Indonesia has three options as it confronts its future relationship within the global economy. One option is to embrace the globalutionaries, swallow the bitter medicine of reform and austerity the IMF insists is necessary for its health to be restored, and then plunge headlong into the global economy. As long as the globalizing economy remains prosperous and vibrant, that strategy probably yields the greatest economic gains for most—but certainly not all—Indonesians. The other side of that choice is that there are no guarantees that the events of 1997 will not repeat themselves, and that the embrace will almost certainly necessitate abandoning some social and economic practices and institutions that are uniquely Indonesian.

The second option is joining the globalizing economy, but with a distinctively Asian flavor, what some call the "Asian model." There are clear incentives to exercise this option, largely on cultural grounds. Joining the West entails becoming like the West, and groups like the *reformasi* are concerned about this erosive effect on Indonesian culture and society. As Smith once again argues, a strong thread of Indonesian opinion believes that "amid great material change, traditional morals and hierarchies must be maintained." The problem is that adherence to aspects of the Asian model that allowed opacity in the financial sector caused the problem in the first place, and that one of the traditional morals turned out to be the "traditional" corruption and nepotism that made the crisis worse than it might otherwise have been. Knowing this to be the case, Western sources are unlikely to be forthcoming of the resources necessary to allow Indonesian recovery should the country choose that option.

The attempt to accept part but not all the Western economic model has already been rejected by the IMF and, by extension, Western investors who must provide the financial lifeblood of investment to fuel any economic progress in Indonesia. As argued in Chapter 8, the IMF insists that countries accept reforms in their entirety. The $5 billion in standby funds that the IMF committed to Indonesia was premised on the Indonesians achieving a series of deadlines for reform of the economy (specifically, features of the financial system designed to promote transparency and thus discourage corruption), but the Indonesian government has lagged behind. As of May 2000, for instance, the *Economist* Intelligence Unit reported the government had failed to meet 42 deadlines and that, as a result, $400 million had already been withheld. This problem has continued into 2002. If the maintenance of a distinctly Indonesian character to economic activity translates into the protection of traditional sources of corruption, then Indonesia and the international economic community are on a collision course the political outcomes of which may be to leave the country culturally pure but economically deprived or culturally compromised but potentially more solvent.

If Indonesia opts for resistance to the requirements of the global community, its effective third option may be a minimal participation in the global economy. Such a course would almost certainly leave Indonesia poorer than and isolated from its neighbors who accept the strictures of the IMF and other international agencies, and it would certainly be opposed by the Westernizers and globalutionaries who favor participation in the global economy as a way to make Indonesia more like the developed world. In addition, one possible manifestation of Westernization that the globalutionaries seek to influence is political, the spread of democracy to the Indonesian polity, and that could also be a victim in an isolationist Indonesia.

Political Reformation

As already noted, Indonesia has less than a rich democratic tradition, and the absence of Western-style democracy is one of the parts of the distinctly Eastern, Indonesian culture that those who have benefited from the traditional system seek to continue and that the globalutionaries seek to change. While the argument that democracy is alien to eastern culture (which arguably places more emphasis on collective, rather than individual, goods and values) is losing ground in many Asian societies, it still has some residual appeal in places like Singapore. At the same time, opposition to Westernization is, in a number of places, little more than the refuge for those whose privilege (including wealth) would be compromised by the greater openness and egalitarianism that democratization would create.

The traditional autocratic nature of the political system forged in the wake of independence has been strengthened by the alliance between the government and an Indonesian military that has long been politically active in support of the traditional system. In the past, challenges to the authority of Jakarta have been opposed and upon occasion even ruthlessly crushed by the Army. The question is whether this will continue in the future.

The answer clearly crosses the political line into the economy. There are clear connections between economic globalization and political democratization. Virtually all the countries at the heart of the global economy are or are becoming democratic, and it can be argued that economic capitalism (the economic philosophy of the globalizing economy) and political democracy are both expressions of the same underlying commitment to individual freedom to choose. Among the world's major powers, only China has sought to separate the two concepts by denying political freedom, and it is arguable that the Chinese communist government will ultimately fail in that separation (see Chapter 1, "China Rising," for a further discussion). In the region, tiny but very wealthy Singapore also manages to enforce the separation between globalization and democratization.

If democratization and participation in the global economy are linked, then the decision either to become a full-time part of the global economy or a partial participant will also help determine the political path for the country. Overcoming the legacy of corruption and mismanagement at the highest levels is clearly part of the problem. In the case of Indonesia, however, this process is further affected by a variable not seen in many other places. The archipelago faces challenges to the territorial integrity of the country that is not shared by many other smaller, less complex countries.

National Integrity

The recently concluded events in East Timor raise questions about whether Indonesia will remain a cohesive unit or whether other areas of the far-flung island chain will spin away by seceding from the union. While the situation in East Timor was unique and the loss of the territory does not threaten the economic or political integrity of the country directly, nonetheless it does potentially provide a precedent that other areas of the country might seek to exploit in the future. As noted earlier, President Wahid, who was elected in October 1999, created a national stir when he suggested that if East Timor could vote itself out of the union, then others presumably could do so as well. What the policy will become since Wahid has been swept from office by charges of corruption before the scheduled next election in 2004 is open to question.

This prospect, which could emerge in Aceh, Irian Jaya or elsewhere, reverberates throughout the Indonesian system and adds to the general uncertainty surrounding Indonesia's future. The Indonesian military has been particularly opposed to secession and has historically used its power to repress separatist movements. It also tends to equate democratization with the freedom to organize seditious movements. At the same time, the kind of campaign that it waged clandestinely to suppress East Timorese separatism clearly blew up in its face, and the military knows that any similar action will be subject to intense international scrutiny that very much limits the future choices it can exercise.

Whether a concern over the relationship between democratization and separatism will provide sufficient weight to slow the processes of political and economic integration into the evolving world system remains to be seen. It is, however, a concern that does not influence the process in many other countries debating globalization but lacking similar divisive forces.

CONCLUSION

Indonesia continues to struggle in the transition from its past to the future. In late 2000, two apparently related incidents provided dramatic, and highly symbolic, evidence of the content and direction of Indonesia's travail. On August 31, the government convened a trial against former President Suharto, who was summoned to answer charges he had stolen $571 million from the government during his years in office and distributed the money to family and friends. Beyond its emphasis on rooting out corruption in the government, investigators hoped to recover all or most of the embezzled funds. Suharto, claiming he was too ill to answer the summons to court, did not appear, to the dismay of his opponents.

The government attempted to begin the trial two weeks later, on September 13. Suharto again pleaded ill health and failed to appear. But on the day the trial was to start, a powerful car bomb exploded outside the Indonesian Stock Exchange in Jakarta, killing 15 people and injuring over 40 more. There were immediate accusations that supporters of Suharto had engineered the explosion to divert attention from the former president, and his youngest son (Tommy Suharto) was arrested by police in an attempt to ensure that a repeat performance did not occur. The symbolism of an attack on the most prominent symbol of Indonesia's flirtation with the globalization system did not go unnoticed. Neither did the fact that the elected government of President Wahid would pursue charges against the leading symbol of the country's corrupt political past. The fact that the Indonesian parliament voted 393 to 4 to investigate allegations of corruption against Wahid in late January 2001 further indicates the pervasiveness of the problem of corruption and the desire to root it out. That the charges sparked a constitutional crisis between the president and the Parliament further demonstrated the fragility of political democracy in the post-Suharto political system. The fate of his successor, Megawati Sukrnoputri, a truly popular figure in much of the country, remains conjectural.

Where is Indonesia headed? Will the country make the successful transition to globalization and democracy, or will it sink back into autocracy and backwardness, a kind of island Myanmar (Burma)? What will the future mean for the centrifugal forces at play in parts of the country?

Indonesia may not face meaningful choices. Unless something dramatic occurs to change the direction of the global economy—an enormous worldwide depression, for instance—Indonesia may have no choice but to jump back on and ride the wave, especially since all of its neighbors in APEC and ASEAN remain essentially committed to globalization. Moreover, acceptance or resistance to Westernization is largely generational in Indonesia, as it is elsewhere. The young, well-educated professionals—the globalutionaries—are committed to full participation in the world order. While their success is not preordained, time is probably on their side.

There is, of course, the matter of Indonesia's special problem, the centrifugal force of areas like East Timor, Aceh, Borneo, and Irian Jaya. The real problem in these diverse areas is, and has been, the treatment the people of these areas have received from the central government in Jakarta, and especially from the military. Whether separatism will continue to mount or wither is probably a matter of the success or failure of reform. Would a truly democratic central government, for instance, have permitted the brutal suppression of the East Timorese by government forces? In a prosperous, open Indonesia, would Acehnese demands for a more equitable distribution of government resources and firmer guarantees of religious freedom not receive a more sympathetic hearing? Would a return to the growing prosperity of the early 1990s heal some of the wounds and moderate some of the centrifugal forces in the country?

Like other countries in the region, Indonesia suffered significantly from the East Asian financial crisis of 1997, and the country continues to strain under the restrictions placed upon it by the international community, which are designed to reform and strengthen the Indonesian economy. Given the trauma the country has undergone, it should not be surprising that at least some Indonesians are reluctant to jump unconditionally back into the globalization system. On the other hand, many Indonesians believe strongly that the country's problem was that it adopted only part of the globalization system before, providing a veneer that obscured the ugly innards of a highly secretive, corrupt system that ultimately undermined the globalization effort. Whether the *reformasi* or the globalizers will prevail in the unfolding debate over the participation of the world's fourth most populous state remains to be seen. The outcome is, of course, important for Indonesia and its large, strategically located population. But it could prove important in a broader context as well. Within the region are the two most populous countries in the world, and each faces deep divisions of their own. Will the fate of Indonesia presage the future for other countries like China, India, and possibly others?

🌐 STUDY/DISCUSSION QUESTIONS

1. Why is Indonesia an important country to study in terms of its transition to the globalization system? How will the outcome of the Indonesian experience affect its region and beyond?

2. The East Asian financial crisis of 1997 had an enormous impact on Indonesia and its region. How was Indonesia in particular affected economically, politically, and geopolitically?

3. One of the effects of the 1997 crisis was to cause a serious collapse of the Indonesian economy and a subsequent debate over the future of Indonesia's participation in the global economy. What are the major arguments in that debate? Who holds which positions? How do they differ?

4. The 1997 financial crisis contributed to the political crisis of 1998 that brought Suharto down. How were politics and economics connected in the crisis? What is the relationship between politics and economics in the globalization process more generally, and how does this affect the future of Indonesia?

5. At least partly because it is a far-flung archipelago, Indonesia has a number of centrifugal forces that are unique to it. What are the sources of separatism, and what can the Indonesian government do to dampen these tendencies?

6. Based on the information provided, draw two distinct futures for Indonesia on the three dimensions discussed, one negative and one positive. Which future do you prefer? Which one do you think Indonesia will follow? Why?

READING/RESEARCH MATERIAL

Bilveer, Singh. "Civil-Military Relations in Democratizing Indonesia: Change Amidst Continuity." *Armed Forces and Society* 20, 4 (Summer 2000), 607–33.

Emmerson, Donald K. "Will Indonesia Survive?" *Foreign Affairs* 79, 3 (Summer 2000), 95–106.

Friedman, Thomas L. *The Lexus and the Olive Tree: Understanding Globalization.* New York: Farrar, Straus, Giroux, 1999.

Menon, Rajan. "Another Year of Living Dangerously?" *National Interest,* Fall 2001, 101–115.

Pei, Minxin. "Will China Become Another Indonesia?" *Foreign Policy,* 116 (Fall 1999), 94–109.

Ravich, Samantha. "Eyeing Indonesia Through the Lens of Aceh." *Washington Quarterly* 23, 3 (Summer 2000), 7–20.

Smith, Patrick. "What Does It Mean to Be Modern? Indonesia's *Reformasi.*" *Washington Quarterly* 22, 4 (Autumn 1999), 47–64.

WEB SITES

Extensive profile prepared by the Federal Research Division of the Library of Congress
Indonesia - A Country Study at http://memory.loc.gov/frd/cs/idtoc.html

Provides basic information on Indonesia and the country's foreign affairs
Department of Foreign Affairs of the Republic of Indonesia at
http://www.dfa-deplu.go.id

Features overview of human rights developments in and current news releases on Indonesia as well as East Timor

Human Rights Watch: Asia at http://www.hrw.org/asia/index.php

Peacekeeping operation administering the territory and exercising legislative and executive authority during East Timor's transition to independence

United Nations Transitional Administration in East Timor (UNTAET) at http://www.un.org/peace/etimor/etimor.htm

PART 4

The Altered Face of Security

Along with globalization, some of the most dramatic changes in the post–Cold War environment have occurred in the areas of national and international security. The Cold War security system was overshadowed by the prospect of nuclear war between the superpowers, a cataclysmic possibility before which other problems paled in comparison. Certainly, there was no shortage of other problems, it was just that they were subordinate to avoiding a possibly nuclear World War III.

Although a nuclear inferno is still a physical possibility, it is now considered far less likely to occur. This has allowed consideration both of some old problems that existed before the end of the Cold War but which received less concern then, and also some matters that have arisen since the Cold War ended. Much of the change is connected to technological possibilities that did not exist before, which have simultaneously made traditional war less likely but more deadly should it occur.

The cases selected for this part of the book reflect this continuity and change. Chapter 10, "Future War," looks broadly at what warfare may look like in the future and how well our anticipation of the future of war in the past century affects our confidence about judging the shape of war in a new century. A good deal of the emphasis is on how the modern technology of warfare, which is known as the revolution in military affairs (RMA), opens new possibilities but may make our ability to predict the outcome of war more difficult.

The other two cases deal with problems that have their sources before the end of the Cold War. National missile defense, the subject of Chapter 11, "When National and International Politics Collide," is a possibility that first appeared in the 1960s, reappeared in the 1980s, and forms one of the major emphases of the Bush presidency in the new century. The case focuses on the evolution of this policy thrust, but with the added concern that the American policy initiative to build a defense system is fundamentally opposed by nearly all the major powers, creating a tension about which priorities are best served in this area.

Chapter 12, "Who Cares about Kashmir?" examines a basic problem of Indo-Pakistani relations that dates back to the partition of the Indian subcontinent in 1948. The princely states of Jammu and Kashmir have been points of contention ever since, but now the problem has been made more dangerous by the addition of the "new teeth" of nuclear weapons on each side. The case looks at how this new "variable" may affect Kashmir in the future.

CHAPTER TEN

Future War:
THE SHAPE OF CONFLICT IN A NEW MILLENNIUM

PRÉCIS

Anticipating the nature of possible future conflict and preparing for that form of combat has always been a primary responsibility of those charged with the responsibility for national and international security. Those who prepare adequately for the future face of war may dissuade those contemplating war against them of the futility of their quest; if they fail in that goal, they may prevail because of their superior preparation. Those who prepare less well may be forced to accept the consequences.

The difficulty of conceptualizing and preparing for future war is the central theme of this case. It is presented in a comparative fashion. The first part of the case deals with the preparation for what became World War II during the two decades after World War I, the interwar years. The central message is that the preparations that were undertaken were clearly inadequate to persuade the Axis not to proceed with the war and that the applications of technology during the planning period did not optimize what might have been done in the war. The second part of the case extrapolates the interwar experience to the present as the basis for comparison. While noting that the conflict environment of today is quite different in that there are no likely scenarios for general war in the foreseeable future, there are great questions about the military applications of technology, the relative balances or imbalances of military power in the world, and the likely faces of future war, particularly in light of the events triggered by the terrorist attacks of September 11, 2001.

Anticipating and preparing for the next war is an age-old problem that has concerned politically organized entities throughout history. Whether states or other political organizations thought about the problem as a means to plan to attack or to defend, knowing who one's enemies are and how they are likely to provide a menace can mean the difference between victory and defeat, even survival or destruction. Understanding the threats present in the environment and acting appropriately to defuse them can also lead to the avoidance of war, clearly the best outcome. For Americans, the events of September 2001 make the imperatives to predict accurately what enemies might do all the more compelling than before.

Why political groups prepare for war will not concern us directly in this case study. Certainly, why one prepares does have a bearing; preparations to deter attack or to defend are different from preparations to act aggressively, although that distinction may or may not have significant meaning for a potential adversary. But regardless of motivations, there are hardly any societies that have not felt the need to address the problem posed by future threats.

It is, and always has been, a difficult problem. The characteristics of future wars must be based on projections into a period of time that does not yet exist and which, by definition, we cannot know entirely in advance. Will the same kinds of weapons be available in the future as there were in the past? If there are new weapons, what will they be like, how will they be used, and what will be their effect? Who will have the new weapons, and will they use them to their maximum effect? For that matter, who will the enemy be? Where will we have to fight the next adversary?

These technical questions take place, and gain meaning, in a political context where the avoidance of war is a major value and *who* one might fight is as important as *how* one might engage a future enemy. The debate about whether preparing for future war makes that bloodletting more or less likely is a perpetual question about which we will make comments. At the same time, properly identifying potential adversaries has a major bearing in the quality of anticipation.

Since we cannot know the precise answers to any of these questions in advance, the result is a condition of uncertainty that becomes a major part of the operational universe of the military planner. These uncertainties produce an environment laced as well with an aura of conservatism and seriousness. It is conservative because reckless innovation and lack of preparedness can lead to vulnerability that can have potentially devastating consequences. It is serious because the wrong decisions—the failure to prepare properly or adequately—can literally endanger national existence. Because of these potential consequences, there is a built-in propensity to overprepare—to anticipate more threats than realistically exist. In turn, this preparation can exacerbate relations with potential rivals who may see even defensive preparations as threatening, a phenomenon known as the *security dilemma*.

Despite the apparently benign environment during the 1990s (and in some sense, because of the tranquility) that was shattered in 2001, the problem of gauging the future of war is especially acute today. There are some clear reasons why many states are grappling very seriously with the future. For one thing, the period that marked the Cold War also marked the "long peace" of the second half of the twentieth century. Since much of the preparation that states undertake in planning for war is an extrapolation of their most recent experience, that means our useful experience, at least in the desperation of a major war that threatens national existence and thus forms what is known as the "worst case," is now over a half-century old. What is the continuing relevance of the most recent experience to the future?

It depends. One of the most important aspects of preparing for future war is anticipating against whom one is likely to have to fight. Although many Americans sought to ignore the warning signs during the 1930s, it was pretty clear that World War II would find the United States on one side and countries like Germany and Japan on the other (at least retrospect suggests that structure of the conflict). During the Cold War, it was absolutely clear that the enemy against whom we had to prepare was the Soviet Union and its communist allies. The structure of the system dictated the content of the planning process.

Not all planning has such a clear focus. In August 1990, Iraq invaded and quickly conquered Kuwait. This act of aggression would ultimately bring together a coalition of over 25 states, none of whom had given much if any thought to the possibility of war with Iraq as little as a few months before the invasion occurred. The lesson was that some problems can be easily anticipated; others cannot. The completely unanticipated terrorist attacks of September 11, 2001 (see Chapter 16) redouble the point.

There is another factor that influences the process today that was a lesser concern in the past: technological change. In the historical past, warfare did not change greatly. As chroniclers of war like the Brodies have suggested, with the exception of an occasional innovation like the catapult or gunpowder, warfare during much of the second millennium did not change a great deal, and most of the changes were gradual and incremental rather than revolutionary and dramatic. Once in a while, a traditional enemy might fashion some new weapon—such as the crossbow—that would make accepted ways of conducting war dangerous or suicidal. At the same time, an outsider might present a military problem with which a society had no idea how to cope—the massed mounted cavalry of Genghis Khan's Golden Horde, for instance. But generally the problem of physical preparation remained relatively the same.

The Industrial Revolution and its adaptation to warfare in the nineteenth century accelerated the impact of technology, and its impact has grown steadily ever since. Our twentieth-century past involved applying inventions like the internal combustion engine to warfare. The twenty-first century looks at a battlefield environment more reminiscent of science fiction motion pictures than of past warfare. New and deadly possibilities like chemical and biological agents applied to war add further to the uncertainty of a future where tomorrow's enemies, like the Iraqis in 1990, are more difficult to anticipate.

All of the past millennium was dominated by a style and philosophy of warfare that was heavily Western and which culminated in the way World War II was fought. Since early in the post–Cold War world, a band of analysts has argued that warfare is changing fundamentally from the confrontation and clash of mass armies to a more asymmetrical form in which weaker foes seek to negate Western styles with Asiatic variants on war. This "fourth generation" of warfare was displayed dramatically for the first time in recent memory on American soil on September 11, 2001.

Thus, the problem of preparing for future war boils down to two basic considerations. The first is the *conflict environment,* and the main factor in that environment is the nature of the adversaries one may encounter in the future, including why and how one may have to fight them. As we shall see, this determination is particularly difficult in the contemporary environment, in which traditional rivalries are muted and the dangers of conflict have moved to the international periphery. The second consideration is the *physical structure of warfare,* which consists of the means available for adversaries to fight one another and the degree to which the means available are appropriately adapted to achieve military ends. The third concern is determining against whom one might have to fight in a major power environment that was remarkably tranquil for over a decade and which has not witnessed a major war in over a half century. The factors are, of course, related to one another, since different adversaries will have different purposes and come equipped with different means and different motives.

These observations form the rationale for the rest of this chapter. In the following pages, we will examine the problem of preparing for future war through two "mini-cases." The first will be historical, and deals with how planners in the 1930s prepared for the likelihood of a second major war in the first half of the twentieth century. Looking at the three basic categories of concern, the conflict environment was, or could have been, fairly clear, but the physical structure of conflict was not. While some argued that war with the Soviets was more likely than war with Germany or Japan and others felt it could be avoided altogether, the combatants were basically locked in by the latter part of the 1930s. Although the last major war was only 20 years in the past, the planners had to grapple with adapting to a number of weapons—tanks, for instance—that were introduced during the Great War (as World War I was known at the time) but not used to maximum effect, and to a number of uniquely new technologies adapted for military use—ultimately atomic weapons. This examination will set the foundation for the second mini-case, the present.

Planning for the wars of the twenty-first century is more difficult because there is a great deal of uncertainty regarding who to prepare to fight and how to prepare to fight them. There are no obvious major adversaries, due in large measure to the ideological harmony among the major powers in the international system that is noted in other cases as well. The long gap between major wars has allowed the accumulation of a large number of militarily relevant technologies that are untested in major wars. Some of the electronically based innovations have been employed in "shooting galleries" like the Persian Gulf War and Operation Allied Force against Yugoslavia in 1999, but none have been employed against a major opponent who could effectively defend against them. As we shall see, it is possible that the physical structure of future warfare will resemble these conflicts, in which case they are instructive. It is also possible that future instances will be sufficiently different that the uses will prove atypical. Moreover, the spread—or potential proliferation—of weapons of mass destruction (WMD) such as nuclear, biological, and chemical (NBC) weapons to otherwise weak potential adversaries adds to the uncertainty.

PLANNING TWENTIETH-CENTURY STYLE: ANTICIPATING WORLD WAR II

Imagine the world from the viewpoint of a military planner in 1919, shortly after the end of World War I. The bloodiest military conflict in human history to that point had just been concluded. It had been a war that had been poorly anticipated; as late as the early 1910s, there was still the widespread belief that economic interdependence had rendered war between the major powers functionally impossible or at least highly unlikely. Although there were some who decried the fact that major war had been absent from Europe for over 40 years, there was little belief that there were any differences worth fighting over.

The war had started almost accidentally; the assassination of Archduke Franz Ferdinand of Austria and his wife by Bosnian Serb terrorists activated a string of alliance commitments that brought the major combatants into confrontation. As the crisis grew, little was done to defuse it. Some attribute that failure to mediocre leadership in the major capitals (see Stoessinger). There was even positive sentiment for war, based on the belief that European youth had gone soft in the interim since the last large European conflict, the Franco-Prussian War of 1870. A war, so the argument went, would infuse Europe with a reinvigorating discipline and sense of national duty and sacrifice.

The greatest tragedy was that Europe had so poorly anticipated the kind of war that it was going to get. From warfare in the nineteenth and early twentieth centuries, there were two models available about what war in the future would be. One model was that of the Franco-Prussian War, where lightning strikes by offensively oriented armies led to rapid and decisive warfare. The Franco-Prussian War lasted only a little over six weeks before the French surrender to Germany, and losses on both sides were minimal by contemporary standards.

The other model combined the experiences of the American Civil War and the Russo-Japanese War of 1904–1905. Both these wars, conducted 40 years apart, were extremely hard fought and costly in terms of casualties, and both featured the increasing dominance of defensive tactics over offense. Indeed, at Petersburg, Virginia, in the winter of 1864–1865, and in the Asian battlefields of the Russo-Japanese War, the first examples of trench warfare, which would ultimately become the grisly symbol of World War I, were seen.

The planners had these models to choose from, and they chose wrong. They dismissed the American Civil War, which one German observer described at the time as "two armed mobs chasing one another around the country, from which nothing can be learned." It was a war between amateurs and hence unlike a war to be fought among the professional armies of Europe. The Russo-Japanese precedent was similarly dismissed because the combatants were either Asian or Eurasian, and hence inferior to European troops.

Preparations and predictions reflected the belief that the war would be short and decisive. In the wake of defeat in the Franco-Prussian War, French General Ferdinand Foch developed the strategy of *offensive a outrance* (offensive to the extreme) as the guiding principle of the French military. In Imperial Germany, Count Alfred von Schlieffen, chief of the general staff, devised a plan for a rapid "right hook" through the Low Countries that would roll up the French forces in a manner not dissimilar to 1870. In Berlin, the Kaiser exhorted troops leaving for war in the summer of 1914 that they would be back before the first leaves fell from the trees in the fall. Everyone anticipated a short, decisive, and relatively bloodless reprise of the Franco-Prussian War.

All of these projections were, of course, erroneous, and planners looking at the scene in 1919 could only shake their heads at the wreckage and begin to plan for the future, hopefully fashioning a system that would prevent a future war or, failing in that, assuring that the conduct and outcome would be very different than what they could survey from the last war. That meant examining the likely environment in the future and the physical structure of the next war.

Largely lost in the bitterness surrounding the environment in 1919 was rebuilding a durable peace that would make a repeat unlikely. In retrospect, World War I had been avoidable if the combatants had tried to avoid it, but they did not. Woodrow Wilson had sought a durable peace through the League of Nations, but U.S. Senate rejection of the peace treaty and vindictive, bitter sentiments in Europe and elsewhere pushed war avoidance to the back burner.

Conflict Environment

The conflict environment facing military planners and political leaders in 1919 bore both similarities to and differences from the prewar environment. The map, for instance, had changed somewhat, but the major players were still intact. The Austro-Hungarian and Ottoman Empires had disappeared, and the Russian Empire had been refashioned as the Soviet Union. Germany was disarmed and had contrition forced upon it by the terms of the peace treaty, but would rise again in the 1930s to the status of a great power. France and Great Britain were physically and financially exhausted by the war, and sought to retreat from major commitments and recover. In the Pacific, Imperial Japan was showing signs of the militarism that would lead to its imperial expansion and the road to war in the Pacific. The United States, of course, was in the process of its retreat into "splendid isolationism."

The geopolitical environment was not entirely unlike the prewar environment. Germany was prostrate and held down by provisions of the Versailles Treaty officially ending the war, but Franco-German animosity remained, and the geopolitical question that had dominated Europe since the Napoleonic Wars—which country would dominate the continent—had clearly not been permanently resolved. The major innovation in the system was the new League of Nations, the twentieth century's first attempt at organizing the peace around an international organization.

Although it is easier to make projections with the assistance of "20/20 hindsight," the geopolitical environment in which conflict might emerge had to be basically familiar to planners in 1919. One might or might not have been able to project with precision what country or countries one might have to fight sometime in the future, but the next war was likely to be between the major European states fighting in familiar ways. Force planning, in other words, was likely to be an extrapolation from the geopolitical past rather than any major deviation from that past. It may have been more difficult to anticipate the growing rivalry between the United States and Japan over the Pacific region, although some historians have argued that war between the two countries was probably made inevitable by American colonization of the Philippines in 1898, since the Philippines archipelago was a clear barrier standing in the way of Japanese expansion in East Asia.

Physical Structure of Warfare

World War I had been a technologically interesting event, as a number of new weapons based on technologies developed in the years leading to the conflict were introduced to the battlefield. As is so often the case, the new technologies were often not employed in the most effective way that they could be, nor were they employed in support of warfare as they would be in the future. For military planners in the years between the world wars, the task was to assess these innovations and how they might be better utilized in a future war. Most tragically, planners did not anticipate the greater lethality of the new technologies and the quantum leap in carnage they would produce.

Although it risks some oversimplification, there were two categories of innovation introduced between 1914 and 1918. One of these was in firepower, and it was represented by two kinds of weapons in land warfare. World War I, for instance, introduced rapid-fire weapons to the battlefield. Modern military rifles of the kind issued to average soldiers could fire up to 20 bullets per minute, an enormous increase over older weapons that could fire only a few shots in that period. More dramatically, the first reliable machine guns were introduced; they could fire as many as 200 to 400 rounds per minute. These weapons were, however, heavy; the machine gun and its mount weighed about 100 pounds, meaning it had to be placed in a stationary position, generally with entrenchment or some other form of protection for the machine gunner. The other innovation was improvement in heavy artillery. The artillery pieces employed in World War I could fire large shells over long distances at the rate of 6 to 10 shots per minute. As the name implies, their weight made them largely immobile, and the result was that large-scale artillery exchanges took place as each side tried to silence the other's big guns.

The tactics associated with the war did not adequately compensate for this change in firepower. The offensive orientation that both sides had adopted before the war put them on the attack as the doctrinally proper way to fight. When the trench lines hardened (and were aided by other innovations such as razor-sharp concertina wire), attacks against these rapid-fire weapons systems were nothing short of suicidal. Planners of strategies like the *offensive a outrance,* however, remained wedded to their ideas, and sent wave after wave of increasingly cynical, disillusioned young men to their deaths at the hands of the machine gunners.

The other innovation was in transportation, inspired by the invention and application of the internal combustion engine and the storage battery to warfare. The internal combustion engine produced three vehicles of war: the truck, the tank, and the heavier than air airplane. The battery made the submarine possible. Each changed the nature of warfare, although with different effects.

The truck served two functions. First, it provided a way to transport troops and supplies to the battlefield. It increased military flexibility, because trucks could go anywhere there were roads. In the setting of the trenches that stretched unbroken from the Alps to the North Sea, trucks could move personnel and materiel to weak spots in the trench line—in other words, to reinforce the advantage of the defense even further.

The British first introduced the tank into the war in 1916. Its promise was as a weapon system that could smash through German trenches and open spaces through which troops could advance, thereby breaking the deadlock and recreating movement on the front. The tank did not, however, fulfill its promise in World War I. The early tanks were very slow, leaving them vulnerable to artillery fire, and their treads often came off, leaving them immobile sitting ducks. But even with their weaknesses, tanks were the centerpiece of Plan 1919, a strategy devised by the British general J.F.C. Fuller to spearhead a breakthrough against the Germans in 1919. The plan was never implemented because the war ended in 1918.

The internal combustion engine also made feasible flight by heavier than air flying machines. The airplane was introduced into the war with little advance indication of what its role would be. The first air warriors were used initially as observers, flying over enemy positions and performing reconnaissance missions. Gradually, airplanes became engaged in air-to-air combat and some limited bombing, but their impact on the war's outcome was minimal.

Finally, the storage battery made the submarine a plausible naval weapon. The submarine's major purpose was attacking shipping across the Atlantic, and especially between the United States and the Western Allies. Fortunately for the Allies, the Germans manufactured relatively few U-boats, because the Kaiser was discouraged from putting his resources into so-called "commerce raiders" by the writings of American naval strategist Alfred Thayer Mahan. Instead, the Germans concentrated on building large battleships (as Mahan suggested they should), the largest of which were the dreadnaughts, which remained bottled up in North Sea, while the submarines were able to slip through the British naval net and wreak havoc on Allied shipping.

Interwar Planning

Each of these innovations underwent reevaluation during the interwar years and, with revisions of hardware and tactics, became part of the backbone of the military machines that prepared for and fought World War II. In the case of each technology, there would be some disagreement about what those roles would be, and only the crucible of war itself would validate some ideas and invalidate others.

Military planning incorporating the new technologies affected all three locations in which warfare could take place: on land, in and under the water, and in the air. Land warfare, especially as it would be applied again in Europe, came to reemphasize the offense in warfare through mobility. The fruits of the internal combustion engine led the way, as tanks, armored personnel carriers, and the like became the spearheads of land campaigns, with infantry acting in a supportive role to armor, rather than the other way around, as had been the case in World War I. At the same time, rapid-fire weapons developed further, so the average infantryman could carry a semiautomatic machine gun into battle rather than having to mount it in an entrenched position. The idea of the defense did not disappear; the Maginot Line, the single deadly flaw of which being that it did not extend all the way to the North Sea, was testimony to the legacy of the first war.

Some of these developments were anticipated in World War I. The German general Oskar von Hutier experimented with highly mobile special forces that infiltrated Western trench lines by avoiding the most heavily defended areas and attacking isolated places instead. Fuller's Plan 1919 similarly relied on the mobility as well as punching power of tanks crashing through German trench lines. Neither development materially affected the outcome of the war in 1918. These ideas would, however, bear fruit in World War II.

Some countries anticipated these possibilities and planned for them better than others. The German general staff was at the forefront, developing principles of mobility and movement into what became known as *blitzkrieg* (lightning war). Other countries, notably France and Poland, continued to rely on mounted cavalry and gave inadequate attention to mechanization of the war machine. When war came, those who had failed to understand the change in warfare suffered the most. On the battlefield, the leaders who understood and accommodated these changes best were generals like the German Erwin Rommel and the American George S. Patton.

Naval warfare was transformed as well. Prior to World War II, naval warfare was typically between surface combatants, where the object was to attack and sink the opponent and where the largest and most heavily armed vessels normally prevailed. Certainly that had been the case in the First World War, where the largest battleships, the dreadnaughts, were the crown jewels of the world's navies.

Technological advancements also rendered battleships highly vulnerable and increasingly obsolete. The battery systems (and the internal combustion engine for providing propulsion on the surface and for recharging the batteries) that made submarines practical in the first war were improved considerably, and the torpedo-armed submarine became a long-range platform that could lurk beneath the surface and put the largest battleships at its mercy.

More fundamentally, the airplane transformed the way naval warfare would be fought in the second world conflagration. As early as the 1920s, air power enthusiasts like the American "Billy" Mitchell were arguing that airplanes could be used to attack and sink surface ships. When he demonstrated the feasibility of attacking a battleship by flying a bomber with its bomb bay open over a battleship and taking a picture of the vessel, the process of transformation was underway. In the years between the world wars, the centerpiece in naval warfare ceased being the battleship and became instead the aircraft carrier. In World War II, carrier-based aircraft became the principal weapons of naval warfare, with other ships relegated largely to the role of protecting the carrier from attack (a principle that remains largely intact today).

The enthusiasts of the airplane were amongst the most active and ambitious planners between the world wars. People like Mitchell, the Italian Guilio Douhet, and Great Britain's Hugh Trenchard led the way, arguing that the ability to attack from the air would ultimately make other forms of warfare obsolete. As part of what became known as the theory of strategic bombardment, they argued that in the future it would not be necessary to defeat an enemy's army or navy to attack the homeland; aircraft would simply fly over the battlefield and attack the enemy with impunity. When this idea was embellished with the notion of attacking so-called "vital centers" (targets which if destroyed would compromise the enemy's ability to make war, such as oil refineries), the air warrior's claims were complete.

The airmen's claims proved to be excessive, and the supremacy of air power remains a contentious issue. Air power eventually did reduce Germany's war industries to rubble, but the detractors counter that Germany had essentially lost the war anyway by the time bombing succeeded in destroying Germany's vital centers. In the Pacific, the atomic bombing of Hiroshima and Nagasaki by the U.S. Eighth Air Force relieved the United States of the need to launch a resisted invasion of the Japanese home islands, but at a terrible cost in civilian deaths.

The atomic attacks provide a vivid example of the other major controversy introduced by the air power theorists. Prior to the concentrated bombings of the enemy's homelands, the laws of war made it illegal to direct purposeful attacks on noncombatant civilians. Certainly those rules had been violated on occasion, but attacking the vital centers of military production inevitably entailed large civilian casualties, euphemistically referred to as "collateral damage" (objects inadvertently destroyed in the process of attacking a military target). The fire bombings of Tokyo by the Americans and Dresden by the British during the war are particularly vivid instances of this practice. It remains controversial to this day, as the reaction to the bombing of Belgrade, Yugoslavia, by NATO in 1999 to put pressure on the Milosevic regime to end its suppression of Albanian Kosovars indicated at the time.

Determining Opponents

The coalitions that would ultimately fight World War II did varying jobs of "sizing up" their potential opponents. The Japanese understood that their expansion would ultimately bring them face-to-face with the United States, but they underestimated the ultimate power the United States would bring to bear against them. Similarly, Hitler underestimated the task of subduing the Soviet Union. Had his hatred for Slavs been less consuming, he might have maintained an uneasy accommodation with the Soviets, in which case the war might have ended very differently. On the Allied side, none of the major powers prepared adequately for war, and when it came, they had to build up their capabilities, thereby almost certainly prolonging the fighting.

PLANNING TWENTY-FIRST CENTURY STYLE: ANTICIPATING FUTURE WARS

The process of anticipating and planning for war during the first half of the last century has a certain comfortableness and familiarity about it. For the most part, wars were fought for traditional reasons between traditional adversaries in basically familiar ways. The same basic coalitions, after all, fought both world wars in Europe, with only the war in the Pacific between the United States and Japan adding novelty to the cast of characters and motivations. The basic function of planning was the adaptation of new technology to its most efficient ends. The result was warfare that was bloodier and more destructive, but it was still warfare in the traditional sense.

Those conditions are not so clearly evident today. If we put ourselves in the shoes of a military planner in the year 2002, the continuities of the past are not clear. Both elements of the planning process, the conflict environment and the physical structure of warfare, have changed, and the composition of likely enemies to be deterred or, if necessary, fought, is nowhere near as certain.

The source of this change and lack of clarity, of course, was the end of the Cold War. Thinking about and planning for future war during the Cold War was very traditional, an extrapolation from the world wars with the conceptually complicating addition of nuclear weapons. The military rivalry between the United States and the Soviet Union had replaced Franco-German rivalry as the primary source of division in the world, and planning for how to deter or fight a war in which the contestants would be coalitions of the communist and noncommunist worlds was the central, concrete military reality with which one dealt. At that, most thinking was about massive clashes of highly mobile armies on the European plains, naval warfare in the North Atlantic, and air clashes over Europe. The only major planning uncertainty was when, how, and with what effect nuclear weapons might enter the fray.

And then the Soviet bloc collapsed. In the words of then Soviet political observer Georgi Arbatov to his American counterparts, "We have done a terrible thing to you. We have deprived you of an enemy." There could scarcely be a more devastating assertion for military planners whose job it is to identify and prepare for conflict with future enemies.

The result has been to advance uncertainty to hitherto unimaginable heights. Who is the enemy today against whom we must prepare? Who will provide military challenges in a decade that we must anticipate and deflect? Where are the major threats to our interests? Who will we fight, and how will we fight them? During the Cold War, all those questions had concrete answers around which some reasonable degree of consensus could be developed. In today's environment, none of the answers is obvious.

Conflict Environment

Traditional geopolitics has taken a beating since the end of the Cold War. Two politicomilitary alliances facing one another is the stuff of traditional calculation, but, as Arbatov points out, that basis has evaporated. The first victim of the end of the Cold War has been the operational environment for military planning, a structure of adversarial relationships that provides concrete military problems against which to prepare. At least among the major military members of the international system, that structure has utterly disappeared, replaced by a more amorphous, uncertain environment that features shadowy opponents like faceless terrorists.

In some ways, this is a considerable improvement over the past. It means that for now, at least, there is virtually no likelihood of major war between the most powerful countries of the world on the scale of the world wars, and made more potentially devastating by the addition of nuclear weapons in the arsenals of antagonists. Certainly the tools for such a war are still available, but it is difficult to conjure the circumstances that would ignite such a conflagration. There are a few places in the world, for instance the Indian subcontinent, where adversaries might become involved in a war of fairly large proportions (see Chapter 12, the case study on Kashmir), but none of those places would raise the distinct likelihood of drawing in other major actors on opposite sides and thus widening the conflict to anything like the scale of World War III (the major planning case of the Cold War). The only exceptions might be the Koreas and China-Taiwan, but those are fairly remote probabilities.

The other side of the equation is the entry of new and frightening agents of war such as chemical and biological weapons and new forms of warfare such as terrorism. The fear, against which planning is extremely difficult, is the proliferation of these capabilities and the adoption of these techniques by rogue states and shadowy non-state terrorist groups like Usama bin Laden's Al Qaeda. Attempts to extrapolate planning forms such as nuclear deterrence to these problems run afoul fears about the rationality of some states or groups who might possess WMDs or practice or condone terrorism.

While this lack of a structure of adversaries may make the world a safer, more congenial place for most purposes, it produces a nightmare for military planners, and when violence breaks out as it did on September 11, 2001, it becomes a terrifying nightmare for everyone. When one knows who the enemy is, planning is concrete. You know the military capabilities of your adversaries and how they would likely use them, and thus you can plan on what you must do to blunt the opponent. In the Cold War, for instance, the Soviet Union had an enormous army of tanks, and it was assumed that if war came, those tanks would lead the thrust into Western Europe. Knowing that, NATO placed considerable emphasis on anti-tank weaponry and tactics to deflect that attack. It is a process known as *threat-based planning,* and it is the most straightforward and easily understandable method to employ.

When there is no adversary, there is no adversary-based capability against which to prepare. In the United States during the 1990s, for instance, two alternatives emerged. One was to devise hypothetical scenarios that would stress American capabilities to the maximum extent (the so-called worst case) and then plan on how to reduce the problem to manageable size (the favorite scenario was a simultaneous North Korean invasion of South Korea and another Iraqi invasion of Kuwait). The other method was *capability-based planning,* devising and building forces based on technological capabilities rather than any known adversary capability (this planning approach was adopted by the U.S. Department of Defense in the 2001 *Quadrennial Defense Review).* The rationale is that the generally superior American technological base would thus produce an arsenal against which no future adversary could compete. Neither alternative planning method achieved widespread support, particularly since it is difficult to tie such planning to hard-to-grasp problems like biological or chemical weapons or terrorist attacks.

A major reason that warfare among the major powers is less likely than it has been in the past is the absence of major political reasons for the major powers to fight one another. As the case study on the democratic peace (Chapter 3) argued, one of the major trends in the post–Cold War international system has been the progressive democratization of the countries of the world. Certainly all the major states in the system—North America, the European Economic Area, Japan, the Antipodes—have full fledged democracies, and democracy has spread or is spreading to other areas as well—much of Latin America and Eastern Europe, and East Asia, to name the most prominent. Where democracy has yet to take hold, it remains the aspiration of growing parts of the world.

The result is a system of fairly uniform political ideology for much of the world. The old divisions between monarchism and democracy of the eighteenth and nineteenth centuries and between communism, fascism, and democracy in the twentieth century are simply not present to create political differences worth fighting about. This at least temporary "end of history" has resulted in an *international* level of tranquility probably not seen since the eighteenth century, when monarchism was the universal ideology of a European-dominated world system.

The result of shrinking ideological difference is not universal peace, but a restriction on where and with whom war is likely or possible. Among the major powers, force or its threat is simply meaningless as a means to wield power; the threat to attack France will not gain increased access for American foodstuffs or motion pictures to that country's markets, nor can Japan meaningfully threaten military reprisals against South Korea for building cheaper cars and in the process undercutting Japanese competitors.

The domestic tranquility is not shared fully by those countries and parts of the world that have been isolated from the growing global economic system. Almost all of Africa and a good deal of central and southern Asia are not part of the growing networks of economic association that increasingly define the global economy. As the material I developed in *When America Fights* has shown, most of the violence in the contemporary system is occurring in the poorest countries of the world, and especially in those parts of the world that are most divorced from the emerging global economy. Parts of the Islamic Middle East demonstrate the quality of violence that rejection of modernity can produce, although recent events in Afghanistan may be changing that exception to tranquility as well.

Most of that conflict is internal in nature. While they have not disappeared altogether, traditional interstate wars have not been an important part of the landscape of violence since the end of the Cold War (one can, of course, argue that they were not the major form that violence took during the Cold War either). Instead, most of the fighting and killing in the world is basically limited to conflict between factions within countries, and most of it occurs in the poorest states of the developing world. Its purpose may be the traditional goal of civil wars, political control of the system, but increasingly it is motivated by less noble reasons, such as the narcotics trade, control of precious physical resources, or other, more venal forms of criminality. Other problems like terrorism and the use of exotic weaponry like chemicals and agents of biological origin remain prospects rather than concrete matters.

How immutable are these trends? If chaotic civil conflict and terrorism are the dominant forms of violence in 2002, will they continue to be the most common, or even the only, forms war takes in the future? If there is little likelihood of a major interstate war between the advanced countries of the world, at what levels do major countries need to maintain armed forces? What must those forces be capable of doing? And against whom do counties prepare? What, in other words, will the future look like?

Physical Structure of Warfare

The literal answer to the question posed above is that we do not and cannot know exactly the answers to any of them. We know the future environment will be different, but how? Then U.S. Army Chief of Staff Gordon R. Sullivan, writing in 1995 with Anthony M. Coroalles, analogized the problem to "seeing the elephant," a phrase borrowed from the American Civil War (the idea was the initial exposure to combat from descriptions by others was like having an elephant described and then physically seen). Of the future, they write, "our elephant is the complexity, ambiguity, and uncertainty of tomorrow's battlefield. We are trying to see the elephant of the future. But trying to draw that metaphorical elephant, based only on the description of the future that we can glean from the trends we see shaping the world, is infinitely harder than drawing a real one. We don't know what we don't know; none of us has a clear view of what the elephant will look like this time around."

Future war—the shape of the battlefields of the future—is thus an uncertain prospect. One can extrapolate technological trends from events such as the Persian Gulf

War of 1990–1991 and see the future of war as an electronic arcade game. The generals sit at computer consoles with real-time images of the vast expanse of battlefields taken from satellites and projected on high definition television screens, make decisions and send precision-guided munitions to attack enemy positions. All the while, our own forces are safely protected out of range of the enemy's weapons. That may be the future of war, or how some wars will be fought. On the other hand, it may also be that future war is like present war, soldiers slogging through steaming jungles in pursuit of irregular guerrillas, where the terror of ambush is the ever-present reality. Or the future may be both of these possibilities.

If we cannot see the elephant with precision, we can make some reasonable projections, which is what military planning is all about in the real world. We can attempt to sketch the broad contours of the future by looking at likely situations where violence will occur and where international actors will have the opportunities to employ force if they choose to do so. The three aspects of the problem that we will explore are the prospect of warfare between opponents of greatly differing military capability (asymmetrical wars), unconventional situations where military solutions are either not clearly appropriate or only partially relevant (quasi-military situations), and internal conflicts where it is not clear that systemic interests are engaged or that international solutions are possible (new internal wars). What are notably missing from the projections are the traditional kinds of wars described in the opening section of the chapter.

Determining Opponents

Each of these cases project the possibility of war with a different kind of opponent—the third concern in planning. Asymmetrical warfare is the most "traditional" of the three, because it likely pits states—although with different levels of capability—against one another. Quasi-military situations involve attacks on states generally by non–state actors, whereas internal wars involve factions within a state. Each poses a different planning problem.

Asymmetrical War. The Persian Gulf War was the contemporary prototype of asymmetrical war. In that conflict, the Iraqi military was totally overmatched in every conceivable manner by the coalition of states that confronted it, but most completely by the leading Western powers, and particularly the United States. In many ways one could almost argue that the contest was not militarily fair and, on the part of the coalition, it was never intended to be. In the years leading to Operation Desert Storm (the American code name for the operation), there had been a concerted effort not only to increase the deadliness and effectiveness of the arsenals of the world's most advanced militaries, but also to protect them from harm from their enemies. The war over Kuwait saw those capabilities reach fruition for the first time.

Although the *structure* of the war was symmetrical (Iraq's forces were organized along Western lines), the *capabilities* of the two sides were clearly unequal (asymmetrical). This gap in military capability between the most powerful states and the rest means that those with relatively modest military means have no realistic chance against the mightiest states when they bring their total strength to bear and the weaker states have not devised effective ways to nullify the advantages they possess. While that has always been true in the world, its effect is all the more dramatic in a system where the most powerful will hardly ever confront one another but where the powerful and the weak may do so from time to time, as they did over Kuwait. Instead, those facing superior Western forces have been forced to adopt asymmetrical *means* to avoid the meat grinder of Western forces.

The world got a second look at this same kind of phenomenon in Operation Allied Force, the air campaign waged against Yugoslavia by NATO for the purpose of trying to influence the Milosevic government in Belgrade to cease its campaign of so-called ethnic cleansing against the Albanian majority in the province of Kosovo. That campaign, almost three-quarters of which was carried out by American air forces, was waged largely out of range of Yugoslavia's air defenses, and the result was that no NATO pilots died in the eleven weeks while the bombing went on. There is some residual disagreement about how effective the bombardment was either in destroying military targets or in forcing Yugoslav compliance with NATO political aims, but the purposes were achieved. There is disagreement is over whether it was the bombing or diplomatic pressure that convinced Yugoslavia to comply. On the other hand, when massive airpower was used against Taliban forces in Afghanistan in 2001, it apparently contributed significantly to the deterioration of the fighting will of those forces.

If the major powers are unlikely to clash with one another directly in the foreseeable future, then asymmetrical applications of force are the likely form that future war conducted by those powers will take. In one sense, the Iraq case is probably closer to the norm than Yugoslavia in the sense that most opportunities to administer force will likely take place in the developing world rather than in the developed world. The Balkans represent the one part of Europe with much violent potential, and about the only place in North America where one imagines violent conflict is that part of Mexico that is revolution-prone. At the same time, most potential developing world opponents are likely to possess smaller forces than did Iraq.

Moreover, this style of warfare is highly congruent with the stated doctrine of the largest of the military establishments, the United States. In what is sometimes call the Powell Doctrine (named after former Chairman of the U.S. Joint Chiefs of Staff and current U.S. Secretary of State Colin S. Powell), the message is captured by the phrase "overwhelming force." According to this preference, the United States should only employ its armed forces in situations where it is willing to use maximum force to accomplish its goals rapidly and with a minimum of risk and casualties to American forces. While the doctrine is not always enforced (it was not in Operation Allied Force, which was a very gradually escalating campaign the pace of which was opposed by the American armed forces as a violation of overwhelming force), it is always the American preference. If one assumes (which it is fair to do) American participation in international military adventures in the developing world, one can predict with some safety the likelihood of asymmetrical applications of force. The Afghanistan air campaign in 2001 reinforced the preference.

This may not seem sporting, but war seldom is an activity in which both sides attempt to "level the playing field." Those who possess technologically superior capabilities are going to use them to tilt the situation as much in their favor as they can; in a world of political democracies, a major reason for taking advantage of superiority will be to minimize casualties. That does not mean, however, that those with the superior technology will always or necessarily prevail. The enhanced technological capabilities are most effective against conventional forces fighting in conventional ways. The ability to take satellite images of enemy troop dispositions is easiest where there are masses of forces in an exposed position, such as a treeless desert; that same image is more difficult to obtain through a jungle canopy (although infrared sensing somewhat overcomes that problem).

Unless the technologically unsophisticated opponent is mentally deficient as well, that opponent is going to take contrary actions to negate the advantages of the technologically superior enemy. The application of technologically based overwhelming force works to greatest effect against massed formations of enemy troops, and one clear way to reduce the effect of superior firepower is through dispersal. A great deal of the developing world where violence is occurring consists of jungle or mountains (or both), thus providing a terrain amenable to effective counteraction to even the most sophisticated of technologies. This was one of the very clear military lessons of the American military involvement in the Vietnam War during the 1960s and 1970s, where U.S. technology was rendered less effective when the enemy applied strategies that minimized the advantages of the technology; it forms part of the asymmetrical approaches to warfare.

Quasi-Military Situations. A second set of circumstances where military force may be employed in the future is in quasi-military unconventional roles and missions. Some of these are outgrowths of the struggles between the haves and the have-nots within developing countries and finds vent in things like terrorist acts either within the society or against outsiders, with the objects normally being the major powers (the African embassy bombings against the United States in 1998 and, most dramatically, the attacks against New York and Washington in 2001). Others are extensions of the general decay of some of the failed states and often manifest themselves in activities such as criminality (the "war" over control of the diamond field in Sierra Leone, discussed in Chapter 14, is an example). Attempts to deal with the prospects of potential WMD attacks also fit into this category. What these phenomena share is that they are only semimilitary, even quasi-military, in content.

The Western, and specifically American, problem with Usama bin Laden illustrates the problem of terrorism. For a variety of reasons that he has publicly stated (see examples in Chapter 16), bin Laden blames the United States for a large number of the problems afflicting the Middle East and is consequently devoted to inflicting as much pain and suffering on the United States and Americans as he can through the commission of acts of terror committed by his followers and associates (many of whom were trained in camps in Afghanistan originally built by the American Central Intelligence Agency to train the Afghan resistance to Soviet occupation during the 1980s). Although bin Laden has staunchly denied any connection to terrorism, he is accused of authorizing and financing bombings of the American embassies in Dar es Salaam, Tanzania, and Nairobi, Kenya on August 7, 1998, the attack on the *USS Cole,* an American warship, in Yemen in 2000, and the events of September 11, 2001. Although events such as the embassy bombings are relatively infrequent, their prospect is an annoying security problem for people around a world that is relatively secure otherwise.

Is dealing with the Usama bin Ladens of this world a military problem? In the 1980s the United States "made war" on drugs, although many argued at the time that the analogy was flawed, implying as it did that the problem was indeed military in nature and thus something on which to make war. Is terrorism similarly military, and can the international system "make war" on terrorists? The answer is ambiguous. There are certainly aspects of dealing with terrorism that have a military cast, but there are also aspects that do not. Counterterrorist acts intended to punish terrorists (the cruise missile attacks against bin Laden's training camps in Afghanistan in 1998 and the military campaign of 2001 to topple the Taliban government) may employ military means, but dissuading terrorists from acting or penetrating and dismantling terrorist groups is not so clearly military. The problem of dealing with WMD is analogous: threats or acts of retaliation against biological or chemical attacks contain military aspects, but it is not clear that stemming the motives that lead states to acquire these capabilities is military.

The other problem is dealing with the criminalization of societies in states broadly described as failing. In the contemporary world, there is no better example than Colombia, where elements associated with the illicit narcotics industry have destabilized that country to the point of making Colombia a virtually lawless land. Worse yet, their criminalization appears to be spreading across the border and infecting neighboring countries like Venezuela. There is a danger of greater or lesser severity (because the phenomenon is fairly new, it is hard to gauge which) that effectively criminalized countries will also destabilize their neighbors. More or less predictable consequences include migration out of the country of those who can afford to do so and the dangers of living in a lawless society.

Internal Wars. The third kind of environment in which fighting will certainly occur is in the *new internal wars* of parts of the developing world. As already noted, these wars became a prominent part of the landscape of violence in the 1990s after the end of the Cold War, and their prevalence continues into the twenty-first century. They are the most numerous wars in the contemporary and probably future environments, and thus produce the most "opportunities" for the application of force by countries around the world, generally for the purpose of ending the violence. During the 1990s, major international efforts were made in places such as Somalia, Bosnia, Kosovo, and even East Timor, while similar outbreaks were ignored in places such as Rwanda and the Democratic Republic of Congo (the former Zaire).

There are several characteristics of these situations that make them problematic as sites for the application of force, especially by major powers. Many of these characteristics are shared by terrorist and other similar organizations. Six of these are worth mentioning in the current context.

First, they will always display dramatically the gaps in capability already termed asymmetrical warfare. Generally speaking, the protagonists in these civil strifes will be armed with little more than hand-carried weapons or light artillery, will be loosely organized militarily if they are organized at all (the participants will generally be "fighters" as opposed to trained "soldiers"), will engage in hit-and-run attacks and terror directed at the civilian population, and will not stand and fight against organized military units intervening to stop the killing. By contrast, intervening forces will be technologically sophisticated, firepower-intensive, and will emphasize high mobility and air power. Because the countries where these wars occur will often be equatorial or mountainous, many of the advantages of the technologically superior will, as noted, be of dubious advantage, and intervening forces will almost certainly have the avoidance of casualties as a primary mission objective.

Second, the decision to become involved in these situations will always be difficult for outside parties, because generally the potential peacemakers will have few if any concrete, geopolitical interests in the situation important enough automatically to justify intervention. In conventional parlance, the operative term is *vital interests* (situations or outcomes so injurious to the state's interests as to be intolerable and thus to justify action). Most of the time, such levels of interest are absent for the major powers in the developing world (a partial exception occurring when former colonial powers are involved), and the answer to the operational question, "How will my interests be affected by any possible outcome?" will be "not very much." This question is especially important in the United States, where involvement in internal wars (should the United States be the "world's policeman"?) was a major issue during the 2000 presidential election. Ending the sanctuary for terrorists in Afghanistan to reduce U.S. vulnerability to attack is an obvious exception where vital interests were clearly engaged.

Third, there is a growing consensus in the developed world that involvement must be relatively (if not entirely) bloodless to be tolerable. This idea, "war without death," was especially prominent during the NATO intervention in Yugoslavia, where particular attention was paid to ensuring that NATO pilots engaged in the bombing campaign were not shot down and killed. The absence of casualties has been a major factor in allied efforts in Bosnia and Kosovo as well. What it amounts to saying is that even if major interests are absent, the relative safety of forces committed makes that absence tolerable politically in potential intervening countries. Strategies that begin with the avoidance of casualties as a first requirement, of course, very severely limit the kinds and quality of military action that can be undertaken.

Fourth, the absence of major interests also dictates that interventions will be multilateral affairs, where coalitions of intervening states provide "burden sharing" by major actors and the problem of the "free rider" (the actor that does not participate in but benefits from an action) is avoided. Once again this is especially a problem for the United States, where there is considerable political opposition to these kinds of activities on the grounds that vital interests are not involved. If it appears that the United States is shouldering a disproportionate burden, the political ability to mount or sustain an operation may be compromised. The other side of this problem is that coalition actions are generally militarily inefficient and sometimes fraught with major operational problems. In the NATO Kosovo Force (KFOR) operation, for instance, all the national units reported to their home defense ministries before accepting orders from the mission command, and occasionally those orders were refused on grounds that might or might not have had much bearing on the situation itself.

Fifth, there will always be international pressures, generally under the rubric of something like *humanitarian interests,* to mount an effort to ease the situation. Whether it is the distended bellies of the starving children of Somalia, the concentration camp–like detainment centers in Bosnia, or the feckless refugees of Kosovo, these situations will always be marked by gut-wrenching scenes of human misery which are difficult to ignore and which trigger a strong inclination to respond in some manner to ease the suffering. This instinct is made all the stronger when the human suffering is recorded and disseminated by global television, as it often is.

Sixth, the outcomes of these missions are highly problematical. International involvement in the internal affairs of countries predates the post–Cold War period (UN interventions in Cyprus and the Belgian Congo during the 1960s, for instance), but those earlier instances did not produce a pattern or a "model" for how to drop in and stabilize these kinds of situations. If the goal of intervention is both to stop the fighting and reasonably assure peace and tranquility after the mission is completed, it can fairly be said that none of the instances of humanitarian intervention has unqualifiedly succeeded to this point. Some may, but none have. There is a suspicion, especially held within military establishments, that these kinds of operations are probably doomed to long-term failure, and thus should be avoided. If that assessment turns out to be correct, it will certainly compromise even further the likelihood that intervention in internal conflicts will constitute the wars of the future.

CONCLUSION

Planning for the wars of the future has always been a difficult business. During humanity's bloodiest century, the twentieth, the difficulty of seeing into the future and determining what kinds of wars to prepare for has clearly evolved greatly. As the first part of this case study demonstrated, the problem was arguably more linear in the first half of the century: the protagonists remained relatively constant, and the major problem was adapting the emerging weapons technologies to their most efficacious applications. Having said that, planning for World War II was not that much different than planning for World War I. Only the scale of violence escalated.

Planning for the future wars of the twenty-first century does not offer the same apparent continuities. The Cold War structure and military planning problem was familiar and represented the kind of continuity that World War II planners faced; the structure of who provided the opposition was the major difference. But the collapse of the communist world and the threat it presented has fundamentally altered the landscape of possible future violence. There are no concrete, compelling enemies (or even potential adversaries) that provide the grist for planning grounded in concrete problems. Instead, we face a shifting set of shadowy potential opponents, the nature of whom and the threats they pose being largely speculative and ever changing. Who will the next terrorists be, and where and why will they strike? Will they attack with exotic WMDs, and what can be done to prepare for that contingency? What kinds of weapons and strategies will we need to deal with primitive but dedicated, even fanatical, forces operating in hostile environments that may negate the advantages that technology has provided us with? *Should* we interfere in the fratricide that has become so common in so much of the developing world? The answers to these questions are not clear at all. What is clear, however, is that these are characteristics of the environment in which future war will occur. They all seem more compelling today than they did before September 11, 2001.

Having said all this, we return to a question raised in the beginning of the case. Is the process for planning for war itself a bellicose act that makes war more likely? Or should our focus be on the avoidance of war, examining how to avoid fighting rather than how and when we might fight? It is an interesting philosophical and moral question. From the viewpoint of the military planner that has been the primary perspective in this case study, the answer comes in the form of the rejoinder by Vegetius, circa 375 A.D.: "Let him who desires peace prepare for war." It is, of course, not the only perspective one might adopt.

🌐 STUDY/DISCUSSION QUESTIONS

1. The past case of military planning between the world wars and the current situation offers points of similarity and contrast. One of these is in the nature of planning; for the familiar in the 1930s, and the unfamiliar now. Discuss these similarities and differences. Which would be a more comfortable planning environment?

2. Put yourself in the position of being a military planner looking at weapons for the future based upon the experience of the past. What kinds of military capability would you like to have to deal with the universe you see 10 or 15 years in the future?

3. If you assume that most of the locations for future conflicts will be in those parts of the developing world between the Tropics of Cancer and Capricorn—terrain dominated by mountains, deserts, and jungles—how would you maximize advantageous asymmetries between the developed and developing world?

4. Should it be a major priority of the most advanced countries to involve themselves in trying to ameliorate internal violence in the developing world? If so, what kind of criteria should be adopted to guide involvements? If not, what should we prepare for?

5. Predict where and in what kind of conflict the United States is most likely to be engaged ten years from today.

READING/RESEARCH MATERIAL

Brodie, Bernard, and Fawn M. Brodie. *From Crossbow to H-Bomb: The Evolution of Weapons and Tactics on Warfare.* Bloomington: Indiana University Press, 1965.

Fukuyama, Francis. *The End of History and the Last Man.* New York: Free Press, 1992.

Johnsen, William T., et al. *The Principles of War in the 21st Century: Strategic Considerations.* Carlisle Barracks, PA: U.S. Army War College, 1995.

Lind, William S., et al. "The Changing Face of War: Into the Fourth Generation." *Marine Corps Gazette,* October 1989, 22–26.

Metz, Steven. *Strategic Horizons: The Military Implications of Alternative Futures.* Carlisle Barracks, PA: U.S. Army War College, 1997.

Scales, Maj. General Robert H. Jr. *Future War: Anthology.* Carlisle Barracks, PA: U.S. Army War College, 1999.

Snow, Donald M. *When America Fights: The Uses of U.S. Military Force.* Washington, DC: CQ Press, 2000.

———, and Dennis M. Drew. *From Lexington to Desert Storm and Beyond: War and Politics in the American Experience.* 2nd ed. Armonk, NY: M. E. Sharpe, 2001.

Stoessinger, John. *Why Nations Go to War.* 7th ed. New York: St. Martin's Press, 1997.

Sullivan, General Gordon R., and Anthony M. Coroalles. *Seeing the Elephant: Leading America's Army into the Twenty-First Century.* Boston: Institute for Foreign Policy Analysis, 1995.

Van Creveld, Martin. *The Transformation of War.* New York: Free Press, 1991.

WEB SITES

Research projects on national security issues conducted by RAND for divisions of the U.S. defense establishment

National Security: Research and Analysis at http://www.rand.org/natsec_area

Provides reports on future trends in terrorism as well as its sociological-psychological aspects

Federal Research Division: Terrorism Studies at http://www.loc.gov/rr/frd/terrorism.htm

Organization for the study of military strategy, arms control, regional security, and conflict resolution

The International Institute for Strategic Studies at http://www.iiss.org

Conducts research on questions of conflict and cooperation affecting international peace and security

Stockholm International Peace Institute at http://www.sipri.se

The Institute's Research Directorate analyzes emerging strategic and international trends that pose long-term challenges for national security

Institute for National Strategic Studies at http://www.ndu.edu/inss/insshp.html

Organization committed to independent research on the social, economic, environmental, political, and military components of global security

Center for Defense Information at http://www.cdi.org

CHAPTER ELEVEN

When National and International Politics Collide:

THE CASE OF MISSILE DEFENSE

PRÉCIS

The question of defenses against ballistic missiles is a recurring theme in international relations. The issue has tended to focus on the United States, which, because of its superior technological base, is the country most likely (or least unlikely, depending on your assessment of the prospects) to be able to field such a system, and on the status of American efforts to build such a system. Proposals to do so have been periodic, culminating in the advocacy of a national missile defense (NMD) by the current Bush administration.

The thrust of this case is twofold. It offers a comparison of the current NMD with previous American programs designed to protect the country from a missile attack. The analysis is theoretical (Is a missile defense desirable?), technological (Is a missile defense possible?), and historical (How do programs compare across time?). The case then takes a different tack by looking at the question as a transnational issue whereby the actions of one state (the United States) could adversely affect the actions of other states, possibly making the world less secure than it was before the program. This goal is accomplished by looking at the objections that a number of former American adversaries (notably China and Russia) and American allies have made to the proposed NMD proposal.

One of the more common scholarly and policy concerns during the Cold War era dealt with the question of the effects that national security decisions made by individual states or groups of states had on other—especially adversarial—states or on the international system as a whole. Much of the concern centered on armaments decisions that states made: What effects would fielding a particular kind or quantity of weapons systems have on friends, allies, or adversaries?

This problem was captured in a number of concepts that fell collectively into the analytical category of *arms racing*. While the literature on arms races is very extensive and complex and thus beyond our detailed consideration in this case study, two concepts—each developed specifically to describe aspects of arms racing in the Soviet-American nuclear relationship—capture the heart of this concern as it applies to a contemporary international issue.

The first concept is the *action-reaction phenomenon (ARP)*, a notion at the core of arms racing. The basic idea here is that a particular decision to deploy a weapons system (an action) will trigger a response by the adversary at whom it is aimed to counter the original action (the reaction), which in turn may trigger another reaction and so on. At the end of the process, either or both parties may or may not be better off in a security sense (in other words, they may not either be or feel more secure).

This leads to the second and related concept, the *security dilemma*. In this construct, a state may take an action to improve its own security that has the effect of making the object of the original action feel more insecure than before, forcing that state to take counteraction to restore that country's sense of security. In extreme cases, the net result can be to leave the initiator less secure than before the original action or, even worse, to leave the entire international system less secure than before the original action.

These kinds of concepts and problems largely disappeared from the public dialogue after the end of the Cold War. The military confrontation rapidly receded with the demise of half the competition. Especially in the area of nuclear weapons, questions of threats and insecurities became subdued, and virtually all countries radically reduced their defense spending in an apparently more benign security environment. The old concepts seemed archaic, a part of history.

These concerns may have been revived with the announced intention of the Bush administration to field a national missile defense (NMD) when the efficacy of a deployment is demonstrated (or even before such a demonstration). The decision, when or if it is made, will be the result of largely domestic political decisions about what strengthens U.S. security. This action will, however, almost certainly trigger a reaction from an international community virtually unanimous in its opposition to the American initiative. In some cases, the responses by states may be so strong as to raise the possible negative consequences of the security dilemma.

The international reaction to missile defenses resembles what are known as transstate issues in a political regard. International opposition to the prospects of missile defenses comes from a variety of concerns, such as their feasibility, cost, or, more importantly, their impact on the stability of the international system. There is, for instance, the fear that an American deployment of a missile shield would force China to expand its small nuclear missile force to be able to penetrate the American shield, thereby avoiding having the Chinese force left impotent (a classic action-reaction phenomenon with security dilemma ramifications). In turn, a Chinese expansion could have ripple effects elsewhere in Asia, with the net result that the international security system is left more unstable than would be the case in its absence.

The advocates of missile defense in the United States, on the other hand, focus almost completely on what they believe will be the salutary effects on the security of Americans provided by the planned ability to intercept small missile attacks by rogue states (now designated "states of concern" by the U.S. Department of State). The prospect of negative international, systemic effects of the unilateral American actions is either ignored or denied. The Bush administration, for instance, early on attempted to assure critics and skeptics that it could convince those countries—like Russia or China—that expressed concern about the destabilizing effects that they were wrong, and then spent a good deal of 2001 in an effort to do so.

In fact, the national missile defense issue may also fall broadly into a new category of transstate issues, what one analyst has called *transnational security issues* in a recent article. Citing examples such as transnational crime and terrorism and transnational migrations and even disease flows, this analyst generally defines his concept as "threats that cross borders and either threaten the political and social integrity of a nation (*sic*) or threaten that nation's inhabitants." A transstate launch of a terrorist missile (one of the problems that NMD is designed to negate) would clearly fall within the purview of such a problem. The same would be the case if a rogue state like Iraq were to obtain a few intercontinental-range missiles and target them on the American homeland.

The missile defense plan is hardly new. In the United States, an interest in developing and deploying a defensive system against attacks by nuclear-tipped (or, for that matter, nonnuclear) missiles delivered by its enemies is at least as old as the missile age itself. Before there had even been a successful test-firing of an intercontinental range missile, the theoretical problems of defending against such a missile had been solved; the only problem, which continues to plague similar efforts in the twenty-first century, is using that knowledge to create a functioning, effective missile defense system.

The intellectual and emotional lure of an antimissile capability is obvious. The ballistic missile, when it was introduced, was an *indefensible* weapon system. What that means is that there were not at the time, and still are not today, effective ways to avoid being destroyed by a ballistic missile launched against a target. The reason is the extraordinary speed at which ballistic missiles travel—the intercontinental varieties reach speeds of 15,000 miles or more per hour. The problem of intercepting and destroying a launched missile drew the analogy of "hitting a bullet with another bullet" (clearly a daunting task) from then-candidate John F. Kennedy in the 1960 presidential campaign. The *Berliner Morgenpost* newspaper (quoted in *World Press Review*) revived the analogy on July 12, 2000, asking "whether a system where a bullet must hit another bullet in flight can ever be made functional." The analogy, of course, suggests that missile defense is a nearly impossible task, an inference often intended by critics of the concept.

In the absence of reliable missile defenses, the only way to avoid being destroyed by missile attacks is to prevent those attacks from occurring in the first place. In the latter 1950s as missiles began entering the arsenals of the United States and the Soviet Union and later Great Britain, France, and to a much more modest degree China, this recognition created a lively interest in the idea of *deterrence*, which evolved to mean dissuading an adversary from attacking with nuclear-tipped missiles for fear of the consequences in retaliation. While the system of deterrence coincided with the absence of nuclear war (or other wars using missiles directed against the United States), the support for deterrence as the basis of national existence has always been tentative. The reason is that deterrence could fail, leaving us completely vulnerable, and thus there has always been sentiment to build a system that could protect the homeland even in the event of an attack from some foreign enemy.

Enthusiasm for missile defenses has never much extended beyond the United States. Part of the reason is technological: even if one doubts (as leaders around the world do) that missile defenses are possible, the United States is more likely to be able to develop them than any other country due to its scientific and technological base. Moreover, it is universally agreed that the development and deployment of a missile defense system would be terribly costly, probably beyond the practical means of any country but the United States. Missile defense, if it is possible, is a luxury only the Americans can obviously afford.

When the missile defense issue remains at the abstract level of American research and testing programs with no particular likelihood of deployment and no overt champion, the international community overlooks the American advantage. These opponents do not raise other objections to American unilateral deployment or what are viewed as paternalistic, probably insincere American offers to share the missile shield with others. At these times, missile defense remains almost exclusively a domestic political issue within the United States. The poles of that debate are, on one side, the irresponsibility of not trying to protect American citizens from attack by hostile states, and the impracticability and expense of a feckless enterprise on the other.

Whenever the United States has announced a decision to attempt to field one form of missile defense or another, the matter has quickly become an international issue as well as a domestic concern. The current NMD advocacy is the third time the issue has been raised, and each time it has followed a similar script. Thus, when the U.S. government continued testing of the national missile defense system in 2000 and announced that if testing was successful, that deployment could begin as early as 2003, the reaction was predictable. If anything, the collision of national and international concerns was intensified by the election to the presidency of Republican nominee George W. Bush, an ardent supporter of deploying the system.

International reactions were predictably negative, as they have been each time the United States has approached the threshold of a missile defense deployment. In many ways, the domestic and international debate of 2000 was little more than a replay of the 1960s and 1970s, when the U.S. government proposed and actually began to deploy a defensive system largely against the threat from a newly nuclear China. It resurfaced again in the debate over the Anti-ballistic Missile (ABM) Treaty of 1972 and regarding the Reagan Strategic Defense Initiative (SDI) in the 1980s. In each case, those favoring missile defense failed to carry the day, not so much because there was general international opposition, but because they could not demonstrate that the system could work or was worth the expense it entailed and because the opposition could raise the further objection that fielding the system would destabilize a deterrence system based in the provisions of the ABM Treaty, from which the United States announced its intention to withdraw in 2002.

The current controversy is the latest chapter in the national-international debate over missile defenses. While it shares a common lineage with the rounds of debate about previously proposed programs, it is different in at least two ways. The first and most obvious is that it occurs outside the context of the Cold War. The clear difference is the focus and rationale for defenses. The answer to "defenses against whom?" was easy to answer during the Cold War; it is neither easy nor obviously compelling now. The other difference is the larger, and more uniform, international opposition to the idea. During the Cold War, American allies could not openly complain about the idea of defense against a known, robust Soviet enemy (although they could complain about whether they would be included in the defenses or not). Freed of that tether, they can now raise more concerns about the systemic influence of missile defenses that they always held but were reluctant to articulate.

Thus, the nature of the national-international policy debate over missile defense has broadened since the last time it arose. The question is whether the generally negative tone of international reaction to the prospect of a U.S. missile defense system, which most see as an international-system destabilizing action propelled by domestic American politics, will affect the outcome more this time than before.

Answering that question will be the burden of the case. Because the current debate resembles others that precede it, we will begin by looking at the previous American missile defense initiatives and their outcomes, particularly in terms of the relative weight of domestic and international concerns. We will then move to the current debate, summarizing the American aspect and dwelling at some length on responses and criticisms from outside the United States. The relative weight of the two aspects of the debate will form the basis for some conclusions couched in concepts like the ARP and the security dilemma that NMD has helped to reintroduce into the international security environment.

MISSILE DEFENSE IN THE PAST: HISTORY AND PRECEDENTS

The issue of missile defenses has gone through three distinct phases, each of which reflected two major schools of thought and advocacy: a growth in missile defense technology that emboldened its champions and growing criticism among its detractors of those proposals domestically and internationally. The domestic criticism has not changed greatly over time. Centered around feasibility and cost and the effects of missile defenses on deterrence, it emerged in the 1960s and has remained so constant as hardly to constitute a variable. Indeed, one is struck by the fact that many of the same critics from the 1960s and 1970s are making the same arguments today.

What has changed is the gradual internationalization of the missile defense argument, which has intensified and spread over time to the point that the only states that openly support the idea are the United States and Israel, which faces a real potential threat of the kind NMD is supposed to solve and which expects to develop its own NMD based on the American system. A quick summary of two of the three historic phases of the debate, the Sentinel/ Safeguard proposal of the 1960s and the Strategic Defense Initiative of the

1980s, demonstrates this evolution and provides the context for understanding the relative place of the NMD proposal in the international and domestic political framework.

The Sentinel/Safeguard System

The spotted history of ballistic missile defense in the American political debate got its start in the middle 1960s in a manner strikingly similar to the circumstances surrounding the national missile defense debate in the new century. The stimulus was the threat posed by the incipient Chinese nuclear force, which caused the Johnson administration to propose to deploy a light missile defense of U.S. (and especially California) cities, an objective modified and eventually abandoned by the Nixon administration. Thus, Sentinel/Safeguard was a domestic political response to a potential international threat; when the system was cancelled in the middle 1970s, the reasons were almost exclusively domestic.

The impetus for Sentinel, the original system, must be seen in the context of the international politics of its day. At that point in time, the People's Republic of China was viewed as an intractable enemy of the United States, one with which the United States had had no formal diplomatic relations since the Chinese mainland fell to Mao Zedong and his communist supporters in 1949. In 1964, the Chinese had successfully obtained nuclear weapons capability and had begun a modest missile-testing program. In 1966, the Chinese had embarked on the highly militant Cultural Revolution, and Mao had even opined publicly that China—due to the size of its population—was the only country in the world that could survive a nuclear war. In addition, the PRC was an open supporter of North Vietnam in the war the United States was waging in Southeast Asia. China appeared to be, indeed, the "Yellow Peril," and an increasingly implacable and threatening power that deserved the attention of the American defense establishment.

Chinese international militancy and possession of nuclear weapons created pressure within Congress and the Joint Chiefs of Staff for an American missile defense response. It came in a speech by Secretary of Defense Robert S. McNamara in September 1967, in which he intoned, "There is evidence that the Chinese are devoting very substantial resources to the development of both nuclear warheads and missile delivery systems. Indications are they will have...an initial intercontinental ballistic missile capability in the early 1970s, and a modest force in the mid-70s."

On the basis of this assessment of what was a *potential future* threat, the Johnson administration announced in December 1967 its intention to erect a missile defense system it called Sentinel around major U.S. cities to protect them from the Chinese menace. When construction began, however, it met widespread public opposition, especially from the places where it was being deployed and that it was designed to protect (much of which was the result of the fact that interceptors themselves were nuclear weapons that no one wanted in their communities). Aside from the questions about the effectiveness of the system, which have always plagued missile defense proposals, there were objections that the defensive missiles might pose as much of a threat to the American population as the Chinese missiles. Moreover, it was argued that the sites in which the missiles were placed might themselves become targets, thus increasing the likelihood of such attacks.

These domestic pressures caused the Nixon administration quietly to dump the Sentinel program, replacing it with another light missile defense it called Safeguard. The major difference between Sentinel and Safeguard was where it would be located. Instead of stationing antimissile missiles around populated areas, Safeguard would be erected around intercontinental missile silos in remote areas far from urban areas. The strategic rationale for the deployment was that protecting missiles from attackers would mean more American forces would survive a nuclear attack and be available after such an attack to retaliate against the aggressor. In turn, the knowledge of that increased availability would contribute to deterrence by promising a more devastating retaliation. The practical political reason was that no voter's backyard would—figuratively, of course—be dug up to place a nuclear missile in it. There was ultimately one Safeguard site built and made operational in Grand Forks, North Dakota, in 1975. Because of "technical difficulties," the site was only active for a few months, after which it was quietly deactivated. The cost to taxpayers was about $5 billion.

The current proposed NMD system bears an eerie resemblance to Sentinel/Safeguard. The first and most obvious similarity is that both are responses to potential, rather than actual, threats to the United States. China posed no nuclear threat to the United States in 1967; it was presumed that they would in the near future. What may be instructive is that the estimates of the threat at the time proved to be gross overestimations of what in fact evolved. According to the prestigious International Institute of Strategic Studies (IISS) in London, the first Chinese nuclear missiles appeared in their arsenal in 1993 or 1994, when the PRC deployed about 14 ICBMs and 12 sea-launched ballistic missiles (SLBMs). The 1999 Chinese nuclear threat consists of 20 ICBMs and 12 SLBMs (the latter with a modest range of 2,150 miles, far out of range of the American homeland), according to IISS. In other words, the threat against which Safeguard/Sentinel was supposed to deal has not yet emerged more than a third of a century after the deployment decision was reached. Will the potential threat against which NMD is proposed be similar? In this case, domestic American politics drove the program from birth to death, and the parameters of the debate, the moral entreaty to protect citizens from a nuclear inferno versus whether a missile defense was feasible, are familiar in the current debate over NMD as well.

The domestic politics of missile defense affected and were affected by one major international factor, the negotiation and adoption in 1972 of the Anti-Ballistic Missile (ABM) Treaty as part of the Strategic Arms Limitation Talks (SALT) discussions between the United States and the Soviet Union. The Soviets have always been opposed to missile defenses, at least partially because they recognize their own technological base is inadequate to produce a workable system. While the Soviets were skeptical of the American ability to field an effective ABM in the 1970s, they did not want to encourage the American technological community to investigate the prospects and thus insisted on a very limited deployment in the treaty. Originally under the treaty, each side was allowed two sites: one around the national capital (Sentinel, in other words) and a second around a missile site at least 1,500 kilometers from the capital (Safeguard). When Sentinel was abandoned, an amendment to the treaty reduced the number of permissible deployments to a single site. Many argue that the ABM Treaty has become the bedrock of stable deterrence and that the NMD system would force the United States to withdraw from the treaty, sparking security dilemma concerns. The Bush Administration denies the importance of the ABM Treaty, with Secretary of Defense Donald Rumsfeld dismissing it as "ancient history," a sentiment echoed repeatedly by President Bush.

The Strategic Defense Initiative

Ronald Reagan's Strategic Defense Initiative (SDI) was announced as part of a March 1983 speech in which he declared his intention to develop a missile defense screen that would render nuclear-tipped missiles "impotent and obsolete" by providing a blanket defense against even the largest of attacks on the United States—specifically an all-out Soviet attack. Reagan reasoned that by denying the Soviets the ability to destroy the United States with its nuclear forces, such a defense would make the maintenance of such forces irrelevant and would eventually lead the Soviets to join in his ultimate goal, nuclear disarmament.

The Reagan proposal, which was quickly nicknamed "Star Wars" by a White House press corps reporter (much to the president's annoyance), was clearly more ambitious than Sentinel and Safeguard. Both of these were "thin" defenses, the purpose of which was to deflect a few warheads launched at the American homeland by China or some other state with a very small arsenal of weapons. The SDI proposed a very thick shield that was analogized to a geodesic dome or umbrella defense that could deflect or destroy a Soviet launch of 10–12,000 warheads in a concerted attack.

The SDI was both similar to and different from Sentinel/Safeguard. Its similarities included that it came from the same prodefense scientific and military community that had favored Sentinel/Safeguard (Reagan, as the governor of California, was an early enthusiastic supporter of the Sentinel protection of California cities from Chinese attack) and that it was produced with little regard to international reaction, which was overwhelmingly negative. Its differences included that it was a response to a concrete rather than a hypothetical threat and that it was conceptually and technologically much more ambitious than its predecessor.

The knotty problem of Star Wars was not its vision, but its realization. Sentinel and Safeguard were designed to deflect very small, "manageable" threats, and they both failed to accomplish their task (a major factor in their demise). The SDI, on the other hand, faced an enormously large and complicated mission. While relatively few could argue that the goal of SDI was not praiseworthy, how could technology produce a system that could deflect thousands of enemy missiles when the same technological base had failed to design one that could shoot down a handful?

The answer lay in a very complex, technologically sophisticated system known as a "layered" defense made theoretically possible by technological developments during the intervening decade. Laser battle stations in space would receive information of a Soviet attack from sensors and satellites in space and then attack and destroy rising missiles and their reentry vehicles, backed up by ground based interceptor antimissile missiles that would "mop up" whatever Soviet forces survived the defenses in space (a vision reintroduced by President George W. Bush as part of a potential NMD design). At one point, it was estimated that the computer program necessary to manage the system would be between 30 and 100 *million* lines long; estimates of cost ranged from $500 billion to $2 trillion over a ten-year deployment period. Ultimately, a combination of projected cost and suspicion that such a system could never be built successfully subverted the project.

International criticism was largely confined to the Soviet Union, and it changed over time. American allies complained that the system would protect the United States but not them (Reagan promised to extend the shield to the European allies), and some analysts worried that there could be destabilization of the nuclear balance while the system was being put in place (e.g., would the Soviets be tempted to destroy the system before it could be made operational and leave their forces "impotent and obsolete"?). Mostly, however, the Soviets provided the intellectual objections. Since these were within the Cold War framework, they tended to be confined to the propaganda level.

Soviet attitudes reflected the succession crisis going on within the Soviet Union during the heyday of the SDI. In 1983, that process had begun with the death of Leonid Brezhnev, and the successors to Stalin were giving way to the leadership of Mikhail S. Gorbachev. In the early years of SDI, the Soviets painted the defensive system in dire, confrontational tones, viewing it as a potential offensive, rather than defensive system (the analogy with the "Death Star" of the 1980s *Star Wars* movies was often drawn). After Mikhail S. Gorbachev came to power, and especially after he brought Soviet physicist Andrei Sakharov out of internal exile, the tone changed as the new Soviet leader became convinced that the SDI would never be fielded and that Reagan was sincere in his desire to use the SDI as a tool for disarmament, a goal with which he was sympathetic.

SDI was almost exclusively the vision of Ronald Reagan, and it did not survive his tenure in office. President George H. Bush maintained the SDI as a research program within the Strategic Defense Initiative Office (SDIO), with gradually decreased funding. When Clinton became president in 1993, he allowed the project to lapse quietly to a shell that eventually became the basis for a return to a more modest system, the NMD.

The National Missile Defense (NMD)

In the American defense community, the advocates of missile defense have consistently demonstrated that they do not give up or go away, they simply regroup. Although the SDI "umbrella defense" proposal fell to the combined suspicion that it would not work and would cost too much, the more general proposition that defending against ballistic missiles was desirable never left the American political dialogue and, indeed, was aided by events that occurred during the 1990s.

The first event was the use of Russian Scud missiles by Iraq during the Persian Gulf War of 1990–1991. While American Patriot antiaircraft missiles were effective in defending against the attacks by the Iraqis, they also increased interest in *theater* missile defenses (TMDs, antiballistic missiles designed to shoot down battlefield and short-range missiles) for two reasons. First, the fact that the Iraqis had employed the weapons against both civilian and military targets indicated a willingness for so-called *rogue states* like Iraq to do so again in the future and thus buttressed the "need" to be able to defend. Second, it was presumed that in the future the missiles available to potential attackers would be more sophisticated and difficult to intercept, thereby justifying efforts to fashion more effective defenders. The result in the United States was passage of the Missile Defense Act of 1991, with an emphasis on TMD.

The current NMD advocacy was revived by two events in 1998. First, a blue-ribbon panel chaired by current U.S. Secretary of Defense Donald Rumsfeld issued a report arguing that rogue states like Iran and North Korea could well be capable of fielding offensive missiles within five years, rather than the fifteen years or so in the future that was commonly assumed in the defense community. As if to accentuate and validate this prediction, the North Koreans test fired a Taepo Dong I rocket over Japan, raising fears they were intent on producing an intercontinental-range missile in the upcoming years. The national missile defense proposal thus entered the American dialogue, and would soon become part of the international stage as well.

Like all the proposals that preceded it, NMD entered the scene in the midst of controversy, with domestic and international supporters and opponents. The cast of characters and their positions were familiar to anyone who had followed the earlier debates, although the nature of the threat and the pretensions of the system were different. In many ways, the NMD is a return to the debate over Sentinel/Safeguard, both in terms of the threat it addresses (a potential threat) and the capability it proposes (a limited system).

NMD is the successor of something called Global Protection against Limited Strikes (GPALS). It is much closer in concept to Safeguard/Sentinel than it is to SDI. As Walter Slocombe, the Clinton administration's undersecretary of defense for policy, explains, it is "designed to counter a few tens" of incoming missile reentry vehicles, not a massive launch. The justification for this more modest shield is twofold: it is designed for the size of attack a rogue state can contemplate in the foreseeable future; and its more modest requirements make it more plausible to design and operate. Its opponents reject both these claims. As John Pike of the Federation of American Scientists and a consistent opponent of missile defenses over the years, puts it NMD is "a system that won't work against a threat that does not exist."

Advocacy and opposition are strong and polarized. Bush administration advocates and their civilian supporters tend to make five supporting assertions. The first is that the threat from the rogue states (Iran, North Korea, and Iraq—Bush's "axis of evil"—are the most frequently cited examples) is real and must be dealt with now, before their missile capabilities become operational and pose a more ominous threat. Second, possession of NMD will insure that the United States will be willing to act forcefully in regional conflicts, since it will not be vulnerable to missile attacks (or their threat) from the rogue states. Third, the supporters say the protection will be extended to allies and others (such as Russia and Israel), thereby widening its appeal. Fourth, they argue that the cost of NMD is a "small price" to pay for a system that will protect the United States from nuclear and other exotic (e.g., chemical and biological) attacks delivered by missiles. Fifth, they argue the system is not designed against Russia and China and thus should not worry them (which, we will see in the next section, they believe is not quite the case).

The opponents are equally detailed in their concerns. Many of the four most frequently voiced objections to NMD reflect the reverse of the claims of the advocates. First and foremost, opponents argue that the feasibility of the system has not been demonstrated even in a testing program designed to maximize the likelihood of success. Further, Richard Garwin, a long-time critic, maintains the current system would fail miserably against any kind of countermeasures (efforts to confuse or disable the defenses) that would certainly be part of any attack. Second, the critics disagree with cost estimates, saying they will almost certainly escalate beyond current projections and citing inflation in the price tags for Safeguard/Sentinel and SDI as precedents. Third, they argue that we are working politically to improve relations with both Iran and the Democratic People's Republic of Korea (North Korea), and that is a better way to deal with the problem than building provocative defenses.

Fourth, they take exception to the assertion of the generally benign effect that defenses will have on the international scene. The Russians, they point out, are adamantly opposed to missile defenses and that erecting them over Russian objections could have serious consequences in the bilateral relations between what remain the two nuclear superpowers. Similarly, the Chinese fear the effect of NMD on the deterrent ability of their currently small nuclear force. In addition, American allies have shown very little enthusiasm about the project, and despite overtures from Rumsfeld and other Bush administration officials, their support cannot be taken for granted.

It is at this level that the national and international political imperatives collide. The essence of the arguments put forward by the advocates of NMD is that these defenses are in the American national interests, since they will protect American citizens from attacks by the rogue states. Critics, as noted, dispute whether the defenses will protect anyone from anything, but they also raise potential negative international effects as well. If there are negative international ramifications associated with the deployment of the NMD, then the decision to build defenses could instead produce a form of the *security dilemma*: the situation where an action taken by one state to increase its stability decreases the stability of others and potentially causes them to take counteractions that decrease the security of them all.

INTERNATIONAL REACTIONS

Part of the international objection to NMD deployment by the United States arises from the sense of American *unilateralism,* the perception that the United States takes actions without thinking about the broader repercussions of the international system. Yoichi Funabashi, chief diplomatic correspondent for the Tokyo newspaper *Asahi Shimbun,* warns in an article in the *Washington Quarterly* of potential unforeseen effects "if the United States proceeds with its own NMD deployment while disregarding the international implications of such an action."

Aside from this general objection of unilateral action, specific states have had different reactions to the NMD proposal. Israel stands out as a strong supporter of the project, on the presumption that the technology will be shared with them, thereby increasing their ability to deal with the rogue states that confront them. Otherwise, all the major states have more or less major objections. These states include Russia, China, India, and American allies. Whether these objections, which are not necessarily universally held in each capital, will have an important bearing in the deployment decision will help determine whether national or international imperatives turn out to be pivotal in the deployment decision.

Russia

During the Cold War, the Soviets generally opposed American missile defense proposals. While their official reasons for doing so were generally couched in terms of the adverse effect on deterrence, at least part of their reasons for wanting to scuttle the projects was technological: the Soviets knew they did not have the scientific manpower or computer power to tackle missile defenses without diverting enormous resources needed for other priorities. Although the Soviets did deploy and the Russians maintain a suspect ABM system (*Galosh*) around Moscow, that perspective holds for Russia today, in some ways even more vividly than it did when their Soviet predecessors were seeking to undermine SDI.

The chief official objection the Russian government has to NMD deployment is its effect on the ABM Treaty of 1972. To advocates of arms control generally around the world, the ABM Treaty is considered the cornerstone of post–World War II nuclear arms control, because it sanctified the system of mutual deterrence between the two superpowers by denying them the ability to field defensive forces that might threaten retaliatory capabilities and thus lower inhibition to starting a nuclear war. Indeed, the ABM Treaty is regarded by many as the *heart* of nuclear deterrence, making any threat to its continuation emotionally and intellectually wrenching.

The U.S. and Russian governments disagree on the effect of NMD on the treaty. The U.S. government argues that the ABM Treaty is the product of a very different security environment and that, given the nature of the contemporary environment, the treaty is largely obsolete. The Russians disagree vociferously. As Sergei Ivanov, secretary of Russia's security council, put it at a conference in Munich in February 2001, "The destruction of the ABM Treaty will result in the annihilation of the whole structure of strategic stability and create the prerequisites for a new arms race." Something has to give, and there was little movement on the disagreement when Bush and Russian President Vladimir Putin met for the first time in June 2001 in Slovenia. Although Putin subsequently agreed in principle to NMD testing that violates the treaty, he has shown no willingness to scrap the agreement itself.

The Russian attachment to the ABM Treaty has other bases. Paramount among them is the need to engage in further nuclear force reductions as a way to save monetary resources desperately needed in other areas of the Russian economy, including the military (as the plight of the Russian submarine *Kursk* in August 2000 demonstrated). The Russian Parliament (the Duma) ratified the Strategic Arms Reduction Talks (START) II Treaty during the summer of 2000, which reduces the number of warheads in the Russian (as well as the U.S.) arsenal to about 3,500 that must be maintained. The Russians are known to want to enter into START III, which will likely reduce the number to about 1,500 apiece, allowing further needed savings. At a slightly lower level of concern, the Russians also worry that continuing research by the Americans on the missile defense problem could lead to a "strategic breakout" that could produce a comprehensive system of the SDI variety that would render their deterrent force "impotent and obsolete," to borrow the Reagan term.

The key element is the ABM Treaty. When the Duma passed START II, one of its specific conditions was continuation of the ABM Treaty. If the ABM Treaty is somehow breached, then ratification of START II is rescinded and so are the needed plans for force reduction and the diversion of funds to other uses. Vladimir Putin, the Russian president, has consistently tied adherence to the Treaty to progress in START III, despite Bush administration attempts to change his mind. He has also stated that a unilateral U.S. decision to deploy NMD could result in increases in Russian offensive forces, a countermeasure with anti-START ramifications. Such a decision cannot fail to strain American-Russian relations. The Russians have been oddly silent on this issue since Bush announced the American intent to withdraw from the treaty.

The outcome of the NMD thus has the potential to affect adversely the relations between the successors to the Cold War rivalry and still two of the world's most powerful states militarily. There were three possible NMD/ABM Treaty outcomes. The United States could have abandoned NMD deployment, leaving the ABM Treaty intact. This would have been the preferred outcome of the Russians and probably most other countries in the world. The United States could have continued discussions with the Russians about altering the treaty so that it would accommodate a larger, more robust NMD deployment than currently is allowed. So far, the Russians have refused to accept any modifications. Finally, the United States could exercise its rights under the treaty and withdraw (after giving a required six months notice), as it has done. This allows the United States to deploy as large an NMD as it wants without violating any treaty obligation. It also probably maximizes international enmity and reactions toward the project.

China

If Russia worries that a breakout could leave its nuclear deterrent impotent against the United States somewhere in the future, China has the same fear about the effects of the current proposed system today. Although China is not the avowed object against which the NMD proposal is designed, as it was in the 1960s, the prospect of the deployment of such a system has a direct effect on the small Chinese nuclear force and its deterrent ability.

The Chinese are on record that they would never initiate nuclear war, thus having disavowed any possibility of launching a first strike against an opponent. The current small size of its force reinforces this statement, since a Chinese first strike could not destroy an opponent and would certainly invite a much larger retaliation. Rather, China maintains its force for retaliation against a first strike against it, promising to punish an aggressor by means of retaliation should it be attacked.

How can China argue it has a credible deterrent given the small size of its arsenal (as noted earlier, 20 ICBMs and about a dozen SLBMs)? The answer, of course, is that it cannot sustain the argument credibly against an adversary with a large, capable arsenal: its ICBMs are at fixed sites that could be targeted by an aggressor, and its submarine-launched missiles are highly unreliable and have a short range. Thus, the retaliatory capacity of the Chinese force is sometimes referred to in the defense community as a "strategic fiction."

The proposal for NMD, however, upsets and undermines that fiction in Chinese minds. China argues that even in the event of a nuclear aggression against it, a few of its missiles might survive and be available for a retaliatory mission. If the initial attack was by the United States and it had an operational NMD, the remaining Chinese force after the initial attack would be the exact kind of force with which the NMD is designed to cope. The prospect that a Chinese retaliation could be picked off by the NMD would, in the words of retired American rear admiral Michael McDevitt, restore Chinese "nuclear vulnerability without a retaliatory recourse" and leave China in a position where it could be subject to "nuclear blackmail." The most common scenario in which the United

States might threaten China would be a renewed Taiwan crisis (essentially a repeat of American threats during the 1958 crisis over the island).

For these reasons, China much prefers that the United States maintain the status quo and refrain from NMD deployment. *Renmin Rabao,* the Communist Party daily newspaper published in Beijing, made the case that presumably reflects official policy in a July 7, 2000, editorial: "U.S. deployment of the NMD system, a plan aimed at strengthening its own offensive and defensive capacity while blunting other countries' offensive weapons, is an act of sheer selfishness and hegemonism. Going against the main trend of the times, the United States will inevitably end up self-injured. The whole world, including the United States, will never be at peace."

One can argue the concern contained in this statement is overblown, but nonetheless an American decision to deploy NMD does put China in a strategic policy bind. If China believes the "strategic fiction" of a retaliatory capability is sufficiently important, one possible, even likely, response would be to modernize and expand its nuclear forces to the point that they would be capable of overwhelming the NMD after an American attack, a possibility that they have hinted could occur. Doing so would come at the expense of modernizing other elements of Chinese military forces (as noted in Chapter 1, "China Rising," military upgrading is one of the "four modernizations" begun in the 1970s), a process to which the regime is dedicated. At the same time, an enlarged Chinese force could be viewed as a threat to some of its regional neighbors, notably India, thereby setting off a ripple effect.

India

Along with Pakistan, India is the newest avowed member of the nuclear weapons "club," as noted in Chapter 12, "Who Cares about Kashmir?" The Indian nuclear program is much older than its recent emergence in 1998 would suggest; India detonated what it maintained was a "peaceful nuclear explosive" in 1974, and it has generally been conceded that India has been a potential nuclear weapons possessor ever since. While the impetus for going overtly nuclear in 1998 has largely been seen in the context of Indo-Pakistani relations and Indian nationalism, the original—and continuing—obsession of Indian military planners has been China and the Chinese nuclear force. Anything that potentially affects the nature of Chinese nuclear capability is therefore also a concern to India.

India considers itself to be in a uniquely vulnerable geopolitical situation. As possibly the most steadfastly neutral country in the world, India does not fall under the nuclear "umbrella" (protection) of any nuclear weapons state, meaning India is on its own to deter potential nuclear opponents. At the same time, its geographic position is such that "few countries [that] confront the multitude of missile threats that India does," according to Brahma Chellaney, a former consultant to India's National Security Council, writing in the *Washington Quarterly.* Among the actual or potential nuclear states that do or might menace India are China, Pakistan, Iran, and Iraq.

To the Indians, however, the real problem is China, a country it fought border wars with in the 1960s and which it considers a natural enemy. The Indian fear of NMD derives from the fact that it might cause China to expand its nuclear forces, as suggested above. Were that the case, India fears the result might well be a new arms race in Asia. Since India's nuclear deterrent could be undermined by a larger Chinese force, the Indians fear they might have to expand their own forces to restore deterrence, a process that could spiral into a classic action-reaction phenomenon that would, in the end, leave neither more secure. At the same time, an expanded Chinese force would presumably also be modernized, and the Indians fear that China might be tempted to sell its old missiles to Pakistan to help pay for modernization.

Moreover, the Indians believe the threat to which NMD is a supposed response is itself overblown, particularly given the potential cost of deployment. Chellaney, for instance, refers to the Clinton justification of the system as a "cry wolf" approach to the problem, suggesting the threat really does not exist. Moreover, they believe the ABM Treaty will be a certain victim of deployment, and given the symbolic importance of the ABM Treaty, Chellaney concludes "NMD's biggest casualty will be international arms control."

The Allies

The proposal to field an American missile defense has not had a tremendous impact on allies in Europe and Japan, since neither area will be directly affected by the protection or costs (at least not initially). In both cases, however, there are residual concerns that suggest to them that NMD is not a good idea.

European concerns have been muted in some measure because they take the threat less seriously than do the Americans. As Francois Heisbourg, a professor at the French *Institut d'Etudes Politique,* argues in an article in the *Washington Quarterly* summarizing European attitudes toward NMD, Europe has "a more laid-back attitude" toward the rogue states and the threats they pose or may pose in the foreseeable future. Nonetheless, there are at least four concerns that NATO allies do raise.

One concern is the opportunity cost associated with developing and deploying the system. Regardless of what NMD ultimately costs, the bill will come at the expense of other investments the United States might have made and which, given their assessment of the threat, the allies think would probably be spent on better allocations of resources. Some Europeans question the strategic impact of erecting a defense against a country like North Korea, which Heisbourg describes as "a famine-ridden Asian backwater with a yearly GDP (gross domestic product) representing one month's worth of Wal-Mart sales." Europeans worry as well about the adverse impact NMD could have on Western relations with China, which have expanded greatly in the economic realm, and also what a European-based NMD might look like some time in the future, should Europe decide to join an NMD regime. Moreover, European leaders believe maintenance of the ABM Treaty is more important than any gains in security that might derive from an NMD deployment.

The Japanese perspective is somewhat different. Japan is, obviously, geographically close to one of the rogue states (North Korea) against which the system is directed, and Japanese policy has been influenced by what it refers to as the three "security shocks" of the 1990s: Chinese missile tests over Taiwan, the North Korean missile tests over Japan itself, and the explosion of nuclear weapons by India and Pakistan. Each of these events alters the strategic equation in Asia in the Japanese mind, if not in altogether predictable ways.

According to Funabashi, the proposed missile defense system has an impact on five areas of Japanese interest:

1. *Impact on extended deterrence.* The Japanese have long relied on the American nuclear deterrent. Their fear is that the United States might retreat behind the missile shield to "fortress America."

2. *Differing perceptions of North Korea.* Many Japanese feel the level of concern the United States is demonstrating over the North Korean missile threat is exaggerated and might upset diplomatic approaches that could lead to more realistic solutions to the problem.

3. *Connection to theater missile defense (TMD).* While Japan downplays the *strategic* threat posed by North Korea (its ability to target the United States), they do worry about the prospects of short-range missiles and fear American preoccupation with NMD will lead to a deemphasis on TMD, which is important to them.

4. *Russian and Chinese reaction.* Japan realizes that both these large and powerful neighbors oppose NMD, and wonder what the negative effects of supporting the United States on NMD will be for their relations with the Chinese and the Russians.

5. *Long-term architecture in Asia.* Were the NMD to become a comprehensive system covering Asian countries including Japan and Taiwan, the Japanese worry about the ramification for dealing with China.

CONCLUSION

As the preceding discussion suggests, the debate over further development and deployment of a national missile defense system is more than a domestic American political issue, even though most of the discussions within the United States have stressed American rather than international effects.

As noted at the beginning, the problem of missile defense has much of the *structure* of a traditional arms issue, bearing a resemblance to the arms-racing issues that roiled the Cold War, including earlier considerations of missile defenses. The similarity is fairly clear on three grounds.

First, missile defense meets the criterion of being a problem with both national and international ramifications which can best be dealt with by the concerted efforts of a number of states. If the solution to deploying missile defenses is not to deploy them, of course, that could be done by a unilateral American decision. If, on the other hand, the problem of missile proliferation that is the reason for a missile defense initiative is included, then the underlying problem can only be solved by the abstention of possible missile proliferators as well. Whether that goal is best accomplished by negotiations that result in agreement to abstain or defenses to hedge against proliferation is at the heart of the international debate about defenses.

A second way in which missile defenses resemble earlier arms race issues is its abstract nature. The problem that missile defenses seek to overcome is a *potential*, not an actual, capability, although one can argue about when (or if) the threat will become real. Many traditional arms race issues—including the debate over Sentinel/Safeguard—are similar, and with a similar effect. The international problems caused by missile defenses are abstract, and exist somewhere indefinably in the future, problems that may or may not materialize. If, in other words, one could argue powerfully and convincingly that erecting missile defenses will have immediate and strong deleterious effects on the international security environment, the debate would be changed to a greater international dialogue. The fact that it does not, allows, for instance, the Bush administration to try to "jawbone" opponents (up to now with little success) without the threat of short-term repercussions.

Third and finally, we return to the basic concern, which is the clash between national and international interests. If the arguments about defenses have merit, whatever decisions are reached will have opposite effects on the two levels. If missile defenses work and are deployed, American national security—narrowly defined as the protection of the homeland—will be arguably strengthened, but at the expense of adverse international reaction that may destabilize the international environment because of the actions it causes other states to take (the security dilemma). Conversely, a decision not to deploy may leave the international system tranquil, while leaving American national security less secure. Who is the more important winner or loser with either outcome?

The proper course of action is not entirely clear. In the Cold War system, national interests were clearly supreme over international ones, but is that true in the contemporary environment? Whether the solution to traditional security issues occupies a higher or lower order of importance than it did during the Cold War is one important measure of how—or whether—international politics has changed much in the post–Cold War world.

Finally, we must end by reinforcing the whole notion that this is a concrete debate over an abstract problem. The problem of rogue states with nuclear missiles is a projection, not a reality, and the earlier projections of Chinese threat that underlay Sentinel/Safeguard advocacies offers some caution. Similarly, even the Bush administration, as chief advocates of the NMD, have cautioned they will not make a positive decision until there is a workable system, which may never occur. Thus, national and international politics collide in a cloud of uncertainty.

⊕ STUDY/DISCUSSION QUESTIONS

1. What is the nature of traditional arms race, including ARP, the security dilemma, and transstate security issues? How does the proposed national missile defense (NMD) proposed by the United States fit into that definition?

2. How are the Sentinel/Safeguard and NMD system proposals similar and different? What lessons, if any, can be learned from the earlier deployment that apply to the newer proposal?

3. How did the Reagan Strategic Defense Initiative (SDI) differ from Sentinel/Safeguard that preceded it and NMD that followed it? How did those differences make SDI simultaneously more and less appealing?

4. What exactly is the NMD? What is it supposed to do, and how? Why does it clash with the ABM Treaty, and why is that important to critics both in the United States and elsewhere?

5. Why do Russia, China, India, and American allies object to the NMD plan? Are their objections reasonable? What are the consequences of those negative assessments?

6. Would the negative reactions that could occur in places like Russia, China, and India if NMD is deployed leave the world a more or less secure place than it is now?

7. Given your assessment of these effects, should the United States pursue or abandon the NMD program, or should it withhold final judgment until the threat materializes or workable NMD designs are demonstrated?

READING/RESEARCH MATERIAL

Eisendrath, Craig, Gerald E. Marsh, and Melvin E. Goodman. "Can We Count on Missile Defense?" *USA Today Magazine* 130, 2676 (September 2001), 10–16.

Gaffney, Frank J., Jr. "Bush, Missile Defense, and the Critics." *Commentary* 111, 2 (February 2001), 29–37.

Guertner, Gary L., and Donald M. Snow. *The Last Frontier: An Analysis of the Strategic Defense Initiative.* Lexington, MA: Lexington Books, 1986.

Ivanov, Igor. "The Missile Defense Mistake: Undermining Strategic Stability and the ABM Treaty." *Foreign Affairs* 79, 5 (September/October 2000), 15–20.

The Military Balance. London: International Institute for Strategic Studies.

"Misguided Missile Defense." *World Press Review* 47, 9 (September 2000), 4.

Mosher, David E. "Understanding the Extraordinary Cost of Missile Defense." *Arms Control Today* 30, 10 (December 2000), 9–16.

The *Washington Quarterly,* a respected foreign policy journal associated with the Center for Strategic and International Studies, devoted much of its Summer 2000 edition (Vol. 3, 3) to the argument over missile defense. The pertinent articles and their authors follow:

Chellaney, Brahma. "New Delhi's Dilemma." 145–154.

Funabashi, Yoichi. "Tokyo's Temperance." 135–144.

Hadley, Stephen J. "A Call to Deploy." 95–108.

Heisbourg, Francois. "Brussels' Burden." 127–134.

McDevitt, Michael. "Beijing's Bind." 177–186.

Nacht, Michael. "The Politics: How Did We Get Here?" 87–94.

Pikayev, Alexander A. "Moscow's Matrix." 187–193.

Slocombe, Walter B. "The Administration's Approach." 79–86.

WEB SITES

Complete online source of information on the national missile defense program
National Missile Defense: What Does It All Mean? At
http://www.cdi.org/hotspots/issuebrief/default.asp

Briefing book taking an in-depth look at each of the four criteria that President Clinton considered in his decision not to deploy a NMD

Pushing the Limits: The Decision on National Missile Defense at http://www.clw.org/pub/clw/coalition/libbmd.htm

Collection of technical analyses, testimonies, and other documents criticizing NMD

Global Security: Missile Defense at http://www.ucsusa.org/arms/0missile.html

Contains latest developments, links to official documents, governmental and nongovernmental resources

Arms Control and Non-Proliferation: Missile Defense at http://usinfo.state.gov/topical/pol/arms/nmd

Offers a wide variety of documents concerning missile proliferation and missile defenses

Ballistic Missile Defense at http://fas.org/ssp/bmd

Official news, briefings, transcripts, and other resources in favor of NMD

Missile Defense at http://www.defenselink.mil/specials/missiledefense/inner.html

CHAPTER TWELVE

Who Cares about Kashmir?

AN OLD PROBLEM WITH NEW TEETH

PRÉCIS

There are some politicomilitary problems in the world that are so deep and fundamental that they appear to be incapable of solution and thus linger on for a very long time. The situation between Israel and its neighbors, the subject of Chapter 6, is one of those kinds of conflicts. The struggle between India and Pakistan over control of the strategically and emotionally important princely state of Jammu and Kashmir (Kashmir for short) is another. Given the depth and diametrical opposition of the various sides on the important issues, it is a truly irresolvable conflict.

The case develops the problem in two ways. The first is historical, looking at the evolution of the problem from the time of the partition of the Indian subcontinent after the end of World War II to the present. The second, and more fundamental, purpose of the case is to look at the prospects for ending the fighting and coming up with a peaceful solution with which all sides can live. This involves looking at the underlying interests of the major players and their desired outcomes. Why do India and Pakistan believe control of Kashmir by them is vital to their national interests? Why do some Kashmiris believe that independence is the only acceptable option? The basic problem is that the outcomes preferred by each antagonist are absolutely opposed by the others, creating an intractable situation that may have parallels to situations like that in Kosovo and between the Israelis and the Palestinians.

It is a war being fought literally at the top of the world, in a land that is home to some of the world's tallest mountains and most awesome vistas. The battlefields are the high Himalaya Mountains, often at altitudes of 16,000–17,000 feet above sea level where the air is so oxygen-poor that normal military activities by combat forces are physically impossible to perform even were it not for the icy, snow-covered, rugged terrain. Given the conditions, much of the fighting consists of long-range artillery duels between the contending sides. The front moves periodically in one direction or the other, but the frontier never seems to move very far. At varying levels of intensity, the fighting has been going on for over a half-century, with no conclusive end in sight to the grim struggle for power and control.

The place is the northern tip of the Asian subcontinent, where India, Pakistan, Afghanistan, Tajikistan, and China meet in the world's tallest mountain range. Forming the geographic cap for the new country of India when independence came to the subcontinent, the point of contention is the princely state of Jammu and Kashmir (hereafter Kashmir). It is a territory about the size of Utah, annexed by India when the subcontinent was subdivided in the latter 1940s by Great Britain as it dissolved its long-held colonial empire there. Because the population of Kashmir is predominantly Muslim, the new government of Pakistan never recognized Indian control and has been contesting sovereign political control ever since, through Kashmiri "freedom fighters" whom India accuses of being agents of the Pakistani government (a charge denied by Pakistan). On at least two occasions, Kashmir has been a major battleground in wars between India and Pakistan. The rest of the time, Kashmir is the site of a low-level war of attrition with considerable explosive potential for the region and potentially beyond.

Why highlight a seemingly parochial dispute over some physically awe-inspiring but economically impoverished territory very far from the center of the international political scene? On the face of it, the answer to who cares about Kashmir would seem to be not much of anyone except the people who live there. Such a conclusion, however, would not be warranted.

What has revived or, for much of the world, created international interest in Kashmir, quite simply, are the "new teeth" demonstrated by India and Pakistan in 1998 when they both exploded nuclear weapons and thus made official the spread of the nuclear arms race to that part of Asia. Kashmir is the most likely flashpoint that could lead to wider war between India and Pakistan, and dealing with the Kashmir problem was one of the major reasons that former President Clinton traveled to the subcontinent in early 2000. Prior to leaving on that trip, he referred to Kashmir as "the most dangerous place in the world today."

Defusing the Kashmir conflict as a means to help lower the likelihood of nuclear war on the subcontinent would seem enough to establish its importance, but there is more. On one hand, the outcome of the dispute, particularly if it resulted in independence for Kashmir or attachment to Pakistan, would provide a significant territorial precedent in the region in at least two ways. Indian possession of Kashmir has been compared to Chinese possession of Tibet (which is not far away physically). At the same time, Kashmir's secession could provide encouragement for other areas within India (or even Pakistan) with centrifugal tendencies.

In addition, there is another significant aspect of the Kashmir situation for the study of international relations. In a world where American power seems to be a factor nearly everywhere, the crisis also demonstrates the limit of the United States to influence events. The United States has always had very limited influence on the subcontinent and especially with the government of India, a lack of affinity between the world's two largest political democracies that might seem strange. Part of the problem has been that the United States has been more interested in improved relations with China, and that has "tilted" U.S. policy more toward China's ally Pakistan. India, in turn, felt the necessity to be closer to the Soviet Union during the Cold War to counterbalance China, and especially after the Soviets took a leading role in mediating the outcome of the 1965 Indo-Pakistani War. Even with the Cold War over, however, U.S. influence on the subcontinent, and especially with India, remains minimal. The U.S. de facto alignment with Pakistan over the 2001 war in Afghanistan (in which India also offered assistance) has increased American visibility and presence in the region. Any long-term change in influence remains to be seen. Unlike in so many other crisis situations around the world, the United States is not clearly an important "player" in resolving the tensions over Kashmir. We will speculate on why this may be the case in the conclusion.

The Kashmir conflict is an extremely intractable situation that has proven very difficult—to this point impossible—to resolve, and it may remain so. To understand both the nature of the problem and the barriers to its solution, we will begin by looking at the historical basis of the disagreement and how it has evolved, including the effects that "nuclearization" has had on it. We will then examine the interests of the various parties to the dispute, and how those interests have served to preclude particular outcomes. We will then look at a series of options for settling or managing the dispute and the political and other barriers to implementing them. We will conclude with some assessment of where the dispute may head in the future.

EVOLUTION OF THE PROBLEM

Kashmir became an international problem with the breakup of the British Raj (the British colonial administration) on the subcontinent after World War II. Before World War II, there were several independence movements on the subcontinent. One of these, the Muslim League headed by Muhamad Ali Jinnah, represented the interests of the Islamic minority on the subcontinent, while the interests of the Hindu majority were represented by the Indian Congress, headed by Mohandas Gandhi. During the period between the world wars, the activism was sufficient to force the British to pass the Government of India Act of 1935, promising independence for the subcontinent. That process was interrupted by the outbreak and conduct of World War II. After the war, it would return and have to be faced.

Subdividing the Subcontinent

After World War II ended, a high level British delegation under the leadership of British war hero Lord Mountbatten was dispatched to the Indian subcontinent. Its purpose was to subdivide what had been a single colonial unit (the Raj) into independent units that represented some reasonable form of self-determination along ethnic and communal lines. The problem was that the subcontinent before (and after) colonialism is an incredibly diverse physical and political place, made of numerous nationalities and religions that have, through history, been more or less antithetical to one another. To get some feel of the extent of this diversity, 562 "princely states" had to decide their political destiny for partition to be complete.

The basic form of partition was conceptually simple enough. The subcontinent would be divided into a predominantly Muslim state (Pakistan) and a Hindu state (India). The basic criterion for drawing the map between the two would be territorial: areas that were overwhelmingly Muslim would become part of Pakistan, and predominantly Hindu areas would accede to India. For a variety of ethnic, cultural, religious, and historical reasons, such a basic subdivision was both necessary and sensible.

No political boundary line could perfectly partition the two groups, and as a result, at the time of independence several million Muslims were left in India and vice versa, causing a panicked migration across the borders that remains the largest such event in human history (most of this occurred in the Punjab region of western India and West Pakistan) and resulted in high levels of tension and fighting there as populations migrated from one side of the frontier to the other. In addition, the principle of territorial majority also meant that the Muslim state would be divided into two physically distant parts of Pakistan, the Punjabi-dominated West Pakistan and Bengali-majority East Pakistan separated by 1,000 miles of Indian territory. In 1971, East Pakistan splintered away from Pakistan to form the independent country of Bangladesh.

The princely states were given two choices. They could accede either to India or to Pakistan; it was understood that they could not choose independence. Further, states that were not predominantly Muslim would become part of India. Based on religion and other factors, most had little difficulty reaching a decision under what was known at the time as the Transfer of Power. In the vast majority of cases, accession to one state or another was accomplished either through popular vote or by an act of accession by the government of the princely states and India or Pakistan. The Transfer of Power guidelines did not specify which method would be used.

The accession process went well for all areas except Jammu and Kashmir, which, along with Janagadh and Hyderabad, had not decided their fate when the Transfer of Power took place on August 15, 1947. All three states eventually became part of India over the protests of Pakistan; of the three, Kashmir has remained the major point of contention since 1947.

The situation in Kashmir was the mirror image of Jungadh in the Punjabi western part of the subcontinent. In Jungadh, 80 percent of the population was Hindu, but the region's ruler was a Muslim. At the insistence of the Indian government, the issue of accession was submitted to a plebiscite, and the population voted overwhelmingly to become part of India. This line of action would not provide a precedent when it came time to decide the political fate of Kashmir.

In Kashmir, the demographics and geopolitics were reversed: about three-quarters of the population of four million in 1947 were Muslims, while the ruler of the state was a Hindu, Maharajah Sir Hari Singh. The maharajah's instinct was to press for independence, but this option was unacceptable to any of the other parties. In 1947, Muslim "freedom fighters" invaded Kashmir to force union with Pakistan, and the fighting became part of the general war on the subcontinent between India and Pakistan that broke out in October of that year. Unwilling to submit the fate of Kashmir to a referendum he knew he would lose, the Maharajah reluctantly acceded to joining India in 1948. The state of Pakistan refused to recognize the accession and demanded a referendum that was authorized by the United Nations in 1949. The Indian government refused to hold the referendum, maintaining Kashmir had legally become part of India by intergovernmental agreement. The basis for the ongoing dispute was established by this action by India.

The Bases of Dispute

On the face of it, the case for allowing Kashmir to be a part of Pakistan rather than part of India would appear to be a strong one. Writing in 1991, Alastair Lamb summarizes these bases of the Pakistani claim to Kashmir: "First, the State of Jammu and Kashmir was a region with an overwhelming Muslim majority contiguous to the Muslim majority region of the Punjab, which became part of Pakistan. Second, the economy...was bound up in what was to become Pakistan. Its best communication with the outside world lay through Pakistan, and this was the route taken by the bulk of its exports. Third, the waters of the Indus, Jhelum, and Chenab [Rivers], all of which flowed through Jammu and Kashmir territory, were essential for the prosperity of the agricultural life of Pakistan."

These reasons are emotional, pragmatic, and geopolitical. Clearly, the desire to have coreligionists united with their religious brethren is a deeply emotional question that has helped fuel continued Muslim activism over the decades of the conflict and which formed the original rationale for partition. Particularly given that India insisted on popular self-determination in other cases where Hindus were in the majority, it contributes to the ongoing sense of distrust and hatred between the people of the country and the Pakistanis. Among other things, that sense of distrust meant that no meetings were held between the heads of states of India and Pakistan between 1947, when partition occurred, and 2000, when such a meeting finally took place. The pragmatic, economic argument, of course, has been overcome with time, as the commercial patterns that formed its base in the 1940s have been supplanted with a reorientation of the Kashmiri economy toward India.

Although it is less often emphasized, the geopolitical argument about the Indus rivers, which contains an emotional element as well, may be the most sustaining part of the Pakistani contention other than religious kinship. The basis of this importance is the enormous reliance of Pakistani agriculture on the waters from these rivers, a dependence brought dramatically home when India interrupted the flow of waters in 1948 during harvest time and almost destroyed a vital crop.

As the accompanying map shows, essentially all the river water flowing into Pakistan has its source in the mountains of Kashmir. Of a total of six rivers, three (the Indus, Jhelum, and Chenab, collectively known as the western rivers) flow directly from Kashmir to Pakistan, while the other three (known as the eastern rivers) flow from Kashmir into the Indian state of Rajasthan, and then into Pakistan. Prior to the partition of the subcontinent, the Indus river system had formed part of the oldest irrigation system in the world, providing irrigation waters for what would become Pakistan and India. When

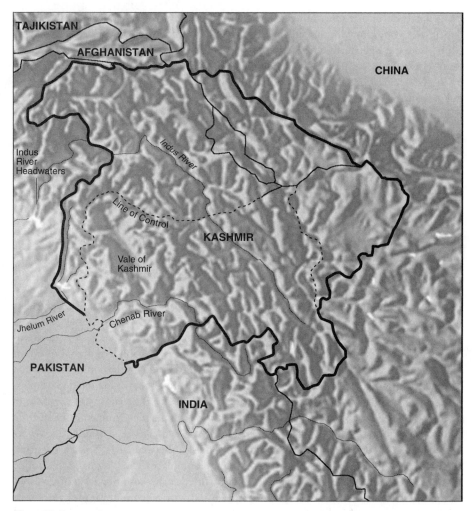

Map 12.1 Map of Kashmir.

the Mountbatten mission provided its final plan for partition, the boundary line cut through the irrigation system, leaving unanswered the question of which states would continue to have access to the waters.

The crisis that brought home to Pakistan the vitality of control of the headwaters of the rivers in Kashmir occurred in the spring of 1948. The Indian government, arguing it needed the extra water to sustain Hindu immigrants who had fled from Pakistan into Rajasthan, cut the flow of the eastern rivers for six weeks at a critical period just prior to harvest, nearly ruining the crops in Pakistan that relied upon the rivers. Although the flow was restored after international intermediation, a Pakistani government already suspicious of Indian intentions learned that they needed to ensure that access to the water could never be interrupted again.

The issue is clearly an emotional one for the Pakistanis as well. Pakistan's need for water from the rivers is undeniable; most of the Punjab region of Pakistan (West Pakistan) is very arid, with an average annual rainfall in the range of 10–15 inches per year (about the same as eastern Colorado), and a good deal of that falls in storms during the monsoon season. Without a reliable source of irrigation water during the year, much of Pakistani agriculture is at peril. The geopolitics of Pakistani survival and prosperity are clearly at work.

Recognizing this problem and attempting to solve it, the International Bank for Reconstruction and Development (IBRD, or World Bank) helped India and Pakistan negotiate the Indus Waters Treaty of 1960. The provisions of the agreement included dividing claims to the waters so that India received all the water from the eastern rivers (a fraction of the total flow), while Pakistan got all the water from the western rivers. Hydroelectric dams were built in Kashmir to create reservoirs that would allow control of the flow of the rivers into Pakistan, and canals were built to redirect water from the western rivers to irrigate parts of Pakistan formerly supplied by water from the eastern rivers.

This agreement would seem to have solved the water problem, but it has not. Since the headwaters of the western rivers continue to rise in Indian-controlled Kashmir, the Pakistanis continue to worry about another interruption and thus insist on de facto control of those headwaters by Azad Kashmir (Free Kashmir) rebels. Their position is more emotional than rational in this regard because the geography of the mountains through which the waters flows makes it physically impossible to divert any of the water into India without boring tunnels through the mountains to redirect the flow, and such a diversion goes well beyond Indian physical or financial assets.

The Indian position on Kashmir is more straightforward. As far as India is concerned, there is no conflict over the status of Kashmir, because that was settled in 1948 with Kashmir's accession into India. Thus, the fracas that flares from time to time is strictly an internal matter, although one that is aggravated by what they see as illegal Pakistani interference in support of "rebels" and proindependence freedom fighters or terrorists (depending on what side one is on) that India considers as agents of Islamabad.

The Indian position has a geopolitical side as well. Part of their reason for insisting upon continuing control of Kashmir is based in geography. Located as it is literally as the "cap" of India, Kashmir also sits astride historic invasion routes into India, notably from China. A Kashmir controlled by a Pakistan in official or informal alignment with China poses a very real military threat to India. At the same time, the idea of Kashmir breaking away from India has precedential value for India, as it does for China over Tibet. There are any number of Indian states with varying levels of secessionist inclinations, and the government of India worries that a breakaway by Kashmir could encourage other similarly inclined areas to follow their lead.

STATUS OF THE PROBLEM

The dispute over Kashmir sporadically breaks out into more or less intense violence, with even the "peaceful" interludes marked by some intercommunal fighting and terrorist attacks. Kashmir was a major object of the first war fought between the two countries shortly after independence was granted in 1947, a conflict that ended on January 1, 1948, with a United

Nations mandate to hold a plebiscite that never, in fact, occurred, as already noted. In 1965, war broke out again between India and Pakistan at a barren area along the border between West Pakistan and India known as the Rann of Kutch; initial Pakistani success in that encounter emboldened them to try to seize Kashmir, making it what turned out to be the inconclusive focus of the war. In 1971, war broke out again, and although its major focus was the secession of East Pakistan to form Bangladesh, much of the tension during the conflict centered on Kashmir as a potential second front in that war.

Kashmir has thus been a major focus in each of the three full-scale wars fought between the two subcontinental powers since their independence. A truce line drawn after the war in 1971 gave de facto control over portions of western Kashmir to the Pakistanis and their Kashmiri brethren, thereby creating a lull in the violence for a time. Kashmiri dissidents under the banner of Azad Kashmir resumed the armed struggle in 1988, and regular Indian and Pakistani units began exchanging fire in 1990. Although violence was suspended in summer 2000 as part of the first-ever meeting between the heads of state of the two countries, tensions remain high and terrorist attacks continued to be reported into 2001.

The potential for resumption of the fighting thus remains. For instance, the relationship between the Pakistani government and Azad Kashmir is not clear, and hence the degree to which the Pakistanis can control the actions of their "allies" is also in doubt. If Indian descriptions of that relationship are to be believed, Azad Kashmir is no more than a puppet organization of the Pakistanis, who recruit, equip, train, and even provide some of the "freedom fighters" that make up the force. Pakistan, of course, vehemently denies these charges, maintaining the rebels are an independent body seeking independence for Kashmir, possibly with the long-term intention of union with Pakistan. As a result, the possibility of renewed violence remains as long as relations between India and Pakistan continue to be problematical.

Part of the problem is that the status quo, while minimally acceptable, pleases neither side. The "line of control" or truce line established in 1971 provides de facto Pakistani control over most of the western portion of Kashmir, giving them (through Azad Kashmir) physical possession of the headwaters (or sources) of the western rivers of the Indus system. Since Kashmir remains legally a part of India, however, that possession is not as firm as Pakistan would like, given the dependency Pakistan has on the irrigation waters from the river system. Moreover, some of the hydroelectric dams created by the settlement of the Indus Waters Treaty to provide electricity and to store monsoon rains for later use are also in the zone. India, on the other hand, maintains physical control of the mountainous regions and thus the geopolitically important passes along their border with China. The fact that part of their sovereign territory is effectively outside their control is annoying to the Indian national ego and creates the motivation to alter the line of control.

The issue of Kashmir was revived in international consciousness by the public display of nuclear weapons capability by India and Pakistan in 1998. On May 11 and 13, India conducted five underground nuclear tests in the desert of Rajasthan, announcing the reason for the tests was growing concern about the Chinese nuclear threat (see discussion in Chapter 11) and alleged nuclear cooperation between China and Pakistan. On May 28, Pakistan also exploded five devices underground at the Chagai test site. Following a protest by the United States government and the threat to suspend economic assistance, Pakistan conducted another test on May 30.

One of the interesting aspects of the Kashmir dispute and its nuclear extension is the impotence of the United States to affect the situation one way or the other. One of the hallmarks of the post–Cold War 1990s has been American global activism in brokering peaceful settlements of international disputes, often through the personal efforts of President Clinton. The most notable instances of this success have been in negotiating agreements on aspects of the Arab-Israeli conflict (not including Palestine) and in Northern Ireland.

The United States has been notably unsuccessful in influencing events on the subcontinent. The United States was, for instance, not even informed ahead of time about the nuclear tests by either India or Pakistan (partly because both countries knew the United States would object), and American intelligence was apparently caught completely off guard and failed to predict the explosions. When Clinton visited the subcontinent in April 2000, going first to India and then to Pakistan, he was largely unsuccessful in moving the peace process along. Besides "photo ops" in front of the Taj Mahal and other Indian sites, he made little headway with the Indian leadership on the nuclear weapons question and was given virtually the cold shoulder by the leaders of Pakistan. The experience suggests that there are indeed limits to the power of the world's remaining superpower to shape events to its particular liking.

PROSPECTS FOR RESOLUTION

Why has the conflict over Kashmir been allowed to fester for over half a century? One possible explanation is that the issues involved are so intractable and the possible outcomes so emotionally charged that none appears acceptable, a situation not unlike the Palestinian question in the Middle East. Another possibility is that resolution of the matter is insufficiently important for the parties to make the necessary sacrifices to achieve closure. Yet a third possibility is that there has been no outside force that has the level of interests or leverage involved to mount an effective effort to mediate the differences.

The Problem Reformulated

Until 1998, some combination of intractability, insufficient local interest, or outside interest or leverage explained why the dispute was not resolved. But things have changed. Most notably, the explosion of nuclear weapons has added Kashmir to the list of conflicts in the world over which a nuclear war might begin. Whether the public demonstration of nuclear capability by the two major regional powers has made any war between them more or less likely is an open question, and one for which a case can be made in either direction. What that demonstration *does* mean is that nuclear war between them is now physically possible. Moreover, the aspect of the Indo-Pakistani relationship that has most often resulted in war has been over Kashmir; the kind of war the next battle over Kashmir could become would seem to make resolution more important than before, both to the principals and the international system as a whole.

There is precedent for international involvement. In the 1973 Yom Kippur War between Israel and her Islamic neighbors, there were two incidents that raised the fear that the situation could escalate to nuclear weapons use, with unforeseeable consequences for the rest of the international system. First, when Israel suffered serious military setbacks early in the fighting, the Israeli government allegedly authorized the arming of Israel's nuclear arsenal (which Israel neither admits or denies it possesses). The arsenal presumably could have reached and destroyed the capitals of all of Israel's adversaries, thus raising the stakes had such attacks occurred.

Later in the war, when Israel's military fortunes had improved significantly, the Israelis trapped an entire Egyptian army with its back to the Suez Canal but no way to get across and escape, and the Israelis threatened to destroy that army "in detail." The Soviet Union at that point threatened to drop Soviet paratroopers into the Egyptian lines to help in their defense. The United States responded by going to full alert status, and its leaders (notably U.S. Secretary of State Henry Kissinger) spent 24 breathless hours of diplomatic activity defusing a situation which some observers maintain was a closer brush with nuclear war than even the Cuban missile crisis of 1962.

Neither Israel activating its nuclear forces nor the Soviet threat to intervene triggered a nuclear war, but the knowledge they could have helped energize, especially within the United States government, a determination that the Arab-Israeli crisis could not be allowed to devolve again to a point where the result could be a general nuclear war that would threaten the international system itself. The seeds of the Middle East peace process were really born in the desperation of the Yom Kippur War. Although that process has not solved all the region's difficulties, it has succeeded in defusing those disputes and lessening the likelihood of their escalating to the nuclear level.

And now Kashmir has potentially achieved a similar status within the structure of international problems. But does settling the differences over Kashmir have the same perceived urgency in 2002 that settling the Middle East crisis had in the 1970s?

The answer is mixed. There are certainly dissimilarities. What made the situation so volatile in 1973 was that the United States was clearly aligned with one side (Israel) whereas the other nuclear superpower was a benefactor of the Islamic states. Thus, the possibility of being drawn into the fray simply because one's "friends" became entangled was a very real prospect. Since we had never been to the brink of nuclear war in this manner before, the dynamics of escalation were unknown (as they basically are today). At the same time, both the Soviets and the Americans had some ability to influence the behavior of their client states. The United States, for instance, was able to restrain the Israelis from destroying the trapped and largely defenseless Egyptian army, thereby providing the breathing room necessary for Kissinger's shuttle diplomacy.

Neither of these conflicting factors is present on the subcontinent today. With the end of the Cold War, there are clearly no client states to draw the superpowers into the conflict on opposing sides. This may actually make the probabilities of war greater, however, since the major powers also cannot as easily restrain the principal actors. At the same time, the prospects of being dragged inadvertently into a war that has gone or threatens to go nuclear would seem to be reduced; the same escalatory potential is missing.

There is one point of commonality, and that is *uncertainty*. The simple fact of the matter is that nuclear weapons have never been used in war when both sides possessed them and could use them against their enemies. Over the years of the nuclear age, we have devised "rational" constructs about how countries should act in different nuclear situations, but given our total lack of experience in the circumstances surrounding the nuclear escalation process, they remain no more than elaborate, articulate speculations.

That means the answer to the question, "What happens to the rest of the world if India and Pakistan engage in a nuclear exchange during the next Kashmir crisis?" must be "there is no way to know." Rationally and analytically, the prospect of escalation to the system as a whole would seem to be fairly remote; what the major—including nuclear—powers *probably* would do would be to marshal as much international pressure as possible to end the nuclear fighting at as low a level of death and suffering as possible. That would make sense, if sensibility were to prevail.

But we do not know that would happen. Everyone might act calmly and rationally, or they might not. What we *do* know for certain is that the most certain way to avoid finding out the answer is to avoid there being another war over Kashmir that could escalate to nuclear exchange. Thus, the search for a suitable option to resolve the dispute takes on added meaning when the "new teeth" are present.

There is yet another possible effect that nuclearization of the subcontinent could have on the Kashmir issue. It is also possible to argue that the overt possession of nuclear weapons will have a calming, sobering, and even stabilizing effect on both India and Pakistan. Both countries are now fully aware that *any* war in which they might face one another is a potential nuclear exchange with incalculable consequences for both of them. This realization forces each side to include in its decision process the question of whether any objectives in any contemplated conflict are worth the risk of nuclear escalation, no matter how small that risk might appear to be in any given situation. It might or might not have much or any impact in any particular encounter, but it is also true that no two states possessing nuclear weapons have ever fought one another. That may be the result of coincidence rather than of the weapons. But it is nonetheless true and can lead to the conclusion that nuclear weapons will stabilize rather than destabilize the subcontinent in the future.

Options for Resolution

The possibility that another war over Kashmir could escalate to a nuclear exchange may make resolution a more important priority although, as noted above, it may also make a renewed war less likely, since both sides presumably recognize what could happen now and may avoid actions with escalatory potential. Regardless of which of these arguments one makes, the clearest way to avoid finding out if Kashmir has nuclear dynamics is to settle the problem in such a manner that the reversion to war is no longer a real prospect—if it is possible to find such a solution acceptable to the parties.

A variety of schemes for settling the problem have been put forward over time. Not all have been formal proposals, nor have any of them enjoyed widespread support. What has bedeviled all the proposals is that none have, to date, been acceptable to the three principal groups to the conflict, the Indians, the Pakistanis, and the Kashmiris. The crux of the difficulty is that each interested party sees the outcomes in absolute and mutually exclusive terms, as a kind of zero-sum game in which one side's gains are inevitably the other side's losses. The Indians optimally want to reassert their sovereign authority over all of Kashmir. The Pakistanis and Kashmiris want that sovereignty reversed, either by accession of Kashmir to Pakistan (the Pakistani preference) or independence for Kashmir (the preference of at least some Kashmiris). None of these outcomes has been acceptable to the others.

The proposals for settling the dispute have generally followed these preferred out-comes. In *The Crisis in Kashmir,* Sumit Ganguly has summarized seven proposals, three of which would reinforce India's continued claim of sovereign control, two of which rep-resent compromises where each side receives some but not all of what it wants, and two of which support the Pakistani/Kashmiri desire to remove Indian sovereignty. In addition, we will explore an eighth outcome, which is a more or less permanent stale-mate that results in continuation of the status quo.

The Pro-Indian Options. The three pro-Indian options involve changing the politi-cal composition of Kashmir in such a manner that some semblance of pro-Indian legit-imate control can be manifested. One possibility, which violates current Indian law and thus cannot be formally advocated, is called *ethnic flooding.* The idea here is to encour-age massive Indian immigration into Kashmir to tip the population balance to the Indi-ans, thereby allowing something like a plebiscite in which the new Indian majority might prevail and legitimize Kashmir's status as an Indian state. Since three-quarters of the seven million current citizens of Kashmir are Muslim, this would require a very large influx of people who would patently not be welcomed by the current citizenry, particularly after the reasons for their migration became known. Implementation of the strategy would require amendment of the Indian constitution, a provision of which (Article 370) pro-hibits, among other things, the sale of immovable properties in Kashmir to non-Kash-miris. The provision, unless rescinded, would virtually prohibit Hindus from establishing homes in Kashmir. Moreover, it is impossible to imagine that organizations like the Jammu Kashmir Liberation Front (JKLF), which seeks independence for the state, would sit idly by while the population flood occurred.

The other two pro-Indian solutions involve military actions the purpose of which would be to destroy the armed resistance to Indian rule. Each strategy is based on a prece-dent that India has employed elsewhere in the country to quell dissent, although the situations from which the precedents derive are arguably too different to be applicable. Also, it is hard to imagine that Pakistan would accede to the reduction and destruction of groups with which it has had, at a minimum, close relations for half a century. Mil-itary solutions, in other words, almost certainly increase the risk of more general war on the subcontinent, with all the dangers that might entail.

One military solution is the *mailed-fist strategy.* Like ethnic flooding, this option, which is the most bellicose of any, has not received any formal endorsement within the Indian political system. The idea, based on a strategy used earlier to pacify the Punjab, would require greatly increased military action against the dissidents, the purpose of which would be to crush the armed resistance completely, as was done to the Sikhs in the Punjab. With the rebels defeated and removed from the scene, the idea is that elections could be held that would hopefully endorse Indian hegemony. History suggests that Kash-miri resistance to such a campaign would be considerably greater than that which occurred in the Punjab, making the possibility of success less likely.

The other military solution, applied in India's northwestern region in the 1960s and 1970s, is a *wear-down strategy* of attrition. The idea in this case is that a patient strategy of military pressure may literally wear down the dissident Kashmiris to the point that they simply tire of the contest and fade away. This suggestion runs in the face of a long-term, tenacious opposition within Kashmir that has shown consider-able resilience over a long period of time. It is even arguable that India, which has plenty of other problems of its own, including a large population segment not all that interested in the fate of Kashmir, might actually be more vulnerable to this strat-egy than the Kashmiris (in the form of public opinion turning against the campaign as it did to the United States in Vietnam).

Compromises. As in any situation where all parties have strong claims to the object at hand, compromise is always an attractive possibility, especially if a compromise can be arranged whereby each party can argue that they prevailed. This is especially the case in an emotionally charged situation where almost any concession will be viewed by some partisans as an unacceptable sellout of a deeply held preference. Finding a solution that represents a compromise with which all feel they can live has proven elusive to this point.

Two ideas, one territorial and one jurisdictional, have been put forward. The ter-ritorial solution involves *cessation of the Vale of Kashmir to Pakistan.* This region is in the western part of Kashmir, thus contiguous to Pakistan, and it is also the region through which the rivers flow (the Jhelum in particular traverses the valley). The tradeoff would be Pakistan's relinquishing claims to other parts of Kashmir, and notably the mountainous areas so important to Indian security. It is a solution with conceptual ties to Israel relin-quishing the West Bank as part of the price of peace with the Palestinians. The prob-lem is that it is politically unacceptable.

There are several objections raised to this compromise raised by the various par-ties. First, it is argued that formally ceding *any* part of Kashmir to Pakistan after a half-century of resistance to just such an outcome would be political suicide for any Indian government that might suggest it. Doing so might be interpreted in Islamabad as a sign of Indian weakness, which was a perception that many Indians believe contributed to Pakistani aggression into Kashmir in 1965. Further, the concession might embolden Pak-istan to try to annex all of Kashmir. At any rate, the solution would be unacceptable to the JKLF, which will accept nothing less than total independence for the province. There is also the objection that the concession would be morally unacceptable for India, since it would involve abandonment of pro-Indian citizens who are residents in the valley.

The other proposed compromise, little more than a fuzzy suggestion at this point, is *shared sovereignty.* The basic idea here would be somehow to come up with a scheme whereby India and Pakistan would jointly control Kashmir, presumably with some par-ticipation by the Kashmiris themselves. Details of how this work—for instance, would there be parts of the country administered by one country and parts by the other?—have not been talked through, and it is difficult to imagine how two countries with as long and bitter a relationship of animosity could suddenly agree to the extraordinary levels of cooperation that any form of joint administration would require. There is also the ques-tion of whether Kashmiri separatists would agree to anything less than full autonomy.

Pro-Pakistani Solutions. The last two solutions favor Pakistan or Kashmir. One of these is to hold a *plebiscite* to let the Kashmiris decide their own fate. This was, of course, the solution favored by the United Nations in 1948, and it has been endorsed in subse-quent UN resolutions as well. The Pakistanis would clearly be most enthused about this option, particularly if the options for voters were limited to those available under the Transfer of Power guidelines crafted in 1948: union with Pakistan or union with India. The problem is that independence for Kashmir has entered the discussion and would be advocated by a large number of natives of Kashmir (and probably opposed by Pakistan). Short of a campaign of ethnic flooding that preceded a vote, the Indians would oppose any form of plebiscite, since regardless of whether the voters favored union with Pakistan or independence, they would clearly vote for disunion with India.

The final option is *Kashmiri independence.* It is opposed by everyone except those Kashmiris who want an independent state. The Indians and Pakistanis oppose the creation of such a state for geopolitical reasons: India would lose control of strategically vital territory in the north of Kashmir, and Pakistan would lose control of the equally vital headwaters of the Indus rivers. In addition, both countries have other regions whose continuing desire to remain part of India or Pakistan is suspect. The creation of an independent state of Kashmir could only serve as an encouraging precedent for separatists elsewhere on the subcontinent. Even neighboring China joins the chorus on this point, because the success of Kashmir's independence movement might also encourage similar sentiments in Tibet.

Perpetual Stalemate. None of these solutions seem especially promising, and it may be that the situation is so intractable and the unwillingness of the parties to compromise so deeply set that no mutually acceptable outcome is possible. Since the imposition of a solution by military force is largely ruled out by the nuclear possibility, Kashmir may be a problem that cannot be solved but instead only managed in a way least objectionable to the most.

The situation may be analogous to the Palestinian impasse that derailed the Camp David process short of peace in 2000 (see Chapter 6). The Palestinians and Israelis could not agree on two of the issues dividing them (repatriation of Palestinians to Israel and control of Jerusalem) because the positions each held were diametrically opposed and uncompromisable. There was ultimately no room to negotiate.

The triangular relationship between the Kashmiris, Pakistanis, and Indians over the political control of Kashmir may be similar. All three sides have irreconcilable positions about who should be sovereign, and none is willing to compromise its preferred outcome. Even if the Kashmiri separatists and Pakistan could somehow reach agreement (the only possible compromise), the Indians would disapprove and block implementation.

Thus, managing a perpetual stalemate based on the status quo established in 1971 may be the only attainable solution. While de facto control of the headwaters provides less security for Pakistan than sovereign control, it is better than Indian control. India wants the whole issue to go away, but it will not and at least they control the invasion routes. The Kashmiri separatists, who are incapable of seizing independence, at least do not have their hopes snuffed out altogether. It is by no means the best solution; but it may be the best *possible* solution.

CONCLUSION

Kashmir has become an internationally important dispute, one of the global hot spots in the post–Cold War world. It was far from the public eye for most of the half-century of its existence, but times have changed. The answer to the question "Who cares about Kashmir?" was effectively only those people and countries directly involved with it. But in the international environment of the 1990s and 2000s, there are less "big" conflicts that span vast areas and even have the ability to disrupt the entire international system in the way the Soviet-American rivalry did for over forty years. Without the larger conflicts, smaller disputes like Kashmir seem more prominent than they did during the Cold War period. In the case of Kashmir, that interest has been piqued by the addition of nuclear weapons by India and Pakistan to the mix.

The dispute has been and continues to be intractable. Each of the sides has distinct positions that have survived for over fifty years, when Kashmir was annexed to India over the protests of Pakistan and Kashmir's ethnic majority of Muslims. The Indian accession was of shaky legality and was and continues to be condemned by the United Nations as a rather clear violation of the principle of self-determination that was supposed to dictate the political affiliation of the princely states at the time of partition. Still, accession to India remains a fact.

Positions have hardened, and circumstances have changed. The longer Kashmir has been part of India, the more Indians think of it as Indian territory; as a result, ceding Kashmir (or even a part of it) to Kashmir would be a politically heinous crime on the order of giving New Mexico back to Mexico. No Indian politician or government could survive such an event, and the prospect is made all the more impossible by probably well-grounded fears that such an action would encourage other dissident groups in other parts of the country to attempt to follow suit out of the Indian state. Moreover, the transfer might be seen as an act of weakness by the hated Pakistanis, and if the territory ceded included the passes between India and China, could be a geopolitical disaster. Any compromise by India would require an enormous act of political courage by any Indian politician proposing it.

The Pakistani position is equally hardened. Pakistan has made itself the principal advocate of Muslim Kashmiris for over a half century and is no more likely to abandon that position than are the Indians to turn their backs on Kashmir's Hindu minority. Politically, the Pakistanis have less to lose by movement toward a settlement, because any solution is likely to come at physical Indian expense (giving away sovereign control over some of Kashmir), which is a net gain for Pakistan. As long as pro-Pakistani elements control the regions of Kashmir that control access to water, the status quo is tolerable if not optimal. The only outcome (other than the reassertion of Indian hegemony over all of Kashmir) that could cause Pakistan potentially to suffer would be independence for Kashmir.

The independence movement is one important way things have changed in the Kashmir situation. As stated earlier, independence for the princely states was ruled out as an option by the British when the subcontinent was divided. It is still opposed by all parties except the Kashmiri separatists, notably the JKLF. Any settlement that does not give at least some consideration to separatist demands may well be resisted violently within Kashmir itself by those who see Kashmiri independence as the only acceptable outcome.

Finally, there is the matter of outside efforts to achieve a lasting peace in the region. Such efforts were minimal during the Cold War, from a combination of lack of interest and of a wish to avoid embroiling the area as yet another Cold War battleground. Cold War reluctance has given way to concern with the possibility of nuclear war on the subcontinent. Is the need to remove Kashmir from the list of potential nuclear battlegrounds sufficiently great to make an attempt to mediate the dispute more attractive than it has been in the past? Does the international effort in Afghanistan make the region more geopolitically important than before?

There is precedent for an international effort about Kashmir, the Indus Waters Treaty of 1960. In that instance, the principal outside mediator was the World Bank, which negotiated a division of the waters that provided India with secure access to the waters of the eastern Indus rivers to irrigate Rajasthan and Pakistan with control of all the western rivers, including diverting some of that flow to irrigate areas previously watered by the eastern rivers. Hydroelectric and storage dams to produce power and regulate the flow of the rivers were an added incentive.

The bank's efforts succeeded because they were able to provide funding from a group of interested countries who were willing to foot the bill for the projects that made the agreement possible. In that case, everyone could view themselves as winners: India got the eastern rivers, and Pakistan got total control of the western rivers, plus funds for diversionary canals to move water to areas historically serviced by the eastern rivers and the dams. The benefits for each outweighed the political costs of consorting with the historic enemy. The World Bank was able to transform the situation from a zero-sum to a positive-sum outcome.

Would a parallel effort work to settle the dispute in Kashmir? If so, who would lead it? As noted at the beginning, American lack of clout in the region is one of the distinguishing characteristics of the conflict. Should the lead role go to some other state, such as the old colonial power, Great Britain? Is there enough interest in settling the problem to produce the funding for some kind of solution, some way to escape the current zero-sum mentality? More fundamentally, is there some mutually acceptable solution that will still the guns at the top of the world?

🌐 STUDY/DISCUSSION QUESTIONS

1. There are four possible long-term outcomes to the crisis in Kashmir: continued union with India, annexation to Pakistan, partition between India and Pakistan, or Kashmir independence. Compare and contrast each. As an outsider with no vested interest in the outcome, which would you recommend?

2. The problem with each possible outcome is the objection which other interested parties have to each solution. Using the four options in Question 1, to whom is each outcome unacceptable? Weigh the objections. Which have the most and least merit?

3. Assume the role of an outside mediator. What would be the position on settling the dispute from which you would begin negotiations? What concessions would you have to be prepared to make to reach a compromise solution? What would be the costs of a solution?

4. Think of yourself as an outsider viewing the problem. How much difference does the possession of nuclear weapons by India and Pakistan make to you? Does the addition of nuclear weapons create enough interest to become involved? If, as is likely, a settlement will require lubrication with outside funds, how much is a settlement worth?

5. The other possibility is that nuclear weapons actually stabilize the situation by making both sides realize the consequences of escalation. Defend and critique the ideas that nuclear weapons make negotiating a settlement more or less important to the subcontinent and the international system at large.

6. Eight potential solutions were suggested as possibilities for solving the crisis over Kashmir. Rate them by two criteria, desirability and practicality, for each party. Is there any basis for optimism? Does perpetual stalemate emerge as the least objectionable solution?

7. Is there any way to create a positive-sum atmosphere in the Kashmir conflict that parallels the Indus Waters Treaty in 1960 and allows agreement to be reached?

READING/RESEARCH MATERIAL

Abdullah, Farooq. "The Stand-off on the Roof of the World: India, Pakistan, and Karshmir." *Economist* (electronic edition), January 19, 2002.

Ganguly, Sumit. *The Crisis in Kashmir: Portents of War, Hopes of Peace.* New York: Cambridge University Press, 1997.

Jha, Prem Shankar. *Kashmir 1947: Rival Versions of History.* New Delhi, India: Oxford University Press, 1996.

Krasner, D. Stephen. *Sovereignty: Organized Hypocrisy.* Princeton, NJ: Princeton University Press, 1999. See especially Jose Joffe, "Rethinking the Nation-State."

Lamb, Alastair. *Kashmir: A Disputed Legacy, 1846–1990.* Hertingfordbury, Hertfordshire, UK: Roxford Books, 1991.

Schofield, Victoria. *Kashmir in the Crossfire.* London: I. B. Tauris and Co., Ltd., 1996.

WEB SITES

Oldest and most widely circulated newspaper of Jammu and Kashmir
    The Kashmir Times at http://www.kashmirtimes.com

Offers an annotated and current record of electronically distributed sources of information about Kashmir
    Kashmir Virtual Library at http://www.clas.ufl.edu/users/gthursby/kashmir

Recent news and commentary from the viewpoint of the Government of Pakistan
    Islamic Republic of Pakistan: Kashmir at *http://www.pak.gov.pk/public/kashmir*

Official website of the Jammu and Kashmir Government, India
    Jammu and Kashmir at http://jammukashmir.nic.in

Organization working to raise awareness of Kashmir's struggle for self-determination
    Kashmiri American Council at http://www.kashmiri.com

Site dedicated to socio-cultural, political, and current affairs in Kashmir
    Kashmirnet at http://www.kashmir.co.uk

PART 5

Transnational Issues

The book concludes with a discussion of a relatively recent emphasis in international relations, something called transnational issues (technically they are transstate or transsovereign issues, since it is states that deal with them, but the term transnational has become conventional in describing them). These issues are defined as problems that transcend international borders in ways over which governments of individual states have little control, and which generally cannot be solved by the actions of individual states working alone.

In most of the literature, the discussion of transnational issues focuses on a few familiar problems such as various environmental difficulties, the human condition (human rights or the rights of certain groups of people), and man-made problems like drugs, to name the most obvious. In an attempt to broaden and extend the discussion, this part addresses four different areas that meet the criteria of transnational issues or which attempt to address transnational issues that are not so commonly found in the literature.

Chapter 13, "The Millennium Summit," examines the meeting held at United Nation headquarters in the summer of 2000 to address a whole range of issues on the international agenda for the new century. Although the meeting did not draw great attention, it was attended by most of the world's leaders and did result in a series of commitments that, if honestly addressed, will provide some dramatic changes in the international condition. The case both examines what was done at the meeting and assesses how seriously its outcomes will likely be taken.

The second chapter in the section, Chapter 14 looks at the transnational issue of resource scarcity in the new century. One such issue is water scarcity, especially in the Middle East, from which the chapter takes its title, "Let Them Drink Oil." Two other mini-cases look at different aspects of scarcity: the problems associated with exploiting the petroleum and natural gas reserves of the Caspian Sea, and the tragedy of attempting to exploit the diamond wealth of Sierra Leone. The purpose of the cases is to suggest different transnational resource problems in the future.

Chapter 15, "Worse Than the Bubonic Plague," is a case study of the AIDS pandemic in Africa. Beyond the reiteration of the enormous social and physical consequences of the problem (projections suggest more people will die from AIDS than perished in the bubonic plague of the Middle Ages), local and world attention (or inattention) will be presented as model for how the international system deals with the problem that "disease knows no frontiers" (the motto of the World Health Organization), with particular emphasis on the possibility of an Ebola virus epidemic.

Finally, international terrorism has emerged as a major transstate problem for which the efforts of individual victim (or potential victim) states have proven inadequate to suppress. Chapter 16, "September 11, 2001," examines the problem through the lens of the terrible events that transpired in New York and Washington, D.C., on the date of the title. It begins by discussing important aspects of terrorism generally, and then applies those observations to the attacks by Usama bin Laden's Al Qaeda terrorists against the American homeland, concluding with some ways the international community can deal with the problem.

CHAPTER THIRTEEN

The Millennium Summit:

RHETORIC OR AGENDA OF THE 2000s?

PRÉCIS

Since the end of the Cold War, a whole series of international issues that affect multiple states but which cannot be solved by the unilateral actions of individual states have come to the forefront of the international agenda. Focusing on matters as diverse as human rights and environmental degradation (the two most frequently mentioned examples), these issues have become known as transnational (or more correctly, transstate, since they are dealt with by the governments of sovereign states) issues. During the 1990s, a series of international meetings were held and more or less controversial agreements were reached on these questions (the Kyoto convention on global warming is the most recent).

The subject of this case is a comprehensive conference—nicknamed the Millennium Summit—on these issues held in New York during September 2000 that produced an extraordinary list of international goals to be reached. These commitments received widespread attention during the three days that the participants—more than 150 heads of government—met, and then the Summit quickly faded into obscurity. The purpose of the case is twofold. First, it reviews the commitments made by the conferees in the context of how the issues had evolved to that point. Second, it raises questions about the sincerity of the Millennium Declaration (the collection of commitments) and how many of these will actually be converted into concrete international regimes.

At the Millennium Summit held at United Nations headquarters in New York during early September 2000, over 150 heads of state, the largest assemblage of its kind in history, met in the Assembly Hall for three days of highly publicized speeches. On Friday, September 8, the Summit concluded its deliberations and adopted a series of resolutions that it called the Millennium Declaration.

Although most of the document is noticeably short on specifics (the conferees, to the extent they took a direct hand in writing the declaration themselves, had less than three days to cobble its provisions together), the contents of the declaration represent a kind of culmination to the international human rights movement that began at the end of World War II in a concerted manner, went essentially into hibernation, and then burst forth onto the international scene in a series of well-publicized conferences during the 1990s.

The declaration addresses a broad range of subjects, many of which are discussed elsewhere in this volume. Collectively, the list encompasses most of the international problems typically subsumed under the rubric transnational issues. It begins by acknowledging the process of globalization and the challenges that process poses to the international system and the welfare of its members. In particular, the introduction to the document emphasizes the need for international cooperation to help ensure that responsive "needs of developing countries and economies in transition, are formulated and implemented with their effective participation."

But that is just the beginning. After its prologue, the declaration moves to a stunning list of what it calls "fundamental values essential for international relations in the 21st century." As summarized by the *New York Times* on September 9, 2000, they are:

Freedom Men and women have the right to live their lives and raise their children in dignity, free from hunger and from the fear of violence, oppression, or injustice. Democratic and participatory governance based on the will of the people best assures these rights.

Equality No individual and no nation must be denied the opportunity to benefit from development. The equal rights and opportunities of women and men must be assured.

Solidarity Global challenges must be managed in a way that distributes the costs and burdens fairly in accordance with basic principles of equity and social justice. Those who suffer, or who benefit least, deserve help from those who benefit most.

Tolerance Human beings must respect each other, in all their diversity of belief, culture, and language. Differences within and between societies should neither be feared nor repressed, but cherished as a precious asset of humanity. A culture of peace and dialogue among all civilizations should be actively promoted.

Respect for Nature Prudence must be shown in the management of all living species and natural resources, in accordance with the precepts of sustainable development. Only in this way can the immeasurable riches provided to us by nature be preserved and passed on to our descendents. The current unsustainable pattern of production and consumption must be changed, in the interest of our future welfare and that of our descendents.

Shared Responsibility Responsibility for managing worldwide economic and social development, as well as threats to international peace and stability, must be shared among the nations of the world and should be exercised multilaterally. As the most universal and most representative organization in the world, the United Nations must play the central role.

At one level, the declaration is little more than familiar rhetoric. It speaks to a broad variety of themes that have arisen in other forums, especially during the 1990s when international activism on a number of issues escaped from the shadow of the receding Cold War into international prominence. At least five themes, familiar to those who have observed this international activity during the 1990s, stand out. They are:

1. an emphasis on human rights, including the universality of those rights;
2. the need for development of the less developed parts of the world, including the obligation of the richest countries to participate in and support that development financially;
3. a recognition, and even celebration, of cultural diversity;
4. the role of sovereign states in solving international problems; and
5. the central role of the UN in international problem solving.

What is notable about this list is its confluence in the Millennium Declaration. Essentially all of these areas have been the subject of UN conferences during the 1990s—the series of UN conferences on the rights of men, children, and women that began in Vienna in 1993 and moved through Cairo to Beijing in 1995, for instance. Each individually focused event has tended to overlap and incorporate other emphases—human rights and cultural differences, environmental problems and economic development—but the sheer inclusiveness of the agenda produced by the Millennium Summit and Declaration makes it stand apart from past efforts dealing with a single issue or narrow group of issues. When one adds to this list of principles the further list of specific goals adopted by the summit (which is the subject of a separate section later in the case), the sheer breadth of what was adopted in New York is more apparent.

Since the conferees departed New York at the end of the meeting, there has been hardly any mention of its accomplishments or progress toward achieving its goals in public sources. Thus, it is reasonable to question how much meaning should be attached to the Millennium Declaration. Its provisions are very general and do not instruct anyone to do anything in a specific manner. Thus, one way to look at them is as essentially empty rhetoric, the entreaties of which are to be taken seriously when some more concrete actions are taken. Although some of them appear, on the surface, to provide additional rights or obligations that have not been universally accepted before (the assertion that political democracy better promotes human rights than other political forms, for instance), it does not compel anyone into compliance (China can still operate an authoritarian regime and directly violate no provision).

On the other hand, the declaration did come out of the deliberations of the heads of state of most of the world's countries. They added their personal *imprimatur* to the positions probably hammered out by staff members from the UN itself and from various embassies in the weeks and months leading to the summit. Heads of state sometimes do sign on to large ideas at similar meetings and then walk away and ignore that to which they have apparently committed—the lack of implementation of the original Summit of the Americas held in 1994, which supposedly laid the foundation for a Free Trade Area of the Americas by 2005 and which is nowhere in sight despite being reiterated at subsequent summits, is a prime example of lofty declaration not translating into concrete action.

Is the Millennium Summit and its declaration high-flown rhetoric or a working agenda for dealing with transnational issues in the 2000s? It is too early to answer such a sweeping question, but the fact that the summit was held and issued the statement it did is itself notable. If nothing else, the declaration provided a kind of summary and punctuation mark for the activities of the 1990s. While linear extrapolation is always dangerous in world politics, this case study will thus try to assess, however tentatively, where the declaration's admonitions may lead based on the record of the 1990s and how those events appear to culminate in the summit's major document. In the process, we will also discuss some of the more ambitious specific resolutions included in the declaration and some barriers to implementation of the agenda.

THE "SUMMITS" OF THE 1990s AND BEFORE

International recognition of the kinds of concerns raised in the Millennium Declaration did not, of course, arise whole cloth from the deliberations in New York in 2000. All of them have histories that go back at least to the end of World War II, and some before. As well, a number of them are inextricably tied to materials discussed elsewhere in this volume and should be considered alongside those discussions. War crimes and human rights, for instance, are part of the same concern (Chapter 4), as are democratization and development (Chapter 3), and humanitarian intervention and national sovereignty (Chapter 5). For convenience and manageability, we have separated them out; in reality they are part of a common phenomenon that is one of the major forces in the contemporary international system.

As noted, most of these problem areas fall into the category of so-called transnational or, as argued in the introduction to this part of the volume, more correctly *transstate*, issues, since sovereign states, not anthropologically defined nationalities, deal with them. In many cases, they have a developed world–developing world overtone that creates a North-South aspect to dealing with the issue. Generally speaking, the most developed states are asking the less developed states to do something that reflects their values or interests—whether it be Western notions about human rights or environmental degradation. In many instances, non-Western countries are being asked to bear the brunt of whatever changes are required. Because they are being asked to make sacrifices, the developing world often insists on compensation; the most frequent form this request takes is an insistence on a greater Western commitment to developmental assistance.

The items contained in the Millennium Declaration appear to move the international dialogue on a number of these issues forward to new levels of concern. Whether the appearance of movement is no more than that is not clear from the brevity of the items in the declaration and the relative silence about what, if anything, is being done to implement it since. Assessing the meaningfulness of the declaration requires comparing its major assertions to the state of the issues before the summit and then to the actual evolution of actions taken to implement the declaration's provisions.

Human Rights

The declaration is more assertive in this area than in any other. Two of the six resolutions included in the declaration speak directly to the issue of human rights. The first resolution, "Freedom," asserts basic human political rights, such as dignity and the freedom from hunger and the fear of violence. What is notable is that the resolution applies these to all categories of human—men, women, and children. This is notable because various efforts of the 1990s progressively sought to extend basic rights beyond adult males to the protection of children and women, both of whom have traditionally not had the same privileges and protections as men in a number of societies in different parts of the world. The first part of the resolution is also notable in its assertion that political democracy "best assures these rights." Acceptance of this principle represents a major concession on the part of the nondemocratic governments that presumably supported the Millennium Declaration.

The resolution entitled "Equality" extends the assertion of human rights to the so-called "positive" or "quality of life" rights through its advocacy of development. The insertion of this provision was undoubtedly insisted upon by representatives of states in the developing world, because it forms the basis for a claim on Western resources for developmental purposes, thereby tying developmental assistance to human rights. This represents a concession by the developed states, because one of the great divides between those on whom human rights standards are imposed and those who propose such standards has been the developed world's preference to separate human rights issues from developmental entitlement. The equality provision ties the two issues back together. Further, the resolution makes developmental access a gender-neutral issue by suggesting equal access to developmental assets for the sexes (a concession by those states that have traditionally not accorded equal rights to women).

In many ways, the human rights features of the Millennium Declaration represent the culmination—or at least a highlight—of the international human rights movement that began after World War II and blossomed during the 1990s. As noted in Chapter 4 on war crimes (which are, of course, a subcategory of human rights), the assertion that there are universal human rights and the advocacy of international standards based on that premise is relatively new, and did not become part of the international agenda until the United Nations was formed at the end of World War II. To Americans, for whom the idea that "all men are endowed with certain inalienable rights, among them life, liberty, and the pursuit of happiness" is a tenet that is 200-plus years old, the absence of universal claims elsewhere may seem odd and out of place. But then, the idea of universal human rights and democratic principles of governance are highly related practically and philosophically (see the "Democratic Peace" case study, Chapter 3), and the widespread ascendancy of political democracy is a post-World War II, and more specifically, post-Cold War phenomenon.

Because most standard textbooks provide a description of the evolution of post–1945 human rights evolution, it does not need to be described in detail here. It is useful, however, to think about that evolution in two "waves," akin to Samuel Huntington's waves of democracy. The first wave occurred during the infancy of the UN system, before the Cold War was forcefully joined. As a result of international conferences held in the period immediately after the war, the first two major human rights documents were drafted and adopted by the General Assembly (for ratification by the members). The Universal Declaration of Human Rights asserted broad political rights (mostly borrowed from the U.S. Bill of Rights) and added a series of qualitative conditions of life to which humans were said to be entitled. The political rights were labeled negative rights by some, because they detailed things governments were prohibited from doing to their citizens. The entitlements were called positive rights, because they posited qualities of life to which everyone is entitled. In a separate action, the UN also passed the Convention on Genocide, which prohibited systematic acts of deprivation (up to and including systematic elimination) against definable groups within or between states. These prohibitions are included in the list of crimes against humanity that are part of war crimes. Both documents were produced in 1948.

As some countries passed and embraced the Universal Declaration and Convention and others (including the United States) did not, the question of human rights lay fallow for nearly three decades. The major, but certainly not exclusive, reasons for this were the Cold War and decolonization of the remainder of the European empires. The Cold War competition tended to turn human rights questions into propaganda exercises between the blocs, and the clear absence of enforced human rights in the colonies and most of the postcolonial governments that came to power after independence further darkened the prospects of progress.

In 1975, however, an event occurred with major human rights and geopolitical importance. At Helsinki, all the countries of Europe and North America met and reached two major agreements. One agreement, and certainly the one of greatest importance to the Soviet Union and its satellites in 1975, was an accord on permanent boundaries in Europe that reflected the status quo and thus legitimized the permanent frontiers of the Soviet East European empire. In order to gain agreement on this concession to the East, the Western countries insisted on a second agreement: that all the signatory countries honor the basic human rights of their citizens as reflected in the Universal Declaration on Human Rights. This became known as the Basket Four of the Helsinki Accords.

The Helsinki Accords did a number of things, but Basket Four turned out to be the matter with the most profound impact. In order to guarantee that its provisions were implemented, the accords created the Conference on Security and Cooperation in Europe (CSCE) as a watchdog organization to guarantee the provisions were enforced. The CSCE, which included all the members of NATO, the Warsaw Pact, and European neutrals, was widened to include the successor states to the Soviet Union (and Yugoslavia). It became the Organization of Security and Cooperation in Europe in 1995, and plays a major role in European affairs (it has, for instance, major responsibilities in Kosovo).

The extension of human rights to the communist countries is the lasting legacy of the Helsinki Accords and could conceivably provide a precedent for measuring the effectiveness of the human rights provision of the Millennium Declaration. Although it was hardly recognized as such at the time, the human rights provisions in Basket Four are now widely credited with loosening and undermining those aspects of authoritarian communist rule based in human rights violations and thus encouraging the development of dissident movements that could not be suppressed without violating the accords and that eventually shunted aside communist regimes.

Could the Millennium Declaration have the same impact on authoritarianism in a new century? The answer begins with an assessment about whether the declaration is a serious statement of international policy or rhetorical puffery from a "summit" that was little more than a photographic opportunity. To those who would argue the latter, it is worth pointing out that hardly anyone believed in 1975 that the Helsinki Accords would have any particular impact on the quality of life under communist rule. The parallel, of course, is that human rights violators signed in 2000, as they did in 1975. If there is an apparent major structural difference, the Millennium Declaration contains no provisions for a watchdog, monitoring organization such as the CSCE other than the parent body, the United Nations.

The atmosphere in which the Millennium Declaration could be passed, of course, was the remarkable change in the content of international politics in the post–Cold War world. The removal of the Cold War overlay from the international agenda allowed and encouraged a frank international dialogue on a variety of subjects, and human rights were a prominent part of the new agenda. To be sure, ideological differences were superseded by other forms of cleavage, including cultural and religious disagreements, but a much more frank dialogue has been progressively possible, with the United Nations serving as the frequent sponsor of international events. Thus, in 1993, the human rights dialogue was joined with the Vienna Conference on Human Rights, the 1994 Cairo Population Conference (which dealt, among other things, with reproductive rights and the rights of children), and in 1995 the Beijing Conference on Women. All served as precedent and preface to the actions of the New York summit in the area of human rights.

Development

The question of the degree of responsibility that the most developed countries have for raising standards of living and productivity in the less developed parts of the world has been a prominent part of the international dialogue since the process of decolonization began a half-century or more ago. The declaration, of course, suggests that access to the possibility of development is an entitlement of sorts, which, interestingly, it asserts must be equally available regardless of gender. It also ties the developmental obligation to the Western idea of "sustainable" development—that development should be environmentally sustaining rather than destructive of the environment where it occurs.

Calls for developmental assistance have historically been tied to the process of decolonization and the Cold War. The relationship to decolonization is obvious; most of the lesser developed countries were former colonies of the European countries, and their demands for improvement in their status required that they first achieve independence. All of the developed countries of whom developmental assistance was demanded were also part of the anticommunist coalition in the Cold War, thereby assuring a Cold War overlay as well.

During the Cold War period, the tone of the developmental debate tended to be conducted on a moral level. From the less developed countries, the basic argument was that that the former colonizers *owed* the countries of the Afro-Asian world material assistance in developing to greater levels of wealth because the deprivations associated with colonial bondage impeded their growth. The Marxist *dependencia* theorists went a step further and characterized colonial malevolence as a conspiracy to make and keep lesser developed areas in a permanently dependent, subservient position. The Soviet Union, all of whose colonies were republics of the union itself, cheerfully encouraged this verbal assault on the West and portrayed itself as the champion of the downtrodden (but not their economic bankroller).

There tended to be little direct dialogue between the developed and developing countries on this subject, except in international organizations such as the World Bank. Rather, the developing countries developed forums from which they issued developmental demands that were, by and large, ignored by those countries that were the objects of the demands. This process was launched when 23 African and Asian states attended the Bandung Conference in Indonesia in 1955 and issued the first demands for assistance (the meeting was more famous for revealing for the first time the Sino-Soviet split). The Group of 77 (after the number of countries present at the first meeting) followed in the 1960s, and demands for a New International Economic Order in which the most developed countries were to transfer 1–3 percent of their GDP annually to the developing world followed.

These Cold War era efforts were doomed to general failure, because despite one's assessment of the moral obligations the colonists might have toward their former colonies, the simple fact was that the developing world had little leverage to force compliance with their demands. Moreover, many of those demanding assistance ran thoroughly corrupt, even venal systems (as noted in Chapter 9, "Debating Globalization," Indonesia was something of an exemplar of corruption), making the case for transferring large sums to such regimes a very questionable proposition on economic grounds as well.

The end of the Cold War has altered the atmosphere in which the developmental debate occurs, just as it has the human rights debate, thereby providing an altered context in which the drafters of the Millennium Declaration crafted their developmental provisions. Stung by their lack of success in trying to shame the developed world into compliance with their development demands, the developing countries also lacked a reliable cheerleader with the Soviet Union gone. The other communist giant, China, was developing quite nicely without public developmental assistance and thus seemed to give the lie to the need, and stayed on the sidelines of the debate. The old strategy had to be abandoned.

What has gradually taken its place is tying developmental assistance to other global issues, and that is exactly what the Millennium Declaration does. Thus, human rights promotion is tied to improvements in standards of living, which require outside assistance to accomplish. In the environmental area, the developing world has to deal with, as reflected in the declaration, the Western (largely American) position of "sustainable development." The heart of this idea is that development is to be encouraged, but only in ways that will not permanently degrade aspects of the physical environment, so that the globe can sustain development while replenishing resources that are employed in development.

This shift in the developmental debate also reflects the influence of economic globalization. During the first 30 years or so of discussions about development, the presumption was that the bulk of developmental assistance would come from governments and be given to other governments. As the wave of privatization and deregulation of economic activity washed over the developed world and began to mature as globalization in the most developed and gradually the developing worlds, that assumption has changed. In the contemporary setting, a great deal of the investment that occurs comes from private sources, and the secret to development has become how to fashion countries to make them attractive to that investment. This movement from public to private development is both philosophically more comfortable and cheaper for developed countries in which there was never much public support for so-called "foreign aid" anyway.

Cultural Diversity

The declaration also extols the idea of cultural and other forms of difference among peoples and the desirability of maintaining those differences. Of the items included in the declaration, it is clearly the most abstract and hortatory of the entreaties, in the sense that there are no specific actions to be taken to implement this provision, and there are also few ways to measure its accomplishment (other possibly than subjective assessments of whether cultures and their symbols seem to be disappearing).

There are two ways to look at calls for cultural diversity as an item on the international agenda. One is as a quite understandable reaction to the cultural assault that seems an inevitable part of economic globalization. It is clear from the global experience to date that one of the victims of the globalization process is the destruction of some aspects of the cultural distinctiveness of those societies that undergo the process of joining the global economy. This assault is most obvious in cursory ways: McDonald's Golden Arches and billboards advertising Coca-Cola popping up in foreign urban centers like mushrooms, businessman eschewing traditional clothing in favor of Western business suits, people walking about with cell phones glued to their ears. To the degree that such societal icons simply bury and destroy long-standing, valuable cultural artifacts, one can understand the trepidation that many feel toward their intrusion on traditional values and ways of doing things. When the intrusion of American cultural symbols in particular seems to act like a computer virus that appears to destroy what exists but does not replace it with anything of value, then a certain amount of resentment is not entirely surprising.

It may also be disingenuous. A second way of looking at cries of outrage about the assault on culture is to see it as a smokescreen to obscure less desirable aspects of culture that are quite rightly being undercut by globalization. As noted in several other places in this volume, one prominent cultural aspect of many Eastern societies is secrecy, particularly among prominent individuals and institutions. This often manifests itself in concepts like deference and respect for elders, which is good, but it also allows those individuals to whom deference is accorded to make decisions that do not come under public scrutiny. In the financial sector, the result has often been the considerable practice of corrupt acts. Western insistence on societal transparency thus demands transparency in financial transactions to guarantee accountability and expose corruption. Defenders of cultural diversity respond with wounded cries that cultural deference is being destroyed. Is this honest criticism or something else? Or is there some truth in both claims?

It is also possible to argue that the intrusion of Western cultural symbols augments, rather than replaces, cultural manifestations. Harvard historian James L. Watson makes this argument in a recent issue of *Foreign Affairs.* Observing the uses of McDonald's in Beijing and Hong Kong, he finds the Chinese use McDonald's to enhance personal experiences: the restaurant is a favorite place for children's birthday parties and a gathering place for retired citizens during the day, for instance. Moreover, he argues, cultural intrusion is a two-way street; he cites the profusion of Chinese restaurants in the United States as evidence. At the same time, he argues the destructive impact attributed to Western intrusion insults the intelligence of its purported victims. "The explanation of 'cultural imperialism' is little more than a warmed-over version of the neo-Marxist dependency theories that were popular in the 1960s and 1970s," he maintains. "People are not the automatons many theorists make them out to be."

Questions of maintaining or destroying cultural diversity will continue to be highly emotional matters as the globalization process continues to unfold. In some cases, the concerns will be sincere; in others they will be cynical attempts to resist needed change. It is not an issue that has any real form of resolution. As a result, the debate is likely to remain largely at the emotional, exhortatory level, which is where the Millennium Declaration leaves it.

Role of the United Nations

The declaration also envisages a prominent lead role for the United Nations itself in the area of leadership in assaulting the world's problems. In this regard, it makes specific reference both to UN leadership in the economic and social realms and in confronting the rash of "threats to international peace and security" represented by internal wars in areas of Africa and Asia. Its assertion that the world body, by virtue of its universal membership, is uniquely equipped to take such leadership, however, is controversial on several grounds.

Hardly anyone disputes the greater prominence of the United Nations nor its centrality, given its nearly universal membership. Both during and since the end of the Cold War, for instance, the UN has been a useful forum for publicizing issues such as development and in providing a platform for the presentation of views and a place for the exchange of ideas and advocacies.

That position has not, however, translated into UN leadership in the development and especially implementation of programs in either the social and economic or the political and military realms, a role the declaration suggests it should perform. Indeed, there have been long-standing and serious objections to UN leadership in *both* arenas, and especially in the military realm. This reluctance to put the UN in charge extends particularly to situations, such as in Kosovo, where the world body has primary responsibility for complex missions involving both dimensions.

One historic objection to UN administration of programs lies in *resource availability.* Major program leadership in the social and especially the economic realm requires access to large amounts of money. Military operations, such as involvement in complex peace-keeping operations (PKOs), require access both to military personnel and the monetary resources to support them. As an organization, the UN is perpetually on weak ground financially, and of course has no independent military forces. The only way the organization gains either money or personnel is through assessments of the members that must be approved and paid for by the membership. Historically, the membership has been unwilling to provide such resources systematically to the UN.

Reluctance to provide resources has been justified by questioning UN efficiency and competence to manage resources and programs. A long-term allegation against the UN has been that it does not use its resources efficiently, but rather is entirely wasteful and inefficient with any monies provided to it. This criticism has been levied most loudly in the United States Congress and especially by the volatile chair of the Senate Foreign Relations Committee, Jesse Helms (R, North Carolina). At the same time, it is often argued that the organization lacks adequate or competent (or both) personnel to take on complex operations successfully. This charge is made with particular vigor about UN stewardship of PKOs and other military operations.

These charges are reinforced by a third objection, which is the UN *track record*, especially in the area of military operations. It is alleged that the UN has neither adequate expertise nor enough empathy and understanding of military affairs to organize or oversee military affairs. Most UN officials, so it is alleged, are primarily interested in peace, and as such find military matters (even if they are directed at creating or sustaining peace) distasteful. As evidence of UN ineptitude, one particularly gross example is often cited about the organization's early oversight of the UN Protection Force (UNPROFOR) operation in Bosnia. In that case, the office in UN headquarters in New York to whom the force had to turn for decisions about what it was doing was only open for business from 9 A.M. to 5 P.M. Monday through Friday; at other times, it was unmanned. Warring elements in Bosnia quickly realized that the best way to frustrate the UN force was to conduct operations against it when the office was closed and UNPROFOR could not gain authorization to respond.

These allegations against the organization, regardless of merit, are widespread and are unlikely to disappear in the near future, meaning the exhortation to UN leadership is likely to be more ceremonial and symbolic than substantive. The most extensive objections have been against the quality of UN endeavors in military affairs, but questions of competence, for instance, have been extended to the economic and social realms as well. The General Assembly may pass resolutions regarding economic development, but the funding must come through organizations such as the World Bank and the International Monetary Fund (IMF). While both these institutions are affiliated with the UN as specialized agencies, they are operationally independent of the world organization. Similarly, the Security Council is likely to provide the leadership in authorizing PKOs in various Third World countries, but the implementation of these missions is likely to be handed over to other organizations; NATO has become a major surrogate in this regard in places such as Kosovo.

Specific Recommendations

The Millennium Declaration also made six more specific priority recommendations that fall into the general category and four more general entreaties in the area of human entitlement. The six priorities are:

- To halve, by the year 2015, the proportion of the world's people whose income is less than $1 a day and the proportion of people who suffer from hunger, and to halve the proportion of people who are unable to reach, or to afford, safe drinking water.

- To ensure that, by the same date, children everywhere, boys and girls alike, will be able to complete a full course of primary schooling; and that girls and boys will have equal access to all levels of education.
- By the same date, to have reduced maternal mortality by three-quarters, and under-5 child mortality by two thirds, of their current rates.
- To have by then halted—and begun to reverse—the spread of HIV-AIDS, the scourge of malaria and other diseases that afflict humanity.
- To provide special assistance to children orphaned by HIV-AIDS.
- By 2020, to have achieved a significant improvement in the lives of at least 100 million slum dwellers as proposed in the 'Cities Without Slums' initiative.

Each of these goals shares the characteristics of dealing with the quality of individual human life—certainly a major component of the positive human rights contained in the UN Declaration on Human Rights—and of being largely measurable in terms of their attainment. How much of the credit or blame for achieving or failing to achieve these ends will be attributable to the UN is problematic.

The Declaration concludes with four other, more general entreaties. They are:

- To promote gender equality and the empowerment of women, as effective ways to combat poverty, hunger and disease and to stimulate development that is truly sustainable.
- To develop and implement strategies to give young people everywhere a real chance to find decent and productive work.
- To encourage the pharmaceutical industry to make essential drugs more widely available and affordable by all who need them in developing countries.
- To develop strong partnerships with the private sector, and with civil society organizations, in pursuit of development and poverty eradication.

These less specific resolutions, while generally aimed at the same human rights objectives as the more specific ones, are more exhortatory and less amenable to measurement of achievement.

IMPEDIMENTS TO IMPLEMENTATION

With the substances of the outcome of the Millennium Summit described, the discussion returns to an original concern: will it be implemented? It is one thing to commit verbally to achieving the ambitious agenda proposed in the various parts of the Millennium Declaration, and it is another to bring those promises to fruition by carrying out the actions those promises dictate. The failure to do so could be the result of insincerity; it could also be because the goals are unrealistic given barriers to their achievement. In this section, we will look at some of the problems that could get in the way, recognizing that any list we might put forward is likely to be incomplete.

Sovereignty Backlashes

The political area the Millennium Declaration most obviously comes into direct conflict with is its impact on state sovereignty, especially when the assertion of universal rights are attached to means of enforcement of those rights within and against states. It is one thing to exhort countries to honor the "inalienable" rights of their citizens, but when these entreaties are accompanied by international actions, then cries of national sovereignty are likely to be heard.

The arguments in defense of state sovereignty are most often heard (but certainly not exclusively) in the context of Asia, where the cultural diversity argument is used, either honestly or disingenuously, to justify exceptions to various internationally defined rights. In extreme cases, such as the long-running debate in the United States linking Chinese trade rights to human rights abuses (a debate effectively ended in 2000 when the U.S. Congress passed, and President Clinton signed, a bill granting most favored nation and permanent trade status to the PRC), there can be real or threatened sanctions for human rights abuses. As the net of international standards expands to areas such as war crimes, international efforts to enforce human rights standards regardless of sovereign state borders will also increase. This issue has been joined specifically in the case of alleged war crimes violations by the state of Yugoslavia and, specifically, its former president Slobadan Milosevic.

The sovereignty defense can also be extended to other areas, including development. During much of the 1990s, for instance, Prime Minister Mahathir bin Mohamad of Malaysia refused to comply with standards adopted at the Earth Summit of 1992 to protect the world's dwindling rain forests. Mahathir justified overcutting of Malaysia's forests on the grounds that the revenues obtained from the lumber were necessary to provide resources for economic development that were unavailable to his country elsewhere. His defense of defying international standards was that the rain forests were part of sovereign Malaysian territory and that, as such, Malaysia could do anything with them that they liked.

Differential Impacts of Multinational Corporations

The influence of multinational corporations (MNCs) on attainment of the kinds of matters suggested in the Millennium Declaration is decidedly differential. On the positive side, MNCs can be a force for the kinds of change advocated within the declaration, such as providing jobs that increase standards of living. There have been occasions, however, when that was not clearly the case.

One of the clearest instances of the positive impact occurred in South Africa during the 1980s, where the actions of MNCs doing business in that country contributed to the downfall of the *apartheid* system of racial discrimination. The vehicle for this contribution was enforcement of the so-called Sullivan Codes (named after a Philadelphia minister and civil rights activist, Leon Sullivan, who devised the rules). Under the codes, any international company doing business in South Africa was required to treat all its employees equally in the workplace, specifically in terms of conditions of work and rewards for labor. Since blacks were discriminated against in South African–owned companies (in petty ways such as separate drinking fountains and in profound ways such as much lower wages), they flocked to companies enforcing the Sullivan Codes. Since they also made up the preponderance of the industrial work force, eventually South African businesses were forced to loosen restrictions in order to attract workers. Economic betterment became part of the springboard toward ending political aspects of *apartheid*.

There have also been some well-publicized exceptions to this positive role. One of the cornerstones of economic globalization is the Ricardian theory of comparative advantage, which says that production should move to places where it can be done with the best quality at the lowest cost. Operationally, that has entailed moving certain industries, notably those that are labor-intensive but that do not require a particularly sophisticated workforce to perform adequately to produce quality goods in parts of the developing world.

Apparel manufacturing stands at the top of the list of industries meeting those criteria: making clothes (or shoes) requires a fair amount of labor cutting and stitching materials, but it is not very difficult work, and all societies have seamstresses available. Thus, moving clothing factories to the poorest countries makes economic sense in the globalizing economy.

It also creates enormous opportunities for real or apparent abuse. In 1996, for instance, the Walt Disney Company was accused of paying workers less than Haiti's minimum wage (which was a princely $2.40 *per day*) to produce Disney logo wear. Television personality Kathie Lee Gifford was caught up in a similar scandal when it was revealed that a line of clothing bearing her name was produced by Guatemalan workers at sweatshop wages. Athletic apparel maker Nike is regularly accused of such practices in the manufacture of shoes and other equipment bearing its name.

These kinds of problems will continue as globalization spreads. The country with the lowest wages at any point in time is a moving target; as development occurs, countries move up a notch, and the hunt is on for the cheapest place to manufacture clothing or other commodities. To this point, the greatest untapped market for cheap labor is Africa, and the main impediment to its exploitation is the amount of violence and instability on the continent. If that violence abates, however, can Nike and others be far behind?

Globalization Backlashes

As the globalization system becomes more pervasive in the world, it is almost certain that the world will become more homogenous. Such a condition is beneficial when the results are positive and conform to people's expectations; the obvious examples are increased wealth and standards of living and political democratization, including the expansion of human rights.

Questions about inclusion in the globalizing economy overlap significantly the concerns expressed in the declaration. The human entitlements approved in New York, for instance, are best achieved in conditions of growing prosperity and in the presence of the processes of democratization that are also promoted by globalization. Thus globalization and implementation of the Millennium Declaration should be mutually reinforcing.

But are the influences always positive? Although the answer one conjures reveals a great deal about your perspective, the answer is not clearly yes. Even the chief advocate of globalization, Thomas L. Friedman, realizes that not all will benefit. Some countries, and some individuals within countries, simply will be unable to compete, because they lack the skills to participate in even the most rudimentary way, or because they try to enter the general prosperity too late. And there are those who, by virtue of belief and conviction, will never join the globalization system—fundamentalist Muslims come to mind as a primary example, since their cultural and religious beliefs virtually preclude embrace of the values of globalization. A country that combines both characteristics has been Afghanistan. Due to centuries of isolation and now decades of turmoil, its infrastructure and economy lie in tatters, and a fundamentalist regime that destroys television sets because of their insidious effects on people's spiritual purity was hardly likely to embrace the Internet. Even though the Taliban regime has been overthrown and replaced by a more progressive government, it may be too late for the Afghans to catch up in a system that has passed them by, or at least their attempts to do so will be much more difficult. Post-Taliban Afghanistan could stand as the standard, one way or the other, of the effects of globalization on development.

It is not entirely clear that the evolving system cares about the losers. Harvard political scientist Samuel P. Huntington, for instance, argues that globalization promotes economic values at the sacrifice of all other values. As he puts it, "In case after case, country after country, the dictates of commercialism have prevailed over other purposes, including human rights, democracy, alliance relationships, maintaining the balance of power, technology export controls, and other strategic and political considerations." While Huntington is rarely accused of understatement, it is not clear that the globalizing system has much provision to accommodate those who cannot compete. For those who choose to remain outside the globalizing system or are excluded, the association between globalization and the rights incorporated in the declaration will be tenuous at the very best.

American Constancy?

For better or worse, the ability of the global system, working through the United Nations or some other mechanism, to implement the Millennium Declaration depends critically on the leadership role taken by the United States. Stating this is not a matter of chauvinism, but rather a frank admission that the actions of what former U.S. Secretary of State Madeleine Allbright calls the "indispensable nation" make a difference. In the areas affected by the Millennium Declaration, the American record is decidedly ambivalent.

It is clearly not the case that the United States (or essentially all Americans) oppose human rights, economic development, and the other items included in the declaration. Nevertheless, the U.S. record on human rights, for instance, has not been consistently supportive for reasons that have little direct relationship to the substance of the issue. Instead, the United States sometimes finds itself on the "wrong" side of some of these issues for other reasons, notably sovereignty and questions of national interest.

The question of sovereignty, as noted in other cases in this volume (notably Chapter 5), has interfered with American participation in a number of policy areas, and especially in international conventions on human rights. It took the United States over 40 years to ratify the UN Declaration on Human Rights and the Convention on Genocide, on the curious grounds that these agreements infringed on American sovereignty. The same standard currently precludes American approval of or membership in the International Criminal Court that seeks to bring war criminals to justice (this position is described more fully in Chapter 4, "War Crimes").

In other instances, narrow interpretations of what constitute American interests may also make American leadership impossible. In the area of economic development, negative assessments about how much the United States should invest in foreign aid has labeled the country the "stingiest rich nation" in the world, with a foreign assistance budget that declined by an average of 8 percent per year during the 1990s. According to the World Bank, the average amount of individual taxes devoted to developmental assistance fell from $42 per American in 1993 to $32 in 1998. While it can be argued that bolstering economies with public funds runs counter to the expressed American preference for privatization, such niggardliness does clash with the United States' role as a global leader.

CONCLUSION

In the end, we return to the question raised in the beginning: Are the pledges made in the Millennium Declaration meaningful statements of international priority or high-blown but ultimately vacuous rhetoric? The concerns raised in the declaration are, of course, not at all new. As noted in previous sections, all have been debated for some time, and international calls for action on them have been frequently raised and debated in international forums. What is different is their grouping in a single document and the endorsement of that document by most of the world's heads of government. How much of a difference will that difference make? The answer is almost certainly that there will be varying degrees of success in attaining different goals, partly because some are more concrete than others and partly because the international consensus on some is greater than on others.

Take the case of development as an example. Less than a month after the Millennium Summit issued its proclamation, the World Bank and the IMF held a joint meeting in Prague that was greeted by numerous rancorous protesters demonstrating against various aspects of the globalizing economy, including what the protesters viewed as a dismal record of alleviating the suffering of the world's poorest countries. The world's bankers were stung by criticisms of their policies, which the *New York Times* described as, "In return for long-term loans, poor nations got mandatory lessons in capitalism, what might be called the teach-a-man-a-trade theory of aid." Instead, the consensus with which the participants left the Czech Republic was threefold: a shift away from loans to grants; an accelerated commitment to debt relief; and a sensitivity to two-way trade with the poorest countries. These policies are aimed at the world's poorest people, those with a per capita income of less than $2 a day that comprise about half of the world's population.

While it would be a stretch to draw a direct causal link between what happened in New York and Prague three weeks apart, at least the deliberations at Prague offer some indication of sympathy for the developmental aspects of the declaration. The atmosphere for improvements in human rights seems to be generally greater now than in the 1990s and certainly before that, but progress in that area will be less systemic and more the result of actions taken in individual countries. The same is largely true in the area of environmental degradation. The degree of UN leadership will depend upon how much leadership the members decide to delegate to the world body.

In the end, the degree to which the provisions of the Millennium Summit are realized will likely be an evolutionary matter in which progress is more rapid in some areas and slower or nonexistent in others. The declaration agreed to by the world's leaders does provide a raised standard for the international community to attempt to hurdle.

STUDY DISCUSSION QUESTIONS

1. What are the major provisions of the Millennium Declaration? Are they new concerns? What makes their inclusion in the declaration unique?

2. What are the elements of human rights concerns that arise from the Millennium Declaration? How do these fit into the broader movement toward human rights that has emerged in recent years?

3. What are the major assumptions and concerns that underlay the emphasis on development in the declaration? Are these valid concerns? How do they compare with similar concerns raised in this area in the past?

4. What are the major impediments to realizing individual items in the declaration and the overall document? Can you think of others? What do you think of the United States' role in this process?

5. Assess the subtitle of this case study. Is the Millennium Declaration mere rhetoric or a blueprint for the 2000s?

READING/RESEARCH MATERIAL

Diefenbeck, James A. *Rights, Politics, and Economics*. Lanham, MD: University Press of America, 1995.

Donnelly, Jack. *Universal Human Rights in Theory and Practice*. Ithaca, NY: Cornell University Press, 1989.

Friedman, Thomas L. *The Lexus and the Olive Tree: Understanding Globalization*. New York: Farrar, Straus, Giroux, 1999.

Gentry, John A. "The Cancer of Human Rights." *Washington Quarterly* 22, 4 (Autumn 1999), 95–112.

Huntington, Samuel P. "The Erosion of American National Interests." *Foreign Affairs* 76, 6 (November-December 1997), 37–51.

"In Statement Made By the U.N: The Need for Balance." *New York Times,* national edition, September 9, 2000, A4.

Kahn, Joseph. "The World's Bankers Try Giving Money, Not Lessons." *New York Times,* electronic edition, October 1, 2000.

Lauren, Paul. *The Evolution of International Human Rights*. Philadelphia: University of Pennsylvania Press, 1998.

Spar, Debora L. "The Spotlight on Human Rights: America Bows Out." *Foreign Affairs* 77, 2 (March-April 1998), 7–12.

Watson, James L. "China's Big Mac Attack." *Foreign Affairs* 79, 3 (May-June 2000), 120–134.

WEB SITES

Offers information on the Summit's thematic framework, organization, and structure

The Millennium Summit at http://www.un.org/millennium/summit.htm

Overview of relevant reports, background documents, and General Assembly resolutions

The Millennium Assembly at http://www.un.org/millennium

Gathering of global civil society representatives held in preparation for the Millennium Assembly

The Millennium Forum at http://www.millenniumforum.org

Special report looking at what the UN does and what it could do better

The UN Millennium Summit at
http://news.bbc.co.uk/hi/english/static/in_depth/world/2000/un_summit

Comprehensive collection of speeches, papers, and articles relating to the UN Millennium events

The Millennium Forum, Summit and Assembly at
http://www.globalpolicy.org/msummit/millenni

CHAPTER FOURTEEN

"Let Them Drink Oil":

RESOURCE CONFLICT IN THE NEW CENTURY

PRÉCIS

The desire, even necessity, to control vital natural resources, and conflict over those resources, are as old as recorded history. Major wars have been fought over access to precious gems and metals and food and exotic spices, to name only a few examples, throughout history. In the second half of the twentieth century, the most well-publicized resource conflict was over access to the oil reserves of the Persian Gulf region. What types of resources will cause what kinds of conflict in the first part of the twenty-first century?

The case examines three "mini-cases" of resource conflict with roots in the last century but which continue into the current era. The first deals with access to water in the Middle East, and it is primarily a conflict between Turkey and downstream riparians within the Tigris-Euphrates river system and, to a lesser degree, between Israel and Syria over the headwaters of the Jordan River. The second mini-case deals with the familiar example of petroleum, but within the context of the large reserves in the Caspian Sea. This case combines the desire to exploit the oil with the geopolitical struggle to determine how the oil will be moved from its central Asian location to potential consumers. The third case has to do with the desire for diamonds in the international market and the extraordinarily brutal methods that have been employed to guarantee access to them. The focus is on the recently concluded internal war in Sierra Leone.

Conflict and war over the ability to control, monopolize, or deny access to valued resources is as old as recorded human history. Men have fought and died, armies have swept across countless expanses, and empires and states have risen and fallen in the name

253

of precious resources. Whether it was the silk route across Asia, the exotic foodstuffs of the Spice Islands, the diamonds and gold of southern and central Africa, El Dorado in the New World, or the petroleum wealth of the Middle East, the struggle for control of natural, scarce, and valuable resources has been a recurrent theme of human history and the relations between individuals and groups.

How will this historic theme be enacted in the twenty-first century? Resources clearly remain scarce (meaning there are more claimants to them than can simultaneously be accommodated), and some are becoming scarcer as natural stores are depleted (petroleum and other forms of fossil fuel, for instance) or as increasing numbers of people with increasing demands put additional pressures on existing stores (rare gemstones). At the same time, there is little indication that human greed to control and profit from those resources that others want is on the wane.

At this early juncture, we cannot confidently project very far into the new century in terms of the kinds of conflicts that will occur over scarce resources. Instead, the best we can do is to look at the kinds of resource conflicts that have emerged from the end of the twentieth century, and extrapolate from them into at least the near future. Such an examination will provide the context for speculating about resource conflict in the new century.

To explore this subject, we will examine three "mini-case studies" of these conflicts drawn from the 1990s. All three share their location in the developing Afro-Asian world, but they differ significantly in content and in the current severity that they present to their region and to the international system generally. Hopefully when viewed in combination, they will provide some insight into the future.

The cases are presented in reverse order of their current trauma to the international system. The first, from which the title is drawn, analyzes the problem of water scarcity in the Middle East, and more specifically the division of water from the Tigris and Euphrates River system between Turkey and the downstream riparians, notably Syria and Iraq. (The quote in the title has been attributed to an unnamed Turkish official reacting to Iraqi demands that Turkey provide more water for their use.) The second case moves northward and eastward and involves the oil reserves in the Caspian Sea, and, more specifically, the continuing difficulty of finding a geopolitically acceptable way to get this alternative source of energy to Persian Gulf oil to market. The third case looks at a very different kind of resource, diamonds, and the tragedy their exploitation has created in Central Africa, and especially Sierra Leone.

The cases also vary considerably in the violence or potential for violence they threaten in their region and more broadly. While the question of water rights produces a good deal of heated debate in the Middle East that will doubtless increase as time goes by and demands for the basically inelastic supply of water further outstrip supplies, Turkey is so much more powerful than the other states with claims to the water that violence seems a remote prospect, at least for the foreseeable future. In Azerbaijan, the possible renewal of war between that country and Armenia lurks behind plans for shipping Caspian Sea oil to market; activation of the Turkish pipeline solution (see below) contains within it the likely possibility of Armenian efforts to disrupt the flow (or certainly of their threats to do so), and other "solutions" are mired in the problem of Chechnya's attempted secession from Russia. The pursuit of diamonds in Sierra Leone has already produced one of the grisliest civil "wars" of the era, and it is a conflict that could return at any time and that currently has engaged the attention of UN peacekeepers.

MIDDLE EASTERN WATER

The adequacy of supplies of potable water to grow food and to provide for basic human needs is a growing global concern for the present and certainly for the future. In the arid Middle East, a combination of factors has made the problem a current, rather than a future, area of major concern. In a nutshell, growing populations and increased demands for additional water fueled by both population and economic factors are placing greater and greater demands on a water supply that is finite and, in its present form and usage, inadequate for the future. The problem is simple: the demand for Middle Eastern water exceeds supply, and the problem can only get worse as time goes by. Many projections suggest that water could soon supplant oil as the region's most valuable commodity.

In this circumstance, access to and control of water becomes a major geopolitical matter; as the quote in the title suggests, water could also easily supplant petroleum as the major geopolitical concern of states, as well as their most valued asset. The oil-producing states have held sway in the region for years, sometimes with considerable haughtiness, but by and large those same states are the most water-poor ones in the region. It is by no means fanciful to suggest they may find themselves digging into their oil profits to buy water in much the same way in which other states have had to come to them for oil.

Statement of the Problem

The water problem is endemic to the Middle East. The region is surrounded by seas and oceans, but those waters are saline and unusable. Within the region itself, there are only two major river systems (if one excludes the Nile, which flows through only two regional states, Egypt and Sudan): the Tigris-Euphrates river system, which provides most of the water for Turkey, Iraq, and Syria; and the Jordan River Basin, which contributes to the water supply of Syria, Israel, Lebanon, and Jordan. Most of the region is arid or semi-arid.

Of the two systems, the Tigris-Euphrates is the subject of the most immediate physical and geopolitical concern. The Jordan system came into conflict in the 1960s, when the Islamic countries contemplated restricting or cutting off Israeli access to this water source, which was vital to Israel's survival. One of the major purposes for which Israel fought the 1967 Arab-Israeli War was to gain Israeli control over the river and its tributaries (including the Sea of Galilee and streams flowing into it). This end was accomplished with the occupation of the Golan Heights, which gave Israel secure control over the headwaters of its water supply. Finding a way to reconcile Syrian demands for a return of occupied territories with Israeli insistence on control of vital water access remains one of the hurdles—possibly the most important one—confronting a Syrian-Israeli peace accord.

The major regional conflict is over the uses of the Tigris-Euphrates system. As the map indicates, the headwaters of both the Tigris and Euphrates are in eastern Turkey, which is the largest and most powerful country in the region. The Euphrates, which at

1,800 miles in length is the longest river in southwest Asia, flows south from Turkey into Syria, and from Syria into Iraq, where it eventually meets the Tigris at the town of al Qurnah, forming the Shatt al Arab waterway that flows into the Persian Gulf and is the boundary between Iran and Iraq. The Tigris, on the other hand, begins its 1,180-mile flow in eastern Turkey but flows south directly into Iraq (although it briefly forms a boundary between Turkey and Syria).

    Water from the Tigris-Euphrates system is important to all three states, although it is not equally vital to all. Access to the waters is particularly important to Syria, and even more so to Iraq, since the majority of the water each uses for irrigation as well as drinking water comes from this source, for which there are no ready substitutes. Expansion of the agricultural sectors for each depends on a reliable supply of water, and the growing populations in each country place additional stress on current available supplies.

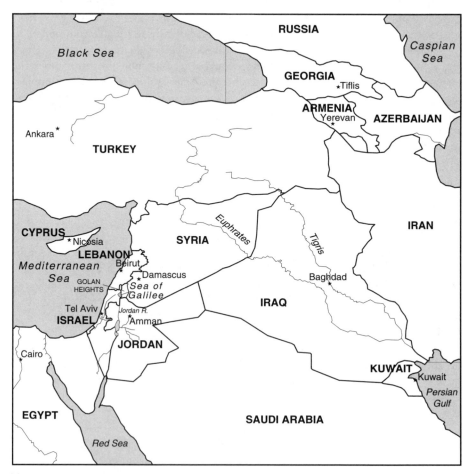

Map 14.1 Map of the Middle East, including the Tigris–Euphrates and Jordan Rivers.

Both Syria and Iraq demand that Turkey increase the amount of flow of the river out of Turkey and guarantee the amount available to them.

Turkey is much less dependent on the system, because it enjoys more rainfall than Iraq and Syria and because it has other river systems that run through the country. Although Turkey is classified as having a water surplus, the Turks have claims on and plans for the system that threaten the access of downstream riparians. For the Turks, the waters of the Tigris and Euphrates river system are an integral part of their plans for the economic and political development of eastern Turkey. The mountainous area is the site of the Greater Anatolia Project (GAP), and central to that project is the development of a series of hydroelectric dams and reservoirs on the two rivers. In addition to allowing Turkey to control the flow of the rivers, these dams are designed to allow agricultural development of the eastern part of the country through irrigation and also to promote recreational uses of the resulting lakes and thus tourism in the country's poorest region.

The GAP has geopolitical ramifications and purposes as well. The area in which the development is taking place is known to many of its inhabitants as Kurdistan, and the Turkish Kurds have been engaged in a long-term civil war against the Turkish government that has resulted in many deaths and alleged atrocities that have blackened Turkey's eye in international circles (ending the civil war, for instance, is one of the preconditions for consideration of Turkey's admission to the European Union, a primary objective of the regime in Ankara). Part of the Turkish government's strategy for ending the civil conflict with the Kurds is to make their homeland in Turkey prosperous enough that they will perceive a stake in remaining a part of the country and thus will abandon their insurrection.

Other regional countries gain a stake in the resolution of the problem in a kind of ripple effect that arises because Syria has claims against both Euphrates and Jordan River waters. In the absence of a satisfactory guarantee that Turkey will keep the water flowing (and Turkey is capable physically of reducing or interrupting the flow altogether), Syria continues to demand a share of the water from the Jordan Basin, which is a matter of considerable concern for Israel, Jordan, and Lebanon (the other users of Jordan River water). To make matters even more complicated, Israel has a nascent alliance with the Turks that may, among other things, result in the importation of Turkish water directly to Israel, providing for them a further interest in Turkey's water situation. Since Saudi Arabia is also a water-poor, oil-rich state that has some interest in importing Turkish water, even it has at least an indirect stake in the problem.

The situation has been intractable, because geopolitics becomes intertwined with the issue of water equity. The issue is clearly defined: Syria and Iraq want and demand concrete, inviolable guarantees to an increasing portion of the water from the two rivers, a demand that reverberates through the interests of the others. Turkey, on the other hand, is perfectly content with the status quo, because that status quo leaves the Turks in control of the situation regarding the supply and control of the water and maximizes their freedom of action.

The problem thus becomes one of claims and counterclaims and leverage. The downstream states base their claims for additional water on demographics like population increases, which no one denies. The Turks, however, counter that the problem is not how much water the Iraqis and Syrians have from the river system, but how they use it. To cite two Turkish examples, the Turks allege that both the downstream states grow crops that are inappropriate in their use of water for the amount of water available (cotton, for instance), and the Turks allege that downstream riparians use primitive irrigation techniques that result in a large amount of water being wasted through evaporation. The Turks thus claim that Iraq and Syria already receive enough water to sustain themselves if they use it properly.

With good arguments on both (or all) sides, a resolution incorporating change requires leverage to induce agreement. To this point, all the leverage has resided with the Turks. They control the source of the water, they are the most militarily powerful state in the region (thereby ruling out military action to seize the water), and there is nothing that Syria and Iraq have that Turkey needs badly enough to compel the Turks to concede on the water issue. In this region where water is king, the Turks would seem to hold the upper hand.

Possible Means of Resolution

Although discussions have been held periodically between Turkey and the downstream riparian states about the Tigris-Euphrates system, the discussions have not yet approached the point where anything resembling a solution about equitable distribution has been found. Partly, this is the case because the needs of the downstream states have not become so critical that Iraq and Syria feel the need to try to force the issue. At the same time, both complainants have other, more immediate concerns: Syria has been in the middle of the succession of the late Hafiz al-Assad to his son Bashar, and has the settlement of hostilities (which incorporate a water dimension, of course) with Israel on its diplomatic plate as well. Iraq and its embattled leader Saddam Hussein are in the midst of stifling United Nations sanctions; any inconveniences caused by water flows from the Tigris and Euphrates pale by comparison with those concerns. There are no particular outside pressures on Turkey to accommodate either the Syrians or the Iraqis, since both are considered international rogues and have few friends who will bring pressure to bear on the Turks.

What, then, are the possible alternatives that might lead to some form of agreement dividing the waters of the Tigris-Euphrates in a manner that would satisfy all parties? One can safely omit the possibility of military action—an attempted seizure of Turkish land to gain control of the waters, for instance. The armed forces of Turkey are much larger and more powerful than those of either Syria or Iraq (whose military was, of course, decimated by the Persian Gulf War and has never truly been rebuilt). As a member of NATO, Turkish forces are much better equipped than the others. Military threats would be greeted with derision in Ankara, although the successful development of weapons of mass destruction by Iraq could alter that calculation.

Although none are very likely, there are four other possibilities for bringing resolution to the water issue. The first is a *negotiated reallocation* of the current formula for allocating flow from the rivers. Such a negotiation would almost certainly have to be multilateral, probably with outside help provided by some general agency like the United

Nations, a regional actor like the Arab League, or a more specialized intergovernmental organization (IGO) like the Water Resources Working Group (WRWG), an organization founded in 1992 to "foster cooperation on water-related issues while creating confidence building measures, and cooperative efforts to alleviate water shortages." The problem with this solution, of course, is the asymmetry of incentives to enter into negotiations; the Turks, after all, see no need to change the formula under which water is currently allocated, and the Syrians and Iraqis can offer few incentives to convince the Turks to change their position. In those circumstances, Turkey would likely be especially unwilling to enter into any discussion the end result of which might be some mandatory reallocation that they might oppose. In such circumstances, the Turks might well decide that no negotiations are better than negotiations that might provide an unacceptable outcome.

A second approach, advocated vociferously by Turkey, is *improved usage of existing supplies.* As already mentioned, Turkey has maintained all along that the problem Syria and Iraq face is not how much water they receive from the Tigris and Euphrates, but how efficiently and effectively they use it. Turkish charges are twofold. First, they maintain that neither country has taken sufficient steps to modernize its irrigation system. Irrigation water from the rivers instead is allowed to flow through open ditches and evaporate in the Middle Eastern heat. In the Turkish view, the solution to the downstream water problem is agricultural modernization. Further, they maintain that both countries need to concentrate on growing crops that require less water, such as wheat, rather than crops that require extensive irrigation, like cotton. While these charges are largely valid, it is not clear where either Iraq or Syria would obtain the resources necessary to engage in the modernization it is alleged they need to undertake. Syria has largely isolated itself from global sources of funding, and UN sanctions assure that Iraq cannot gain support either.

A third approach to the problem is *alternate sources of water.* This supply-side approach is one being pursued throughout various parts of the Middle East, since very few states in the region (Turkey, ironically, is one of the few exceptions) have adequate water within their boundaries. Desalinization of seawater has been a popular proposed enterprise (especially in Israel), but has been dogged by problems of expense; if Israel has trouble paying for desalinated water, how could much poorer Syria and Iraq afford the effort? The fact that Syria is landlocked further complicates its problem—unless it controls Lebanon—and Iraq has a very short coastline as well on the Persian Gulf. Bringing water from countries where it is in excess to the Middle East has attracted attention in countries like Saudi Arabia, and Israel and Turkey have been pursuing the possibility of transporting Turkish water to Israel. The problem with both these "solutions" is that they are expensive and thus are available possibilities only for the richer countries of the region; Iraq, and especially Syria, clearly do not fall into that category.

Finally, some have suggested *regional cooperation* as a potential solution. The idea here is that if all the states of the region (probably excluding Israel) could come together and view their mutual water problem as an integral, regional problem, then possibly they could fashion regional solutions from which all would benefit. The problem here is that the incentives to cooperate are, once again, differential. Certainly, mutual cooperation among those who are water deficient might yield benefit. In this particular situation, however, the problem is that Turkey is *not* water deficient, and it is hard to see what benefit they would derive from mutual action and thus what their incentive would be to become involved in the enterprise.

The Prospects

The ongoing barrier to solving the problem of water from the Tigris-Euphrates system is creating incentives for Turkey to agree to change. At the moment, they have little incentive other than humanitarian concern for their neighbors, and that is normally insufficient to bring about change, especially when the deprivation being endured by the others is not yet critical.

There is some irony and bitterness in the phrase, "let them drink oil." While Turkey has adequate water supplies, it is not one of the petroleum-rich countries of the region and has not benefited from the prosperity heaped upon the oil producers. Now the shoe is on the other foot, and the Turks have to be enjoying the discomfort of their fellow Muslims.

To make progress, Turkey will require some geopolitical incentive to accommodate the downstream riparian states. The hinge may be Turkey's desire to become a prosperous, developed state that can, as Turkey has sought to do for a decade, become eligible for admission to the European Union. One requisite for economic development is reliable access to sufficient energy resources to fuel a modern state. In the form of petroleum, that is something the water-poor states (other than Syria) have. A water-for-oil deal may be the best incentive the downstream states can offer. Whether that is attractive enough to whet Turkey's interest depends on whether there are alternative sources for Turkey. The most obvious alternative is the petroleum wealth of the Caspian Sea area, to which the discussion turns as the subject of the second mini-case in this chapter.

CASPIAN SEA OIL

Petroleum was the most geopolitically potent natural resource of the twentieth century, and especially the latter half of that century, when the concentration of production shifted to the Persian Gulf littoral and the oil-rich states of that region gained control of the wealth under their soil from the major Western oil countries (known in the area as the Seven Sisters). Previously poor and underdeveloped countries became strategic prizes in the East-West competition, favor was curried, wars were fought, and American President Jimmy Carter declared the security of the Persian Gulf vital to U.S. interests. As if to prove the gravity of his assertion in what became known as the Carter Doctrine, the United States led a coalition of over 25 states to expel the invading Iraqis from Kuwaiti soil in 1990–1991.

Western dependence for energy on the Persian Gulf, which possesses nearly two-thirds of the world's known petroleum reserves, has never been entirely comfortable for the oil consumers. This dependence ties the developed countries to the often volatile politics of the region, leaves them subject to periodic extortion and increased prices at the pump when oil supplies are withheld, and necessitates the devotion of military and other resources to a region of the world that would not otherwise warrant the expenditure. The problem and the solution, of course, is how to reduce that dependency.

The basic problem is not, as is sometimes advertised, a shortage of alternate sources of energy. There is, for instance, a large amount of unrecovered oil in the United States, but the cost of extracting it is either too high to make it economical (there is plenty of oil under Texas, but no one wants to pay the $40 a barrel or so to recover it), or the effort runs afoul of environmental or other concerns (the current controversy over exploiting the Alaska wilderness, for instance). There are also large reserves in or adjacent to the west coast of Africa, Venezuela, Indonesia, and a number of other places where the politics are nearly as complicated as in the Persian Gulf. There is also, of course, the possibility of reducing dependency by reducing levels of usage and hence demand, a source many governments (especially the U.S.) have been politically unwilling to embrace and champion seriously.

In these circumstances, the desire to break dependence on Persian Gulf oil has led the world's oil consumers to the small Soviet successor state of Azerbaijan. Its capital, Baku, sits on the banks of the Caspian Sea (which is actually a salt lake and the world's largest inland body of water), under which some of the richest deposits of petroleum and natural gas left in the world lie. The largest of these deposits are about sixty miles offshore from Baku, making it the focus of concerted exploration and exploitation.

The existence of Caspian Sea petroleum is nothing new. In fact, oil was discovered in the area in the second half of the nineteenth century, and by the beginning of the twentieth century the region supplied most of Russia's oil needs (Imperial Russia completed its annexation of Azerbaijan in 1828). Although Azerbaijan declared its independence in 1918, it was absorbed into the Soviet Union in 1920. During the period when it was a republic of the Soviet Union, Azerbaijan was clearly not an alternative source of petroleum for an increasingly addicted West, however, because of the nature of the Cold War competition and thus Western unwillingness to become dependent on Soviet-controlled petroleum reserves.

The demise of the Soviet Union opened the floodgates for Western entrepreneurs to be drawn to Baku. When Azerbaijan declared its independence from the Soviet Union on August 30, 1991, the oil companies were not far behind, engaging in a flood of speculation and exploration that many veteran oilmen say had not been seen since the opening of the Texas oil fields in the early 1900s. By the middle 1990s, the Caspian Sea fields were widely being extolled as the means by which the developed world would break the stranglehold imposed by the Persian Gulf oil-producing states. Yet, in 2000, hardly a drop of Caspian Sea oil was finding its way to the West, and the prospects for that situation changing very much in the short term were increasingly bleak.

Why is this the case? There is certainly no lack of interest among Western governments and the private oil companies in exploiting and bringing to market the petroleum riches lying beneath the Caspian Sea, and there are no major technical or engineering barriers present either. But there are geopolitical problems; one is the political instability of the region, and another is the geopolitics of piping the riches to market because of competing routes with different advantages and barriers.

Regional Instabilities

The major geopolitical liability for Azerbaijan centers on two enclave areas that are points of major contention between Muslim Azerbaijan and neighboring Christian Armenia, Nagorno-Karabakh, and Naxcivan (sometimes known as Nakichevan). Of these two disputes, the ongoing conflict over Nagorno-Karabakh has been the more serious and has created the most difficulties for Azerbaijan generally and for exploiting the oil in particular.

Nagorno-Karabakh (hereafter Nagorno) is an enclave with a majority Armenian population that is located physically in Azerbaijan. There has been a long history of accusations by residents of the enclave that they have been mistreated by their Muslim rulers, and this has accompanied an unease with being physically separated from their Armenian brethren, as the accompanying map shows.

The contest over the status of Nagorno, which was treated as an autonomous region within Azerbaijan by the Soviets, goes back to the latter days of the Soviet Union. In 1988, the Armenians petitioned Moscow to cede Nagorno to Armenia and

Map 14.2 Map of Azerbaijan and surrounding areas (Armenia, Chechnya, and Turkey).

were rebuffed by the Soviets. When Azerbaijan declared its independence, it announced that Nagorno would lose its autonomous status and become an integral part of Azerbaijan, an action that sent residents into opposition, a reaction not unlike what occurred in Kosovo in the early 1990s, when Yugoslav President Slobodan Milosevic revoked that area's autonomous status. War broke out between secessionists from Nagorno and Azerbaijan, and Armenian troops entered the fray in support of the Nagorno Armenians. By August 1993, Armenian forces had occupied Nagorno and had also taken control of the corridor linking Nagorno to Armenia. A ceasefire was arranged in 1994, but the issue has never been permanently settled. In the meantime, Armenia remains in control of the 20 percent of Azerbaijani territory that constitutes Nagorno and the corridor, and the possibility that fighting will resume remains an ever present likelihood.

The fighting over Nagorno has left two legacies with which Azerbaijan must struggle. Of the most immediate concern are Azerbaijani refugees from the war zone. It is estimated that the refugees number over a million, which is the largest percentage of refugees (as a part of the population) in any country in the world, and most of them live in the most wretched of conditions within Azerbaijan. Getting the oil to market and hence gaining the revenues that oil will put into government coffers has the potential greatly to ease this problem.

The other legacy of Nagorno is the danger of renewed violence, which affects thinking about where pipelines can be constructed to get the petroleum to the West. The Armenians have made no secret that they are in a physical position to disrupt any lines going near Armenian territory and that they would not be reluctant to engage in disruption if they feel they need to.

The situation in Nakichevan is the reverse of that in Nagorno. As the map also shows, Nakichevan is an Azeribaijani enclave entirely surrounded by Armenia, and its citizens feel the same kind of apprehension about the Armenians that the residents of Nagorno feel toward the Azerbaijanis. The government of Azerbaijan has not, however, been able to do anything to rescue the Muslims of Nakichevan, and the situation there remains one of potential disruption as well.

The other political problem in Azerbaijan surrounds the government of the country itself. The head of government is Heydar Aliyev, a former first secretary of the Azerbaijan Communist Party who was removed from office by Mikhail Gorbachev in 1987 on charges of rampant corruption. Aliyev returned to the political arena in 1995 as the leader of something called the New Azerbaijan Party (NAP) and was elected president of the country. According to the *CIA Factbook 2000*, corruption in the country is "ubiquitous." The 1999 Corruption Perceptions Index, produced by Berlin-based Transparency Inc., rates the Azerbaijan government as the third most corrupt regime in the world after Cameroon and Nigeria and right before Indonesia (see Chapter 9, the case study "Debating Globalization"). In addition, there have been charges of nepotism and cronyism against the Aliyev family. Dealing with the regime is a major source of frustration for the oil industry and casts doubts, among other things, about how much of the projected oil revenue would be applied to problems like the refugees as opposed to lining Aliyev's pockets.

The Pipeline Problem

The problem of exploiting the Caspian Sea oil and gas fields is not technical in nature; rather, it is almost entirely political, or, more specifically, geopolitical. In the decade or so since the demise of the Soviet Union, the major global oil companies have descended on Baku, generously laden with Western expertise and funds, and have transformed the rickety petroleum industry run by the communists into a modern Western-style operation. Although it is true that the Abseron Peninsula on which much of the refining capacity resides has been proclaimed one of the most polluted places on earth, the oil companies are ready and eager to make the oil flow.

The problem is finding a way to get it safely and securely to market that will help relieve the world's dependence on the Middle East. To this point, there have been three proposals for a pipeline to the West; none of them meet the dual criteria of security and avoidance of the Persian Gulf. The three routes under consideration go through Russia, Turkey, and Iran. Each is flawed in some political manner.

The Russian pipeline would run across Azerbaijan's northern boundary with Russia and would make its way to either the Black or the Baltic Sea, from which it could then be shipped to Western markets. As might be imagined, the Russians are very strong advocates of this route, because they would be able to charge a duty on the petroleum as it is transshipped across Russian territory, thereby providing money needed to aid the transformation and development of the Russian state.

Aiding and hopefully stabilizing the Russian state has considerable support in the West, and especially the United States, but the Russian "solution" raises two objections. The first is that the Russian government has proven so inept that it would likely squander the revenues or have them skimmed off by corrupt officials or other criminal elements in the country, a situation that Russian President Vladimir Putin vows to remedy but has not done so yet. More fundamentally, however, the pipeline route traverses the rebellious province of Chechnya. The Russians realize that no one is going to endorse a pipeline scheme that could be held hostage by rebellious Chechens, and the inability of the Russian armed forces to completely suppress the uprising there cools a good deal of the enthusiasm for this solution for getting Azerbaijani oil to market.

The Turkish solution has the same kind of problem. The idea here is to build a pipeline across Turkey that would connect to the country's existing oil refineries in the northwest part of the country (which, unfortunately, have been the site of major earthquakes in the past few years). The oil would then be shipped through the Black Sea into the Mediterranean and to market.

The geopolitical problem in this case is that the Turkish pipeline would have to be built across or adjacent to Armenian territory, thereby enmeshing it in the volatile relations between those two successor states. Azerbaijan has no direct border with Turkey. The shortest route to Turkish soil from Azerbaijan is through Armenia (and possibly Nagorno Karabakh, depending on how a route might be fashioned), which is clearly untenable as long as the conflict between the two states exists. The alternatives would be to go around Armenia to the south through Iran, which hardly solves the problem of dependence on the Persian Gulf, or through Georgia, which is the currently favored solution. Georgia itself has been unstable, with Abkhazian secessionists periodically causing problems that have led to a Russian army occupation of parts of the country, and it is doubtful the Armenians would hesitate to violate Georgian soil to damage the pipeline if they felt the need to do so.

The final possibility is to go south through Iran to the Persian Gulf. This solution avoids the geopolitical tangles of the Turkish and Russian routes, but would mean that Caspian Sea oil would effectively become part of the Persian Gulf supply, thus not ameliorating dependence on the Persian Gulf states, which is one of the two criteria for a pipeline in the first place. Moreover, as long as Iran remains isolated from the international community and hostile to Western interests, it is hard to imagine how any form of agreement might be created that would be acceptable to all parties.

The Prospects

Because the dual criteria of pipeline security and lessening dependence on Persian Gulf oil have not been met, the Caspian Sea fields remain largely dormant, certainly not pumping the quantities of oil that could make a difference in worldwide supply and thus price. Other issues remain that contribute to the standstill. There is currently no agreement on boundaries in the Caspian Sea among the five littoral states (Russia, Azerbaijan, Iran, Turkmenistan, and Kazakhstan), although the Russians and Kazakhs announced an agreement between them in October 2000. Disagreements such as this are not, however, fundamental. What must occur is an agreement on a pipeline route and a guarantee that the route will be secured so that interruptions in supply do not occur.

It is not clear that the principals can make that guarantee at this time. The proximity of Azerbaijan to Chechnya and the Russians' inability to quell the uprising there suggest they would have great difficulty providing adequate assurances that Chechen separatists would not act to interrupt the flow. Georgia does not have the might to block the Armenians. The proposers of alternative routes simply lack the leverage to make the necessary assurances to get the pipeline going.

What will have to happen to break the impasse? The probable answer involves extraregional action. Regional powers cannot or will not act effectively. Russia is too weak to squelch the Chechens, and Turkey is certainly in no political position to suppress Armenian interruptions, given the genocide of the Ottoman Turks against Armenia early in the twentieth century (although Turkey and Armenia are meeting periodically to explore ways to resolve their historical and ongoing differences). That means the impasse will remain until those who have the most vested interest in access to Caspian Sea reserves decide to act themselves. Direct Western involvement opens up so many unpleasant prospects that, for now, it is far easier to dream of the prospects of Caspian Sea oil than to bring it home.

DIAMOND WARS

The third mini-case moves out of the Middle East into Africa, and more specifically the small West African country of Sierra Leone. It is a country that normally would not draw much international attention; one of its major claims to historic fame is the fact that natives of Sierra Leone carried out the mutiny on the slave ship *Amistad*. But a bloody civil war has been raging off and on there since 1991, and it has produced some of the most gruesome carnage in the decade of the 1990s in the forms of mass amputations of innocent civilians by so-called "rebel troops," which has attracted a good deal of international attention. In turn, the violence in Sierra Leone has triggered both African and broader, extra-regional international efforts to end what has gone on, including the fielding of the largest peacekeeping mission in United Nations history in this country roughly the size of South Carolina.

What has caused the atrocities of Sierra Leone? At the most general level, the civil violence of Sierra Leone is simply part of the tapestry of political instability in its part of Africa. When fighting broke out in 1991, many observers considered it an extension of the chaotic bloodshed in contiguous Liberia, and the Liberian government of Charles Taylor (itself the result of a bloody civil conflict that featured the so-called "child soldiers," 10- to 12-year-olds enlisted into the violence) has been one of the few but consistent supporters of the Revolutionary United Front (RUF), the organization that has waged the war.

But the war in Sierra Leone is about more than simply a power struggle among competing tribes in a poor and backward African state. Sierra Leone has a rich supply of a highly scarce and valuable resource—diamonds. The power struggle in that country can-

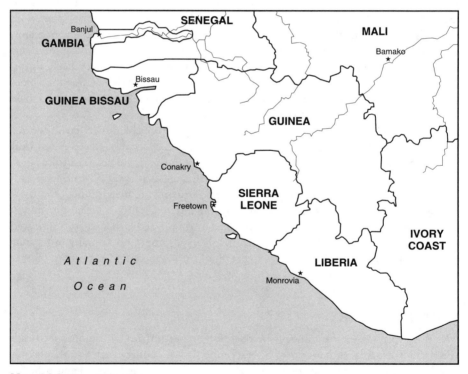

Map 14.3 Map of West Africa.

not fully be comprehended other than in the context of controlling the diamond-pro-
ducing regions that the *Statesman's Yearbook 1997* describes as the country's "primary economic resource" and thus the source of the wealth the country produces. Sierra Leone
would probably be unstable to some extent were there no diamonds in its soil because
of its location; destabilizing the government as a means to exert de facto control over
the gems of Sierra Leone has provided the incentive to conduct a bloody conflict that
could not be justified otherwise.

The Background

A former British colony, Sierra Leone gained its independence in 1961, one of the earlier African states to complete that process. Its early history was marred by instability and
violence, and some semblance of order did not appear until 1978, when it was reorga-
nized as a one-party state. Between 1978 and 1991, the country experienced periods
of civilian and military rule, and in 1991, a new constitution was ratified with the purpose of returning the country to civilian rule. A coup overthrew the government that
same year, and the RUF emerged in the countryside from near the border with Liberia
in opposition to the military government.

Fighting continued between the RUF and the military government of Sierra Leone
(bolstered by observers from the Economic Community of West African States or
ECOWAS and later troops under the ECOWAS authority). In 1995, the UN Secretary General, Boutros Boutros-Ghali, appointed a special envoy to Sierra Leone, Berhanu
Dinka, to negotiate a cease-fire and to return Sierra Leone to civilian rule. To that end,
presidential and parliamentary elections were held in February 1996, and Dr. Ahmed
Tejan Kabbah took power. The RUF boycotted the election and remained in opposition until November 1996, when the government and RUF signed a peace agreement
known as the Abidjan Accord.

The accord did not last long. Unhappy with the accommodation that had been
reached, the Sierra Leonean armed forces once again staged a coup d'etat in May 1997.
The army actually formed a ruling junta with the RUF, and the Kabbah government fled
into exile in Guinea. On October 8, 1997, the UN Security Council imposed an oil
and arms embargo and authorized ECOWAS to employ observer group (ECOMOG)
troops to enforce it. The junta refused to accept the sanctions or an October 23 cease-
fire among the parties.

In February 1998, ECOMOG came into combat with the Sierra Leonean forces,
defeating them and their RUF allies. The junta collapsed and, on March 10, President
Kabbah and his government returned to the country. In order to support the government, the UN established the UN Observer Mission in Sierra Leone (UNOMSIL) in
June 1998. The rebels, forced into the countryside, began their campaign of terror,
including amputating the hands and feet of numerous citizens in a more or less random manner. These actions were witnessed by UNOMSIL members (who were protected
by ECOMOG forces). In order to deal with the chaotic situation, the Security Council authorized the establishment of the United Nations Mission in Sierra Leone (UNAM-
SIL) on October 22, 1999, with an initial force maximum of 6,000 personnel, which
was increased in May 2000 to 13,000 military personnel and 260 military observers,

the largest such mission in UN history. In September 2000, there were discussions of raising the authorized limit to 20,500 troops. A large force remains in place.

Two major points come from this extraordinary chronology. The first is the almost pathetic level of instability in this small country. The term "failed state," originally coined in the early 1990s to describe Somalia and other states chronically unable to govern themselves, clearly applies to Sierra Leone. The country has endured an unbroken string of political woes: elections overturned, coups and countercoups, insurrection, and the alliance between the military and the terrorists-rebels. The second is that outsiders have imposed the only apparent source of stability in the country. ECOWAS (and forces under the banner of ECOWOG) were crucial in restoring order at the end of the decade, and now the UNAMSIL is in place. It is not clear how long it will have to be there; it is clear that their removal would almost certainly result in a return to the chaos of the 1990s.

It's the Diamonds, Stupid!

The conditions in Sierra Leone are objectively horrible enough to raise our sympathies. Christopher Wren recently reported in the *New York Times* that more than 300,000 people have been "internally displaced" in the country, and many more have fled across the border into neighboring Guinea and Liberia. In addition, the terrorist campaign of the RUF has left literally thousands of Sierra Leoneans with neither hands nor feet, creating a prosthetic emergency of the most major proportions.

Given the meager status of Sierra Leone, one initially wonders why it has received the attention it has. Why, for instance, has the RUF and its currently imprisoned leader, Foday Sankoh, engaged in the spectacular, gruesome campaign that has plagued the country for years and is Sierra Leone's principal, overwhelmingly negative, distinction in the new millennium?

The answer, of course, is diamonds. Before the civil war began, Sierra Leone was one of the world's leading producers of commercial and gemstone diamonds, ranking fourth or fifth in total production at different times during the 1970s. The wealth produced by the diamond trade (much of which has traditionally been smuggled illegally out of the country) provides the incentive for fighting, and has enhanced the ability of the RUF to buy weapons and hence carry out their campaign. Recognizing that diamond wealth was being used to underwrite the atrocities, a suspension of the diamond trade emanating from Sierra Leone was part of sanctions imposed on the country during the 1990s, and they have just recently been lifted in an attempt to revive a Sierra Leonean economy that has been devastated by the civil war. Without the lures of diamond wealth, one wonders if the principals would have gone to the ends they have in the war.

The Prospects

The outside world has taken an active interest in Sierra Leone's travail, which may be its major hope for the future. As already noted, the UN has become actively involved through the augmenting of ECOMOG forces into UNAMSIL. As of October 2000, the UNAMSIL force included personnel from 32 member countries as diverse as the People's Republic of China and the Russian Federation to Croatia and Uruguay. Eight of the 32 participating countries are African. In addition, 12 countries have contributed personnel to the civilian police force (six of which are African). The hopes of restoring and maintaining order rest largely with these forces.

On October 5, 2000, the UN Security Council was presented with a plan for a war crimes tribunal for Sierra Leone. Aimed specifically at the atrocities committed largely by the RUF, its jurisdiction will include the crimes of murder, torture, terrorism, rape, sexual slavery, mutilation, hostage taking, pillage, and attacks on civilians. The most obvious objective is to bring to justice those guilty of the enormous number of amputations. Ironically, many of the perpetrators of these crimes recorded their grotesque deeds on videotape or still photographs to impress their superiors, but when this documentary evidence was captured by the UN, it became stark evidence of atrocity. The tribunal, which is the fourth war crimes body formed since the end of the Cold War (see Chapter 4, the case study on war crimes) will be jointly conducted and administered by UN and the government of Sierra Leone. Major questions to be decided include the minimum age of individuals to be tried (since many of the "soldiers" of the RUF were young teenagers) and what to do with Sankoh and the rest of the RUF leadership.

Finally, it is almost certain that a major humanitarian effort will be mounted to deal with the tragedy of the Sierra Leonean amputee problem. In all likelihood, the bulk of the effort will come from nongovernmental organizations (NGOs) that are willing to provide services and manufacturers of prosthetic devices to alleviate the suffering of those victims of the war. The French-based *Medecins sans Frontieres* (see Chapter 2) has announced a major initiative in this regard.

CONCLUSION

In this case study, we have looked at the very different impact that conflicts over scarce resources can have on international or domestic politics. In each case, a resource that more parties want than can have simultaneously (the definition of scarcity) has resulted in conflict. In Sierra Leone, that conflict has been bloody, vicious, and atrocious, tearing apart the internal politics of an otherwise unexceptional West African state. In the Caucasus, the effects of international conflict (Nagorno Karabakh) and internal strife (Chechnya) complicate and, to this point, make impossible the exploitation of a scarce resource to an outside world anxious for its use. In the region serviced by the Tigris-Euphrates river system, the conflict remains dormant and the geopolitics seem to militate against violence, but tension remains.

The point of the discussion is to highlight the diversity of potential situations in which scarce natural resources have affected worldwide situations in the near past and present, as some indication of the kind of role resource scarcity may play in the future. As the world's population continues to grow, there will be an increasing demand for potable water in an environment of limited elasticity. The supply can be increased by bringing water from water-rich to water-poor areas or by increasing the supply through desalinization, but both are economically prohibitive. As the global economy grows to encompass more states, that participation will place added demands for the energy that undergirds much economic activity. Greater industrialization will create the need for more commercial diamonds. And while it is difficult to detail all the possible areas where resource scarcity will result in political conflict in the future, there is no doubt at all that such conflicts will arise and be troublesome.

🌐 STUDY/DISCUSSION QUESTIONS

1. Resource scarcity and its geopolitical implications have not been a prominent topic in international relations to this point. What is the actual and potential problem that scarce resources can have? How might this be a bigger problem in the future?

2. Describe the problem created by excess demands made on the waters of the Tigris-Euphrates water system (including how it spills over into the Syrian-Israeli debate over the Golan Heights). What is the status of the dispute, how can it be resolved, and why is violence unlikely to be the means of resolution?

3. Why is access to Caspian Sea oil and natural gas such a large international priority? What political factors are interfering with the ability to bring this resource to market? What can be done to break the impasse?

4. Given the number of civil conflicts in Africa, what is distinctive about the chaotic conflict in Sierra Leone? Would the war have been the same without access to diamonds? How can the situation be resolved?

5. Can you discern any patterns from the three mini-case studies included in this chapter? Can you think of other examples of resource conflicts that carry out the same or different themes from those presented here?

READING/RESEARCH MATERIAL

"Azerbaijan." *Microsoft Encarta Online Encyclopedia 2000.* Microsoft Corporation, 2000.

"Azerbaijan." *CIA World Factbook 2000.* Washington, DC: Central Intelligence Agency, 2000. www.odci.gov/cia/publications/factbook/geos/aj.html.

BBC News. "Q&A: Why Does Nagorno Karabakh Matter?" *BBC News,* March 31, 1998.

Commission on Global Governance. *Our Global Neighborhood.* New York: Oxford University Press, 1995.

Daniel, D. and R. Matthews. "Environment and Security: Muddled Thinking." *Bulletin of the Atomic Scientists,* April 1991, 8–23.

Homer-Dixon, T. "Environmental Scarcities and Violent Conflict: Evidence from Cases." In Lynn-Jones, Sean and Steven Miller (eds.). *Global Dangers: Changing Dimensions of International Security.* Cambridge, MA: MIT Press, 1995, 144–179.

Elhance, A. *Hydropolitics in the Third World: Conflict and Cooperation in International River Basins.* Washington, DC: United States Institute of Peace Press, 1999.

Lowi, M. "Bridging the Divide: Transboundary Resource Disputes and the Case of West-Bank Water." *International Security* 18, 1 (1993), 113–138.

"Sierra Leone News." October 3, 2000. http://www.sierra-leone.org/slnews.html.

"UNAMSIL." New York, NY: United Nations, October 13, 2000. http://www.un.org/Depts/dpko/unamsil/UNAMSIL.htm.

WEB SITES

Overview of the Euphrates and Tigris damming project provided by the Turkish
Ministry of Foreign Affairs
The G.A.P. Project at http://www.mfa.gov.tr/grupd/dc/dcd/gap.htm

Offers latest information on water resources as well as data on global freshwater issues
The World's Water at http://www.worldwater.org

Primarily focuses on the role of water in the Israeli-Palestinian conflict and the Jordan
river basin
Water and Conflict at http://waternet.rug.ac.be

Provides direction to resources on water issues in the Middle East
IES Water Database Bibliography at http://water1.geol.upenn.edu

Comprehensive analysis of the ongoing dispute over Caspian Sea mineral wealth
EIA: Caspian Sea Region at http://www.eia.doe.gov/emeu/cabs/caspian.html

Links users to vast variety of political, cultural, and humanitarian information
about Sierra Leone
Sierra Leone Web at http://www.sierra-leone.org

CHAPTER FIFTEEN

Worse Than the Bubonic Plague:
AIDS IN AFRICA AS A TRANSSTATE ISSUE

PRÉCIS

By now, the dimensions of the human tragedy being inflicted on most of the countries of sub-Saharan Africa by the HIV-AIDS pandemic are well chronicled and known to most, at least in general terms. The lists of lives lost, and the demographic consequences of those losses for the generations yet to come, have received widespread publicity. Even the major pharmaceutical companies have become publicly involved, engaging in a public relations fiasco of trying to deny Africans access to treatments at affordable prices because it would erode profits slightly; only after being effectively portrayed as heartless and cold did the companies relent.

This case study attempts to examine the AIDS crisis from a different vantage point, as a transstate problem that can only be approached and solved through an international effort. The case reviews the dimensions of the problem and its suggested solutions—a matter made more public by U.S. Secretary of State Colin Powell's public adoption of the pandemic in 2001. It then raises the questions of whether there is sufficient international will and resolve to tackle the problem and whether thinking about this health disaster and its solution as a precedent for dealing with future health disasters (an outbreak of the Ebola virus is used as an example) might produce an international reaction.

It has been described as the world's most severe health crisis since the bubonic plague ravaged Europe during the Middle Ages; current projections are that more people will die from it than succumbed to the black death. Those who observe its deadly progress no longer refer to it as an epidemic; instead, it is now universally called a "pandemic," because its effects encompass a whole continent and threaten to become a worldwide disaster. U.S Secretary of State Colin S. Powell has adopted its solution as a personal cause.

The pandemic's effects, which have been widely publicized in recent years, are staggering in their human toll. Left unchecked, several countries that are most affected could see the average life expectancy, which has been declining for the past decade, dip below 30 years within the next decade. A whole generation of children has been orphaned because their parents have died from the disease, and their countries will soon face a ghastly situation in which the missing leadership of those parents will result in a lost generation. We could even see an absolute decline in population on those parts of the continent most adversely affected.

The problem, of course, is AIDS, and the pandemic is at work on the continent of Africa. It is a human disaster with which we all have by now at least a passing acquaintance, due to the tireless efforts of those with an interest and desire to treat and cure the grisly results. Yet despite a generalized awareness that there is a global problem, AIDS in Africa hardly dents the international agenda. Among the dedicated medical caregivers who seek to lessen the suffering, there are great, even heroic, efforts both to publicize and to treat the disaster. The international community, including those with the ability to address and ameliorate the problem, basically averts its eyes when asked for help, and, if it cannot completely ignore the cries for assistance, it does less than the advocates say it should.

Why is this the case? One part of the answer almost surely comes from the fact that the disaster is occurring far away, in central and southern Africa, in the most distant and obscure part of the world physically and in terms of consciousness for most people who do not live on or study the continent. The AIDS epidemic in the United States, which the African pandemic absolutely dwarfs in scope, has received massive publicity and the concerted medical research and pharmaceutical efforts. Africans, suffering monumentally more, have benefited relatively little from these efforts.

Part of the reason for this inattention is economic. The AIDS "cocktails," widely available to Western sufferers from HIV and AIDS, typically cost between $10,000 and $15,000 dollars a year, a sum far in excess of the per capita income of the people in most African states, which measure annual per capita income in the *hundreds* of dollars. Even the treatments for the side effects of AIDS-caused immunity deficiencies like pneumonia and tuberculosis, which cost far less, are unavailable in most African countries. In the United States, a person diagnosed with HIV or AIDS has the medical doors opened wide, and the treatment options spelled out in detail. In many African countries, all a doctor who diagnoses a patient with the disease can do is to tell the victim's loved ones to take the patient home to die.

One result has been a virtual scandal between the pharmaceutical firms most heavily involved in HIV-AIDS and Third World drug firms intent on manufacturing cheaper versions of medication, pitting international patent laws against humanitarian concerns. The drug companies, buffeted by worldwide accusations of profiteering at the expense of massive human suffering, recanted in 2001 and agreed to sell HIV-AIDS drugs at a greatly reduced price (although still well above the means of many of the victims in Africa).

International inattention to this horrible plague is difficult to understand, and it is the purpose of this case study to try to shed some light on both the pandemic and how it is a broader concern for more than its direct victims. The AIDS pandemic is a classic, although hideous, transstate issue, but it remains in the international shadow of more popular international problems like the environment or human rights. We will try to see why. In order to do so, we will proceed in three steps. First, we will examine the AIDS problem in Africa through the lens of the structure of other transstate issues, in the process trying to establish if African AIDS has the same characteristics as more familiar, orthodox issues spanning the globe and spilling across international boundaries. Second, we will look at some of the characteristics of this particular transstate problem, both as a primer (or refresher) for the reader and as a way to see how this issue differs from or is similar to other transstate issues. Third, we will examine how other transstate issues have been addressed internationally, to see if similar efforts either have been attempted in the AIDS case or whether similar efforts might prove helpful in attacking the tragedy of AIDS in Africa. We will conclude by suggesting that what is learned from treating HIV-AIDS as a transstate issue may provide a relevant model for similar international outbreaks of diseases in the future, such as the Ebola virus that currently also affects Africa and could spread elsewhere.

THE PANDEMIC AS A TRANSSTATE ISSUE

A word about terminology is necessary at this point. The term used more frequently to describe what are called "transstate" issues in this discussion is *transnational,* and while its use is innocuous in general conversation, it is an imprecise and ultimately misleading term. The reason for this is that all definitions of these issues emphasize that they are problems transcending sovereign boundaries in ways that make attempts at solution more difficult, because sovereign boundaries and the dimensions of the problem are not coterminous. Those sovereign boundaries are, of course, what divides *states*, not nations, making the term transstate (some would also argue for "transsovereign") a more appropriate way to think about them.

Although there is not complete consensus on a definition of a transstate issue, this one derived from Snow and Brown, *United States Foreign Policy,* will suffice: a transstate issue is a "problem caused by the actions of states or other actors that cannot be solved by the actions of individual states or other actors within individual states alone." The heart of this definition is its assertion of two common, interrelated characteristics of a classic transstate issue: both its causation and its solution go beyond the ability of individual sovereign jurisdictions.

Not all the problems normally identified as transstate issues meet the criteria of this definition. Some of the environmental problems such as ozone depletion and the greenhouse effect do, but others like human rights do not. In the case of human rights, for instance, it is not physically impossible for individual states to enforce a uniform set of human rights standards; the problem is that some states choose not to do so, and the international community has to this point not been able to agree completely on appropriate standards and the means to enforce them (see the case study on the Millennium Summit, Chapter 13, for a discussion of the current status). Problems which could be solved by individual states but which are not we can refer to as *semi-transstate issues*.

There are also global problems that may rise to the severity of transstate issues but which have not achieved that level of severity or notoriety in people's minds, depending on one's individual vantage point. Global overpopulation is recognized by many demographers and futurists as a grave future threat to the world, and it has engaged the efforts of many population planners and the like. Despite demographic projections of future doom, however, the results have not been so devastating to this point that they activate universal concern or action. Transstate issues in this category can be thought of as *potential transstate issues*.

Clearly, these distinctions form a hierarchy of international concerns. Potential transstate issues are at the bottom of the hierarchy (although by no means necessarily at the bottom of the list of international problems that the international system must consider), because they are less immediate in their effects than full-scale transstate issues. Likewise, semi-transstate issues are less worrisome than full-blown transstate issues because the problems are solvable if the international actors show the willingness to engage in the actions that would solve them.

Transstate issues, on the other hand, are the most intractable and difficult. Partly this is the case because, by definition, they require cooperative actions across sovereign state boundaries, and such actions often generate friction and suspicion of intrusion on state prerogatives. At the same time, the solutions, where they are known, are often controversial. Is, for instance, the problem of global warming caused by the excessive emission of carbon dioxide by burning fossil fuels in the developed countries, or is it the result of the reduction of the rain forests necessary to photosynthesize those emissions in the countries of the equatorial green belt? While the answer is clearly both, there can be substantial scientific and political disagreement about who bears the brunt of the blame. Where solutions to these issues are known, they are often quite expensive, and must compete for scarce resources with other domestic and international priorities for attention and funding. Where the effects of the problem are distant—either in time or in who is affected—attention to the solutions may be disadvantaged in the competition for resources, and especially funds. Finally, when the transstate issue has a North-South, developed world–developing world overlay, as they often do, the heart of the debate often gets swept up in the ongoing differences regarding the "obligations" of the developed world more aggressively to address the developmental needs of the less developed countries, a dynamic raised in Chapter 13.

How does the African AIDS pandemic rate in this scheme of concerns? Clearly, it has moved beyond being a potential problem, since, as noted in the introduction, millions of people have already died from the disease, millions more are infected with HIV or AIDS and likely will die, and the fact and trend of infection will not abate without intervention. One could make a partial case, at least early on in the progression of the pandemic, that African AIDS had some of the characteristics of a semi-transstate issue, in that the efforts of states have either been inadequate to stem the problem before it reached such enormous proportions or, in some cases, in the physical denial that the problem existed (or even that it does exist). That may have been true earlier, but it is no longer the case. One of the major newer sources of HIV infection has been from African soldiers. Some soldiers sent into other African countries as peacekeepers have acquired the virus through sexual contact with infected locals, and then taken it home and transmitted it to their fellow citizens. At the same time, already infected peacekeepers may spread the disease in countries where they serve through sexual contact with local residents. Other than somehow enforcing abstinence or safe sex, it is not clear how the actions of individual states acting alone could stop that problem.

The pandemic thus has risen to the status of a full-scale transstate issue, with all the characteristics and problems associated with such an issue. Clearly, the divisions among states exacerbate the problem by making cross-boundary cooperative treatment programs impossible or ineffective. The motto of the World Health Organization (WHO), "disease knows no frontiers," clearly applies to the pandemic; the response that solutions should be coterminous with the problem has not yet become the norm.

The other common characteristics apply as well. There is basic disagreement not only about the causes of the pandemic but also the solutions. Within the scientific community, there is a small fringe that denies the relationship between HIV and AIDS and also denies that the disease kills anyone, a position endorsed by the president of one African country (South Africa) and vociferously denounced by virtually all of the global medical community. Solutions tend to center on the provision of cheap drugs to treat the disease or its symptoms, putting advocates into conflict with the pharmaceutical firms who produce HIV-AIDS drugs, and activating debates over whether prevention or treatment is the best approach. The matter of treatment raises the question of cost, which most of the African states simply cannot come close to bearing and which can only be approached with either massive subsidies of current drugs by the most developed states or the discovery of much cheaper alternatives. Major drug companies have offered substantial subsidization, but it is not clear this is adequate given the paucity of African health budgets, as noted earlier. Finally, the issue also is tinged by the matter of developmental obligations, since AIDS is arguably the single greatest barrier to African development today and since, it is alleged, ultimately the most effective way to stem the behavior that creates the problem is through the economic development of the societies in which it is occurring.

DIMENSIONS OF THE PROBLEM

For most of the world, the severity of the problems facing African countries is almost inconceivable, and as long as the rampant spread of the disease is essentially isolated to the most marginalized continent of the globe, confronting and coming to terms with its effects will be difficult for most people. Yet there is reason to do so on two counts that go beyond but by no means ignore the immediate horror.

One of these reasons is that the pandemic will almost certainly spread to other continents. There is, for instance, some evidence that AIDS is now increasing in parts of Asia, where there are much larger populations that could be subject to infection but where the resources to deal with the problem are not much greater than they are in Africa.

An AIDS pandemic in a country like China—where cases have already been reported—could be catastrophic. The other reason is that the way the AIDS pandemic is dealt with in Africa may provide a model, for good or bad, of how the world might deal with similar problems in the future.

Directly connected to the immune deficiencies associated with AIDS has been the recurrence of some diseases (smallpox, for instance) that had virtually disappeared from the world but are returning. At the same time, there are other virulent diseases now isolated geographically that could also spread and become transstate problems. Prominent among these currently incurable diseases is Ebola, a highly contagious virus so far isolated to Africa that kills up to 90 percent of those who are infected by it. The West got a chilling portent of this possibility when a Congolese woman, who entered Canada in January 2001, was suspected of carrying Ebola (she was not in fact infected). As we shall suggest in the conclusion, the ways in which the AIDS pandemic is treated may have value as a precedent for dealing with other potentially international pestilences such as Ebola and other diseases that may emerge in the future. How the African AIDS transstate issue is handled, in other words, has both substantive and procedural importance for the future.

Origins and Parameters of the Pandemic

The AIDS virus was first identified in an African country, the then Belgian Congo, in 1959. Although public awareness of the disease in the developed world is generally associated with its outbreak in the United States in the 1980s and 1990s, the fact that the origins of the disease are African has helped mold the way Africans and the world view the disease. The currently most widely held explanation suggests that the disease first occurred in chimpanzees and was somehow transferred to humans, a point of some sensitivity among many Africans because of racist implications concerning the interactions between Africans and the primates. In Africa, there is greater ignorance and denial of AIDS, and at least part of the reason for this denial is the imputation that AIDS is an "African disease."

Certainly the continent has suffered the bulk of the ravages of the pandemic, and there is no predictable end in sight. The raw statistics are staggering. According to UNAIDS—an umbrella group of UN agencies, the World Bank, and the WHO—34.3 million people worldwide had AIDS in 2000, and 24.5 million of them were African (about 71 percent of the total). Already, nearly 19 million people have died from AIDS, of whom 3.8 million were children under 15. In 1999, 4 million out of an estimated 5.4 million infected were African (about 74 percent), and 85 percent of the 2.8 million killed in 1999 by the disease were African. Approximately 13.2 million children have been orphaned by the disease; 12 million of them live in Africa (over 90 percent). Possibly most chillingly, according to a CNN report, "The U.S. Census Board projects that AIDS deaths and the loss of future population from the deaths of women of childbearing age means that by 2010, sub-Saharan Africa will have 71 million fewer people than it would have otherwise." By contrast, 30 million people were estimated to have died in medieval Europe during the bubonic plague, thereby explaining the title of this case study. Since the population of Europe at the time was much smaller than the African population today, a higher proportion of Europeans died of the plague, so the analogy between the two events is not perfect.

Why did this happen and why does it continue to happen? Some understanding of why the problem has reached the proportions that it has and of why it continues largely unchecked is necessary to understand the problem itself, its transstate nature, and how and whether there is an analogy between this tragedy and other similar transstate problems in the future.

There is not general consensus on the reasons why the pandemic has reached the levels it has achieved, and thus any list will be subject to challenge and disagreement. Having said that, we can identify at least six factors that have contributed to the current state of affairs. The reader is encouraged to think of others.

Ignorance and Denial. Part of the problem is ignorance of the disease and its consequences among many African citizens, and especially those who are undereducated and reside in the rural areas of the continent. In most countries (Uganda is a notable exception), governments have not mounted aggressive campaigns of citizen education about the dangers and consequences of HIV-AIDS and how to lessen those dangers personally. Originally, this absence of information itself was a form of denial of the severity of the problem, and it is currently made worse by limitations on government health budgets and the absence of treatments to give hope to those identified as infected.

Some of the results of ignorance and denial are macabre. In some parts of the continent, for instance, there is apparently the belief that having sexual intercourse with a virgin will cure the disease in a male, thereby assuring a maximally high level of infection among young teenaged girls.

The most insidious form of denial comes from a small segment of the scientific community, which denies that the disease exists. The leading spokesman of this position is University of California at Berkeley molecular biologist Peter Duesberg. In his book, *Inventing the AIDS Myth*, he argues that there is no link between HIV and AIDS, and that the only reason the connection is maintained is because of the amount of research funding available to the scientific community to study the relationship. A variation of this theme is propounded by Ghanaian magazine publisher Baffour Ankomah, who maintains there is no such thing as AIDS and that the anti-AIDS campaign is nothing but a foreign plot to "destroy" Africa. In his magazine, *New African,* he has gone so far as to suggest, "What we call AIDS is actually U.S. biological warfare gone wrong." Among highly visible public figures, the most prominent skeptic of the existence and effects of the disease is South African president Thabo Mbeki.

Taboos on Discussion of the Pandemic. In a number of African countries, there is a strong reluctance to engage in open discussions of AIDS. Part of the reason for this reluctance can be found in social taboos about discussing sexuality and death. One result is that obituaries rarely refer to AIDS as the cause of death, preferring vague references to succumbing from a "long illness" or the like. This aversion to discussing sexual matters has also made things like "safe sex" programs promoting abstinence or contraception less effective than they might otherwise have been.

In some cases, the reluctance to discuss the disease has more practical grounds. In a number of countries, public reportage of the pandemic is opposed on the grounds that publicizing it would discourage tourism, a principal source of foreign exchange for some states. Because they generally lack the resources to do anything about the pandemic anyway, many politicians are reluctant to discuss it; their inability to treat sufferers makes them appear less effective as public servants. As evidence that ignoring the problem may appear a viable strategy to African leaders, the 11th International Conference of AIDS and STDs (Sexually Transmitted Diseases) in Africa, held in Lusaka, Zambia, in 1998, was not attended by a single African head of state.

Civil Wars. Particularly during the last decade, a number of African countries have been the victims of internal violence. In most cases (Liberia, Sierra Leone, parts of the Democratic Republic of Congo) these conflicts (which I have elsewhere referred to as "new internal wars") seldom rise to the level of organized conflict that a professional soldier would call war. Rather, they tend to involve attacks against the civilian population by more or less organized armed groups whose members are more likely to be referred to as "fighters" rather than "soldiers." Often, the purpose of these activities is criminal. For instance, a basic motivation of the Revolutionary United Front (RUF) of Sierra Leone is to destabilize governance and thereby to facilitate their plundering of that country's diamond mines (see the discussion in Chapter 14).

In these circumstances, a major purpose of the "revolutionaries" is terrorizing and humiliating the target population (or portion of the general population), and an important tactic of that terror is often the systematic rape of females in the combat zones. Because many of the fighters are young teenagers, the result is increased infection rates among the young, a contributory factor in lowering life expectancy. There is also a chain effect, as young women are infected by HIV-positive fighters and then pass the disease along to other sexual partners. As noted earlier in discussing the transstate nature of the problem, when international peacekeepers are imported to quell the violence, they also sometimes contract the disease and take it back to their countries, or begin the cycle by infecting the local citizens they are charged with protecting. Finally, an important effect of these civil conflicts is to disrupt the provision of public services, including the primitive health care systems found in most African states, and to force the diversion of resources that might have otherwise been devoted to the pandemic to treating the more immediate and direct effects of the war effort.

Debt and Poverty. Even in countries not prone to violence, the existence of enormous poverty, often exacerbated by the widespread foreign debt under which many African countries labor, makes matters worse. Poverty means the resources to try to treat the disease are unavailable, and this in turn has a multiplying effect. As Lawrence Altman explained in the *New York Times* in July 2000, "while a virus causes AIDS, social conditions feed the epidemic. Patterns of behavior—fed by poverty, ignorance, and despair—have resulted in a disease so widespread that it has left millions of orphans and threatens to destroy much of Africa's economy and to wipe out a generation of young people."

A contributing factor to this dismal condition is the crushing levels of external debt that permeates many countries on the continent. As a result, scarce resources that might otherwise by devoted to education about HIV-AIDS, preventive programs such as the distribution of condoms, or treatment of victims are instead funneled into debt service (usually only paying off the *interest* on the accumulated debt, not reducing the principal). There are currently a number of African states that spend as much as four times the amount of money on debt service that they spend on their health systems as a whole, much less on the specific problem of HIV-AIDS.

Expense of Treatment. The extremely high death rate associated with the African AIDS pandemic is the result of the virtual absence of treatment options that are widely available in the West to prolong life and even to arrest the progress of HIV. The culprit, of course, is the cost of the treatments.

Slowing or arresting AIDS in patients in places like the United States is made possible through the administration of a combination of drugs known collectively as a "cocktail." The medicines in the cocktail are, however, quite expensive, with annual costs running at $10,000 per patient or more, as noted earlier. Using this lower figure, the Washington Office on Africa, an advocacy group for the continent, estimates that the cost of providing this kind of treatment for African AIDS patients would be roughly *$220 billion per year.* Given that the majority of the African countries caught up in the pandemic are among the half of the world's population that subsists on an average income of $2 per capita per day (South Africa being the notable exception), the resources are simply not available even to begin reasonably modest programs of treatment. Instead, as already noted, about all the medical system can do is in effect perform triage on sufferers, sending them home to die rather than having them burden an already overly stressed health care system. Although newer and cheaper drug treatments are under development, pharmaceutical firms (as we shall see in a subsequent section) have shown some reluctance to bring these rapidly and widely to market in places like Africa as long as they are recovering their research costs by marketing other, more expensive AIDS medications through the high-priced cocktails, a situation that came to a head in 2001 and that caused embarrassed firms to lower prices.

Relative Powerlessness of Women. One of the more notable aspects of the pandemic is that more women than men are now infected with HIV-AIDS in Africa. The United Nations reported in late 1999 that, for the first time, infection rates for females in Africa exceeded that for males. As reported in the *New York Times*, 55 percent of newly diagnosed infections occurred in women in that year. More dramatically, the UN report also stated that several studies completed in Africa indicate that African girls aged 15–19 are as much as five or six times as likely to be infected than their male counterparts.

The large reason for this phenomenon is the relatively dependent status of women in many traditional African societies. In many places, women have little control over reproductive decisions, and if a woman suggests the use of a condom, for instance, the result may be physical retribution. Despite international emphases on human and women's rights in recent years, translating that movement into sexual empowerment remains an uphill fight in numerous places where HIV-AIDS is rampant.

The list of factors contributing to the severity of the AIDS pandemic is not, as suggested earlier, intended to be exhaustive, and certain factors differ in emphasis from country to country and region to region. In a few countries like Uganda, the pandemic is actually abating, as a large government effort in sex education (centering on the use of condoms) has had the effect of lowering infection rates in important target groups such as teenagers. Nonetheless, the problem remains monumental on the continent. Before looking at what is or might be done to staunch the pandemic, some discussion of its dimensions is in order.

Effects of the Pandemic

When the bubonic plague swept through Europe (and parts of Asia) during the middle 1300s, the "black death" (as it was known) claimed roughly one-quarter of the population as its victims. The epidemic finally ran its course, but since modern medicine had yet to come into existence, there was essentially nothing that could be done either to prevent infection or to treat the disease when it occurred. Today, there are vaccines against the black death and antibiotics to treat anyone who might contract it. At the time, there was nothing but suffering and death.

The AIDS pandemic bears similarities to and differences from the great plague. Certainly the levels of human suffering are parallel; the social and economic fabric of affected African countries are being torn apart as surely as those medieval societies were destroyed. Now, as then, countless lives will be lost or cut tragically short.

There is also a significant difference. Through an aggressive program of biomedical research, there now exist treatments to deal with this disease. Very expensive treatments have been available to those who could afford them for a decade or so, and more affordable drugs are on the way. Although it is impossible to predict precisely when it will occur, research scientists believe a vaccination will soon be available with which to inoculate the uninfected. Both of these latter developments will hopefully bring the pandemic to an end. In the meantime, the suffering continues on a scale rivaling the great plague. This is not the place to describe the structure of human suffering in any detail, since our focus on the AIDS pandemic is as a case in international action. However, we can mention illustrative effects that could recur in the future and which may have accompanied the bubonic plague during its course.

A notable attribute of AIDS is that it is, for many purposes, a young people's disease. Due to the nature of its mode of transmission, it strikes particularly at people in their most sexually active stage of life, from the early teenage years into the 20s and 30s. When there are no treatment options and the infected are just allowed to die, the result is a severe societal and demographic problem and imbalance that it will take years, even generations, to correct.

A major consequence of the pandemic is that it is robbing the countries that are most affected of a future generation of leaders and productive workers. While attention has quite appropriately focused on indicators of the tragedy such the number of deaths, another important factor is the dramatic reduction in life expectancy, a result of the fact that "people are dying in their young adult years, not after leading full lives and then dying," as Karen Stanecki of the U.S. Census Bureau puts it. In 1999, the American Foundation for AIDS Research noted that 80 percent of those succumbing to the disease worldwide are between ages 20 and 50, workers in their prime.

What happens when the time comes for members of the generation who now are dying in their 20s to assume leadership in their countries? Who will provide the working class that can contribute to the economic development of countries desperately in need of economic modernization? Who will serve as soldiers, police officers, teachers, doctors, and nurses? For that matter, who will parent the generation after that, when AIDS is hopefully a matter of history but its demographic consequences are not? And then there are the 12 million orphaned children. What will their psychological and developmental fate be? In the desperate rush to staunch the rampaging disease, many of these questions have only been asked, with the answers unknown or undiscovered.

We have no close parallels from which to devise answers. The black death killed a higher percentage of people than current estimates presume will die from AIDS, but the plague was not demographically selective in the same way; the next generation of Europeans was diminished in numbers but presumably each age group was affected equally. The enormous disruptions caused by forced displacement as the result of Africa's civil wars has affected large numbers, for instance, but the generational gap that the AIDS pandemic is producing is not so obvious.

There is also the question of the broader health implications of the pandemic. As already noted, a major part of the classification of the pandemic as a transstate issue arises from its progression across national borders in ways that have to this point evaded control. At the same time, the immune deficiencies that AIDS creates also leaves the human body vulnerable to other diseases that are now occurring or recurring as public health problems—things like measles and smallpox, for instance. At a time when some diseases are developing resistance to treatment by antibiotics, the revival of old diseases or the emergence of new diseases (drug-resistant tuberculosis and strains of Ebola, for instance) present some chilling prospects for the future.

The AIDS pandemic in Africa has, by and large, been treated as an African problem, but the time may be running out on our ability to sustain that luxury. The disease is spreading to parts of Asia, the continent on which over half of mankind resides. At the same time, the pandemic threatens to affect the rest of the world as well. Speaking in January 2000, Richard Holbrooke, then U.S. ambassador to the United Nations, warned, "If we don't work with the Africans themselves to address these problems, we will have to deal with them later when they get more dangerous and more expensive." Looking directly at the economic consequences, World Bank President James Wolfensohn adds, "Many of us used to think of AIDS as a health issue. We were wrong. AIDS can no longer be confined to the health or social sector portfolios. AIDS is turning back the clock on development."

TRANSSTATE SOLUTIONS

As the discussion immediately above indicates, there is both a growing recognition in the international community of the scope of the AIDS pandemic in Africa, and an increasing awareness that it is more than an African health problem. The result has been a modest international effort to try to come to grips with the problem. Although there is little evidence that the precedent being set in that effort may be important in how we will deal with future crises, that should be a matter of concern for us as well.

The 13th International AIDS Conference was held in July 2000 in Durban, South Africa, to report on the state of the worldwide problem and efforts to control the disease. The location of the conference was of major symbolic importance on two counts. It was the first time that the meeting had been held in South Africa, and it was held in a South Africa, whose president, as noted earlier, has been one of the more prominent figures who are skeptics about the link between HIV and AIDS.

Beyond the recitation of the many horrors associated with the pandemic—including projections of population consequences in Africa—the conference focused on the progress that has been made in developing cheaper medicines to treat the disease. The conference noted that the progression of the AIDS pandemic is far enough along that the population will actually begin to drop in absolute terms in countries such as Botswana, South Africa, and Zimbabwe by 2003. At the same time, the 10,000 conferees were also presented with evidence that more affordable drug treatments that may reduce the rate of progression from HIV to full-blown AIDS are becoming available. The U.S. Centers for Disease Control (CDC), for instance, reported that an antibiotic marketed by Bristol Myers Squibb and Glaxo-Wellcome has been effective in treating a form of pneumonia that "indicates an HIV-infected person has developed AIDS," and can be administered to patients for about $60 a year. While even that reduced price is beyond the public health budgets of most African countries, it is nonetheless an indication of progress. Likewise, drugs cheaper than AZT have been developed that prevent the transmission in HIV from infected mothers to their unborn children.

The efforts reported at Durban are hopeful, but they are not the solution to what Dr. Roy M. Anderson of Oxford University described at the conference as "undoubtedly the most serious infectious threat in recorded human history." That is a very broad, serious statement, and one that you would think would produce a worldwide crash effort to contain the threat. While the research efforts to treat and eradicate AIDS are not inconsequential, neither are they of the monumental dimensions the disease would seem to merit. Why not?

The general experience with transstate issues suggests at least some partial answers to this question. Undoubtedly, they are inadequate to explain the phenomenon fully, and they are offered more to stimulate discussion than to foreclose investigating other solutions to the problem. To this end, two observations that have emerged over transstate issues like the environment may be relevant to understanding international reaction to the AIDS pandemic.

The first is the *seriousness and immediacy of the problem*. In problems as diverse as dealing with carbon dioxide emissions and chlorofluorocarbons (CFCs), a major barrier to action is that the problem does not have an immediate injurious effect on those causing the problem and whose behavior will have to be amended to solve it. People who drive large sport-utility vehicles (SUVs), for instance, might be persuaded to change to a more fuel-efficient and environmentally friendly form of transportation if it somehow physically hurt when you drove the SUVs, and if you felt physical pleasure when you drove 70-mile per gallon vehicles. Obviously, this does not happen, and advocates must rely on more abstract, less immediate arguments such as the effects of global warming on future generations.

The AIDS pandemic is the same way for most people outside Africa. One can read the kind of horrible tales and demographic consequences that have been detailed here, but they have no serious effects on the reader. Just as the producers of carbon dioxide (in the developed countries) tend to blame the countries of the equatorial green belt for cutting down rain forests that are natural "traps" for carbon dioxide rather than blaming their own driving habits, there is a tendency to treat the AIDS pandemic as someone else's problem. When the Clinton administration publicly elevated the pandemic to the status of a threat to U.S. national security in 2000 (on the grounds that the demographic effects could destabilize African states and thus threaten U.S. interests in those states), hardly anyone outside the AIDS community took notice.

This leads to the second and related problem, the *lack of personalization* of the effects of the problem on most people. The worldwide drug epidemic, which is arguably a form of transstate issue, offers an example. Drug enforcement officials maintain that their problem would be much easier if the immediate personal effects of drug use were negative; if, for instance, smoking marijuana caused respiratory congestion or ingesting cocaine caused sharp pain. This is not the case, and so entreaties to avoid use fall on at least some deaf ears.

The problem with AIDS in Africa is in some ways similar. The impact of the pandemic is certainly affecting people on that continent, but the effects remain essentially isolated and concern is not personalized outside the continent. What this may suggest is that the only, or at least most effective, way to gain and focus global attention is to show that there will be concrete negative consequences to not solving the problem. The journalist Robert D. Kaplan (in *The Coming Anarchy*), for instance, argues that a good reason for the rest of the world to deal with the general deterioration of the quality of life in much of Africa is that eventually it will spill over into the rest of the world in the form of migration from that continent to the developed world. Similarly, as the immune deficiencies central to AIDS spawn the birth or rebirth of other diseases that could spread outside Africa, the problems of the lack of seriousness and personalization may be overcome as well in developed societies suddenly vulnerable to those diseases.

The professional AIDS community knows what steps must be taken to gain control of the AIDS pandemic in Africa. The infection rate must be reduced through education about how AIDS is transmitted. Some countries, such as Uganda, have made major progress in "safe sex" education programs that have reduced infection rates, as already noted. Other countries, unfortunately, have not. In order to lessen the impact of AIDS infection, cheaper, more universally available treatments need to be made available, both to reduce suffering and to prolong useful life. Such treatments are available at great expense in the West; they are currently unavailable to almost all Africans. Ultimately, the pandemic can only be halted and the disease eradicated through the development of a preventive vaccine. AIDS researchers are reportedly not far from developing such a vaccine. Whether such a vaccine will be affordable and available where it is most needed is not yet certain.

It is easy to recite the steps necessary to cope with this catastrophic health problem, and what is frustrating is that it is a tragedy the effects of which can be ameliorated, even if they cannot be eliminated. In that sense, the parallel between the AIDS pandemic and the black death of the Middle Ages does not hold. There simply was no possible way that the people of the thirteenth century could begin to cope with the plague, treat its victims, or find ways to eradicate the problem. AIDS can be, and eventually will be, eradicated. The question that will be asked in retrospect is why more resources were not made available more rapidly and massively to confront the problem. Why did it take so long?

CONCLUSION

The African AIDS case is fascinating for a number of reasons that include the dynamics of why it came about, what is being done about it, and how it can be viewed as a form of transstate issue. But the pandemic is more than a case in medical or international dynamics. In addition, there is the possibility that we may learn from the handling of the AIDS crisis how we should and should not deal with future health crises with international repercussions.

One health threat that currently holds great potential horror is the Ebola virus. Like AIDS, it is a disease that is recent in origin (it was first observed in 1976), and its origin is African (its first outbreak occurred in Zaire in the area adjoining the Ebola River, from which it takes its popular name). Ebola has not yet spread beyond Africa nor has it taken lives in the staggering numbers that AIDS has. It is, however, an enormously infectious disease that is easily transmissible (much more easily than HIV), its existence is very difficult to detect until its symptoms appear in an infected person, and it has a very short and painful effect on its victims, most of whom die (in recent outbreaks, upwards of 90 percent of those infected have died). There is no known cure for the disease.

Because there is an incubation period of several weeks between exposure to Ebola and the appearance of its symptoms, it is entirely possible for a person to have the disease and not know it, thereby raising the possibility of "innocent" infection of others by an unaware carrier of the virus. At the same time, medical personnel treating a victim who do not know that Ebola is present are particularly vulnerable to infection themselves (it is passed from person to person through the body fluids of the infected victims, including their corpses).

For these reasons, it is only a matter of time until Ebola escapes Africa, unless a cure or preventive vaccine is found. Because this has not yet occurred, the prospect of an Ebola epidemic breaking out at any of a number of places around the world remains a potential transstate issue for the present. The Canadian case, where the woman suspected of having the virus had arrived only weeks earlier on a commercial airliner, an ideal closed environment for spreading the virus from unaware carrier to unsuspecting victims, may be a harbinger of things that may occur in the future.

Ebola has currently not risen to the status of a full-scaled international issue for several reasons. One is its relatively recent discovery and the isolation and comparative infrequency of outbreaks of the disease. There have been outbreaks in Zimbabwe,

South Africa, and Kenya, and as of late 2000 there was an epidemic in Uganda as well. The disease tends to appear in rural areas where sanitation facilities and practices are reasonably primitive. The practical result is that outbreaks do not receive the publicity and public outcry they would if they happened in urban settings or more geopolitically prominent locations. Also, the nature of the disease and where it has occurred have resulted in comparatively small numbers of deaths, generally in the hundreds in each individual outbreak. Partly, this is the result of outbreaks in rural areas where the population is not concentrated and there are consequently fewer potential victims. In addition, however, the disease kills so quickly that epidemics tend to run their course in short periods. As one newsletter devoted to the study of the virus puts it, "Ebola's virulence may also serve to limit its spread: its victims die so quickly that they don't have a chance to spread infection very far."

The Ebola problem thus clearly does not yet rise to the level of transstate concern that AIDS has, and quite possibly it never will. The AIDS pandemic is of a vast order of suffering and consequence, whereas Ebola strikes quickly but also passes quickly. Nonetheless, it is probably just a matter of time until there is an outbreak somewhere else in the world. If the disease is misdiagnosed in new places (are any hospitals in the United States, for instance, currently geared to look for it or related hemorrhagic diseases among patients?), the result could be an outbreak in which hundreds or thousands would die an excruciating death. At that point, would there be an international cry for a concerted effort to find a cure? There has been some promising research using steroids in the United States that seem effective in treating Ebola. Would that research be greatly accelerated in those kinds of circumstances?

There is the broader precedent that might be set. Will the AIDS pandemic provide the international community with a "wake-up call" regarding the consequences of not engaging the problem with all available resources earlier than it has? Will our retrospective on the devastation of Africa reveal that it might have been mitigated had we acted sooner and placed greater resources into finding vaccines and cures? Will our analysis provide some useful guidelines for dealing with present problems like Ebola before they emerge as larger, more hideous disasters? Or, will we require a major Ebola outbreak in a European or North American location before we mount a major effort aimed at eradicating the problem?

And then there is the future. AIDS and Ebola are unlikely to be the last major health problems with some or all the characteristics of a transstate issue. Will the experience to date inform the approaches the international community takes to the problem? It will be interesting to see.

Finally, there is a question that has only been addressed by indirection. Is the reason for the relative slowness and inattention to AIDS, and by extension Ebola, the result of where the outbreaks have taken place? When AIDS was detected in the United States, action was initially less rapid than it might have been because it was equated, rightly or wrongly, with the gay community. When the disease reached significant numbers in the heterosexual community, then efforts appeared to redouble. Is that the problem, in a geographic sense, with AIDS in Africa? It is a terrible moral indictment to suggest the treatment of great suffering depends on where one is from, but that may have been the case with this disaster.

STUDY/DISCUSSION QUESTIONS

1. What is a transstate issue? What are its characteristics? How well does the AIDS pandemic in Africa meet the criteria?

2. How did the AIDS pandemic come about? How has it progressed? What are its demographic consequences?

3. Part of the problem of AIDS in Africa arises from impediments for dealing with it on that continent. What are these? Are they similar or different from other transstate issue impediments? Can you think of other barriers to confronting the problem?

4. Think about the long-term effects of the pandemic on Africa. What will it take for Africa to recover from the effects (if they can)?

5. What international efforts have been undertaken to deal with the pandemic? Based on the experience of dealing with other transstate issues, what can one expect in the future? Have, for instance, the major pharmaceutical firms done a responsible job of responding to the pandemic?

6. Apply the experience of AIDS in Africa as a transstate issue to other current and potential health disasters like Ebola. What can we learn from one experience to help with others?

READING/RESEARCH MATERIAL

"AIDS Orphans in Africa." *The Washington Office on Africa,* 2000. http://www.woaafrica.org/Aorphans.htm.

"AIDS Pharmaceuticals and AIDS in Africa." *The Washington Office on Africa,* 2000. http://www.woaafrcia.ord/Atrade.htm.

Christensen, John. "AIDS in Africa: Dying by the Numbers." *CNN.com,* November 8, 2000.

———. "Scarce Money, Few Drugs, Little Hope." *CNN.com,* November 8, 2000.

"Ebola." http://www.nyu.edu/eduation/mindsinmotion/ebola/htm.

"International AIDS Conference Offers Good News about Cheap Drug Treatments." *CNN.com,* July 11, 2000.

Kaplan, Robert D. *The Coming Anarchy: Shattering the Dreams of the Post Cold War.* New York: Random House, 2000.

"Report: AIDS Pandemic Declared Threat to U.S. National Security." *CNN.com,* April 30, 2000.

Snow, Donald N. and Eugene Brown. *United States Foreign Policy: Politics Beyond the Water's Edge.* New York: St. Martin's Press, 1999.

Wehrwein, Peter. "AIDS Leaves Africa's Economic Future in Doubt." *CNN.com,* November 8, 2000.

Wooten, James. "Africa's AIDS Tragedy: Monumental Health Crisis May Become Moral Catastrophe." *CNN.com,* November 8, 2000.

WEB SITES

Official website of the Joint United Nations Programme on AIDS/HIV
   UNAIDS at http://www.unaids.org

Links users to a wide variety of reports, fact sheets, U.S. government agencies, and
   other on-line resources relating to HIV/AIDS

   Global Issues: HIV/AIDS and other Infectious Diseases at
   http://usinfo.state.gov/topical/global/hiv

Information on official efforts to address the national and international AIDS
   pandemic

   Office of National AIDS Policy at http://www.whitehouse.gov/onap/aids.html

Provides regional AIDS updates as well as an overview of World Bank HIV/AIDS
   activities and publications

   World Aids Day at http://www.worldbank.org/worldaidsday

BBC special report on the scale of the AIDS crisis in sub-Saharan Africa

   BBC: AIDS in Africa at
   http://news.bbc.co.uk/hi/english/static/in_depth/africa/2000/aids_in_africa

Conference focusing on translating the knowledge gained from science and experience
   into action

   XIV International AIDS Conference at http://www.aids2002.com

CHAPTER SIXTEEN

September 11, 2001:

THE NEW FACE OF WAR?

PRÉCIS

The terrorist attacks on the World Trade Center in New York and the Pentagon in Washington, D.C., on September 11, 2001, shocked the American people and brought into personal relief both the problem of international terrorism and America's vulnerability to terrorists. The events and their aftermath filled the consciousness of countless people around the world, and the responses both domestically and internationally focused on assessing what had happened, what could be done to suppress the perpetrators, and how such attacks could be avoided in the future. Given the gravity of the issue, it is therefore fitting that the concluding chapter of this text be an expanded case study of the attacks and their aftermath.

International terrorism is a transstate issue: it goes beyond national boundaries and cannot be fully contained or eliminated except by the concerted efforts of many states. In this case study, we will begin by identifying and explaining a number of characteristics of terrorism. That effort will be followed by an application of those principles to the tragic events of September 11, 2001, including the assertion that the campaign against terrorism represents a "new kind of war." The case concludes with a discussion of how to try to deal with terrorism.

Terrorism, the use of unpredictable violence to achieve political ends, is certainly not a new phenomenon, even if it has achieved a new and heightened awareness among Americans in light of the events of 2001. The root of the term itself is from the Latin word *terrere*, which means "to frighten," and inducing fright is the clear underlying intent of all those who commit acts of terror. Moreover, events that we would now label terror are probably as old as the interactions between groups and individuals seeking to impose their chosen ideas and ideologies on others of different persuasions.

Prior to September 11, 2001, terrorism was an abstract concept for most Americans. Certainly there had been, in recent years, isolated instances of terrorist acts by isolated individuals, such as Theodore Kaczynski, the single-cell terrorist Unabomber, or Timothy McVeigh (and his associates), who exploded a truck bomb that killed 159 people in the Murrah Federal Building in Oklahoma City in 1995, or the 1993 attack on the World Trade Center (WTC). These acts enraged our senses, but they all seemed at the time to be individual acts by psychotic individuals acting alone, and they seemed to possess no further significance or foreboding (although the WTC attack was later revealed to be part of a broader international conspiracy). They had a significant impact on us as we viewed and recoiled from the carnage, but we could eventually take some solace in realizing they were not part of some broader campaign. More systematic acts of terror were foreign, alien, and unreal—the terrorist attacks by the Irish Republican Army (IRA) against London subways or the spraying of sarin gas into the Tokyo subway system by Japanese extremists.

The horrible attacks against the World Trade Center twin towers and the Pentagon in September 2001 changed our view of terror. These were attacks of unprecedented scale and audacity that revealed a massive, sophisticated plot and an operation of such proportions as to be well beyond what most Americans, including our leaders and experts in the field, could envision. Al Qaeda (the Base), the loose-knit network of terrorist "cells" organized by bin Laden and his closest associates, revealed both our vulnerability to the unthinkable and, more profoundly, the realization that it could happen again, at any time, in any place, and in ways that we might not be able to thwart in advance.

The impact was largely but not only solely on Americans. Americans were not the only ones who died when the four United and American Airlines jets collided with the World Trade Center towers in New York, the Pentagon in Washington, D.C., and the Pennsylvania countryside; citizens of 80 other countries perished as well. The terrorism was international in origin and in effect. Dealing with it clearly requires an international effort, making the terrorism problem clearly a transstate issue.

We have struggled to understand what happened and why. Our initial reaction was shocked disbelief: How could this have transpired? Shock rapidly turned to rage: Who did this and how can we exact revenge for the thousands who perished? But the instinct to avenge quickly has now given way to a deeper understanding in the general public that not only was September 11 a day of incredible tragedy, but that the responses that we could possibly mete out were not as obvious as our conventional thinking suggested. Much of our frustration came from looking for appropriate targets at which to aim our anger but finding only shadows instead.

In the days immediately following the attacks, Americans came to conceptualize the events in terms of "war." The analogy was understandable given the scale of the atrocities and the sense of beleaguerment and siege under which we felt we had been placed. At the same time, however, the analogy tended to channel our thinking into conventional military concepts—targeting the enemy and attacking him through the air and on land, for instance, and that was at least partially misleading. Unfortunately, in this case the opponent was not and is not a conventional military organization, and military action in any conventional sense will not "defeat" the enemy and "win" the war, even if it may eliminate the immediate problem posed by bin Laden and Al Qaeda. There will be and can be no decisive victory that ends the war on terrorism writ large and allows us to execute some kind of "exit strategy" that provides the transition from the contest to the normality of peace. In that sense, this is indeed the new face of war.

The fight against terrorism, as French President Jacques Chirac reminded American President George W. Bush in the days immediately after the attacks, is better thought of as a long campaign, an open-ended event that will not be "won" so much as contained. Just as there was terrorism before Usama bin Laden, the exiled Saudi terrorist responsible for the attacks, burst upon the scene, it is virtually certain there will be terrorists among us after he has exited the scene. What the events of September 11, 2001, have done is to raise that observation about the world in which we live from the abstract to the concrete. We hardly realized we were in a potential terrorist environment, because we had never experienced or contemplated terrorism of this nature and on this scale on our own territory before. Now that fact is indelible and undeniable. That is the enduring legacy of September 11.

These observations help form the way this case study will proceed. In the pages that follow, we will attempt to do three things. First, we will look at the nature and characteristics of terrorism as they have evolved and as we understood them before the attacks against New York and Washington. Included in the discussion will be the suggestion, made by a small but growing number of observers, that terrorism forms the core of the so-called "fourth generation" of warfare that they maintain will be the dominant form of warfare in the future. Second, we will look specifically at the events surrounding the attacks, to understand better what occurred, to see how September 11 does or does not exemplify the general phenomenon of terrorism, and to assess how the attacks may have transformed how we need to think about terrorism in the future. In the process, we will mention the anthrax attacks that began in October 2001 as a further example of terrorism at work. What we will see is that the campaign launched by bin Laden and his associates largely conforms to general patterns of terrorist activity historically; it is, in important ways, "textbook" terrorism. Finally, we will try to extend the analysis to see how it can be applied to dealing with the problem of confronting and containing terrorism in the future.

WHAT IS TERRORISM?

Much of the difficulty we have in understanding and coping with terrorism is that the whole idea is totally alien to most Americans. The heart and core of terrorism lies in the commission of atrocious acts against target populations in order to gain compliance with some set of demands or conditions that the terrorists insist upon. The actual terrorist acts are normally acts of violence intended to maim or kill members of the target group (who, by and large, are lay people guilty of no particular crime other than being members of the target population). The overt purpose is to frighten other members of the group with the threat, implied or explicit, that the same fate may befall them if they do not comply with the terrorist's demands. The threat is based on the future commission of random acts of mayhem that the potential targets can neither anticipate nor prepare for—they could happen anywhere at anytime, and to anyone. The purpose is to induce such a level of fright in the target population that it concludes that submission to the terrorist's demands is preferable to living in this continuing climate of anxiety and uncertainty. If the population reaches this conclusion and capitulates to the terrorist's demands, or if the government overreacts, destroying the principles it seeks to protect, the terrorists succeed. If the targets refuse to submit themselves to the demands, then the terrorists fail to accomplish their goals and must either continue their campaign or abandon their goals.

The activities of the terrorist wing of the Irish Republican Army (IRA) represent one of the clearest examples of this dynamic in action. For years, this group's demands have focused on the renunciation of British Protestant rule in Northern Ireland. One of the tactics that has been employed to achieve this end is through acts of terror in Great Britain such as the bombing of London subway stations. These attacks have been purposely random, with the objective of convincing Londoners that any time they elected to use "the tube," they might be victims of an IRA bomb. The idea was that if Londoners became sufficiently frightened of the prospects of being victims of an attack, they would conclude that agreeing to independence for Northern Ireland (and subsequent annexation to the Republic of Ireland) is preferable to living in continued fear of violent death at an IRA bomber's hand. The IRA campaign, of course, was unsuccessful in reaching its final goal, but the IRA was recognized as a key player in negotiations. Ultimately, the IRA's campaign increased, rather than decreased, British resolve to resist these demands, a not uncommon response to terrorist campaigns.

It is difficult for most of us to identify with terrorism. For most people, the idea of randomly taking the lives of innocent people in the pursuit of some ideal is so alien and even contradictory to our values as to be unthinkable. When the terrorist acts are also acts of suicide, the whole idea becomes even more unfathomable. Moreover, the reasons and motivation for terrorism, when they are made public at all (which they sometimes are not), are often obscure, unorthodox, and intellectually alien to the point of appearing bizarre or totally incomprehensible to nonmembers of the terrorist cause. The net effect of engaging in atrocious acts for bizarre motivations only adds to our inability to understand and especially to empathize with terrorists.

Gaining an understanding of terrorism requires looking at the problem from several angles. These include the objectives of terrorism, justifications for terrorist acts, the contrast between terror as a strategy or a tactic, sponsorship of terrorists and their organizations, and the forms terror may take. In addition, we will examine categories of responses available to those who are victimized by actual or potential terrorist attacks against them. Finally, we will raise the question of whether terrorism is the new form of warfare for the twenty-first century, as many are now suggesting in the wake of the September attacks and American military responses that began on October 7, 2001. Collectively, examining these factors will allow us to begin to get a grasp on the question: Why terrorism? Also, it may help us understand both the nature of the events of September 11, 2001, and how we can deal with them.

Terrorist Objectives

Terrorism is a political act. The purpose of terrorism is to induce political change that the proponents have determined cannot be accomplished in ways other than the application of terrifying violence. Depending on the nature of the group, the political purposes may be more or less articulate and more or less public, but at some level there will always be a political agenda that terrorists seek to implement (or at least some political justification that may hide criminal activities, such as in the case of narco-terrorists operating to protect drug producers in South America under the guise of freedom fighters).

The political purposes of terrorists often get obscured by the hideousness of their acts. Sometimes it is difficult to distinguish dispassionately between the acts and their purposes. One of the political goals that some terrorists have pursued across time has been anarchy, the total breakdown of governance. The removal of government is, of course, a political goal, but in the assassination of political leaders (a favorite tactic of anarchists), the goal may be overwhelmed by the acts taken to achieve it.

At least within a Western philosophical context, terror is a political approach of last resort, an act of desperation when no other more orthodox and acceptable means will achieve the end. Why is this the case? The answer, as hinted earlier, has to do with the nature of the political objectives that terrorists have.

Generally speaking, terrorist goals have a decidedly minority appeal, at least within the target population, and that means their goals can never become public policy through standard, prescribed political processes. In the minds of those who select terrorism to achieve their ends, the ideals may be entirely reasonable. That judgment is usually not shared by the object population. There is the further recognition that standard means of persuasion are unlikely to produce conversion to the cause championed by the terrorists. Moreover, the political goal is likely to be sufficiently unpopular in the target population for conventional coercive power (e.g., military power) to be effective. Terrorism thus becomes the last resort to induce political change.

Terrorism as political process get further obscured when a great misunderstanding or a basic conflict of values exists, especially when the emotions raised by the horror of terrorist attacks on innocent people intensify the adversarial content of the relationship. To anticipate material in the next section, Usama bin Laden and his followers have articulated two basic grievances with the United States that have caused them to pursue so-called "holy war" against Americans. These goals are the eviction of all Americans from Islamic holy lands, notably Saudi Arabia, and American abandonment of Israel. Such goals have a reasonably large appeal in parts of the Islamic Middle East, but are either incomprehensible or unacceptable to Americans and many others in the region and beyond who could also be victimized. The idea that the Americans in Saudi Arabia (who are, by and large, invited guests of the Saudi government) can be viewed as desecrators of holy lands they were asked to protect is beyond our imagination; and the idea we should stop supporting Israel is simply unacceptable to the American government, no matter how disenchanted some Americans become over specific Israeli actions or policies.

Even if we understand terrorist demands, terrorist actions do not justify them in our culture. Western culture has, upon occasion, used terrorism to achieve political goals: the liberation of the Holy Land during the Crusades and the Spanish Inquisition were certainly terrifying to those against whom they were directed, and the sound of B–52 bombers over Vietnam certainly frightened many Vietnamese and undoubtedly resulted in the deaths of innocent civilians. Even after admitting that, the idea that the systematic killing of Americans guilty of no greater sins than being American to achieve alien goals still goes beyond the conceptual abilities of most of us.

Justifications of Terrorism

Whether terrorism can be justified as a means to achieve political ends is largely a question of the legitimacy of terrorism. The answer clearly differs between the proponents and supporters of terrorism and their detractors, and is sometimes captured in the spirited debate over the assertion that "one man's terrorist is another man's freedom fighter." Basic disagreement about that assertion focuses upon whether one views terrorism as a political act of war or whether terrorism is nothing more than common crime hiding behind political ideals. The imputation that terrorism is an act of war has the effect of legitimating it as a political act, whereas treating it as crime delegitimizes—quite consciously—its political content and its assertion of legitimacy. The distinction also has major implications for national and international treatment of terrorists.

Champions and opponents of terrorism are ambivalent on this distinction between terrorism as war or crime, because it has different implications at different times. For the most part, terrorism apologists prefer to think of terrorism as an act of war, which means those who carry out terrorist acts are soldiers (freedom fighters), thereby according them a higher and more legitimate position than if they are considered mere criminals, or worse, mass murderers. Declaring "war" on terrorists indirectly, at least, provides support for that assertion. On the other hand, when terrorists are pursued or captured and brought into the docket for prosecution, they prefer that the entirety of the body and limits (e.g., burdens of proof) accorded through the processes of criminal law be applied to them, especially in a democratic society. The laws of war, on the other hand, provide less protection in critical areas such as search and seizure, detention, and the admissibility and burden of evidence at trial. Suspending civil liberties and trying supposed terrorists before closed military tribunals on the justification that a state of war exists in fact if not in law, as the Bush administration proposed in late 2001, carries this characterization to its extreme.

Opponents of terrorism take the opposite view that since terrorist acts invariably involve breaking the laws of the countries in which they are committed (or international law when they occur on or over space not part of any state jurisdiction), they must be considered criminal acts prosecutable and punishable under criminal law. The opponents, however, recognize that the rules and protections in criminal cases are much more stringent and difficult, and so there is an instinct among some in the counterterrorist community to allow the pursuit and suppression of terrorists under military standards.

Evolving international law provides something of a compromise solution, and it is one that has been heard increasingly in the September 11 context. International law now recognizes certain acts that may occur in a military context as "crimes against humanity," and these acts include the systematic killing of members of groups within society—genocide and mass murder. The International Criminal Court, colocated with the International Court of Justice at the Hague in the Netherlands, has the authority to try cases involving these and other forms of war crimes. Yugoslavia's former president, Slobodan Milosevic, is the most prominent public figure to be charged in this manner; international terrorists would seem to be an eligible category for the future.

Is terrorism crime or war? The answer is that it is both. Clearly, terrorist acts violate criminal laws and are thus, by definition, criminal offenses. But are they justified by the political nature of the objectives they pursue? The answer to that question is a matter of perspective, and depends on your philosophy (Can the killing of innocents ever be justified? Is there a distinction between innocents and combatants in modern war?) and on your position as either a perpetrator or a victim of terror.

Terror as Strategy or Tactic

Although it makes little difference to its victims, terrorist acts can represent either a strategy for achieving political goals, or a tactic that is part of a broader strategy intended to reach particular ends. Strategy, in the military sense in which it has the most obvious meaning, refers to a plan of action to achieve a goal. Tactics, on the other hand, refer to specific actions taken to implement the strategy and thus achieve the objective for which the strategy is designed.

This distinction may seem confusing initially and peripheral to the overall goal of understanding the dynamics of terror, but it is not. One of the charges that is often made against the United States is that its military has engaged in acts of terror parallel to those committed by professional terrorists. Although in some ways this may be true, that truth is conditioned by how states use terror tactically, particularly in times of war.

For instance, is the attack on New York and Washington the equivalent of the American nuclear bombing of Nagasaki and Hiroshima? Certainly to the victims, both sets of acts were terrifying in their execution, resulting in massive death and despair among people whose individual guilt was being in the wrong place at the wrong time. The attacks on American and Japanese cities, however, occurred within different contexts and for different ends, which the strategic-tactical distinction helps illuminate. When Hiroshima and Nagasaki were bombed with atomic weapons, a legal state of war existed between the attacking and the attacked state, and the bombings were an alternative to a forced invasion that could have cost upward of an estimated million lives. These conditions were not present in September 2001, loose discussions of "war" notwithstanding. At the same time, terrorism is the apparent strategy of the New York and Washington bombers, whose plan is to continue to terrorize the American people until the United States accepts their demands. The atomic bombing was, on the other hand, a tactical act seeking to implement the military strategy of capitulation of the Japanese armed forces in order to achieve the political goal of unconditional surrender to allow the overthrow of the Imperial Japanese government. The terrorizing of the civilian population was not the goal of that particular action (although bombing to frighten the population was common on both sides during World War II), as was the case in 2001. The extent to which this distinction mitigates the atomic bombings by the Americans and sets them apart from recent terror in the United States is, of course, a matter of debate.

Sponsorship

Terrorism is by no means the exclusive preserve of shadowy private groups of individuals. States practice terrorism in tactical ways during war, as the last example suggested, and terrorist campaigns aimed to suppress or eliminate (either by killing or by physically removing) segments of national populations are not uncommon in world history, including modern times. Systematic terror against a population was instituted by the Ottoman Empire against Armenia in the years before World War I, and Saddam Hussein's use of chemical weapons to murder the inhabitants of selected Kurdish villages in 1987 were conscious acts of state terrorism or crimes against humanity. Further examples of the systematic use of terror are the genocide campaigns of Hitler in World War II and of Cambodia's Khmer Rouge in the 1970s. In fact, many experts would argue that governments are directly responsible for more acts of terror than any other source.

The sponsorship of terrorism can be viewed along a continuum of levels of involvement by the governments of countries. At one end of the continuum are instances of direct state sponsorship, where governments may use parts of their formal governmental apparatus such as the secret police to terrorize a population (usually their own). Modern examples of direct state sponsorship include the "dirty war" in Argentina in the 1960s and Chile in the 1970s (both involving the capture and disappearance of political foes to still dissonance). In other instances, the state may commission individuals or groups that are not otherwise connected to the state to carry out terrorist acts on their behalf. This method was particularly associated with Libyan dictator Muammar Qaddafi during the 1970s and 1980s, in operations such as the bombing of a nightclub in Berlin in 1986 that killed several American servicemen. This act resulted in an American retaliatory raid against his home and the subsequent destruction of Pan American flight 103 over Lockerbie, Scotland, by Qaddafi-sponsored terrorists.

The other extreme is the complete absence of governmental participation, where terrorist groups act without the encouragement, assistance, or solace of any government. Usually, such privately based movements are very small and isolated, and because they lack outside backers willing to finance their enterprises, the scope of their activity is very limited. Timothy McVeigh's bombing exemplifies this limited-scale type of terrorism. The terrorist wing of the IRA, which has friends in some governments but is officially condoned by none, provides a large-scale example, because it received considerable outside funding from private sources in the United States and elsewhere.

Lying between these extremes is a third form of sponsorship—state-sanctioned terrorism. This form is found most prominently in the Middle East, where terrorist organizations are not arms of any government taking direct orders about whom to attack, how, and why, but they are shielded from outside interference and harassment by governments sympathetic to the particular cause the terrorists champion. A number of states on the U.S. State Department's terrorist states list are accused of this activity. The most notable are Syria, Iran, Libya, Iraq, and most recently Afghanistan.

One of the most notorious places where state sanction of terrorist groups occurs is in Syrian-occupied Lebanon. Groups financed both by governments and private contributions find safe havens in Beirut, where a number of groups accused of terrorism have their headquarters, and in the Bekaa Valley, where many terrorists are trained and harbored. State sanction of terrorism, which is routinely denied by those states accused of it, is particularly vexing to countries that are the objects of terrorism, because sanctioning states will not allow outsiders access to the areas where the terrorists are, in effect providing sanctuaries where they are protected from infiltration and suppression. In many cases, the states seeking to suppress terrorists do not have diplomatic relations with the sanctioning states, making it more difficult to develop the kinds of spy networks among natives that are critical to penetration and thus suppression.

Terrorist Forms

One of the great frustrations about dealing with terrorism is the wide variety of forms that terrorist acts can take. In the contemporary setting, Americans have become familiar with several of the forms—the hijacking and destruction of airplanes, the commandeering of airplanes to be used as guided missiles, and truck bombings. The latter tactic was introduced to us in the bombing of the U.S. Marine barracks in 1983 in Beirut (arguably a military act) and was repeated as a direct act of terrorism in the original attack on the World Trade Center in 1993, the destruction of the Murrah Federal Building in Oklahoma City in 1995, the attack on the Khobar Towers apartment building in Saudi Arabia in 1996, and the bombings of the American embassies in Nairobi, Kenya, and in Dar es Salaam, Tanzania, in 1998. The use of a bomb-laden boat against the U.S.S. Cole in Yemen in 2000 was a variation on that theme. Using a commercial airliner with a large amount of jet fuel on board as a missile against prominent buildings was a significant innovation; the likelihood of its success may have been enhanced by the fact that no one had thought of it before, except in works of fiction (for example, Tom Clancy's *Debt of Honor* features an airliner that is flown into the U.S. Capitol).

Dealing with terrorism would be considerably simpler if these were all the contingencies with which one had to deal, but they are not. In a 1992 book, *Low-Intensity Conflict,* James J. Gallagher provides a representative list of potential terrorist acts of differing levels of severity and against different targets. In addition to bombings (which can take on a wide variety of guises against different targets) and hijackings, his list includes arson, kidnapping of public officials, corporate executives, or common citizens, hostage taking, assassination, raids against installations, property seizure, and sabotage. When one realizes that many of these actions can be taken against a wide variety of targets ranging from urban complexes to government facilities to water supplies to crowded sports stadiums to major bridges, the complexity of methods and countermethods becomes obvious.

The formidability of the forms terrorism may take is compounded by the idiosyncratic nature of many of the methods. The problem is that the methods used to combat one form of terrorism (airplane hijacking, for instance) may be of no use in protecting a city's water supply from contamination. Moreover, the lessons learned from protecting airports from terrorist penetration may have little carryover value in learning how to protect corporate executives from being kidnapped, and hardening the protective efforts may even produce what Steven Sloan calls "target displacement," where efforts to protect one kind of target causes terrorists to look for other, less well protected alternatives.

The result is clear. The variety of ways and means and places where terrorists can strike makes it impossible for any country, and especially a free and open society, to be completely terrorist-proof. While it is possible to make aspects of society highly invulnerable to attack—such as airports—there are simply too many potential targets to make it possible to remove all vulnerability. It is delusional to believe otherwise.

The problem of vulnerability has been made more dramatic because of the possibility that terrorists in the future may have access to so-called *weapons of mass destruction* (WMD), chief among which are nuclear, biological, and chemical (NBC) weapons. This prospect became less abstract with the spread of anthrax spores in the United States in October 2001. That the problem will recur in other, related forms is now more likely than ever, leading former U.S. Secretary of Defense William Perry to conclude in a recent *Foreign Affairs* article that these weapons "constitute the greatest single danger to American—indeed world—security."

The possibility that a terrorist organization will again gain access to and attempt to attack the United States (or somewhere else) with one of the NBC agents is undeniable—it could happen, and if it did, the consequences potentially would be great. The possibilities alone justify a live, very serious concern. At the same time, there are mitigating factors that suggest one should not become hysterical at the prospects. Four are worth mentioning.

First, there is a kind of inverse relationship between the likelihood of each kind of agent being used and its likely effects. Of the three NBC agents, chemical weapons are the easiest to fabricate (or buy) and the easiest to access and apply on a target, in most cases. They are also the weapons that have the least deadly effects against most targets. A sarin gas attack against a football stadium, for instance, would have little effect, as most of the gas would dissipate into the atmosphere, and it would take a very large amount of chemicals to contaminate a reservoir. Biological weapons can be horrible in their effects, but they are very difficult to make (or to buy or steal), and many of them are highly unstable to handle and have very unpredictable effects. Moreover, vaccines exist for nearly all of them. The anthrax outbreak stimulated ongoing research on a vaccine that reportedly may protect against most pathogens. Even if the physical problem is solved, however, the anthrax case shows the profound fear these pathogens produce in potential victims. The most consequential weapons—nuclear bombs—require fissionable material, which is extremely difficult to obtain. The bombs terrorists are likely to be able to design and build would be very large and heavy, making their concealment virtually impossible. Horror scenes such as suitcase nuclear bombs or people dropping vials of pestilence into water supplies are possible, but not as technically feasible as some public representations suggest.

Second, there is a problem of access. Once again, this is less of a problem with chemical than biological and nuclear weapons, since a number of chemical agents can be made by combining legally available chemical compounds. Getting access to agents of biological origin is obviously possible, as the anthrax outbreak demonstrates, but weapons-grade nuclear fuel is heavily guarded and very difficult to obtain. Moreover, nuclear weapons are very difficult to fabricate and require a team of experts to build.

Third, and as suggested above, the delivery of such agents to targets is not as easy to accomplish as popular depictions would suggest. Feasible nuclear weapons would be very heavy and bulky to move about, and many biological weapons might well infect and disable the terrorist before he could employ them, for instance.

Fourth, because most of the agents that are commonly discussed as potential weapons have never been used in the manners proposed, the predicted effects are really hypothetical. They could be as bad or worse than predicted, or they could be lesser in effect. The early experience in treating victims exposed to anthrax, for instance, suggested that containment of the effects may be plausible in at least some cases.

None of this suggests that the possible use of exotic substances can be discounted. The sheer malevolence of terrorist organizations, the wide variety of potential activities in which terrorists may engage, and the vast array of targets, all of which cannot simultaneously be protected, mean that the vulnerability of our society to such attacks, including attacks by WMD, are a permanent part of our future environment. The question is what we can do about the problem.

Dealing with Terrorism

As the discussion of terrorist forms should clearly indicate, the effort to shield the population from terrorist violence is complex and difficult. The complexity of dealing successfully with a terrorist threat has at least two aspects worth highlighting and exploring. The first is the forms of counteraction that are possible in the face of terrorist acts or threats. The second deals with how governmental authority is organized to coordinate and activate whatever means are chosen.

Conceptually, there are two ways to try to cope with terrorism. One of these is *antiterrorism*, defensive measures used to reduce the vulnerability of potential targets to attack and to lessen the effects of attacks that do occur. Antiterrorism focuses on making it more difficult for terrorists to commit their acts successfully, so that they are dissuaded from trying to launch them in the first place. An example of antiterrorism designed to make such attacks more difficult is enhanced airport security measures that make it impossible (or at least very hard) for potential perpetrators to gain access to airliners or airplane cockpits. Another is the practice of armor plating and putting solid rubber tires on the automobiles of business executives to protect them from kidnapping (a particular problem in Europe historically). An example of making terrorist attacks less successful is the practice of prohibiting vehicles from parking close to public buildings, so that an explosion will not destroy the target building. Closing Pennsylvania Avenue to traffic in front of the White House is a concrete example of such an effort.

The other form of response is *counterterrorism*, offensive and military measures taken by the military and other agencies against terrorists or their sponsoring states to prevent, or deter, or respond to terrorist acts. The focus of counterterrorism is on disabling (or dissuading) the potential perpetrator from acting in a terrorist manner by eliminating his or her physical ability to carry out these acts. Counterterrorism may use offensive tactics to attack terrorists, but it is usually reactive, responding to some terrorist act or revelation about a terrorist plan. An example would be the penetration of terrorist cells by intelligence agents to learn of terrorist plots and foil them before they occur. The monitoring and surveillance of known and suspected terrorists and taking preemptive actions if they act suspiciously qualifies as counterterrorism. A more extreme form involves the capture or killing of terrorists after a terrorist incident to send a message to other potential terrorists of the fate that awaits them if they engage in acts of terror. Direct military assault on terrorist-sanctioning states is the most extreme form of counterterrorism.

Each approach has its advantages and limitations, and neither is probably sufficient by itself in the face of a concerted terrorist threat. While antiterrorist actions can significantly enhance security where they are implemented (e.g., the security measures taken at American airports after the September 11 attacks), the range of potential targets is so vast that it is likely physically impossible to protect them all, especially when resources for the effort are limited. How, for instance, can we simultaneously protect all the sources of water supply in the United States and have enough personnel and money left over to deal with other forms of attack which, by virtue of removing water supplies from the list, become more likely targets? Antiterrorist actions are typically very expensive, and the more categories of potential targets we seek to protect, the more burdensome the effort becomes.

Counterterror has an appealing, active ring to it, but "terrorizing terrorists" is often easier said than done. By their nature, terrorist organizations are small, secretive, usually compartmentalized (i.e., one component knows little or nothing of others), physically mobile, and located in countries that protect them from outside penetration by outsiders (state sanction). As the United States had learned from years of trying to hunt down and capture Usama bin Laden even before the September 11 incidents, truly effective counterterrorism is much easier to conceptualize than it is to execute. Since neither approach is sufficient to deal comprehensively with the problem, an effective organized effort will have to contain elements of both antiterrorism and counterterrorism.

Historically, the U.S. government's efforts in dealing with terrorism have been hampered by the diffuse, uncoordinated nature of the response and turf battles over jurisdiction, and the situation has been made worse by the uneven nature of international cooperation to contain terrorism. Within the American government, for instance, over 46 executive branch agencies have historically had some responsibility for different aspects of terrorism, but with little coordination or common direction.

The most publicized examples of failure to cooperate result from mutual rivalry and the absence of effective cooperation among the Central Intelligence Agency (CIA), which has prime responsibility for monitoring terrorist activities overseas that might affect the country; the Immigration and Naturalization Service (INS), with prime responsibility for cataloguing who enters, remains in, and leaves the country; and the Federal Bureau of Investigation (FBI), which tracks suspected terrorist activities within the United States. Some critics describe the failure to anticipate the bombings in New York and Washington as a major intelligence breakdown of the magnitude of Pearl Harbor. Much of the blame is being directed at the failure of major government agencies to share or respond to information that might have made detection and prevention possible. The new Office of Homeland Security headed by former Pennsylvania governor Tom Ridge is a direct response to this problem, although the scope of his authority and thus his power to induce common efforts has not been clearly established or demonstrated. In the wake of the September events, there have also been renewed commitments by the intelligence agencies of various governments to cooperate on matters such as the location and movement of suspected terrorists.

The New "War" on Terror

Immediately following the attacks on September 11, the events were widely depicted as acts of war against the United States, and the war analogy almost immediately took hold and has endured as the major paradigm for understanding the events and American responses to them. Although the scale of the calamity and the level of commitment needed to deal with it made the analogy appealing, it quickly became evident to all involved in the policy and expert community that this was not war in the common, conventional sense of that term. President Chirac's preference for "campaign" may have been closer to the mark conceptually, but the war analogy has been hard to shed, especially as the major media continue to use the term to organize their coverage of related events. When the response became overtly military with the American and British bombing campaign in October, 2001, this image was further reinforced, despite efforts by responsible officials such as U.S. Defense Secretary Donald Rumsfeld to emphasize that military action was only a small part of the overall campaign against terrorism. The purpose of air, and subsequent ground, actions was to bring pressure on the Afghan Taliban government to hand over Bin Laden and his Al Qaeda cohorts. When the Taliban refused to comply, the purpose became to force the Taliban from power, so that Bin Laden could be captured or killed.

If the United States and its allies are at war with terrorists, it is a very different kind of war than any previously conducted. The term "war" conjures an image of sustained military actions taken by opposing military units in battles, the outcomes of which lead to victory or defeat on the battlefield. Since the terrorists (or Afghanistan, for that matter) possess nothing resembling a standard armed force in the Western sense, the analogy quickly breaks down. There may well be no pitched, set-piece battles in this campaign involving regular American combat forces, even if the campaign by the Northern Alliance against the Taliban aided by American airpower had characteristics of conventional warfare. As the allied bombing campaign was being organized, there was a problem identifying meaningful military targets to attack in one of the world's most primitive societies. In the end, once the few military targets were destroyed, about all that was left were people (Taliban armed forces, for instance). The internal Afghan conflict between the Taliban and its opponents has some resemblance to common images of war, but conventional images have been largely irrelevant in helping to describe the terrorism campaign itself.

This new kind of war had been discussed and debated for a decade or more within the professional defense intellectual community. The overarching term used to describe it is *fourth generation warfare* (the first three generations are warfare as it was fought up to the end of the Napoleonic wars, warfare as introduced in the American Civil War, and the German blitzkrieg campaigns of World War II). Previous generations of war, which have been dominated physically and conceptually by Western military thought, have been refinements on the traditional application of increasing amounts and kinds of orthodox forms of warfare. The new fourth generation of warfare stands in sharp contrast with previous warfare, threatening to make conventional thinking obsolete and even irrelevant.

A major statement on this new form of war first appeared in a 1989 edition of *Marine Corps Gazette.* The authors of the article argued that future warfare would share several characteristics different from earlier forms: (1) it would involve attacks on entire societies, whereas conventional military encounters would virtually disappear from warfare; (2) that distinctions between military and civilian targets and combatant and noncombatant statuses would virtually disappear; and (3) that success or failure would be measured more in terms of affecting the morale and the will of target societies than in terms of outcomes on the battlefield. In the words of the *Gazette*, "Television news may become a more powerful operational weapon than armored divisions." Martin van Creveld, whose 1991 book *The Transformation of War*, is one of the more articulate statements about the fourth generation of war, also argues that states are losing their monopoly on the use of force in this kind of war.

Fourth generation war, in a word, is less conventionally military than previous visions of war. While specialized forms of military action—special forces raids and highly selective bombing—may be part of the equation, much of the activity will be nonmilitary in the standard sense, with forces that are very different in composition and strength facing one another in asymmetric warfare, as described below. Secretary of Defense Donald Rumsfeld has even argued that military action may not even be the most important element in this kind of warfare. Instead, the "war" on terror will have decidedly political aspects: lining up opposition to and undermining tolerance of terrorist activity in states, and pursuing international cooperation in identifying, locating, and monitoring the activities of suspected terrorists, for instance. Much of the activity will be conducted by police and security specialists rather than by soldiers.

The traditional war analogy breaks down in another critical area as well: the termination of war. In conventional war, armed forces clash to achieve the political outcomes they have defined as their goals in war, and once these are achieved, the war ends. One of the most articulate statements of this view is the so-called Powell Doctrine, named after the secretary of state while he was still in uniform during the1980s and early 1990s. The correct use of force, he argued, is the swift and overwhelming application of military power to achieve goals in as rapid and as decisive a manner as possible, after which that force can be withdrawn. Clearly, that condition does not apply when dealing with terror. Even if bin Laden is eliminated and Al Qaeda destroyed, that will not be the end of terrorism, but just the removal of one of its faces.

THE TERRORIST ATTACKS OF SEPTEMBER 11, 2001

The terrorist attacks on New York and Washington and the terrorist campaign that has accompanied them represent, in retrospect, almost textbook applications of the principles of terrorism discussed in the preceding pages. The objectives of the attackers, if not widely known by most Americans before the attacks, had been clearly stated in the months and years leading to the commission of the atrocities, and were certainly known to the U.S. government. These objectives produced their own justification for the perpetrators, who apply terror as a strategic weapon to achieve those goals. The terrorist organizations have clear sponsors providing funds and sanctuary for them and have engaged in a variety of forms of terrorist acts. The responses by the United States fall within the categories identified above, and the campaign is increasingly phrased in terms compatible with fourth generation warfare concepts.

The acts themselves are tragically familiar to us now. On the morning of September 11, 2001, 19 members of the bin Laden network boarded four commercial jetliners at East Coast airports. Each jet was bound on a cross-country nonstop flight, which meant that they all had maximum loads of jet fuel on board, making each plane an incendiary device when slammed into its target. After takeoff, the airplanes were commandeered by the terrorists, some of whom had received pilot training in the United States, and redirected toward their targets. Two of the planes slammed into the World Trade Center towers within 18 minutes of each other, causing both to collapse, killing nearly 3,000 people in those buildings. One plane, which had taken off from Washington Dulles airport, was flown into the side of the Pentagon, killing 189 more people, although it is not entirely clear whether the Pentagon or some other government building in Washington was the primary target of the attack. The fourth airplane crashed in the western Pennsylvania countryside after passengers apparently thwarted the terrorists, who were directing that plane toward Washington as well. All 266 people aboard the four aircraft died in the crashes. It was, by far, the largest terrorist act ever carried out against American citizens on American soil and arguably the largest single terrorist episode in modern world history.

The response was swift and emotional. In the days immediately after the incidents, Americans reeled trying to understand what had occurred and why anyone would commit such atrocious acts. As television footage of the second airliner crashing into the north tower of the World Trade Center and the subsequent collapse of both structures was replayed over and over, disbelief turned to anger and the desire for revenge. With the bin Laden network identified as the perpetrators (despite bin Laden's denial of responsibility), the "war" on terrorism was born and calls for military action rang out as National Guard and reserve units were urged to prepare for activation.

The difficulty of the task of retribution and removal of the threat quickly became apparent. Countering the terror that had been inflicted was not going to be the result of conventional military action, as the original "declaration" of war suggested to many. Rather, the effort would be a long, tedious, and difficult process directed first against Al Qaeda and bin Laden, but also against future terrorists who may come forward to replace them. This is a campaign without a definite end.

This brief description suggests the utility of examining the horrific events within the categories established in the first section of this study. The first five categories will be discussed in this section, because they collectively define the acts of terrorism themselves. The last two categories from the first section deal with conceptualization and implementation of responses, and they will be discussed in the conclusion.

Terrorist Objectives

When the attacks of September 11, 2001 occurred, Americans were so stunned by the savagery and utter disdain for human life they exhibited that it seemed impossible to imagine that the events could be attached to some articulated political purpose. When the renegade Saudi extremist Usama bin Laden was quickly identified as the motive force behind the attacks, there was a vague recognition of the man from his alleged conspiracy in the bombings of the two American embassies in Africa in 1998 and elsewhere and that it was his terrorist camps in Afghanistan (along with targets in the Sudan) that had been bombed in retaliation for the embassy bombings. In the days that immediately followed the attacks, no one outside the professional terrorism community seemed to know why bin Laden was conducting his campaign, and the administration did little to inform the public on the matter, despite the fact that his demands had been publicly available for five years prior to the attacks.

Bin Laden's underlying motivation was by no means anarchical. Rather, it was the use of terror to force compliance with a set of political demands that he had been publicly articulating over a period of nearly five years in a series of proclamations and interviews. In the wake of the September 11 attacks, he has reiterated his demands—most eerily in a prerecorded videotape released after the bombing campaign against Afghanistan began— and has promised continued acts of terror until the United States meets his conditions.

What does bin Laden want the United States to do? His first elaborate description came in the form of a three-part document released in 1996, which MSANEWS called "The Ladenese Epistle: Declaration of War." The three parts of the document are sequential. The first is a kind of indictment of the past and present sins of the United States and Israel, what he refers to as the "Zionist-Crusader alliance" that have occupied "the land of the two holy places," referring to Mecca and Medina in Saudi Arabia, Jerusalem, and possibly Iraq, which also contains sites extremely important to Shi'a Islam. In the minds of bin Laden and his followers, the presence of American military forces in Arabia (the birthplace of Islam) and along the route Muhammad took to Jerusalem desecrates these holy lands and is intolerable. In the videotaped interview first broadcast on October 7, 2001, he added the granting of Palestinian statehood to his list of demands, in an apparent attempt to broaden his appeal in the region and to get the United States to put greater pressure on Israel to grant Palestinian demands. In addition, he condemns the government of Saudi Arabia both for having abandoned pure Qu'ranic practices and for allowing the American presence on holy ground.

The second part is a charge to action, explaining both what must be done and why it can succeed. The goal of the campaign is clearly established: "Today your brothers and sons, the sons of the two Holy Places, have started their Jihad (Holy War) in the cause of Allah, to dispel the occupying enemy out of the country of the two Holy Places." Thus, the campaign's goal is the removal of all Americans from Arabia and of the Israelis from Jerusalem (at a minimum), with a focus on liberating the al-Aqsa Mosque in Jerusalem, from which legend has it Muhammad ascended to heaven. The campaign will continue until these goals are achieved. Virtually mocking the United States military, bin Laden contends his campaign will succeed because of the American inability to accept casualties. As evidence, he cites the withdrawal of the United States from Beirut in 1983 (after the attack against the Marine barracks that killed 241 Americans) and from Mogadishu, Somalia in 1993 (after 18 Rangers were killed in an ambush). Of the Mogadishu experience, he says, "You left the area carrying disappointment, humiliation, defeat, and your dead with you."

The third part of the letter is a chilling exhortation to his followers. It begins by asserting, "Our youths believe in paradise after death," and adds, "they have no intention except to enter paradise by killing you (Americans)." The goal of these followers is clear: "They will continue to carry arms against you until you are—Allah willing—expelled, defeated and humiliated." Further, the campaign has what he views as a lofty goal. "Terrorising you, while you are carrying arms on our land, is a legitimate and morally demanded duty."

The means to conduct the campaign of terror are explicit as well. In issuing a *fatwa* (religious decree) on February 23, 1998, titled "Jihad Against Jews and Crusaders," bin Laden and the leaders of several other like-minded groups declared, "The ruling to kill all Americans—civilians and military—is an individual duty for every Muslim who can do it in any country in which it possible to do it." In a television interview on June 16, 1998, bin Laden reiterated the threat: "We do not differentiate between those dressed in military uniforms and civilians. They are all targets in this *fatwa*."

The demand (or objective) and the threat to force compliance are thus clearly stated and publicly available. The objective of the terrorist campaign is the removal of the United States presence from Islamic sacred lands, along with the physical removal of Israel from the holy shrines in Jerusalem. The threat is the promise of indiscriminate killing of Americans until they agree to accede to the demand and leave the holy places. To Americans, it is a chilling and hideous warning, but it is also congruent with terrorist practice.

Justifications of Terrorism

The justification of the terrorist actions being undertaken by bin Laden and his associates follow closely from his stated objectives in this campaign. Both the objective and justifications are religious in origin, although there is great debate in the Islamic world whether the ends that bin Laden demands justify the means. At the same time, the basic objective of the jihad—changing the United States and its policies—is shared by many in the Islamic Middle East who do not accept the methods being implemented. This latter factor makes most governments in the region, which by and large have limited popular support, reluctant to embrace the American counteraction openly and wholeheartedly.

The bin Laden group clearly considers their actions to constitute acts of war. His religious decree (*fatwa*) that exhorts Muslims to arms calls specifically for a holy war (*jihad*) against the infidels. The lack of distinction between the military forces and civilians of the target states would seem to raise some questions within the laws of war about whether this campaign can correctly be depicted as a war, but bin Laden offers a twofold explanation. Civilians and the military are equal targets, he maintains, because the desecrating influence of the Americans affects Islamic civilians and the military equally. Since American presence influences Muslims universally, so should Americans be universally vulnerable. Moreover, he contended in his June 16, 1998, television interview, "We must use such punishment to keep your evil away from Moslems, Moslem women and children."

These justifications evoke a mixed reaction within the Muslim world itself. The idea that Islam justifies offensive violence, particularly against innocent women and children, is rejected by mainstream, moderate Islamic leaders and followers, as is the practice of committing suicide in the name of jihad. These rationales have some appeal within fundamentalist sects of the religion, notably the extremely conservative, ascetic sect of Wahhabism, the official state religion of Saudi Arabia. The extreme fundamentalism of

Wahhabism, as taught in religious schools (the *madrassas*) in Pakistan (and funded in part by wealthy Saudis) and also in Saudi schools, provides a breeding ground for adherence to interpretations of Islamic duty described by bin Laden and Al Qaeda. It is notable that the hijackers of the September 11 flights were mostly Saudi and virtually all Wahhabi.

Anti-Americanism in the Middle East provides some support for expelling the corrupting influence of the United States from the region. On the "Arab street" (opinion voiced by ordinary Muslims in the region) there is opposition to the United States that has numerous sources but tends to focus on U.S. support for Israel (which is translated into opposition to the aspirations of the Palestinians) and the intrusiveness of American culture on Islamic societies. This opposition places several Islamic governments, and especially the Saudis, in a bind. On the one hand, many governments are aligned with the United States politically and militarily and, in the case of the oil-rich states, depend heavily on American consumption of their petroleum for their wealth. On the other hand, these regimes rarely have majority support among their populations—partly because of their relationship with the United States—and are viewed (sometimes rightly) as relying on the Americans to keep them in power. The result is a tightrope act that is very frustrating to the United States. Governments like that of Saudi Arabia publicly support the United States, but refuse to allow the Americans to stage overt military actions from their soil (since military attacks against Muslims are the ultimate expression of American presence). At the same time, they seek to avoid alienation of their populations by turning their backs on large monetary contributions to the terrorist organizations made by some of their citizens (presumably with some of the money coming from petroleum—including American—revenues).

Terrorism as Strategy or Tactic

It is clear that the Al Qaeda's use of terrorism is a strategy to attempt to achieve its ends. It has suggested in its official pronouncements that it has no plans or intentions to assault the United States frontally in the kind of clash of armed forces that Westerners associate with the term war. At one level, this simply reflects the military balance worldwide; bin Laden and his active "soldiers" probably number around 5,000, according to published estimates, and they would stand no chance of defeating the West on the open field of battle. This, if nothing else, is a lesson that Saddam Hussein provided all too clearly when he attempted to engage in conventional, symmetrical warfare against the Desert Storm coalition in the Gulf War.

Lacking the ability to compete on equal terms, the terrorists must engage in asymmetrical warfare, where their objective is not to overcome the enemy's armed forces, but rather to attack his will to continue. Bin Laden's objective, as noted earlier, is to convince the United States that bowing to his demands is preferable to continuing to live in the dread and fear of random terrorist attacks against America and its citizens. It is his hope and plan that a campaign of terrorist acts will cumulatively convince the United States to relent. In his own words in his declaration of war, he asserts "great losses induced on the enemy side (that would shaken and destroy its foundations and infrastructure) will help to expel the enemy defeated out of the country." The part of the quote in parentheses could be interpreted as a guideline for target selection on September 11, 2001.

The British military historian John Keegan offered an additional and compatible explanation for the style of warfare chosen by bin Laden in an opinion piece in the October 11, 2001, *London Daily Telegraph*. His argument is that Asian armed forces have consistently eschewed the kind of direct military confrontation of armies central to the Western military tradition, preferring more indirect approaches that surprised rather than directly crushed enemies in open combat. In the Middle East, he argues, "The Arabs were horse-riding raiders before Mohammed." Tactics of hit-and-run and retreat, and especially surprise attacks, were a staple of that warfare and, he asserts, still are the preferred style of war in the area. As he states, "On September 11, 2001 it [the Arab form of war] returned in an absolutely traditional form. Arabs, appearing suddenly out of empty space like their desert raider ancestors, assaulted the heartlands of Western power in a terrifying surprise raid and did appalling damage."

Sponsorship

The movement represented by bin Laden and his Al Qaeda network appears to be a sort of a hybrid in terms of sponsorship. It is clearly not a state-run organization that professes allegiance to and receives instructions from the government of any particular country, as had been alleged to be the relationship between Iran and a number of terrorist organizations operating out of Lebanon against Israel, such as Hizb'allah. On the other hand, it has received sanctuary from a regime, the Taliban government of Afghanistan, which shielded bin Laden and his fighters, even in the face of an American military onslaught. Funding for Al Qaeda does not come from an impoverished Afghan government or from any other known state source, but instead is alleged to have come both from bin Laden's personal fortune and contributions from wealthy private citizens from countries in the region, notably Saudi Arabia and Egypt.

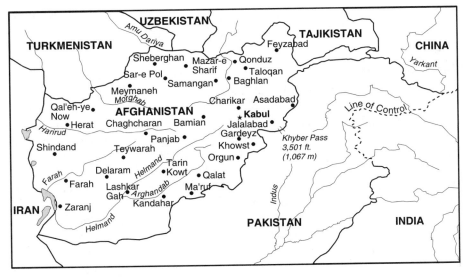

Map 16.1 Map of Afghanistan.

Thus, the organization emerges as a hybrid. It was state-sanctioned by the Taliban, but it is apparently unconnected to other governments in the region in terms of funding and command. Other governments in the Middle East explicitly condemn it with varying degrees of intensity. In structure and especially in funding, Al Qaeda is a private actor claiming it represents the Islamic *nation* (all those with common Islamic culture) but no Islamic *state* (or government).

Al Qaeda's unique status apparently reflects both its founding and its mission. Although publicly available details are sketchy and unreliable, Usama bin Laden started the process that led to his current quest in the 1980s, when he migrated to Afghanistan to join the *mujahadeen* (freedom fighters) opposing the Soviet occupation there that began in 1979. He showed apparent skill at recruiting people and raising money for the cause, and after the Soviet withdrawal from Afghanistan in 1989, had a loyal following of fundamentalist Muslim fighters. He was also closely associated with the Taliban during the anti-Soviet struggle, since they had also been recruited by the West to throw out the Soviets.

When Saddam Hussein invaded Kuwait in 1990, bin Laden apparently offered the services of his followers to defend Saudi Arabia against an Iraqi incursion into his native land. The Saudi government rejected this offer and instead invited the American armed forces to defend them. This snub and invitation both alienated bin Laden from the Saudi government and created the influx of Americans onto the soil of the "Holy Places" that became the basis for his campaign. When he was expelled from Saudi Arabia in 1995, he retreated to Sudan (which expelled him under Saudi pressure in 1996) and eventually to Afghanistan, and with the apparent approval of the Taliban government, began converting the *mujahadeen* camps they had shared (and which had been largely funded and set up in the 1980s by the CIA to aid in the expulsion of the Soviets) into terrorist training camps. Much of the early effort was apparently underwritten from bin Laden's personal inheritance as the son of a wealthy Saudi contractor. Reports on how much of his fortune remains to fund ongoing operations vary, as do reports about how much funding support the organization receives from outside sources.

Terrorist Forms

In its campaign against the United States, the bin Laden organization has employed only a few types of potential terror to this point. It has, however, demonstrated a willingness to go beyond the bounds of previous terrorist organizations in two significant ways, one of which speaks to the kinds of targets he attacks, and another that seems to suggest how he attacks.

Historically, his choice of targets shows a willingness to engage in actions that produce massive numbers of deaths among innocents who just happen to be in the vicinity. The willingness to kill thousands of people has been demonstrated both in the attacks against the American embassies in Kenya and Tanzania and the atrocities of September 11, 2001. Assuming the truth of accusations regarding his involvement in the attack against the Khobar Towers apartments in Dhahran, Saudi Arabia (where 129 American servicemen were killed in 1996) and the attack against the U.S.S. Cole, a U.S. naval destroyer, in a Yemeni port in 2000 (where 17 American sailors were killed), he has also shown a willingness to attack smaller concentrations as well. A common thread in target selection seems to be a preference for highly visible symbols representing American power and, by virtue of his success, its vulnerability. Such a preference is highly congruent with his stated intention to defeat the United States by attacking its "foundations and infrastructures," as described in the earlier section on justifications for his actions.

His choice of methods has also shown a commonality that combines established ways to carry out attacks with some innovation. The pre-September terrorist attacks listed above all involved the use of suicidal terrorists driving vehicles laden with explosives up to the target and then detonating them, destroying the target, and usually killing the terrorists who served as detonators of the devices. The Khobar and African bombers, of course, used trucks as their attack weapon, while the attack on the Cole was accomplished by sailing a small boat loaded with explosives alongside the American warship and detonating it. These attacks represented no particular innovation in terrorist methods. Timothy McVeigh, for instance, used a truck bomb in Oklahoma City (although he did not kill himself in the process), and suicide bombers have been a common element in the terrorist campaign against Israel in the name of Palestinian autonomy.

His real innovation, which was the cause of much of the shock of the September 11, 2001, was a new way of using airplanes as weapons of terror. Airplane hijacking and blowing up airplanes has been an established tactic of terrorists for decades, but hijacking airplanes and turning them into what amounted to explosives-carrying cruise missiles directed by suicidal pilots was an extension of the use of airplanes for terrorist purposes. The careful selection of transcontinental flights heavily laden with fuel that, once impact was made, turned into deadly incendiary bombs and initiation of the hijacking missions before much fuel was expended was clearly part of a well-planned attack. Since some of the perpetrators had backgrounds in engineering, it is almost certain that they knew that crashing their missiles into the upper floors of the World Trade Center towers would lead to the collapse of the structures, thereby magnifying the effects. The audacity and innovation in the form of the attack undoubtedly helps explain the lack of anticipation of the attack, despite some fairly suspicious actions by the hijackers before the attack (e.g., while in flight school, one of them requested instruction in flying and steering an airplane in flight but not in learning how to land or take off).

The follow-on campaign of mailing anthrax-infested letters to prominent American officials and institutions follows the same pattern, except for the number of deaths it caused. The letters were sent through the mail (thus involving the U.S. Postal Service, a symbol of the government) and to high-profile institutions (the television networks) and individuals (Senate Majority Leader Thomas Daschle), thereby guaranteeing maximum sustained publicity. Although actual incidents were very few given the volume of mail delivered every day, most Americans became distressed, fearing they might be victimized. As a result, the campaign achieved maximum effect with minimal effort.

What do these observations tell us about future forms of attack by the bin Laden organization before or until it is successfully suppressed? If he follows his past preferences, it suggests that his future targets will be high profile, highly visible public (both governmental and nongovernmental) symbols of American power in the world. As his history has shown, those symbols may be either on American soil or overseas. If the September attacks represent a shift in campaign emphasis to target the American people directly and to convince them to force their leaders to abandon Saudi Arabia rather than to live in continued fear of future mayhem, targets on American soil may be more likely than remote, overseas targets.

How much comfort can we take from extrapolating from the past actions of the Al Qaeda organization in preparing for the future? As the foregoing analysis fairly clearly indicates, bin Laden and his followers are indeed virtually textbook terrorists in the general terms in which we have described the dynamics of terrorism. One of the principal lessons in the "book" on terrorism is that terrorist actions are most effective when based on threats of absolutely random, and thus unpredictable, violence that potential victims can neither anticipate nor prepare for. The earlier bin Laden campaigns suggest he and his organization understand this dynamic. The U.S.S. Cole, for instance, was a much less visible target than had been the U.S. embassies, and the attackers did use a boat rather than a truck as their weapon. Whether the outbreak of anthrax infections, initially in Florida and around the country later in October 2001, is ever convincingly tied to bin Laden or not, it would be a form of terrorism compatible with a strategy of unpredictable actions. Moreover, the anthrax outbreak demonstrates a further goal of the terrorist, who succeeds when any adverse actions (including ones the terrorist could not possibly have committed) are attributed to the terrorist, thereby heightening the fear he hopes to induce in the target population.

CONCLUSION: RESPONDING TO SEPTEMBER 11, 2001

As the months since the national horror turn into years, the U.S. government has, along with a growing coalition of other concerned states, mounted a wide-ranging set of responses. The immediate reaction, as already noted, was to "declare war," suggesting the gravity of the acts and the level of our resolve to deal with them. The war analogy, of course, was useful for mobilizing public support behind resolute action that the public quickly demanded after shock turned to rage. The inappropriateness of the response when taken in the literal sense of a conventional military campaign rapidly became evident to the administration and other observers. As the campaign has gained shape and definition, reactions have begun to fall within familiar categories for dealing with terrorism. Lurking behind this pattern of response are questions about whether this new form of warfare is really the "fourth generation" and whether it is indeed the wave of the future as the United States faces an international environment with hostile elements it had not previously contemplated with the seriousness ascribed to them since the terrorist attacks.

Dealing with Terrorism

In responding to the September 11 attacks, the United States has begun to evolve an increasingly complex and sophisticated pattern of responses in hopes of suppressing or rendering ineffective future actions by Al Qaeda and provide the basic framework for dealing with future terrorist activities. Because neither approach is sufficient by itself, the evolving strategy contains elements both of counterterrorism and antiterrorism, as well as terrorist preemption (through efforts to remove the historic ban on assassinations, for example). The strategy contains an overtly military component that reverses the historic use of terror as a tactic to further military goals by making the use of military strikes from the air and on the ground as a tactic to assist in the strategy of counterterrorism.

The strategy contains both organizational and operational elements. One of the most consistent criticisms of American efforts to fight terrorism emerging from the community of scholars and professionals who study terrorism has been the diffusion of responsibility among various agencies and the absence of any overarching authority to enforce cooperation and coordination, as the CIA-FBI-INS example in the first section suggested. This organizational deficiency was addressed by the creation of the Office of Homeland Security and the appointment of Governor Ridge as its director. Whether this appointment will prove to be no more than a largely symbolic act to rally the population and agencies into common cause for the moment, or a major attempt to restructure the terrorism effort into a more efficient and effective operation, remains to be seen as the duties and powers of the Homeland Security office evolve.

Operationally, the response has combined highly visible (and highly invisible) counterterrorism and antiterrorism elements. Antiterrorism efforts have been directed at protecting the most obvious and visible potential targets from attack, but have also recognized the enormity of the potential target list that cannot be comprehensively protected—particularly if the terrorists randomize their victims. Counterterrorism, on the other hand, has focused on the physical suppression of the bin Laden organization to make it incapable of mounting future operations while simultaneously creating a global network that hopefully will allow identification and suppression of future organizations before they can become active problems.

The international counterterror campaign has developed along two distinct lines. One has been the overt campaign to suppress the Al Qaeda organization by capturing or killing its core members, with American and opposition Afghan military forces playing the most visible role. The military campaign, of course, focuses on the Afghan headquarters and sanctuary of bin Laden and is accompanied by a worldwide effort to identify and suppress members of the network in other places. These efforts have been hampered by the lack of accurate intelligence (including a shortage of area and language specialists) about the location of members and leader of the network, especially but not exclusively in Afghanistan. This has necessitated a second counterterrorism emphasis on improving the capability to identify, surveille, and capture or otherwise suppress terrorist operatives. Much of this deficiency results from the absence of intelligence agents on the spot who can collect human intelligence (or HUMINT).

The military effort has had two principal targets: the bin Laden organization and the Taliban government of Afghanistan that has provided him with a sanctuary. When the Taliban government refused American demands to turn bin Laden and his associates over to international authorities without conditions (the Taliban initially insisted the U.S. government provide proof of bin Laden's responsibility for the attacks), the U.S. military began its bombing campaign against both the terrorist camps and the regime. The purpose of attacking the Taliban was to convince its leaders to change their minds about harboring bin Laden by threatening to continue military pressure leading to their overthrow if it refused and to cease it if they complied. The latter effort has included forging arrangements with Afghan opponents of the Taliban, including the so-called Northern Alliance of rebels who have been resisting the government in Kabul since it came to power in 1993. The Bush administration recognizes that the bombing campaign and insertion of Special Forces into the country to capture or kill bin Laden is only part of the counterterrorist campaign, since there are known bin Laden associates outside Afghanistan and his capture or death might well result in a new leader or leaders rising to take up his cause.

The other, far less visible aspect of counterterrorism involves improving our intelligence capabilities. One of the military problems of suppressing Al Qaeda has been the lack of good intelligence about the situation in Afghanistan and the physical whereabouts of bin Laden. The United States has had no official presence in that country since January 1989, when the American embassy in the capital of Kabul was closed for security reasons. Since embassies are generally critical as physical headquarters from which to recruit and supervise spy networks, the United States has been deficient in that area for over a decade. The same can be said of American intelligence capabilities in other countries contiguous to Afghanistan, such as Iran, Tajikistan, Uzbekistan, and Pakistan.

The intelligence problem has several aspects. One is in internationalizing intelligence collection and sharing about terrorist organizations and their memberships (as well as sharing information *within* the U.S. intelligence community). Pakistani intelligence, for instance, is clearly more capable of monitoring activities in the *madrassas* (which have apparently become a prime recruiting ground for suicidal terrorists) than American agencies could ever be, and they could assist in providing rosters of potential perpetrators in them. Other intelligence agencies can track suspects in their countries, provide surveillance and warnings of movements, and the like. All of this, of course, involves considerable coordination and cooperation among countries, and establishing such connections has been a central thrust of U.S. Secretary of State Colin Powell's policies in the aftermath of September's events. Although there are limits to the degree intelligence agencies can share information without compromising themselves, better intelligence cooperation, particularly featuring operatives from the region, will facilitate the penetration and the crippling of these organizations. Intergovernmental cooperation can lead to crippling actions such as identifying and freezing or seizing their financial assets. All of these actions clearly fall within the category of counterterrorism.

Antiterrorism is part of the U.S. strategy as well, and many of the most highly visible responses to the terrorist attacks in the United States are antiterrorist measures. In direct response to the September 11 incidents, for instance, airport security has been increased substantially (although early reports suggest unevenly), and security procedures for gaining access to large buildings such as the Sears Tower in Chicago have become much more restrictive. The exposure of a number of people around the country to anthrax has resulted in greater mobilization of medical resources, such as antibiotics, to lessen the effect. In addition, a number of communities have begun guarding their water supplies to protect them against chemical or biological contamination. Other similar measures will undoubtedly be devised by the Office of Homeland Security to protect nuclear power plants from attacks by airliners or penetration by terrorist bands. Institutional and legal barriers, such as the ways military forces can be used in the United States in a policing role, should not be underestimated as new measures are fashioned.

These antiterrorist actions are understandable and of value, but they also speak to the limits of antiterrorism as a strategy. As already mentioned, there are a very large numbers of targets that terrorists simply intent on wreaking havoc on American society may choose. Those seeking to inflict maximum fright among the population will simply look for targets that have not yet been protected. Though airports may now become very difficult to penetrate, what about a major bridge into Manhattan or in the San Francisco Bay area or the dam for a hydroelectrical plant? The problem for the antiterrorist is that planning is largely reactive. If that planning attempts to become anticipatory, there will always be a real danger of protecting the wrong target or, by virtue of the effort, causing the terrorist to move on to another high-value target not included in the antiterrorist list.

The New "War" on Terror

As the duration of the effort to deal with the terrorist attacks of September 11, 2001, lengthens from days and weeks to months and years, the complexity of the task and the difficulty of achieving durable results become more obvious. The task of hunting down and punishing those who perpetrated the terrorist crimes operates on one level that approximates traditional war in its objective and employs military means as part of its approach. It is obvious, however, that eliminating Usama bin Laden and his Al Qaeda network is only part of the task before us; simply removing him is not enough. In the words of Mohamed Zarea, a human rights advocate from Cairo quoted in an October 14, 2001, *New York Times* article, "This war on terrorism may eliminate a few terrorists. But without basic reforms, it will be like killing a few mosquitoes and leaving the swamp."

The broader task for the United States and other potential victims of terror is removing the causes of terrorism, the complex of conditions that has given rise to substantial hatred of the United States and Americans and that motivates people to engage in acts of terrorist self-immolation because of those hatreds. While satisfying and fulfilling our sense of justice, capturing and killing bin Laden and his associates will not end that hatred; bin Laden feeds off it, but he did not invent it. Unless other conditions change, some other individuals will likely arise to take his place. Counteracting this problem will require a multidimensional approach, the outline and details of which are in development. While it is impossible to suggest a comprehensive strategy for this campaign against something like fourth generation warfare, we can at least list a few of its features.

The campaign will have a *military component*, although it will not necessarily be the most prominent aspect at different stages of the campaign. Military action was necessary to bring pressure on the Taliban government to relent or step down and to facilitate the search for Al Qaeda. If the task eventually turns to state building in Afghanistan, as has been suggested, the military's role will be much more confined to something like the peacekeeping function it performs in places like Bosnia and Kosovo. State building itself is a highly controversial approach due to the difficulty of building a viable state, which would be especially difficult in a highly factionalized, poor state such as Afghanistan. (For a discussion of the problems of state building, see Donald M. Snow, *When America Fights*.)

Diplomacy will play an important part in the strategy. Efforts are underway to forge new relationships with a broad coalition of states to develop a united stand against terrorist activities. These efforts will likely deepen as they are operationalized in areas such as cooperation on intelligence activities tracking and monitoring terrorist activities across international boundaries. The result, as Edward Luttwak has suggested, may be a new pattern of international relationships, where those states that support and condone terrorism are confronted by an international coalition of most of the rest of the world. This diplomatic activity will likely include *international political pressure* for reform or replacement of governments like the Taliban and *law enforcement* activities aimed at suppressing terrorist organizations (counterterrorism) and at making it more difficult for terrorists to achieve their goals (antiterrorism).

State building (actions intended to produce the conditions for a peaceful, stable country in a formerly unstable state) will also be part of the equation to remove the "swamp" of conditions in which terrorism breeds and flourishes. The Bush administration embraced this concept with some initial reluctance, given what it had viewed as the morass of similar efforts in Bosnia and Kosovo during the 1990s. The aim of state building is to uplift conditions for citizens economically, politically, and otherwise to the point that they develop a greater stake in continued peace and tranquility than they have in continued violence and chaos. In the case of Afghanistan, this means building virtually from scratch both a viable political system and economy. It is a daunting task at best.

The difficulty is accentuated by the phenomenon of the *madrassas* operating along the border between Afghanistan and Pakistan. Prior to the reactions to the terrorist attack, few American had heard of these Qu'ranic schools, where the impoverished, often abandoned sons of people in the region are housed, fed, and indoctrinated in a curriculum almost exclusively composed of studying the Koran and radical interpretations of the faith, including anti-Americanism and the virtues of martyrdom. There are around 7,500 of these schools in Pakistan, and they have an enrollment of between 750,000 and a million Islamic youth. They have become the training grounds for *mujahadeen* to fight around the globe and the recruiting grounds for Al Qaeda. As long as the *madrassas* continue to function as they do and spew out an unending stream of anti-American fanaticism, there will be no end to the terrorism.

But what to do about them? The obvious answer is to do away with them, but that is easier said than done. They do serve a socially valuable function by taking in and providing shelter and sustenance for children who otherwise might live and die in the streets. The Pakistan government, which spends nearly nine-tenths of its budget on debt service (paying the interest on international loans) and the military, can neither care for nor educate those waifs (most of their funding comes from private donations, notably from Saudi Arabia). Part of state building must be directed toward handling these repositories of hatred and venom. But exact solutions are not going to be easy.

Our world was turned on its head on September 11, 2001. We learned that a portion of the world deeply hates Americans and is willing to engage in unspeakable, despicable acts to hurt and kill Americans, even if it means committing suicide in the process. A new kind of war has begun that is fought by state and non–state actors and makes no distinction between combatants and non-combatants or soldiers and civilians. Whether this phenomenon represents a fundamental shift to a new, fourth generation of warfare that will dominate how military force is used in the future or not, it will certainly continue for a long period of time. We will try to reduce our vulnerability to those who would harm us, but we know our preparations will not be perfect. That is simply the world in which we now live. Maybe the best we can do is to try to manage a condition of permanent conflict, but maybe we can eliminate or shrink the "swamp" of conditions in which the problem has bred and festered. At this point, we do not know which alternative describes the future.

STUDY/DISCUSSION QUESTIONS

1. Is terrorism ever justifiable? If so, when? Is it more acceptable as a tactic to achieve ends, or as a strategy toward an end? Is it more justifiable during times of war than when war does not otherwise exist?

2. How is the campaign against terrorism currently being developed like and unlike war? How appropriate is the "war analogy" for describing our efforts?

3. What are antiterrorism and counterterrorism? Which is more effective, and in what circumstances?

4. One of the most difficult problems facing the United States in dealing with terrorism is how to deal with Saudi Arabia, which is a close U.S. ally but also the source of much of the funding for terrorist causes. How should the United States deal with this seeming paradox?

5. Given Usama bin Laden's choice of targets in the past (large symbols of American power) and the various forms terror may take, are there potential targets of terrorist violence in your community? What can be done to make them less vulnerable to attack?

6. Read "The Roots of Muslim Rage" by Bernard Lewis, cited in the reading list. What does the author argue creates the rage? Can we "mollify" the rage? How? If not, how should we treat those who experience the rage and hate us as a consequence?

7. Is the removal of the Taliban government in Afghanistan a justifiable objective to achieve the broader goal of destroying the bin Laden organization? Will a successor regime better serve American interests in removing that country from the list of terrorist sanctuaries?

8. What are the *madrassas* (see the Smucker and Satchell article for a description)? Is it possible to end terrorism against the United States as long as they exist and teach what they do? What can we do about this aspect of the problem?

9. Using his own proclamations found on Web sites listed in the reading list, construct bin Laden's objectives and justifications for his campaign against the United States. Do they make sense?

10. How would you advise Governor Ridge to organize for and conduct the operations of the Homeland Security office? How would you suggest he begin the task of devising a strategy to deal with terrorism?

11. Afghanistan has always been one of the most difficult places in the world for foreign military forces to operate successfully. Read the Bearden article, and then discuss whether, or to what extent, the United States should have committed ground forces to Afghanistan to overthrow the Taliban and destroy Al Qaeda.

12. Should the United States directly address Usama bin Laden's demands? How? If he would abandon his campaign against the United States if we agree to leave Saudi Arabia, should we consider doing so?

READING/RESEARCH MATERIAL

Ajami, Fouad. "The Sentry's Solitude." *Foreign Affairs* 80, 6 (November-December 2001), 2–16.

Bearden, Milton. "Afghanistan, Graveyard of Empires." *Foreign Affairs* 80, 6 (November-December 2001), 17–30.

Betts, Richard. "The New Threat of Mass Destruction." *Foreign Affairs* 77, 1 (January-February 1998), 26–41.

Deutch, John. "Terrorism." *Foreign Policy*, 108 (Fall 1997), 10–23.

Gallagher, James J. *Low-Intensity Conflict: A Guide for Tactics, Techniques, and Procedures.* Harrisburg, PA: Stackpole Books, 1992.

Hendrickson, Ryan C. "American War Powers and Terrorists: The Case of Usama bin Laden." *Studies in Conflict and Terrorism* 23 (September-October 2000), 161–176.

Hoffman, Bruce. *Terrorism.* New York: Columbia University Press, 1998.

Huntington, Samuel P., et al. *The Clash of Civilizations: The Debate.* New York: Council on Foreign Relations Press, 1993.

Keegan, John. "In This War of Civilisations, The West Will Prevail." *The Daily Telegraph (London)*, October 10, 2001.

Laqueur, Walter. "The New Face of Terrorism." *Washington Quarterly* 21, 4 (Autumn 1998), 169–178.

Lewis, Bernard. "License to Kill: Usama bin Laden's Declaration of Jihad." *Foreign Affairs* 77, 6 (November/December 1998), 14–19.

———. "The Roots of Muslim Rage: Why So Many Muslims Deeply Resent the West, and Why Their Bitterness Will Not Easily Be Mollified." *Atlantic Monthly* 266, 3 (September 1990), 47–60. Electronic edition: http://www.theatlantic.com/issues/90Sep/rage.htm.

Lind, William S., et al. "The Changing Face of War: Into the Fourth Generation." *Marine Corps Gazette*, October 1989, 2–26.

Luttwak, Edward N. "New Faces, New Alliances." *New York Times* (national edition), October 2, 2001, A27.

Perry, William. "Preparing for the Next Attack." *Foreign Affairs* 80, 6 (November-December 2001), 31–45.

Powell, Colin L. "A Long, Hard Campaign." *Newsweek*, October 15, 2001, 53.

Reeve, Simon. *The New Jackals: Ramzi Yousef, Osama bin Laden, and the Future.* Boston: Northeastern University Press, 1999.

Sachs, Susan. "The Despair Beneath the Arab World's Growing Rage." *New York Times* (electronic edition), October 14, 2001. http://www.nytimes.com/international/middleeast/ 14ARAB.html.

Safire, William. "For a Muslim Legion." *New York Times* (national edition), October 1, 2001, A26.

Sloan, Stephen. *Beating International Terrorism: An Action Strategy for Preemption and Punishment* (revised edition). Montgomery, AL: Air University Press, 2000.

Smith, James M., ed. *Searching for National Security in an NBC World.* Colorado Springs, CO: USAF Institute for National Security Studies, 2000.

—— and William C. Thomas, eds. *The Terrorism Threat and U.S. Government Response: Operational and Organizational Factors.* Colorado Springs, CO: USAF Institute for National Security Studies, 2001.

Smucker, Philip, and Michael Satchell. "Hearts and Minds." *U.S. News and World Report,* October 15, 2001, 28–29.

Snow, Donald M. *When America Fights: The Uses of U.S. Armed Force.* Washington, DC: CQ Press, 2000.

Van Creveld, Martin. *The Transformation of War.* New York: Free Press, 1991.

Zakaria, Fareed. "The Allies Who Made Our Foes." *Newsweek,* October 1, 2001, 34.

——. "Special Report: Why They Hate Us." *Newsweek,* October 15, 2001, 22–40.

WEB SITES

Office coordinating national strategy to strengthen protections against terrorist threats or attacks in the United States

The Office of Homeland Security at http://www.whitehouse.gov/homeland

Updates users on current developments in the U.S. fight against terrorism

Response to Terrorism at http://usinfo.state.gov/topical/pol/terror

Outlines U.S. counterterrorism policy and links users to other relevant information

Counterterrorism Office at http://www.state.gov/s/ct

U.S. government profile of Afghanistan, including its people, government, and economy

CIA World Factbook: Afghanistan at http://www.cia.gov/cia/publications/factbook/geos/af.html

Extensive country profile provided by the Library of Congress

Afghanistan - A Country Study http://memory.loc.gov/frd/cs/aftoc.html

Text of the "bin Laden Epistles"

http://msanews.net/MSANEWS199610/19961012.3.html

Index